THE SILENCE OF
BARBARA SYNGE

THE SILENCE OF
BARBARA SYNGE

W. J. Mc Cormack

Manchester University Press
Manchester and New York

distributed exclusively in the USA by Palgrave

Copyright © W. J. McCormack 2003

The right of W. J. McCormack to be identified as the author of this work has been asserted by him in accordance with the Copyright, Designs and Patents Act 1988.

Published by Manchester University Press
Oxford Road, Manchester M13 9NR, UK
and Room 400, 175 Fifth Avenue, New York, NY 10010, USA
www.manchesteruniversitypress.co.uk

Distributed exclusively in the USA by
Palgrave, 175 Fifth Avenue, New York NY 10010, USA

Distributed exclusively in Canada by
UBC Press, University of British Columbia, 2029 West Mall, Vancouver, BC, Canada V6T 1Z2

British Library Cataloguing-in-Publication Data
A catalogue record for this book is available from the British Library

Library of Congress Cataloging-in-Publication Data
A catalog record for this book is available from the Library of Congress

ISBN 13: 978 0 7190 6279 7

First published in hardback 2003 by Manchester University Press
This paperback edition first published 2009

Printed by Lightning Source

FOR
MARGARET LAWRENCE
ETHEL STRAHAN
AND IN MEMORY OF
LILY WEBSTER

In the early eighteenth century, when the word was gaining acceptance ... people retained habits of thought that made clear the direction of the comparison implied by 'decadence'. Family trees were drawn up in detail because important matters depended on them, such as the man your daughter could marry, the job your son could accept, your own liability to the tax laws. (Robert M. Adams, *Decadent Societies*, 1983)

Contents

LIST OF PLATES—*page ix*
ACKNOWLEDGEMENTS—*xi*
ABBREVIATIONS—*xiii*

INTRODUCTION
The Synges from Bridgnorth, Shropshire—*1*

PART I
SETTINGS

1 Lands elsewhere: Wicklow—*18*
2 Other people: the Hatches—*24*
3 A little learning—*38*
4 The mill at Animo—*46*
5 The state of the roads—*50*

PART II
HATCHED, MATCHED AND DESPATCHED

6 An MP and his wife—*58*
7 Death in the mountains, 1769—*73*
8 A battle of wills—*80*
9 On debt—*92*

PART III
THE DEVIL'S GLEN

10 Roundwood and after—*98*
11 Her brother's will, 1792—*108*
12 Rebellion, union and family romance—*113*
13 Proprieties—*127*

Contents

Part IV

AFFAIRS WITH THE MOON
JOHN SYNGE, 1788–1845

14 How Pestalozzi reached Wicklow—*134*
15 Melmoth the stay-at-home—*157*
16 In Darby's field—*168*

Part V

LITERATURE AT NURSE

17 John Hatch, a country doctor—*186*
18 Windfalls—*194*
19 Workhouse insurgency—*201*

Part VI

CONCERNING J. M. SYNGE
1871–1909

20 Madness and local government—*210*
21 Instituting 'The Playboy'—*221*
22 A county in romance—*226*
23 The wounded dramatist takes a bow—*241*

A PERSONAL APPENDIX
Method, error and offence in literary history—*249*

NOTES—*255*

INDEXES
I General—*285*
II Wicklow place-names—*296*
III Members of the Hatch and McCracken families—*298*
IV Members of the Synge family—*301*

List of plates

Market Street, Ardee, County Louth, with Hatch Castle
– its present name – on the left, c. 1890—*page 10*

Death notices, including that for Barbara Synge (Mrs John Hatch),
and adjacent items, in *The Freeman's Journal* (Dublin), 21–25 April 1767—*11*

Undated entry in the 1765 diary of John Hatch (d. 1797).
Courtesy Trustees of the National Library of Ireland—*11*

The West Front of Saint Patrick's Cathedral, Dublin, in 1791 (detail from
James Malton, *A Picturesque and Descriptive View of the City of Dublin*,
London 1792–1799). Courtesy The British Library—*12*

A map of Roundwood, County Wicklow, 1731.
Courtesy Trustees of the National Library of Ireland—*12*

The Pestalozzi school-room at Nun's Cross, County Wicklow.
Courtesy Board of Trinity College, Dublin—*13*

Roundwood Park, County Wicklow (before the fire of c. 1950).
Courtesy John Millington Synge Trust / Board of Trinity College, Dublin—*13*

Glanmore Castle, County Wicklow, 1805
Robert Owen's proposed model Irish village (1823).
Both courtesy The British Library—*14*

Drawing by John 'Pestalozzi' Synge (1788–1845), from his Italian sketchbook.
John Hatch Synge (1823–1872).
Both courtesy John Millington Synge Trust / Board of Trinity College, Dublin—*15*

Ballincor North and Newcastle, and adjacent Baronies, County Wicklow,
in the late nineteenth century. Courtesy Simon Mc Cormack,
House Manager, Kedleston Hall, Derbyshire—*16*

Acknowledgements

I owe numerous debts to individuals – nearly all of them women – who have made the present book possible. Marie-Louise Legg advised on matters of eighteenth-century family property. Niamh Kirk of Moore, Kiely & Lloyd (Solicitors) Dublin very amiably provided access to dormant Synge Estate papers, at the prompting of Ms U. Brown of Donegal. To all three I am grateful for clarification of the Synge family's Dublin possessions. It was my erstwhile solicitor, Judge Catherine Murphy, who suggested where Synge papers might yet be located in non-public collections, and to her I owe a special word of gratitude.

Kate Manning, newly appointed archivist of Saint Patrick's Cathedral, Dublin, answered queries with great alacrity, and Susan Hood of the Representative Church Body Library made facilities available for my inspecting material relating to the Cathedral and to various parishes with which Synges and Hatches were associated. In the Archives Department of University College Dublin, Helen Hewson assisted my research into the Synge-Hutchinson collection. Carmel Rice of the Meath County Heritage Centre was particularly helpful with matters of Hatch and M'Cracken family history (or, rather, the sparsity of it!).

Jenny Scott guided me to Darby's Field on the Powerscourt Estate in Wicklow. Joan Kavanagh of that county's Heritage Centre drew my attention to various details I would otherwise have missed, and opened up to me the records of Rathdrum Union. Domestically, Jane Haville watched with more tolerance than I deserve as I pursued yet another Irish paper-trail.

Large collections of Synge (and Hatch) papers are carefully preserved in the National Library of Ireland, where Noel Kissane and Tom Desmond were exceptionally kind in giving me access to obscure sources, including maps. In the Library (manuscripts department) of Trinity College, Dublin, I was greatly helped by Felicity O'Mahony and Bernard Meehan in my efforts to read the Synge and Stephens collections in a different light to that previously focused on them: Dr Meehan also eased my access to the papers still preserved in the offices of Moore, Kiely & Lloyd. For more than thirty years, Trinity Library's Department of Early Printed Books and Special Collections has provided a homely environment from which I have been able to work while revisiting Dublin: to Charles Benson and the late Vincent Kinane I owe a scholar's special debts of hospitality. Down in County Wicklow, Chris Lawlor of Dunlavin shed additional light on the career of Dr John Hatch; while George Huxley provided details of late nineteenth-century and early twentieth-century Ireland which continue to intrigue me.

Material quoted from the Hatch Papers, the Synge Papers, with some related documentation, is the property of the National Library of Ireland and has been reproduced with the permission of the Council of Trustees of the National Library of Ireland.

Acknowledgements

In addition to the individuals and institutions already mentioned, the staff of Dublin City Archives, the Registry of Deeds, the Northern Ireland Public Record Office, the library of Magdalen College Oxford, the Society of Genealogists (London), and the Public Record Office (London) were helpful as ever.

At Goldsmiths College I was supported in my research by a number of colleagues whom I value equally as friends, notably Conor Carville, Howard Caygill and Alan Downie. In Ireland, Gerry Dukes and Deirdre MacMahon offered support at crucial moments, and Paddy Gillan continued to supply reports from unexpected sources of enlightenment.

W. J. Mc Cormack
Monaghan

Abbreviations

For economy and clarity in a book where similar names recur in numerous permutations, the dramatist John Millington Synge (1871–1909) is referred to as JMS.

Sources frequently cited are referred to in the notes by means of the following codes:

DRD (Dublin) Registry of Deeds.

Elphin Letters Marie-Louise Legg (ed.), *The Synge Letters: Bishop Edward Synge to His Daughter Alicia, Roscommon to Dublin, 1746–1752*. Dublin: Lilliput Press in Association with the Irish Manuscripts Commission, 1996.

Family K. C. Synge, *The Family of Synge or Sing* (privately printed, 1937).

Fool W. J. McCormack, *Fool of the Family: A Life of JM Synge*. London: Weidenfeld & Nicolson, 2000.

Letters Ann Saddlemyer (ed.), *The Collected Letters of John Millington Synge*. Oxford: Clarendon Press, 1983 (vol. 1) and 1984 (vol. 2).

My Uncle John Andrew Carpenter (ed.), *My Uncle John; Edward Stephens's Life of JM Synge*. London: Oxford University Press, 1974.

NLI National Library of Ireland.

O'Faolain 'A Broken World', in *The Collected Stories of Sean O'Faolain, Volume 1*. London: Constable, 1980. pp. 163–173.

PRONI Public Record Office of Northern Ireland.

RCB Representative Church Body (Dublin).

Stephens (TS or MS) Edward Millington Stephens's biography of his uncle in its original form (Typescript or Manuscript, with call number) as preserved in Trinity College, Dublin.

TCD Trinity College Dublin (library).

UCD University College Dublin.

Wicklow Essays Ken Hannigan and William Nolan (eds), *Wicklow History and Society; Interdisciplinary Essays on the History of an Irish County*. Dublin: Geography Publications, 1994.

Works (1–4) J. M. Synge, *Collected Works* (ed. Robin Skelton and Ann Saddlemyer). London: Oxford University Press, 1962-1968. 4 vols: 1 – *Poems*; 2 – *Prose*; 3 – *Plays I*; 4 – *Plays II*.

Introduction

The Synges from Bridgnorth, Shropshire

There was one Synge, a hatter at Drogheda, who was my relation and I acknowledg'd him as freely as if his rank had been equal to mine own, and supported his son, till I found him worthless. I then dismiss'd, and know not what is become of him. This is the right temper with respect to poor relations. I observe with pleasure that you have it. (Edward Synge, Bishop of Elphin, to his daughter, 1752)

THE temptation to write a book which is in some sense a model for other books should probably be resisted, for it is likely that the imitation (if there should be one) will prove better than the original. Yet even if this fate befall the present brief enough exercise in Irish literary history, something may have been gained. Years ago I had hoped to compile a complex of inquiries into the material and cultural histories of certain families whose names are famous usually for just one individual – the Edgeworths (Maria), the Joyces (James), the Moores (George), the Persses and Gregorys (Augusta), the Shaws (Bernard), the Synges (John Millington), the Wildes (Oscar), not forgetting the Yeatses (several candidates here, despite WB's efforts.) I quickly found that the surviving material for such an undertaking was vast, much of it daunting in the complexity of its financial and legal detail. The present book concentrates on just one of these genealogies, with the implication that others may be adopted by better qualified sponsors.

The exemplary aspect does not end with the isolation of Synges from the rest of the 'indomitable Irishry'. Humans do not spring from the soil, despite what the Athenians believed about their own origins. Populations, citizenries, migrations, settlements and colonies all come about through movement and through encounters with different populations, citizenries and so forth. Apart from very particular exceptions such as Australia, aboriginal peoples have not existed anywhere for many centuries, even millennia. It is true that some migrations are brutally enforced or sponsored, whereas other populations are oppressed *in situ* militarily

Introduction

or economically. But even in Elizabethan Ireland, there was already in existence a hybrid body of people, with intermarriage between Celts, Normans, 'Old English', and – soon – newcomers like the Synges.

Not that Ireland in the sixteenth or seventeenth century was a sweetie bazaar where one might pick 'n mix. The context in which George Synge (1594–1652), from Bridgnorth, Shropshire, went to Armagh in 1621 was relatively peaceful. Yet the background was one of intense religious conflict, manifest in several prolonged wars, and projected into confiscations of land, plantations of settlers. He became a cleric of the Church of Ireland, eventually becoming Bishop of Cloyne in 1638, just in time for the next outbreak of war. He had never been a soldier. Indeed, soldiering was rarely to appeal to the Synges until Charles Synge (1789–1854) won his spurs in the Peninsular campaign against Napoleon, to become *post-bellum* a lieutenant-colonel.

George is buried in Saint Mary Magdalen, Bridgnorth. In the royalist insurrection of 1641 – which broke out in Ulster – he lost his wife and several of his children. (They drowned at sea while fleeing from the rebels.) Though he remarried in Ireland, he returned home to die in England. His first wife had been Anne, daughter of Francis Edgeworth (died 1627) who held the office of Clerk of the Hanaper and was an ancestor of the great novelist, Maria Edgeworth (1767–1849). Such families bounced between the two islands as advantage suggested, and occasionally skittered between the rival versions of episcopalian Christianity. Of the two, the Synges cleaved to Ireland and to protestantism more resolutely than the Edgeworths.

A striking feature of cultural activity in and about Ireland has been a compulsion to justify claims to Irish identity made by various groups and individuals. Latter-day historians of the nationalist or republican kind specifically tend to play down the royalism of 1641's insurrection, presenting it instead as a pre-emptive confrontation with Oliver Cromwell (aka The Devil Incarnate.) The synthesis of national sentiment and Catholic suffering, far from being native and archaic, has been ascribed to the work of seventeenth-century Franciscans working in the Low Countries, their compelling motive being what Joep Leersen has wittily called 'vestigial bardic chauvinism'.[1] All of this may strike the gentle reader as heavily pedantic, carrying the terrible twins of abstraction and generality. However, what follows is a highly specific narrative, dedicated to illuminating a family history. It is not an official version. Those who were denied fame are given their chance. Ideas, unable in their time to boost the particular 'identity' then deemed useful, are reconsidered. The woman named in the book's title may not acquire any more extensive biography in the course of the pages which follow, but her condition emerges as indicative of how family history is channelled towards celebrated figures (the dramatist, J. M. Synge, 1871–1909) through others whose fate is to remain uncelebrated, even suppressed.

Introduction

The Synges had arrived in Ireland as servants of the Reformation; they acquired landed property both in their personal and professional capacities. Midway on the scale of success and prosperity would appear to be Samuel Synge, sometime Dean of Kildare, who died in 1708. His name shines from the published record as a model of unremarkable probity. Yet diligent research by the most recent family historian suggests that the dean's ecclesiastical superiors felt differently and with some passion, regarding him as unworthy of promotion.[2] To cut a swathe through accepted reputation and the fruits of incomplete research one needs to focus sharply on particulars. A truncated family tree would appear as below.

Some of these are manifest losers, despite the episcopal regalia of their celebrated kith and kin. Women feature disproportionately among the unnumbered dead. Is there no life to be found for the christian-nameless Miss O'Doherty whom Edward Synge *may* have married? Did she speak Gaelic? And, to take the case which we will regard as symptomatic – why were Barbara Synge's date of death and place of burial untraceable even by diligent family chroniclers? Her life-story is a central concern, even if it also remains a substantial blank. The obverse of the blank raises male questions – to what extent did her husband, John Hatch, benefit from the doubtful last will and testament of a semi-literate suicide? Why did Anne Kennedy (niece of the suicide) declare to Hatch, 'Delicacy forbids me to mention the Degree of affinity subsisting between me & your Honours Family'?

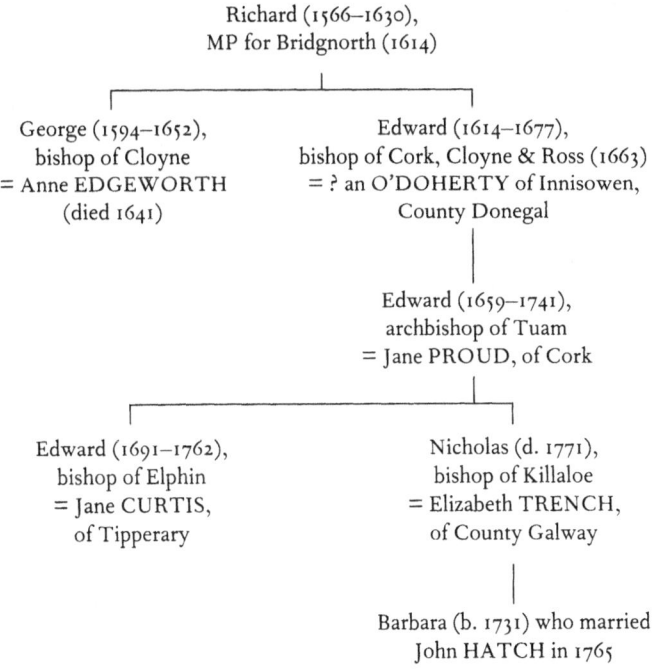

Introduction

These questions were, or would have been, important to the individuals concerned. Answers were not available in every case, and certainly not in that of Barbara Synge, great-great-grandmother of the playwright hereinafter referred to simply as JMS. She, we may provisionally conclude, went to the grave unaware that her entry in the family annals would lack that very detail. The questions, the silences, the concealments (of at least one will, authentic or forged) would in time preoccupy unsung Barbara's most celebrated descendant. By *his* time, the population of Wicklow could not be conceived in terms of the protestant hegemony implicit for the earlier period examined here. Thus, to the questions and silences one should add those absences from the present book – the Catholic tenants, the descendents (not all of them tenants) of Gaelic chieftains like Fiach Mac Hugh O'Byrne (c. 1544-1597) whose disturbingly inter-language name haunts the pages of *An Irish Utopia* (1906) published more than three centuries after the Wicklow leader's beheading.

There were also lesser figures who bore the name. For example Joseph Synge, an apothecary of Meath Street, advertised an award when his apprentice, John Coffey, absconded.³ Socially, he was closer to the Drogheda hatter whose son had offended the Bishop of Elphin than to the episcopal Synges who inhabited a grand tomb in nearby Saint Patrick's Cathedral. Perhaps he was the ancestor of those nineteenth-century Dublin Synges who died in humble, even abject, circumstances, some of whom are traced in chapter 18. The point, of course, is not to fill the absences with retrospective figures and calculations. Indeed, for all the excitements of the chase, fact-hunting is only as valuable as the effect it has on later minds. If the O'Byrnes, O'Tooles and Kavanaghs whom we can infer as populating the valleys of upland Wicklow in the eighteenth century cannot legitimately be dragooned into the argument, this is more than an oblique acknowledegment of the means employed in banishing them to the margins. Others disappear also. The Synges of Bridgnorth soon drop out of sight in *The Silence*, not because there ceases to be any survival of the family in England, but because the reflexive dimension has been organised round the Synges of Wicklow on the east coast of Ireland.

Reflexivity here might be glossed as (in old-fashioned terms) the transformation of quantity into quality, in the sense that the first three Parts of *The Silence* are primarily concerned with history and the last one primarily with literature. These figures – the acute reader has already observed – do not account for all of the Parts, and it should be emphasised a different book could treat the Irish eighteenth century in terms of an undeniable cultural amplitude (e.g. Swift, the Sheridans, O'Carolan, etc.) not to be discovered through my focus on Henry Hatch and other money-grubbers. In other words, a period which literary historians may treat for their immediate purposes as a 'producer' is also and already a 'product' of a distinct but related historical process. Yeats acknowledges such a dialectic in 'Meditations in Time of Civil War'

Introduction

> Some violent bitter man, some powerful man
> Called architect and artist in, that they,
> Bitter and violent men, might rear in stone
> The sweetness that all longed for night and day,
> The gentleness none there had ever known:
> But when the master's buried mice can play,
> And maybe the great-grandson of that house,
> For all its bronze and marble, 's but a mouse.[4]

The poet's fear of 'declension', dwindling authority and (in its place) new commonness is only one version of a wider anxiety which pervaded much of Europe in the late nineteenth century. Decadence was at once a supposed disease and the preferred antidote of many who complained of its enervating symptoms. The cultural productions of a particular group or class may be read at several levels, not the least important being that at which its former 'natural' productivity can be written off.

This transformation is not simply to be identified with the literary genius of JMS, author of *The Aran Islands* and 'The Playboy of the Western World' (both 1907), even though it is through his work that the complex history unfolded in the succeeding pages was first observed. For example, there is a moment in the play when Pegeen, cross-questioning a newcomer in the isolated public house, addresses Christy Mahon as 'you with a kind of quality name, the like of what you'd find on the great powers and potentates of France and Spain'. This is apiece with the deliberate exaggeration of Synge's drama, but it also indirectly connotes awkward legacies – fallen status, foreign origins, present resolution and mobile identity.[5]

Between the marriage of Barbara Synge and John Hatch in 1765 and the birth of JMS just over a century later, there rose and fell three generations of the family. There's no real difficulty in tracing them – in *Burke's Landed Gentry* and similar reference books, and also in *The Family of Synge or Sing* (1937), a privately printed set of genealogical tables. Barbara and John Hatch had two daughters who married two of their own first cousins, the brothers Francis and Samuel Synge. Francis's son – just to summarise one line of succession briefly – was John Synge (1788-1845), whose son John Hatch Synge (1823-1872) was the father of JMS. This is the line which becomes known as the Synges of Glanmore, in County Wicklow. Its central figure is treated in Part IV, 'Affairs with the moon', below.

But the sources mentioned above are selective, incomplete and, to a degree, self-serving. The *Landed Gentry* originated as *Commoners*, and the change of title signalled much. Information derived ultimately from the subjects themselves, or from their increasingly sensitive descendents. This was the age of pride and anxiety. Not for nothing did Sir John Bernard Burke augment *Peerage* and *Gentry* in a book called *Vicisssitudes of Families* (1859). In many commonplace yet agonising ways, the nineteenth-century Synges suffered the ills of the age – deaths in infancy, bankruptcy, lifelong spinsterhood, mental illness, and so forth. Less predictably, they became involved in experimental education, in evangelical revival and – with JMS – in the Celtic Revival also.

It is with the last-named movement that the business of reflexive history really got under way in Ireland. Did Yeats's Revival revive a Celticism of the 1790s, or did it secularise the evangelical movement of the 1820s and 1830s? A list of distinguished names – Augusta Gregory (1852–1932), George Moore (1852–1933), Edward Martyn (1859–1923), W. B. Yeats (1865–1939), and JMS – testifies to the pull of the religious past. Martyn, a pious Catholic, is best commemorated today in a Palestrina Choir which he endowed in Dublin's Pro-Cathedral. The novelist Moore, his cousin, wrote historical romance in which the first generation of Jewish Christians were fictionalised. Gregory (born Augusta Persse), Yeats and JMS all came from landed families of recent evangelical activism. Of course, there was another list of contemporaries – Oscar Wilde (1854–1900), George Bernard Shaw (1856–1950), and James Joyce (1882–1941) – whose backgrounds were very different, being middle-class, professional/commercial, with a tinge (or binge) of Bohemianism.

JMS acts as the most mutually acceptable negotiator between the two lists, especially if the diversity of his family background is called into play. His brothers were all professional men, and their shadowy ancestor (John Hatch) a man of business, a manager of other people's affairs. Yet any attempt to realign these titan personalities as 'Celtic' or 'Anti-Celtic' results less in a discovery of their greater coherence as a single group, and more in an awareness of social disintegration and individual uniformity. Celtic Twilight Ireland in the 1880s and 1890s was the poor relative of Britain under High Capitalism, America of the Gilded Age, Bismarck's goose-stepping industrial democracy. Read within this broader context, the vicious squabbles of Irish sectarianism are but marginal notes in the decline and fall of the Christian empire. The – purely aesthetic – urge to rediscover a Jesus who had not died on the cross led Moore in *The Brook Kerith* (1916) to invent a Pre-Raphaelite Palestine. And the exercise is typical of an important strand in the reflexive history-making characteristic of so much Irish cultural endeavour.

No family offers a better opportunity for tracing ironies and omissions than the Synges. To put it positively, there are two vast collections of papers open to view. One was deposited in the National Library of Ireland by – or on behalf of – Edward Millington Stephens (1888–1955), JMS's nephew: it is made up primarily of business and legal papers. The other, a literary archive with substantial associated papers of family interest, was sold in 1968 to Trinity College Dublin by the Synge Trustees, amongst whom Lilo Stephens, Edward's widow, was a notable facilitator.[6] To put it less positively, these transfers were made in the knowledge that depredations had been wreaked upon the dramatist's papers in the period following his death in 1909. Edward Stephens's name will recur with increasing frequency.

These losses reflected anxieties about JMS's apparent embroilment in literary 'decadence' during his Paris years, and perhaps after. Decadence, however, should not be regarded simply as hashish and soft porn – no evidence of either in his case; it more strictly involves an intense awareness of decay. For a family which had wielded great powers of ecclesiastical patronage throughout the eighteenth century, acquired two baronetcies at the beginning of the nineteenth, and held property in at least half a dozen Irish counties, Victoria's long reign heaped trial upon tribulation. Lands were now lost in the Encumbered Estates Court (1848/1849). The State Church, to which the Synges had contributed archbishops, bishops and archdeacons, was disestablished by parliament in 1869. Tenants began to withhold what rents were still due, and to argue morality as their case, not that of the landlords. John Hatch's success threatened to re-present itself as ancestral guilt.

Seen in this light, *The Silence* is a family history. But the book could as well be described as a study in locality, its focus being County Wicklow. Though the Hatches and Synges had property and business interests in many parts of Ireland (and England), the particular line which runs from John Hatch to his great-great-grandson, the dramatist, can be traced in detail in connection with the acquisition of Wicklow land. The starting point now is not just biographical but political. We observe the erratic development of the Temple estates in that county. We investigate at least one intervention into these affairs by Jonathan Swift, sometime secretary to Sir William Temple. We trace in more detail the activity of Hatches as managers for superior landlords, and the inheritance of parts of this property by Francis Synge (MP) at the beginning of the nineteenth century. Hardly had that process of acquisition begun when it assumed the counter-dynamic of loss and dispersal, accelerated by the Great Famine of 1845.

The third way of reading *The Silence* is as history of ideas, with particular emphasis on changes of religious sensibility within Irish protestantism during the first half of the nineteenth century. The birth of the Plymouth Brethren in the mountains of County Wicklow may come as a surprise to some, but the participation of the Synge family in a complex of heterodox activities – Pestalozzian schooling, dispensationalist theology, 'moral agency', to name but three – demonstrates the inadequacy of standard accounts of Anglo-Irish protestant culture in the nineteenth century. Against this refocused background, it will become easier to follow Yeats, JMS and Joyce on their early continental pilgrimages.

Somewhere or other, Raymond Williams observed that nobody ever became a Marxist by conviction alone. In his craggy way, what he was striving to emphasise was a Marxist interpretation of his own Marxism, a recognition of those complicated necessities which contribute to the intellectual decisiveness in which we may

Introduction

take pride, comfort or refuge as the circumstances require. Williams is dead of course, a circumstance which does not automatically invalidate him. He was by no means a fellow-traveller with Moscow orthodoxies, nor was he a comfortable passenger on the British New Left. His version of dialectical thinking cannot be *précised* or appropropriated. But his general example remains attractive, not least his example of a local and residual element sustained even as it was being anatomised. Williams's Wales could be seen from the hill above my grandparents' Wicklow home.

There is, perhaps, one further way of reading *The Silence*, or way of combining the three readings already suggested. That is, to regard the book as reflective rather than narrative or analytical. The written history of any period or subject can augment one's apprehension of the period in which it was written, and this without any capitulation to postmodernism. Certain chapters here derive from papers which were actively used by Edward Stephens in the 1930s and 1940s when he was compiling a dossier of material relating to the life and background of his uncle JMS. A judiciously abbreviated version of this appeared in 1974.[7] But certain questions were not raised by Stephens, though to his legally-trained mind their relevance was obvious. The simplest instance of this diplomatic omission arises in his treatment of John Hatch's death in 1797: did Hatch leave a will or did he not? The matter is elided into Stephens's account of how Francis Synge (Hatch's son-in-law) acquired a seat in the House of Commons and how, after the 1800 extinction of the Irish Parliament, Synge nurtured a country seat in Wicklow instead.

These tactics of narrative legitimation go further than simply to celebrate the good fortune of the Wicklow Synges. They consolidate a view of late eighteenth-century Ireland, and of protestant gentry conduct specifically, a view which had comforted Irish Unionists during the heyday of Parnell and the Home Rule crises. Further, we gain an insight into Stephens's own attitude to politics in the 1920s when, as a southern lawyer who had been close to Michael Collins, he played an important role in the affairs of the Boundary Commission, whose Report (1925) consolidated Unionist dominance in Northern Ireland, at the same time making permanent the partition of Ireland. It is no disparagement of Edward Stephens to say that his intended Life of JMS was part of an even larger 'project', the narrative of transition and legitimation by which the Irish Free State became an acceptable home to descendants of 'the Big House', on terms which permitted them to criticise the new polity because they had also interrogated their own past. Such terms, of course, included (on both sides of the deal) some unstated terms, reservations and residual prejudices. Yeats's *The Tower* (1929) is the poetic sublime equivalent.

While Stephens was quietly at work on his never-to-be-published Leviathan, a new literature was coming into existence in Ireland. Close associates of JMS were

Introduction

still pre-eminent in the world's view of Irish culture – notably Yeats, but also Joyce. Thanks to the latter, a new genre of writing had been taken up by the younger generation. The short story was to become – for good and ill – a favourite medium of both literary expression and social critique. First Moore and Joyce. Then – from the 1920s onwards – Elizabeth Bowen, Mary Lavin, Frank O'Connor, Liam O'Flaherty, Sean O'Faolain, and James Plunkett explored the problematic identities of Ireland through this demanding art-form.

This latter perspective, or prospect, takes us into the academic zone known as Anglo-Irish Literature. I am well aware that the usual suspects will grab hold of 'Anglo-Ireland' in the hope of turning it into a pretty penny – I mean tour agents, rectors of old decency, heritage industrialists, and the like. In the historical analysis on offer here, Sean O'Casey's birthplace in rundown Dorset Street is not eclipsed by Lissadell or Derrynane. Neither are the downtrodden masses assumed to be pregnant with revolution. In the end, the risen people give rise to Archbishop MacQuaid and Charlie Haughey more often that they donate revolutionaries. By a depressing corollary, certain kinds of Irish radicalism derive more energy from comfortable discontent, from resentment and injured hubris, than they do from unmediated suffering. (To that end, the system is careful to ensure that all suffering is mediated, not least these days by the media.) Out of this paradox may spring the concluding volume of – potentially – a trilogy, the third volume to re-open the question of JMS's experience in Paris, and to examine Gentry Republicanism in twentieth-century Ireland, with particular reference to the Bartons, Childers, Robinsons (and others) of County Wicklow. These are not separate worlds. Should the hidden god of Cronemore, Ballinatone, Macreddin and Roundwood deprive Himself of my company for sufficient years, the three volumes would constitute *The Broken World of Irish Literary History*.

Whatever about its general aptness, the title of the trilogy derives from a short story by Sean O'Faolain (1900–1991). The narrator of 'A Broken World' (1937) meets a retired priest in a train. Though their journey is taking place elsewhere in Ireland, the focus of their conversation is Wicklow. The priest had served there in his early days, the period – roughly – when JMS was enjoying his last summers in the county. The story is at one level an example of O'Faolain's short-story art of engraving character, disappointment, and innocence on to simple material, written during or in response to his brief residence at Killough House, in north County Wicklow. 'It had a neglected orchard, a crumbling glasshouse with vines, therefore a vinery, and a lawn with a swing.'[8] That is to say, its twentieth-century remnants constitute an unintentional memorial to untraceable Barbara Synge for whom another Wicklow was intended in the 1760s but which she probably never saw.

At another level, O'Faolain's story is a form of history, local without doubt, but by implication a larger history also. It displays its debts to James Joyce,

Introduction

especially to 'Ivy Day in the Committee Room' and 'The Dead'. In 'A Broken World', O'Faolain sought to write, or at least to palimpsest, a chapter in the moral history of his country. Such an undertaking nowadays would fly in the face of too many fashions. The significance of the story was brought home late in 1999 with the destruction of a Wicklow mountain farm-house – complete with its older cattlesheds – known to me in childhood, and its replacement by an eighty-bedroom hotel. *Pace* Raymond Williams, research has its personal calendar.

Market Street, Ardee, County Louth, with Hatch Castle – its present name – on the left, c. 1890

Plates

James Baron, on the High Road leading from Waterford to Dungarvon.

DUBLIN, April 25.

17th.] In the Morning, a new-born Infant was found dead, with several Marks of Violence, at the Foot of the Steeple of St. Patrick's Cathedral.

18th.] An Adjournment of the Quarter Sessions was held at the Tholsel, when Thomas Connor, Hugh Ryan, Michael Clancy, and James Corrogan, were found guilty of Felony, and ordered for Transportation; and two were acquitted. The next Sessions will begin on Tuesday the 28th Instant.

19th.] The Body of the Mate of a Vessel, who fell yesterday off a Plank into the Liffey, was this Morning found standing erect in the Mud.

MARRIED.] A few Days ago Mr. Christopher Casey, Wigmaker; to Miss Anne Jones; both of Britain-street.—At Waterford; Mr. Elliot Blackmore of Carrick, to Miss Sibella Gibson.

DIED.] A few Days ago at Montruby near Mallow; Mrs. Mc.Carthy Wife of Ruby McCarthy, Esq;—At Dunleer; Mrs. Magahre.—In Essex-street, Mrs. Gough, Wife of Alderman Gough of Limerick.—The Wife of Mr. John Finlay, one of his Majesty's Messengers.—At Feathard, aged 90, Mr. Henry Sheppard.—In Patrick-street, Mr. Wade, Poulterer.—Mrs. Lettice Sankey, of Kilmore in the County of Longford:—At her House in Suffolk-street, Mrs. Sarah Bull; a Maiden Lady.—At Stephen's-Green, Mr. Hatch; wife of John Hatch; Esq;

THEATRE-ROYAL.

Death notices, including that for Barbara Synge (Mrs John Hatch), and adjacent items,
The Freeman's Journal (Dublin), 21–25 April 1767

Undated entry in the 1765 diary of John Hatch (d. 1797)

The West Front of Saint Patrick's Cathedral, Dublin, in 1791

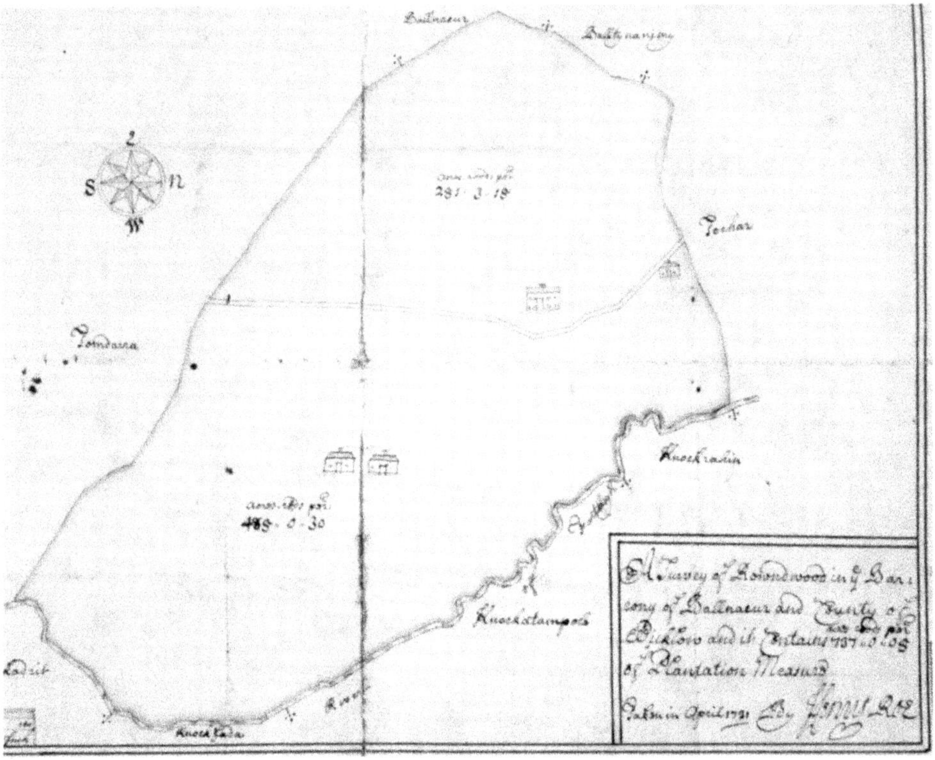

A map of Roundwood, County Wicklow, 1731

The Pestalozzi school-room at Nun's Cross, County Wicklow

Roundwood Park, County Wicklow (before the fire of c. 1950)

Plates

Glanmore Castle, County Wicklow, 1805

Robert Owen's proposed model Irish village (1823)

Plates

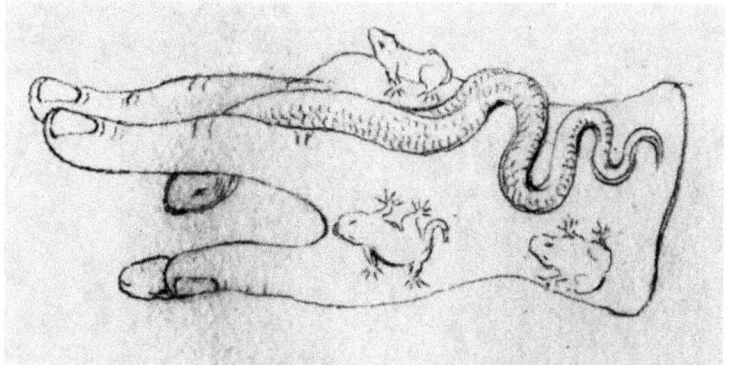

Drawing by John 'Pestalozzi' Synge (1788–1845), from his Italian sketchbook

John Hatch Synge (1823–1872)

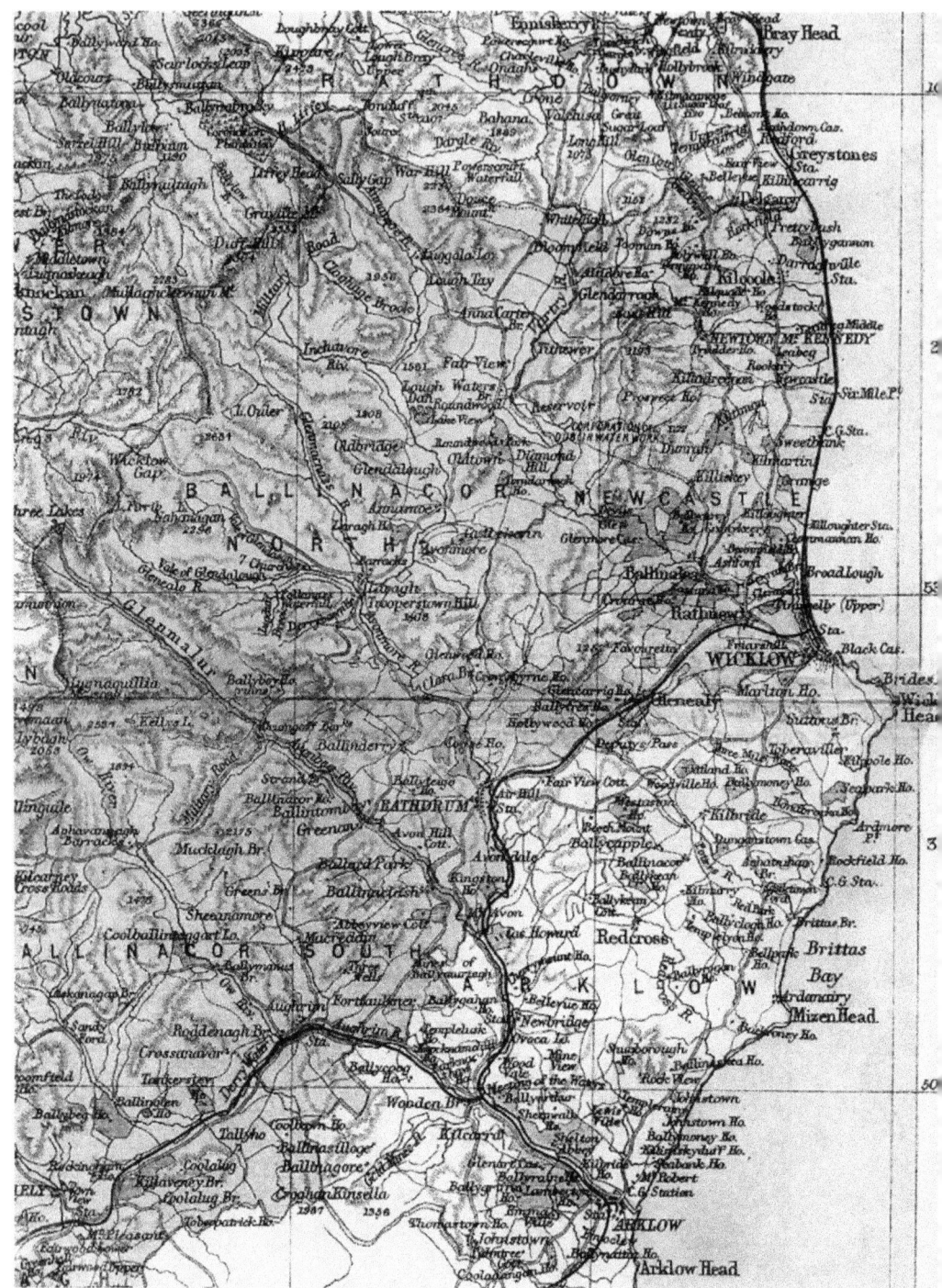

Ballincor North and Newcastle, and adjacent Baronies, County Wicklow, in the late nineteenth century

Part I

SETTINGS

2

Lands elsewhere: Wicklow

From my presbytery window I could see the entire coast, a long straight beach, miles to the north, miles to the south, with a headland at each end stuck out into the sea. By the sea it was marsh. Then comes the first wave of high land around villages like Newtownmountkennedy. The land isn't bad on those hills, though it isn't what you would call really good land. They grow good turnips and potatoes and mangolds; the greens are not bad; but they cannot grow wheat. You need a good marl bottom for wheat. I was a young man then, and keen, so I studied these questions. (*O'Faolain*)

LAND is no absolute. It is a means of distinguishing between one human location and another, one historical process and another. Wicklow was the last area of Ireland to be incorporated (1606) into the county system. For this reason its shape was determined by a series of earlier demarcations and boundaries. Though its northern edge lies scarcely more than fifteen kilometres from Dublin, the lateness of its submission to the administrative sway of Jacobean power was a testimony to the county's impenetrable fastnesses and its uncertain coastline. Though the Temple family were granted Wicklow lands in the seventeenth century, no house was erected by them nor estate cultivated. Later landlords engaged in various minor 'plantations' of tenants loyal to reformed church and state. Nothing flourished, little failed to endure.

This paradoxical condition affected ecclesiastical affairs also. The ancient see of Glenadalough, in turn deriving from the monastery founded in the Wicklow hills by Saint Kevin, was united with the metropolitan diocese of Dublin in the thirteenth century. Unity, however, led to much anomaly. While religious and even theological questions will preoccupy us in due course, the particular importance of the ecclesiastical establishment in the argument which unfolds here lies in its consubstantiality as property. Church offices, and not only church lands, potentially constituted wealth which might be alienated. Of course, in the post-Reformation period, religion (or Christianity, to be exact) also became a field of conflict, political, social and personal.

Lands elsewhere: Wicklow

Despite its remoteness, 'ordinary' crime also flourished in Wicklow. The Dublin newspaper, *Pue's Occurrences*, reported on 8 January 1741 that 'Tuesday night last, the House of Mr. Freeman of Tomdaragh ... was set on Fire by some Villains, this is the third time his House and Barns have been ... within this Year ... burnt down.' On a Sunday morning in August of the same year, Robert Usher was killed near Rathdrum; before the month was out an elderly man had his throat cut at Powerscourt 'and his Skull broke in a most barbarous manner'. In the latter case, crime of a more general kind provided the background. When Michael Kerwin was brought from Liverpool to face the murder charge, his father and brother awaited him in Wicklow Gaol – detained there as horse-thieves – and the victim had been Kerwin's uncle.[1]

Wicklow became infamous or, in other circles, renowned at the very end of the eighteenth century. Rebellion stubbornly resisted suppression here in the aftermath of sectarian conflict during 1798. Nevertheless, it has been shown that the county's levels of violent crime were comparatively low throughout the nineteenth century.[2] The Gaelic language lingered in isolated pockets, detached from the self-consciously besieged cultural 'last ditches' of Munster and Connacht. Circa 1907 JMS reported that in the port of Arklow in the southern part of the county, 'some of the comparatively recent immigrants have revived Gaelic in this neighbourhood'.[3] His observation, however, fails to reveal that the immigrants in question were probably a very small number of internal migrants, moving from the West of Ireland under the influence of protestant evangelicalism. Up-river from Arklow, near Avoca and Woodenbridge, the Plymouth Brethren and other such sects maintained a presence.

Alongside this exotic aspect of Wicklow's cultural diversity, the county inevitably became a recreational retreat for discontented Dublin intellectuals. The great parliamentarian, Henry Grattan (1746-1820), had been fixed up with a country residence near Enniskerry, in recognition of his services to a short-lived colonial nationalism. A little further south, Romantic painters sketched at Glendalough. The first players of the Abbey Theatre, like many others of their Edwardian generation, took walking expeditions in the Dublin-Wicklow hills. After independence, some writers (less than convinced of the new state's good will) sought their tiny thatched *dachas* or their secularised *dyserts*. For many, Wicklow had been a place of last resort.

Sean O'Faolain's short story is dominated by the conversation of his elderly priest, travelling with the narrator and a third passenger in a train through a snow-covered Irish landscape. The setting of the story is not specified as to place, though the south-west of Ireland is initially implied through descriptions of the landscape, afforestation, weather and so forth. No date is suggested, beyond that implicit in the references to government attitudes towards landed estate: some time in the early to mid-1930s. The priest had served in County Wicklow, and the view from the carriage window – a snow-covered rural desolation, dark even at midday – prompts him to reminisce.

Everything in 'A Broken World' is refracted through the priest's broken career. He had been silenced for his youthful political opinions, though it is also clear to the narrator that the man is held in awe by railway officials and the people at the station where he dismounts. His account of Wicklow is arranged in terraces which rise from the marshy coast, through the well-to-do estates of the gentry, the respectable farms and cabins on the lower hills, reclaimed bog and upland, and (above that) 'the utterly, miserably ... wretched moor'. The one topographical name he provides – Newtownmountkennedy – fixes the area reasonably well. There, in the last decades of the eighteenth century, General Cunningham cultivated a great pleasure ground, with eye-catching temple and contrived vista to the sea. The General's sight failed, ruling him out of the military leadership which crushed the rebels of 1798.

Yet in many ways, O'Faolain's Wicklow is untypical of the county's representation in literature. He describes a series of social terraces, leading upwards from the coast through gradations of cultivation (both agricultural and cultural) on to the moorland or mountain. Certainly the mountains feature in fictional and poetic accounts of Wicklow more often than the well-watered estates near Bray, Delgany and Enniskerry, or Tinahely and Shillelagh further south. This is partly to emphasise that the literature in which the county features is Romantic or post-Romantic, indebted to Wordsworth and Scott. Even Gothic fiction exploited the county's wild proximity to Dublin, as in C. R. Maturin's famous *Melmoth the Wanderer* (1820), a novel which will repay closer attention (see chapter 15 below). Thomas Moore's drawing-room song 'Vale of Avoca' may be mellower than Standish O'Grady's Celtic Revivalist novel *The Flight of the Eagle*, but both illustrate how Wicklow was imaginatively conceived in terms of valleys and glens, precipitous descents from an uninhabitable upper world. Here early Irish Christians built their monasteries, here Gaelic heroes eluded the Elizabethan invader.

It is no mere coincidence that the final violation of this constructed reality is linked to 1798 and its aftermath. The rebellion did not commence in Wicklow, but its suppression was graphically encoded there in the form of military roads. These were built across the high wasteland to link the city of Dublin with its dangerous hinterland and – within the county – to link glen to glen in the name of state security. The Romantic era has been brilliantly characterised in terms of incompleteness and fragmentation, and nowhere is this diagnosis more thoroughly vindicated than in the fate of the Wicklow landscape in the decade following publication of *Lyrical Ballads* (1798). The roads simultaneously broke the county apart and bound it in an adamantine system of control.[4]

The present book deals with both the anterior condition of Wicklow and its later literary eminence, with the death of forgotten John Hatch in September 1797 acting as the pivotal event. It does not, of course, deal with the entire county, but

Lands elsewhere: Wicklow

rather with a pattern involving accumulation, dispersal and transmission of lands along a line extending roughly from Calary at its northern end to Drumgoff some twenty or so kilometres to the south. This is upland country, a landscape of bog and hillside, rather than mountain – though mountains (vindictively out of sight) contain the area. Perhaps a more recognisable set of co-ordinates would cite Enniskerry (close to the Dublin-Wicklow county boundary) and Rathdrum, the market town adjacent to the Parnell estate at Avondale, but these names suggest larger fields of operation than will in practice be entered upon. Even if substantial holdings (notably those of the Synge family) will be discussed, the inquiry which follows is an experiment in micro-history, focused as often on a townland, a mill-building or a cottage as on the great estates and 'Big Houses'.

As everywhere in rural Ireland, the names of places are striking, potent and disputatious.[5] The gradations of territorial unit inscribed a history of displacement. The fundamental unit, the *baile* or townland, reached back to the pre-Viking Celtic realm. Parishes were a twelfth-century development, near-coincidental with (but not resulting from) the Norman invasion; later the Reformation brought further distinctions, so that it is now necessary to refer distinctly to civil or ecclesiastical parishes and (within the latter) to Catholic or Church of Ireland ones. Larger units – provinces and baronies – were alike different in their origins, the former having a very ancient history, the latter term introduced in the sixteenth century. Wicklow lies wholly within the province of Leinster, and the specific area investigated in this book is mainly to be found in the baronies of Ballinacor (north and south). There is, of course, a townland called Ballinacorbeg (beg, or properly *beag*, being the Gaelic for little or lesser) and the name Ballinacor was used casually for both the townland and the Kemmis family's estate further south. Such nominal profusion is often the mark of real contention.

This is a terrain everyone should get to know, though it will prove treacherous, elusive and hypnotic. As with a language, the process of familiarisation can be based on essential elements. Recurring names will include:

Annamoe, previously spelled Animo (e.g. in Laurence Sterne's 'Memoir' of 1758); a small village whose name derives from Gaelic *Ath na mBó* (Cattle-Ford) (*Price*, I, 34).
Calary, a townland in the barony of Rathdown, where a Church of Ireland church was erected in 1832 (parish of Enniskerry; Calary became a parish in its own right in 1831), the point from which the Revd John Nelson Darby launched the campaign resulting in the foundation of the Plymouth Brethren (see *Price*, V, 305 for earlier history).
Castle Kevin, now a house close to the village of Annamoe, but previously the name related to an ecclesiastical territory of far greater extent, taking its name from the patron saint (Kevin) of Glendalough and linked to the medieval archdiocese of Dublin (and Glendalough) (*Price*, I, 30–32).

Settings

Derrylossary, a parish (based on an ancient church) incorporating Annamoe and 'Seven Churches'. In 1231, it became part of the Corps of the Chancellor of Saint Patrick's Cathedral, Dublin (*Price*, I, 27–28).

The Devil's Glen, a steep defile running from Glanmore westwards and uphill in the direction of Annamoe. Not to be confused with Paradise Glyn.

Drumeen, a townland north of Roundwood, where, in the latter half of the eighteenth century, Thomas Hugo had a house – burnt 1798 by Joseph Holt who appears to have been a native of the same district (*Price*, I, 34). The property was subsequently bought by the Barton family.

Glanmore, previously Glenmouth; here Francis Synge developed a Gothic-style residence with attached estate, in effect eclipsing Roundwood Park as his family's seat in the county.

Glenmalure, a long secluded valley running NW-SE, with the Avonbeg river flowing towards Greenane (and onwards to the sea).

Laragh, a village at the eastern end of the road leading into Glendalough; defensive buildings were erected after 1798; Laragh East is an adjacent townland.

Newtownmountkennedy, a relatively modern village on the lowland road from Arklow to Dublin; developed by Robert Cunningham.

Powerscourt, estate of the Wingfield family, with Enniskerry serving as its village; the lands ran southwards to meet the (future) Synge property of Roundwood.

Rathdrum, a small market town with rail links to Dublin and Wexford, at the southern extremity of the terrain examined in these pages. In the late eighteenth century, a stronghold of protestant loyalism. With the establishment of institutions such as the workhouse and railways, the town grew in importance during the nineteenth century. C. S. Parnell's estate lay immediately to the south.

Roundwood, a village in the barony of Ballinacor North, with a house (Roundwood Park) lying to the south-east. It seems reasonable to assume that Barbara Synge's husband, John Hatch, intended to develop Roundwood Park after their marriage in 1765. The village is sometimes known by the Gaelic name, An Tocher – *tocher* meaning a raised area created to make bogland accessible (*Price*, I, 42).

Tomriland, a townland to the south of Glanmore Castle, part of the mid-eighteenth century Hatch/M'Cracken holding where, in the summer of 1769, Cornelius Connor contracted with Sam M'Cracken to roll stones.[6] In Tomriland farmhouse, JMS wrote 'In the Shadow of the Glen' (1902).

While these and other local spots will exert their own fascination, the history of one out-of-the-way place may stand as a testimony to the complexity of the area as a whole. According to records in the Dublin Registry of Deeds, on 15 February

Lands elsewhere: Wicklow

1748, Henry Hatch (father of the obscure John Hatch who will marry into the Synges) acquired a 99-year lease to 309 acres of Wicklow mountainside. However, a later memorial (no. 94, 277, oddly mis-indexed in the Registry) records an endorsement of the original date, written on the back of the deed: by these documents, John Xemenes of Kilkenny and his eldest son, Charles, had granted to Hatch a lease of Glassnamullen, a townland lying on an east-facing lower slope of Djouce Mountain. Though Hatch paid £300, the endorsement declared 'that the said sum ... was the proper money of Samuel McCracken of the City of Dublin Perukemaker and not of him the said Henry Hatch [and that his name was made use of in the said deed in trust for the said Samuel McCracken]'. While the original deed had been witnessed by Henry Stearne, clerk to Christopher Dalton, a Dublin public notary, the later documentation was not sworn nor lodged in the Registry until 27 March 1750, when John Hatch was one of the witnesses.[7] It remains to be seen why the lease-purchase was first registered in Henry Hatch's name, only to have the record amended two years later with M'Cracken declared the purchaser and beneficiary. It was on this second occasion that the younger Hatch began his investments in Wicklow. And while the plot of land seems obscure and uninviting, Glassnamullen had its own ancient history. It featured in a medieval list of 'feoffees in the tenement of Castlekeyvyn'.[8] The Sutton family, who feature in the margins of this story, were early associated with the townland (its name variously spelled), and their burial rights endure at Calary churchyard. A few consecrated square yards act as the latter-day assembly point for a series of names which will occur in this centuries-long chronicle: twentieth-century burials include Cuthbertson, Delemere, Johnston, Pollard, Sutton and Synge.

Not that local history remains out of the way, divorced from the world of wars and exterminations. In the stage directions, etc., for 'In the Shadow of the Glen', a play owing not a little to Henrik Ibsen, JMS referred to 'the last cottage at the head of a long glen'. This is a two-storey (four-room) house, sometimes known as Ballinagoneen, at the northern end of Glenmalure. Maud Gonne bought it in October 1919, together with fifteen acres of land, and grazing rights on nearly 12,000 acres of mountain. She sold it in 1928, probably as part of the transactions which included the purchase of Laragh Castle for her daughter Iseult Stuart and Francis Stuart, the novelist. Though Stuart left Ireland for Germany in the late 1930s, and remained outside Ireland until after his wife's death, Iseult continued to live in Laragh Castle (with her mother-in-law and children) until the end.[9] She died in March 1954.

The Glenmalure property also passed through dedicated hands. Before its conversion into Ireland's smallest youth hostel, the cottage was owned by Kathleen Lynn, socialist daughter of a Church of Ireland rector, medical attendant to Connolly's Irish Citizen Army in 1916, and later a thorn in the side of De Valera's regime. While holidaying in Glenmalure, Dr Lynn attended morning service at Ballinatone, where the present writer was baptised in 1947.

2

Other people: the Hatches

History and ult. signification obscure, Cf Heck and Hack, sb2. (OED)

TO BE vulgarly cryptic, Barbara Synge disappears through a Hatch. The relationship between people, names and things has never been simple. The Oxford Dictionary lists several related meanings for the not uncommon noun, hatch, ranging from a half-door with an open space above it to a wooden bed-frame. But it begins by frankly announcing that the origins of the word are unknown. Much the same obscurity marks the Irish family of the same name. Nothing daunted, this chapter attempts to bring together the sometimes conflicting evidence regarding JMS's lesser known eighteenth-century ancestry. It does not pretend to answer all the questions it raises. The results are deliberately left in relatively unprocessed form, not out of respect for some aboriginal virtue which they might thereby manifest but, on the contrary, with the intention of emphasising the extent to which any kind of data already is possessed by earlier intentions, needs or anxieties. 'Being past, being no more, is passionately at work in things', Walter Benjamin noted. 'To this the historian trusts for his subject matter.' Or, rather for objects of knowledge. Despite the vapidities of Visual Culture and Cultural Studies, such objects endure, though not unchanged. 'And', Benjamin continues in connection with these things, 'the energy that works in them is dialectics.'[1] So far is reading from any kind of empirical activity.

SEVENTEENTH-CENTURY DUBLIN AND AFTER

Though William de Hatche served in a medieval Irish parliament (1297), and was also Sheriff of Louth, there is no reason to believe that any line of JMS's ancestry extended in Ireland earlier than the seventeenth century. It remains possible to find a Norman ancestry more venerable than the Synge-come-latelys of the sixteenth century, but the genealogist's neglect of the possibility – indeed of the whole Hatch line before our John Hatch – argues against it. Hatches and Synges

Other people: the Hatches

may have come to Ireland more or less simultaneously, give a decade or two and a considerable distance between their stations in life. There was a Hatch in Dublin sometime in the 1640s, for he is mentioned in the infamous Depositions, taken down in the years after the 1641 Rising and in turn exploited by Sir John Temple (1600–1677) to justify the confiscation of Irish estates. Sir John's family featured among the beneficiaries, and acquired land in County Wicklow later owned by Hatches or Synges. The list of so-called '49 Officers – that is, those who had served before 1649 and were rewarded with property in the walled towns (such as Ardee) includes one John Hatch, without any further particulars.[2] The name is suspended in paper history, like a villain in some Gothic novel, absent and ineradicable.

The earliest person of the name whom I have traced in Dublin is Richard Hatch, father of David Hatch baptised 27 March 1635 in the parish of Saint John the Evangelist. This is quite early enough for our purposes, which are not to constuct yet another family tree, but rather to challenge the self-legitimation buried in the foliage of such post hoc constructions. In any case, the Christian names Richard and David do not recur among the Hatches we are concerned with.

Two years later, Nicholas, son of John and Mary Hatch, was baptised in Saint Michan's on 5 May 1637. This is probably the Nicholas Hatch who, on 27 June 1678, married Mary Pullen in Saint Bride's church. Nicholas (dates otherwise unknown) was the father of John Hatch (1680–1719), who has the distinction of being the only known member of the family to take holy orders. Born in Dublin, but educated in Drogheda by Mr Waller, the Revd John Hatch graduated a BA of Trinity College Dublin in 1702, and was perpetual curate of Duleek (diocese of Meath) for the last two or so years of his short life; his wife's Christian name was Catherine.[3] Others less easily assimilated to a family tree include Benjamin who witnessed the will of Thomas Houghton, Dublin merchant, in October 1667, and Margaret Hatch (of New Street) who was buried on 23 November 1711 in the parish of Saint Bride. John, son of George and Ann Hatch, was baptised on 24 September 1726 in the parish of SS Peter and Kevin. A different Ann Hatch married James Boyle by special licence on Saint Stephen's Day 1728 in Saint John's parish, Dublin.

Returning from Ringsend races in July 1764, a Hatch of Sycamore Alley was thrown from his horse. In the early summer of 1768, a fruiterer named Hatch (also of Sycamore Alley) married the Widow Aspel of Essex Street.[4] Apprenticed to a printer, Charles Hatch broke into his master's closet in August 1772 and fled the city, having found no money. Though an accomplice in this escapade was subsequently admitted a member of the Guild of Saint Luke, no further trace of the absconded Hatch has been established.[5] Perhaps he prospered abroad after this youthful indiscretion, but his brief Dublin career in many ways epitomises the humble or middling station which the Hatch tribe generally occupied in the city's life, and also the obscurity which descended upon their one *eminence*, the MP for Swords.

Settings

Some later Dubliners bearing the name were Catholics, for example, Bridget Hatch who lived at 3 Catherine's Lane in 1802 is recorded as a sponsor.[6] But these probably represented a deviation from the family's unremarkable protestant traditions, a deviation associated with social non-advancement, at least in the eighteenth century. The Convert Rolls include 'Catherine Nugent, otherwise Hatch' who conformed to the Established Church on 18 May 1774. Nicholas Hatch, a merchant, was in business in Amiens Street during the 1840s. Two women (or perhaps just one) are listed in later directories – Mrs Hatch of No. 1 Brookville, Monkstown (1850) and Mrs H. Hatch, Brookfield House, Blackrock (1855). Sarah Hatch, who died on 20 June 1862 and is buried in Carrickbrennan church (Monkstown), may be one and the same.

HATCHES OUTSIDE DUBLIN

A local historian has concluded that, as the town of Ardee in County Louth was allocated to what were known as the '49 Officers under the Cromwellian Settlement, the presence there of the name Hatch in the late seventeeth century originated in that fashion. Certainly, one list of these Officers mentions a John Hatch, though it does not link him to Ardee. As we have found pre-Cromwellian Hatches in Dublin, it would then seem as if some of the family moved from the capital out to this rural town (whether as beneficiaries of Cromwell or not) rather than the other way round. Instead of promoting themselves through university education and other forms of gradual infiltration into the city, the Hatches may have 'devolved' from Dublin in search of minor rewards. Though the only member of the family who achieved a measure of distinction was the Dubliner John Hatch, the dramatist's great-great-grandfather, lesser members of the family – notably country members – impacted on their Dublin kinsman with, at times, an embarrassing effect. These can be considered under three sub-headings.

ARDEE, COUNTY LOUTH

Although JMS's ancestors of this name were closely associated with Dublin, his brothers attended Rathmines School where a Hatch from elsewhere was also a pupil. While it is not yet possible to complete the family forest, some details of ex-Dublin Hatches are included here. Leaving aside the thirteenth-century sheriff, of the Hatches of Ardee the earliest record tells of Mary Hatch who died in childbirth on 17 March 1695 and is buried in Saint Mary's churchyard.[7] A list of 'Gentlemen of County Louth c. 1600' does not include the name, though its omission may signify lack of status rather than absence from the county. By 1717, John and Edward Hatch sat as representatives of 'the commons' on Ardee's corporation.[8] A list of inhabitants for 1760 establishes that at least seven bearers of the name were residents/householders in Ardee – these were Ann Hatch, Debby Hatch, John

Other people: the Hatches

Hatch, Jonathan Hatch, Thomas Hatch and his mother (living in what is later known as Hatch's Castle), and Terence Hatch. The 1767 listing of a Thomas Hatch among supporters of a defeated political faction (the Fortesques) indicates respectability, little more. A William Hatch of Ardee, who died in September 1769, was sufficiently notable to have his passing recorded in a Dublin newspaper.[9]

From Old Saint Mary's we additionally learn of another Thomas Hatch, said to have been a student at Trinity College Dublin, who died on 13 June 1778 at the age of 19. Jonathan Hatch died in July 1739 aged about 70, and Richard Hatch in 1772. In addition to these, gravestones, etc., record Jeremiah Hatch (d. 30 May 1811, aged 56), Jane Hatch (d. 4 May 1817, aged 59: this is probably the Jane Pepper referred to below), and Ann Hatch (d. 10 August 1840, aged 85, the wife of Jeremiah Hatch). Jeremiah Hatch of Ardee, gent., witnessed the will of Bradston Cheney on 24 March 1796. Of more than casual interest is John Hatch who died 9 September 1819 aged 70, but is curiously commemorated at Old Saint Mary's as 'an Honest Man', as if to distinguish him from someone less honest who might be confused with him.

One family will be of particular interest, though its relationship to the MP has not yet been established. Jeremiah Hatch married Jane Pepper; on 20 August 1793 their son Jeremiah married Ann, daughter of Thomas Hatch of Ardee and his wife Rose (née Williams): these latter had issue:

Thomas MB (23 July 1794–18 August 1817)
William (1 July 1795–1870 'aged 73') – see pp. 28–29 below
John MD (20 July 1796–30 October 1874), married Harriet Freeman
Jeremiah AB (1797– ?)
Rose-Anne (who married James Cuthbertson MD of Dublin)

Names are not just data, they are statements (however cryptic) of relationship. We may not yet know what 'cryptography' is appropriate to the recurrence of medical qualifications of the last few nominees, nor can we predict what follows from this brief glimpse of Cuthbertson. Nevertheless, a social context, a texture of class begins to form. It could be summarised in the concept of *occupation*, meaning both the manner by which a person earns his or her living and the place of abode, or degree of possession which he or she holds. Occupation, of course, smacks of a latter-day sociology rather than the traditional image of Ireland still deduced by too many from their highly selective reading of Yeats and his Celtic Revival contemporaries.

A STORM IN THE BELLEWSTOWN CUP

Ecumenical relations in 1822 can be judged from an incident when person or persons unknown broke into Ardee's Catholic chapel to place a calf's head on the altar in protestant protest at some confused notion of transubstantiation beloved of the perpetrators.[10] It comes almost as a relief to learn that, in 1828, Mr William Hatch mounted two four-pounder ornamental cannon on the east tower of Ardee Castle. The authority for this display of authority is a Victorian guide to Louth which credits Cromwell with granting the castle 'to an ancestor of the Hatch family'. Here at last is something more than atomised fact, arranged in mere lists. But if the Hatches held the property throughout the intervening years, then testimony from the 1750s strongly indicates that they presided over some kind of local gaol. Thomas Wright reported that 'here we found a poor old grey-headed Man imprisoned for a Debt of six English Shillings whom we released'.[11] The same William Hatch corresponded with Lord Oriel (John Foster, 1740–1828) to establish his voting rights as a freeman.[12]

Such attention to civic dignity did not go without hostile comment. The social climate was disturbed. At Ardee Fair in 1831, a man was stabbed in the stomach till his bowels tumbled out, in a riotous situation quelled eventually by a new partnership of local magnate (Ruxton) and Catholic curate (exotically named Deccluzeau). During these days of pervasive uncertainty, William Hatch's activities on the turf led to heated dispute, during which he published items in the local press. 'A Subscriber to the Bellewstown Cup' replied, mocking the manner in which Hatch had alleged religion to be sole cause of the 'anti-feeling' he had stirred up. Hatch had entered his horse – significantly named *Sir* Nicholas – in several heats for the same race. Protestant susceptibilities were clearly linked to social pretension in this case, with the horse knighted in anticipation of its owner's triumph over new commonness. In response to Hatch's styling himself a gentleman, the broadside declared, 'that cannot be the echo of another person's saying'. The question now posed was, 'are you admitted as a guest into the house of any acknowledged gentleman in the county[?]' Fine repartee was marred by colourful abuse scarcely matched by Michael James in 'The Playboy of the Western World' – Hatch's face resembled 'a human excrement after four or five days bleaching by a March wind'.[13]

Despite the sub-Swiftian humour, urgent political matters were under discussion between Hatch and his assailant. Three years earlier in 1829, Catholics had won the right to sit in parliament; eight further years would pass before the exclusively protestant corporations (like Ardee) fell to the Reformers. This was a dangerous *entr'acte* between political innovations of the greatest consequence, a period of resentment which, in different registers, gave rise to the Tithe War and the *Dublin University Magazine* (*DUM*). Hatch, in his concern with others' religious antagonism and his own doubtful status as gentleman, manifested exactly the small-town hubris associated with 'protestant ascendancy' in the early nineteenth century. By the end of the Victorian era, the term would be transvaluated to accommodate Lady Gregory, W. B. Yeats and JMS. Perhaps William Hatch's ornamental cannon, drawn by Sir Nicholas, pointed the way.

Other people: the Hatches

In more immediate terms the tentative rapprochement between Irish Toryism and native culture, best seen in Samuel Ferguson's contributions to the *DUM* during the 1830s, touched the world even of the rates-collector turned patron of horse-racing. In the summer of 1831, the historian John Dalton spent extended periods of time in Louth in preparation for a study of the county's antiquities: his progress was reported in the local press.[14] When scouts for the Ordnance Survey visited Ardee in late 1835 or early 1836, they listed Hatch among the principal family names in the parish, even giving a Gaelic equivalent in Na Hatchaigh. Their informant appears to have been one S. Hatch.[15] The Gaelic neologism is in its own pioneering way an act of appropriation, a bid to incorporate a borough-freeman family into the emergent idiom of cultural nationalism. Ordnance Survey etymology might as well have been the object of Nietzsche's thought when, in the 1870s, he observed how 'all that is small and limited, moldy and obsolete, gains a worth and inviolability of its own from the conservative and reverent soul of the antiquary migrating into it and building a secret nest there'.[16]

DULEEK, KELLS, ETC., COUNTY MEATH

Totting up graveyard tributes to an obscure Irish Georgian small town household, one is not remote from the 'will to power' of a later cultural politics. The Modernism practised (however bitterly) by D. H. Lawrence, Ezra Pound and W. B. Yeats had its affinities with Jacobitism and its underlying doctrines of pre-ordained authority. At one point at least, the Hatches of an even earlier period became embroiled in the fate of kings. After the flight of James II from England, through Scotland to Ireland, efforts were made to raise taxes for the cause. A commission was issued in April 1690 – three months before the Battle of the Boyne – to generate £20,000 per month from personal estates. Among the nine commissioners for County Meath was one John Hatch.[17] This may have been the John Hatch of Kells (died 10 March 1708 aged 70) who is buried in the parish church. It is scarcely credible that the shadowy John Hatch who features in O'Hart's list of '49 Officers could be the same John Hatch who served the Jacobite cause in 1690. If they are not one and the same, are they doppelgangers, cousins, or harbingers of ancestral anxiety?

Joyce Metge, alias Hatch, died 23 January 1735 aged 60, is buried in Dunshaughlin. It seems reasonable to assume that the Joyce Hatch of Kells, who married Peter Ievers (a surveyor of excise with a Dublin address in Capel Street) in 1766 is a relative, though it may be more important to note how Meath-born members of the family at large were acquiring Dublin connections.[18] Writing to John Hatch (our silent MP of chapter 6), James Hatch of Kells, County Meath, refers in 1770 to his own son (name not yet established): this James may be the one who was appointed Commissioner Extraordinary for taking affidavits in the court of Exchequer four years earlier, further evidence of social and professional advance

Settings

beyond the walls of Kells.[19] On 14 April 1770, Elizabeth Hatch married John Power of Kells, gentleman, in Saint Michan's parish, Dublin: John Hatch Power (Florint, 1860), the Dublin physician, was their son. He appears to share with only three other traced individuals the distinction of bearing the Hatch name as a second Christian name, the most significant in the present context being the dramatist's father, John Hatch Synge (1823–1872).[20]

We know of one family in some detail. Mark Hatch (died 27 June 1823) and his wife Jemima had a son Richard who died on 13 March 1891. Related to these were Nicholas Stephen Hatch (killed in France on 1 July 1916), Minnie (died 20 July 1919), and Mark Pendry Hatch (captain in the A. V. C.) who died on 30 December 1922. With them it must seem that we have returned to atomised facticity and little more. Yet, in the very sparcity of family records, we trace a Zephyric movement (soon to reach Storm Force 10) which whips from pre-Jacobite Ireland to the Western Front.[21]

Among the properties with which 'Silent' John Hatch was involved, either as agent or proprietor (or both), was that of the Barry family in Meath to which he was related.[22] This side of his activities will receive less attention here than that involving Wicklow on the one hand, and Ulster on the other. Nowadays, Louth and Meath are counties securely integrated in the Republic of Ireland and – in less functionally important ways – in the province of Leinster. In the eighteenth century, however, the frontier between north Leinster and south Ulster did not in terms of cultural identity conform with county boundaries. Thus the Hatches of Ardee would have looked west towards County Monaghan (an Ulster county, and part of the present Republic), and felt no sense of division or separation. Even areas of Meath participated in a northern-orientation which, thanks in part to increased road building and the railways, has been replaced by a Dublin-centred network of communications.

THE LINE WHICH MARRIES INTO THE SYNGES

It is one of the horrors of genealogy that ancestors multiply by a geometric progression, like waves breaking as they reach dry land. Thus while the modest researcher aims to clarify the position of one person – in this case, ultimately, JMS – a plethora of relationships are disinterred and their dust scattered over the very object of concern. Here we shall restrict inquiries to a small group of Cork families, significant because a great deal of Synge wealth came out of that county. Of one family they married into it has been said by a learned genealogist, 'it is difficult to discover exactly what was the Meade religion at the close of the seventeenth century'.[23] Colonel William Meade (1612–1692) may be assumed to be have been a protestant because he acted as trustee for some of the soldiers known as 'the [16]49 Officers', with others of whom the town of Ardee was associated. Yet his eldest son

Other people: the Hatches

married first Mary Coppinger, a Catholic, while a granddaughter married George Synge, rector of Tisex and Kilmacabea. In the late eighteenth century, two Coppinger cousins were distinguished by being known as Catholic Tom and Protestant Tom.

Another of the Coppingers (John of Ballvolane) married Mary Blundell (d. 1734) whose larger family – Jacobite, or at least Stuart-supporting, in part – ultimately married with the ambitious Hills of County Down. Though they do not persist in the story, the Blundells serve to illustrate the diversity which lay behind the supposedly hegemonic Irish eighteenth century. They were of English but also of Catholic/Stuart background. Mary Blundell married John Coppinger of Ballvolane, County Cork: their only surviving child, Frances (d. 17 April 1773) married Henry, grandson of Thomas Peppard (MP for Drogheda in 1640), who died 23 November 1771. The Peppards were Liverpool merchants c. 1737 when the name Blundell was assumed by a Nicholas Peppard.[24] John Coppinger married, second in 1736, the daughter of Michael Moore of Drogheda: their daughter, Marianne, succeeded to the Ballvolane properties and married into one of the oldest of English aristocratic families.[25] John Hatch (d. 1797) regarded a later Miss Blundell as his employer in effect, reporting to her on the condition of the Blundell estate in King's County (now Offaly). Some of these relationships were close (e.g. the Catholic Coppinger and the Revd George Synge), others more remote (the several Blundell branches): they illustrate a prolixity which befalls any individual who looks backwards for a simple answer. When JMS looked back in the 1890s, it was not always his titled and high-born ancestors who swam into view.

If gilt-by-association is an adornment then, by the end of the eighteenth century, some of these non-Synges were moving in glorious circles. By a marriage of 1786, Mary Turnbull (1764–1836), daughter of a viscount Blundell, became the future Marchioness of Downshire; meanwhile in 1767 Marianne Coppinger (d. 1769) of Ballvolane had become the first wife of Charles Howard who (despite the strong recusant traditions of his family) became not only a protestant but, in 1798, an outspoken democrat: as the 11th Duke of Norfolk he was a racing crony of the Prince of Wales and President of the Society of Arts. Another marriage, closer to the Synges and Hatches, established links with the decidedly undemocratic Lords Kingsborough (see chapter 12 below.) Such attachments have tended to obliterate from view the commercial and untitled among the Synge progenitors.

Thus – antiquarianism apart – we are ultimately interested in the eighteenth-century and provincial Hatches because, from their low number as well as from better-known names, JMS's non-Synge ancestors (or some of them) stepped forward. The father of 'Silent' John Hatch is described by Andrew Carpenter as 'a successful land agent from the north of Ireland'.[26] Born round 1680 in Dublin, and graduated from Trinity in 1702, by 1717 Henry Hatch (now of Peter Street, Dublin) was granting leases at Rathfarnham, south of Dublin, an area in which his granddaughter's husband (Francis Synge) later held land on the river Dodder. He also acquired land in County Meath by buying up the arrears owed to an improvident or incompetent owner and within a year acquiring the freeholds and leaseholds also.[27] He served as man of business for members of the Temple family in the early decades of the eighteenth century. Edward Stephens presented him as 'a shrewd self-made man from the North, who would not be likely to allow sympathy with a tenant to delay *ejectment* proceedings when rent was overdue'.[28] Given that a good deal more is known of the younger Hatch's activities, this twentieth-century characterisation should be seen as assisting a progressive pedigree; that is, Henry Hatch can be acknowledged as tough, his son as succcessful and their Synge descendents as fortunate. A more recent study of the Marquis of Downshire's properties seems to confuse Henry and John Hatch – 'for fifty years Henry Hatch acted as agent for the Edenderry estate, assisted in his old age by his son-in-law Francis Synge who continued after Hatch's death in 1797 to run the estate from their law office in Dublin ...' Later the agent is named John Hatch, 'a Dublin solicitor'.[29]

We shall look more closely at John Hatch in due course, but it may be helpful first to clarify the issue of the Synges' involvement in his mid-career business dealings. There is in fact little evidence that Francis Synge played an active role in managing the Downshire estates; when Hatch died in 1797, Synge specifically denied any knowledge of the business while nonetheless seeking to take over the agency. In the winter of 1792–1793 great hardship afflicted the tenants at Edenderry, to which Miss Blundell responded by sending John Hatch funds for relief of the poor. On 30 May 1793, he informed her that he had instructed his nephew at Edenderry to draw up a list of worthy recipients.[30] Hatch had no brothers, and the only son of his only sister took holy orders. The nearest thing to a nephew he could have cited might have been a nephew of his wife's. Francis Synge meets that description but, as Synge had married Hatch's daughter six or seven years earlier, one would have expected him to be regarded as a son-in-law, especially in a communication designed to assure the philanthropist that her money was applied to charity by the best and closest assistant Hatch could find.

If Synge was not the nephew at Edenderry, then who was? To answer this question, we will need to explore the Hatches' extended operations in County Wicklow. In the 1730s, Henry Hatch and some member(s) of the Hutchinson family were engaged in land transactions, including land at Coolmodry, in the western part of County Wicklow.[31] This was a partnership which, however informal, was to flourish in years to come when Francis Hutchinson (d. 1807) ensured that his baronetcy was devised by special remainder to Samuel Synge, son-in-law to Henry Hatch's son. Sir Francis, who held land both in west and east Wicklow, also thrived as the representative in Ireland of Lord Lansdowne, a powerful and unpopular minister who devoted much of his wealth to patronage of the fine arts. Perhaps it was through Hutchinson's role in Lansdowne's affairs,

Other people: the Hatches

and the marquis's family connections with the political economist, Sir William Petty (1623–1687), that a six-volume set of Petty's maps of Ireland were to be found in 1797 securely locked in a chest of Sir Francis's. Perhaps it is mere coincidence that the first volume of these – which specifically covered County Wicklow – did not pass with the others into the possession of the British Library.[32]

These are matters of high uncertainty. We were in search of an obscure nephew. As early as the 1730s, Hatch involvement in Roundwood (further east) might be deduced from a portfolio of maps in the National Library of Ireland. This includes a map of Henry Temple, Viscount Palmerston's property at Rathmines (1742), 'A Survey of Roundwood ... 1731' (see p. 12 above) which shows four scattered houses, and maps of the properties in County Meath which formed the basis of John Hatch's subsequent estate there.[33] This Henry Temple (1673?–1757) was the grandson of Sir John of the Depositions.

But the story which unfolds relates to figures of no such eminence. Events at Roundwood in the late 1760s will reveal several shadowy figures, loosely described as nephews of an unfortunate suicide who had repeatedly styled himself John Hatch's cousin. These are disappointingly vague terms of kinship, but they throw up a candidate for the role of an obscure nephew at Edenderry, one who may be proven also to have sought the agency in 1797 when Francis Synge denied any knowledge of the place.

More is now known of the earlier (Henry) Hatch's activities as an agent on the Blundell/Downshire estate at Edenderry in King's County (modern Offaly). On taking up the agency in 1746, he had found matters in a confused condition, and set to put them to rights. A threat to murder him was faced down, and collection of rents regularised with full power of attorney vested in the new agent. Evidently he prospered, for he loaned money to Counsellor Anthony Foster and received annual payments of £50 interest for the years 1758–1760.[34] On Monday, 1 February 1762, Henry Hatch died 'in an advanced Age, at his House in Patrick-street' just a week after Edward Synge, Lord Bishop of Elphin who had expired 'in a very advanced Age' scarcely four hundred yards away in Kevin Street. Hatch was succeeded by his son, John – the sometime MP for Swords.[35] Despite running the estate for half a century between them, the Hatches were subsequently written off by the third marquess of Downshire in 1823 for having as their 'great object' the levying of fees on leases.[36]

What is the status of these early Hatches, their 'signification'? So far from being a land baron (a recent American biographer's description), Henry Hatch is regularly deprived of his Christian name on the few occasions when Jonathan Swift condescends to mention him in correspondence – 'Here lives one Mr Hatch who is a manager for the Temple family, he came lately to the Deanry and talked with great melancholy of Mrs Fenton [Swift's sister] not having received any money from me in a long time whereupon I payd him ten guineas for her use, and took his Receit ...'³⁷ As we have seen, when his business expanded through the Edenderry agency, he remained a Dublin-based middleman, a manager not a landlord.

Henry Hatch married twice: first to Dorothy Reading on 6 August 1719; and, second, to Elizabeth Hore (a widow) on 20 August 1737, in Saint Bride's church on both occasions. Between these dates, Henry Hatch served as a churchwarden in this parish in 1729. Dorothy Reading has not been further identified, but it may be worth noting that the lawyer Daniel Reading was, in Swift's words, a 'useful and excellent friend' of the Temple family. He was in fact Deputy Chief Remembrancer in the Irish Court of Exchequer.³⁸ If Henry Hatch married into this well-placed family, his star was rising to a degree which displeased the dean of Saint Patrick's. We catch another unflattering Swiftian glimpse of Henry Hatch in a letter to Revd Thomas Sheridan on 16 June 1735 – 'And one Mr Hatch's niece is run away with a hedge attorney's clerk.'

At this period, Henry Hatch became a subscriber to the Incorporated Society for Promoting English Protestant Schools in Ireland (founded 1733). Among the original members were George Berkeley, Jonathan Swift, Edward Synge (archbishop of Tuam), the younger Edward Synge (bishop of Elphin) and his brother Nicholas Synge (later bishop of Killaloe). The latter was father to Barbara Synge. Other subsequent member-subscribers included figures of consequence for the present story – two members of the Wicklow-based Acton family, John Ellwood (vice-provost of Trinity College), Robert French (a lawyer), Luke Gardiner (a Wicklow landlord), Samuel Hutchinson (dean of Dromore), Walter Harris (historian), the Revd Gabriel James Maturin, George Morgan, Lord Palmerston and the Honourable John Temple (the last two members of a great family holding land in Dublin and Wicklow). It is unlikely that the Society met collectively or that it provided a social forum in which the relatively humble Hatch rubbed shoulders with the ermine of Tuam and Elphin.

Clearly, it was a useful circle in which to do business. While its official concern was proselytism 'among the lower Sort of People', its foundation was bluntly justified in economic and demographic terms. Following less than four years after Swift's *Modest Proposal for Preventing the Children of the Poor from Being a Burthen to their Parents or the Country*, the Society blithely repeated declarations which Swift had satirically anatomised. The need for this body, to which at least three of JMS's ancestors simultaneously subscribed, arose at a critical juncture 'when the Protestants of this Kingdom are deluded to transport themselves to the American Plantations'. In a footnote worthy of Swift's cannibalistic projector, the Society calculated that '7260 Persons will be the Produce of twenty original Couples in the space of one Century ...'. Its schools project aimed to ensure that the prolific youth of Ireland should engender themselves within the reformed church and so replace deluded emigrants.³⁹

Other people: the Hatches

Of Henry Hatch's second marriage, less is known. The Hores or Hoares were related to a London banking firm which also supported the Incorporated Society in Ireland. Relations between the Hatches and Hores were further extended when, on 15 September 1744, Edward Hore married Elizabeth Hatch (a spinster) in Saint Bride's. Though these second marriages between families draw attention to the need for procreation and fecundity among Irish protestants, Elizabeth was John Hatch's only sibling.[40] Mrs Henry Hatch (alias Mrs Elizabeth Hore) probably died in 1759, for her will was being administered in that year. But matters now become more certain – however briefly.

John Hatch had entered TCD on 15 May 1736, and the register of alumni adds 'No Further Particulars', implying that his age and previous education went unrecorded, for whatever reason. It would have been usual for a freshman to be aged c. 16. Given that Henry Hatch had married in 1719, we might assume that John was the son of Henry's first wife, Dorothy Reading who would be thereby established as an ancestor of JMS. He entered College just under seventeen years after his parents' marriage. However, at the time of his death in 1797, John Hatch's age was stated in the *Gentleman's Magazine* to be 74 (i.e. he was born in 1723 or 1724, and so would just have been an impossible twelve or thirteen on matriculation).[41] He graduated BA in 1739 (i.e. after three years on the College books), and was admitted to Lincoln's Inn, London, in the same year. In 1749, he was called to the Irish Bar, but was listed as retired from the profession by 1784.

Though it is rarely wise to apply Occam's Razor to family trees, we are offered a relatively uncluttered line of descent, as shown below:

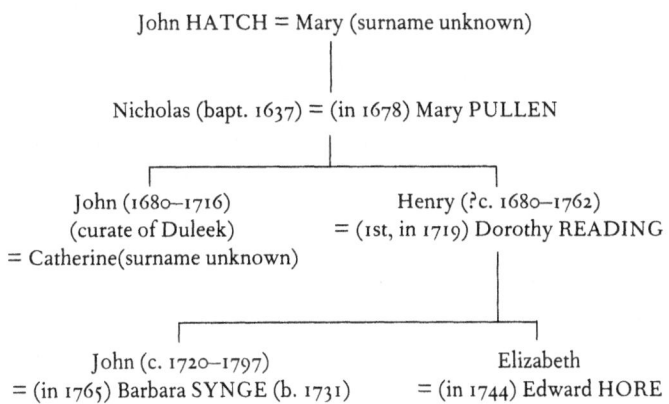

In connection with John Hatch and Lincoln's Inn, it is noteworthy that he was the only bearer of his surname to be admitted (in 1739) within the period covered by the printed register (i.e. lxxx–1893).[42] Nothing is known of him at the Inn until,

Settings

on 13 July 1748, he petitioned for permission to remove himself 'to another Society of the Law' – that is, the King's Inns, Dublin. Nevertheless, he proceeded in fact to be called to the bar in London, on 24 November 1748. Apart from these formalities, over a period of more than nine years – seven years' registration was the requirement – the Lincoln's Inn records tell us nothing, except that standard fees were paid in lieu of having a chamber. This strongly suggests that Hatch was a non-resident while on the books of the Inn.

However, in the chapel of Lincoln's Inn, two eighteenth-century marriages were celebrated involving persons of the same surname – on 13 November 1728, a John Hatch married Mary Fox (both of Staines, Middlesex); on 24 February 1730, Thomas Pritchard (widower) married Susannah Hatch (both of the parish of Saint George the Martyr, Middlesex, virtually the local church). Given the non-appearance of the name elsewhere in the Inn's register, it seems reasonable to infer some family connection among the Hatches of 1728, 1730, 1739 and 1748, unless it is accepted that these were servants or the descendants of servants in the Inn. However, if it is supposed for a moment that, to apply William of Occam's principle, one should not multiply John Hatches without necessity, then it looks as if John Hatch (married, 1728) could be the uncle of John Hatch (entered the Inn, 1739). However, the future MP's uncle John had died in 1716 according to Church of Ireland records. The Inn's records have nothing further to add about the Hatches who married in the chapel. The only direct descendant of John Hatch MP known to be given his surname as a Christian name was John Hatch Synge who, on 18 January 1845, was also admitted to Lincoln's Inn. He left on 8 May 1846 to join the King's Inns, Dublin, having completed the formal requirement (not abolished until 1885) that a member of the Irish bar should have resided at an English inn of court.

It is not yet clear how the Hatches (Henry and John) were related to Samuel M'Cracken, but kinship wass acknowledged on both sides. M'Cracken wrote on several occasions to his 'cousin' in the early 1760s when he appears to have been holding property at Roundwood, County Wicklow, on John Hatch's behalf. 'Mr Hatch has a mill at Annamoe, otherwise Ballynacor', writes Samuel Hatch on 6 December 1777. It had been (re)built for Hatch in 1765, with M'Cracken in charge of hiring craftsmen and labour, and paying for materials. Consequently it cannot be identified as the mill-race at Animo into which the celebrated Laurence Sterne (1713–1768) fell as a child.[43] Samuel Hatch may be the attorney of that name who entered the King's Inns in 1761. If so, he cannot have prospered, for we will later find him acting as clerk to another attorney in Dublin, and ultimately falling foul of John Hatch's acquisitive diligence. For John Hatch quietly persevered in patching together a portfolio of Wicklow properties. By an undated letter of roughly this period from Joseph Mason, it is established that he held land at Glenmalure.

Other people: the Hatches

Two further names appear in letters to John Hatch which recur in JMS's experience of the Roundwood/Annamoe area of Wicklow. Samuel Hatch (writing from Wicklow town on 6 December 1777) refers to John Harding as a resident of the Annamoe area, and this suggests that Harry Harding (who looked after Castle Kevin during the Synges' vacationing in the 1890s) was (like the Frizell owners) of long standing in the district. Daniel Bourne (Byrne?), writing to Hatch on 19 July 1791, refers to Mr Weekes and the imminent Wicklow assizes. We shall meet the Revd Ambrose Weekes, perpetual curate of Derrylossary, in several contexts, some redolent of lofty Enlightenment projects, others of concealed crime. The Revd Mr Weekes's violent conduct in 1798 has become folklore, and was available to JMS in this form.

3

A little learning

In every one of these cabins they earned money by taking in boarded-out children – children unwanted by poor parents, or simply illegitimate. There was hardly a cottage without one, two or three of these stranger children. They were well looked after, and the people often grew so fond of them they wouldn't part with them; and I suppose, that was a nice trait too. But the point is that the only fresh blood coming into the county was ... Well ... a curious county, as you can see, and the morals were a bit curious too. However, that's enough about them. (*O'Faolain*)

And the songs of the temple shall be howlings in that day. (Amos 8:3)

THE victory of William over James in the 1690s inaugurated a long period of domestic peace in most of the British Isles. The cultural efflorescence conventionally associated with such diverse beauties of the age as the *Dunciad*, Blenheim Palace, 'The Beggar's Opera' and Kneller's English Academy of Painting (1711) was – as even these examples reveal – a great deal less unified than convention liked to admit. Bad nerves demanded reassurance. When the age of Pope and Swift acquired its familiar Latinate name, astute historians remembered that the victory of Caesar Augustus had resulted from years of civil conflict. Contradiction persisted. The two great writers of triumphant British protestantism were an Irishman and a Catholic. The newness of the regime depended on the willingness of older power systems to endorse change in order to maintain their own place in the sun. But the thoroughness of James's defeat in Ireland left the island particularly vulnerable.

The Temple family of Surrey were long connected with Ireland, Sir William Temple (1555–1627) having served as fourth provost of Trinity College, Dublin. His son, Sir John (1600–1677), navigated the storms of mid-seventeenth-century politics, assisting the king's government at the outbreak of the 1641 'troubles' but taking the parliamentary side in the ensuing Civil War. In 1646, he published in London *The Irish Rebellion; or, An History of the Beginnings and First Progresse of the Generall Rebellion Raised within the Kingdom of Ireland, upon the Three and Twentieth Day of October in the Year 1641, Together with the Barbarous Cruelties and Bloody Massacres which Ensued Therefrom.* This highly partisan and self-serving narrative acted in practice as the justification for extensive confiscations of land from Catholics. Among the beneficiaries were the author's own family. Temple's *Irish Rebellion* was regularly reprinted in the century and a half following, whenever the relaxation of anti-papist laws was under discussion.

Several members of the family became intimately involved in Irish affairs. Two brothers (and their future brother-in-law, Thomas Giffard) sat in the General Convention of 1660.[1] The second Sir William Temple (1628–1699), a traveller, diplomat and writer, sat in the Irish House of Commons as an MP for County Carlow. In 1668, he effected the triple alliance of England, Holland and Sweden. After some reversals in his professional career, he went to The Hague in 1674 and played a major role in securing the marriage of Princess Mary and William of Orange. Marginalised by Charles II, Temple took no part in the Revolution of 1688, but presented himself thereafter to William at Windsor. In other words, he was a major figure on the political stage of Stuart-becoming-Williamite England.

Nor was his domestic life without enduring consequence. At Moor Park in Surrey, he employed the young Jonathan Swift as a secretary, during which period Esther Johnson was in the service of Temple's sister, Lady Martha Giffard. As the result of a suicide, Moor Park was inherited by a nephew, John Temple (died 1753, without issue), who had married Sir William's daughter. Though Jack Temple inherited Irish lands, he never took up residence in Ireland. In June 1706, Swift advised him against setting his property 'at a Rack-rent; they that live at yr distance from their Estates would be undone if they did it, especially in such an uncertain Country as this'.[2] The family featured in seventeenth-century redistributions of Wicklow land, but commercial activity rather than confiscation appears to have marked their activities in the county under the Williamite Settlement.[3] The Temples were granting leases to land in Wicklow as early as 1713, when John Temple and his wife Elizabeth (residing at Saint James, Westminster) conveyed woods at Ballynacor to Thomas and William Hatton who were already apparently living there.[4] The Hattons will recur in this narrative as suspects in a scandal of the 1760s.

A kinswoman of Jack Temple married William Flower (of Ashbrook, County Kilkenny) who in October 1733 was elevated Baron Castle Durrow. Henry Hatch acted in business for Flower and other members of the Temple circle in Ireland.[5] It is in this context that we discover Swift in reluctant contact with Hatch. In the summer of 1735, lamenting the absence of any real gossip, Swift reported to the Revd Thomas Sheridan that 'one Mr Hatch's niece is run away with a hedge Attorny's clerk'. In October of the same year, he informed a London bookseller that 'here [in Dublin] lives one Mr Hatch who is a manager for the Temple family,

Settings

he came lately to the Deanry and talked with great melancholy of Mrs Fenton not having received any money from me in a long while …'.[6] The repeated phrase 'one Mr Hatch' – there is never a Christian name – inscribes a measure of scorn. Somewhat over a year later, Swift wrote to Jack Temple describing a portrait of Lady Giffard, and suggesting that Temple pay some money to Rebecca Dingley, the life-long companion of Esther Johnson, Swift's 'Stella'. From this Harold Williams concluded that, about this time, the dean had presented the portrait (by Sir Peter Lely) to Temple in recognition of the latter's kindness to a friend, the gift having been made through Henry Hatch. Yet Hatch had been unable to inform Swift of the Temples' circumstances, and was evidently at some distance from the English and more elevated side of the family.[7]

The gap between high and low was perhaps more treacherous than great. Though Swift had been employed in a relatively menial capacity at Moor Park, he subsequently enjoyed the confidence and friendship of powerful ministers of state. Nevertheless, he preferred to avoid the Temples (especially Jack) and even confided to Stella that he was glad to 'have wholly shaken off that family'.[8] Sir William had left to his sister's servant 'a lease of some lands … in Monistown, in the County of Wicklow' which, years later, Esther Johnson converted into hard cash. Edward Stephens, preparing his long life of JMS, noted this literary precedent for his uncle's association with County Wicklow, for he located Moneystown 'adjoining Castle Kevin', the Synges' preferred holiday place.[9] The desire for continuity from Swift to JMS is palpable. Moneystown was not Swift's only traffic in his friend's business affairs. Some years after, he sold a property called Talbot's Castle for £223, acquired a few months earlier by Stella for £65. In the biographer's judgement, this was simply a device for 'putting gold in Mrs Johnson's pocket'. The property, unlike Monistown (or Moneystown), was not in Wicklow, but on the green grassy slopes of the Boyne.[10]

Property, however, may not be the most volatile of impositions within a contested society. In 1736, Jack Temple 'repurchased a plot of land on an estate which he had leased some twenty years before and on it established, near the demesne and house of Roundwood, one of those charter schools which were the cause of inexpressible bitterness and suffering, but were intended by the landlords to teach an illiterate Catholic peasantry to be industrious and educated Protestants'.[11] So wrote Edward Stephens, preparing the ground for his interpretation of JMS as Wicklowman and ecumenist. The charter system targeted 'the children of Popish and other poor natives', in a phrase which unconsciously sought to identify settlers with prosperity and consign to native status any non-Catholics who failed to prosper. In the later 1760s, a Mr and Mrs Edward Rooney, attached to the Roundwood school, were involved (innocently enough, perhaps) in the contrived discovery of a forged will, with consequences reflected in JMS's first attempt at a play in the 1890s.[12] This affair is discussed at length in a later chapter.

A little learning

The numerous Charter Schools have been examined in great detail by the Church of Ireland's historiographer, but the establishment near Roundwood does not feature anywhere in his account.[13] For accounts of the early days at Templestown, we have to rely on the Society's own reports. A Wicklow landowner Thomas Acton put up £100 for 'a School-house and other convenient Buildings' in the summer of 1737. These opened to receive twenty pupils (ten boys, ten girls) on 29 December, and the following summer a Master 'who understands the Improvement of Land' was busily at work. A report on the first year of the school's existence records that 'four cows have been bought for the use of the Family' – family being the term used for the whole school community, pupils and teachers alike.[14]

The supplier of the cows was Edmund Kavanagh who, in May 1737, was paid £8 16s 0d for them. His surname strongly suggests a local man – JMS will have a Pat Kavanagh in his first attempt at Wicklow drama – but the subsequent decision of the Incorporated Society to pay him a half-year's salary also suggests that he was engaged as a teacher when the first pupils were arriving. Certainly efforts were being made to clothe the newcomers at Roundwood, £1 5s 0d for forty pairs of stockings, two shillings for a boy's suit, eighteen shillings for pewter chamber pots. Kavanagh was paid eight guineas for 'Sustinence of Children'. Perhaps the most revealing detail in the Society's records is the purchase – two weeks before Christmas – of twenty 'economy spoons'.[15]

In the first three months of its operations, the School appears to have received further support from Jack Temple, who contributed £22 15s 0d. This relatively trivial sum was routed to the Society through Henry Hatch, the earliest evidence of any Hatch involvement with the Roundwood area. Later in March 1738, Hatch was also involved in transmitting money from Thomas Acton, the resident benefactor in Wicklow. Payments to a Mr Synnot indicate that a regular teacher had taken over from Kavanagh.

Later evidence strongly indicates that investment was quickly replaced by cheese-paring. An unusually lengthy report for the year ending in October of 1740 did not appear until 1742. Drawn up by the Revd David Stephens, curate of Derrylossary, it provided extensive lists of tasks undertaken by the pupils. Among the boys' achievements were

> [Number] 10. With the help of one Labourer for four Days, (who was only emplyed before it was known that the two Biggest Boys could do without him), they cut, reared, carried home, and stacked up all safe, three hundred and twenty five four-barrel Kishes of excellent Turf, all of which cost the Society three Shillings, neither more nor less.
>
> [Number] 12. They burned and saved about half a Barrel of Fern Ashes for Lye, to lessen the Expence of Soap, in washing Linnen, and whitening Yarn.[16]

This set a pattern. Yet Stephens comses across as a decent man, attentive to his duties, if not a regular composer of annual reports. He notes that 'Though much is done both by the Boys and Girls, yet they are never hurried, or in the least checked for their Slowness, the Direction of the Local Committee to the Master, in their own Presence, being to keep them always employed in something or other, but then as slow as they please themselves, and to contrive to make their Work only a kind of Diversion to them.'[17] The only committee member named is John Belton, a clothier rather than a gentleman of the Acton class: members of the same family lived in the same parish in JMS's time. The Society's charity sermon preached at Christ-Church in Dublin on 18 March 1743 was eventually printed the following year; among the appended reports for the schools, Templestown was noted for having 'a large Local Committee of the neighbouring Gentlemen' with little by way of detail. The children and their masters are never named in these publications.

The name of the school in early records is Roundwood, and it is only in 1741 that Templestown appears. As Jack Temple's involvement does not appear to have been either lavish or attentive, we may deduce that the renaming was designed to attract his attention and to configure an identity for the area immediately round the school. The Actons lived quite some distance away near Rathdrum and, if Roundwood Park was already in existence, there is no means of telling who lived there. When a porch was added to the school building in April 1742 the builder, John Houghton, bore (like Edmund Kavanagh) a distinctively Wicklow name.

Within a few years, 'some Ground for Rye [had] been prepared here by the Boys: they likewise cut their own Turf for firing'. The boys brought a plot of mountainous land to 'a high degree of fertility' and also saved fifty tons of hay – probably in 1746.[18] This commendable industry suggests that there were few other labourers in the area at the time, a factor of some consequence when the career of Samuel M'Cracken is examined. Yet Belton's involvement at the beginning of the 1740s indicates that M'Cracken had not betaken himself to an utter wilderness.

The social historian, Joseph Robins, is inclined to see links between the Dublin Foundling Hospital and these remote Charter Schools, with the implication that the latter were used not simply to convert Catholic children of low degree but also to absorb the capital's bastards and other unwanted babies of whatever religious persuasion. Infants were not officially admitted to the Schools, but a sub-system of nurseries fed into the Schools proper. One of these nurseries was active in York Street, Dublin, by 1749, where M'Cracken had property. York Street houses will constitute a major part of the Synge family's urban wealth, right into the twentieth century when a great swathe of it was acquired by the public authorities under the Housing of the Working Classes Act.[19] Though the street was designed to civilise the rougher, west side of Saint Stephen's Green, early and late it had contact with the sufferings of the poor, exemplifying the causal relationship between wealth

A little learning

and social exclusion. Like the Foundling Hospital, the Incorporated Society's schools and nurseries formed the *terminus a quo* of an unhappy production line in human servitude. As we shall see in connection with the village of Dunlavin, County Wicklow was never short of missing babies, abandoned charges and the innocent victims of adult behaviour.

Long before Synge the dramatist began to explore his shadowy background, the issue of education had impacted dramatically on local society. If his ancestors had taken no particular interest in the Charter School at Roundwood, the name of Synge was nevertheless prominent in the materials disseminated to local households. Quite apart from proselytism among children, the school possessed a standard pack of books for circulation to reading adults. No fewer than four of the twenty titles were the work of Edward Synge, archbishop of Tuam. If these included the relatively mild *Charitable Address to All Who Are of the Communion of the Church of Rome* (1728), Tuam's nice-policeman tract was accompanied by Archbishop Tillotson's *Hazard of Being Saved in the Church of Rome*. How these difficult theological controversies were read in the larger houses of Wicklow in the latter part of the eighteenth century is near impossible to reconstruct though we do know that Francis Synge, Tuam's great-grandson, turned to Tillotson in the dangerous year of 1798.

Heartily and understandably detested by Irish Catholics, who saw the schools as a direct threat to their own families, the Charter institutions acquired an unsavoury reputation in Britain and further afield. In the course of his long campaign for prison reform, the English philanthropist John Howard (1726–1790) twice examined the Incorporated Society's nurseries and schools. His *Account of the Principal Lazarettos of Europe* (1789) devoted an entire chapter to them, citing damaging evidence taken even from members of the Society's ruling body. Quite apart from the undeniable brutality of their regimes, changes in sensibility affected the general issue of child-care, as the age of revolution dawned. Nothing so incensed the early nineteenth century than the Incorporated Society's casual manner in reporting the disappearance of institutions under their authority – 'Sixteen national schools have been lost to Ireland between 1775 and the time of the Union.'[20] Nothing, that is, except the loss of children.

Edward Stephens makes no reference to his own forebears' leading role in the propagandist drive of the Incorporated Society and its schools. In the increasingly bitter political conflicts of the years following the Napoleonic wars, rival schools systems – some new, some fugitive – added fuel to the sectarian bonfires. The Roundwood (or Templestown) school did not survive into this era, having been superseded within the county by a newer school at Arklow. To judge by figures readily available for 1785 and 1788, this was primarily a school for girls – only nine of the thirty-three pupils in April 1785 were boys, and evidently none of the forty-nine on the roll in May 1788.[21]

Settings

The history of education in County Wicklow is not an extensive one. The absence of a school in Wicklow town was bemoaned in *The Freeman's Journal* in the early 1760s.[22] According to Stephens, attempts to secure protestant control were 'particularly vigorous in Wicklow where the Evangelical movement acquired great strength among the settler Protestant farmers' of the upland interior where the Synges had inherited from John Hatch.[23] Oddly enough, Stephens here may have been more concerned to mark off his forebears from secessionist evangelicals like John Nelson Darby (1800–1882) than roundly to condemn the Establishment. Yet it is indisputable that schools controlled by the Incorporated Society fomented a great deal of resentment and – just as significant – practised a great deal of physical cruelty and neglect. So much was tacitly admitted in a published internal inquiry in 1818, where the widespread occurrence of eye-disease among pupils was particularly noted.[24] The inevitable public outcry was not to be postponed. An Irish Education Inquiry of 1825 led to the speedy withdrawal of state support.

Thus, in less than a century, a grand scheme to provide rustic academies dedicated to the manufacture of protestant menials (tradesmen at best) from even rawer material lay not only in ruins but in disgrace. Jack Temple's particular contribution to the cause had been among the first casualties. Its history, in positive as well as publicly condemned ways, continued to bear upon the Synge family. When from 1815 onwards John Synge, grandfather of JMS, helped to introduce the Pestalozzian scheme of teaching into Ireland, he was able to draw on a tradition of local, 'popular' education at Roundwood even as he simultaneously sought to refine it and redeem his own inheritance.

The need for reform in the schools, and the general state of civilisation, can be gauged from the Incorporated Society's rules as promulgated in 1826 under pressure from government. 'It having appeared to the Committee of Fifteen by Returns from some of the Charter Schools, that Children had been admitted of unsound Mind and Ideots [sic] ... it is ordered that every Child hereinafter to be admitted ... who shall within three Months after its admission, show the smallest symptom of Ideotism, Insanity, or defect in its natural Understanding, or to be affected with the Evil, Scald or other Scofulous Complaint, shall be immediately returned to its Recommender.'[25] As ever, no specific school was named when abuses were acknowledged. County Wicklow acquired a reputation in the nineteenth and early twentieth centuries for high levels of mental illness, without the provision of a dedicated county asylum. If it survived into this era, Arklow was scarcely exempt from the Committee's embarrassed public admissions. Templestown, which had been Arklow's out of the way precursor, had happily dropped from view, its closure said to have resulted from anonymous complaints and allegations.[26]

John Synge's Pestalozzian approach can thus be seen to have had a dramatic local justification, even if he never entered the arena of popular education. Other initiatives in the area, including Sir Francis Hutchinson's erection of Kilfee school in 1807, and the printing of classroom materials in Glanmore Castle during the 1830s, testify in their different ways to a rural milieu in which the landlords' interest in education was active and far from mechanical. Hutchinson had been a member of the Committee of Fifteen in the 1780s.[27] His initiative followed (slowly enough) on his dissatisfaction with conditions endured by girls at the Arklow school. At least half of the gowns were too small to protect the wearers from cold, and some had been torn 'in endeavouring to make them cover their shoulders or breasts'.[28] In 1845 Eliza Davis, unmarried and epileptic, who was certainly a product of the Foundling Hospital and possibly of a Charter School also, murdered her infant son at Cronelea in the southern part of the county. Sentenced to death after a nonsensical trial, she was the subject of a petition signed by many of Wicklow's notables, including young Francis Synge (1819–1878) who had been appointed High Sheriff the previous year. Though the sentence was commuted, the woman's ultimate fate remains obscure.[29] She stands as a suitably ambiguous representative of those who endured a system of ideological engineering which the Synge family had sponsored and would seek to replace.

These matters were certainly not unknown to JMS who, as an undergraduate at Trinity, augmented his college reading with Sir Richard Musgrave's wildly partisan *Memoirs of the Different Rebellions in Ireland* (1802). After a long loyalist account of the events of 1798, Musgrave added an appendix in which he warmly commended the Incorporated Society, and noted that Sir Francis Hutchinson was one of a triumvirate whose 'great zeal and unabated exertions' were dedicated to superintending its operations.[30] Hutchinson's strictures were forgotten in Musgrave's commendation of all things protestant. For JMS as a reader of Musgrave, the 1890s were tense but fertile times in which to reflect on scrofula as an antidote to revolution. Decadent conclusions might result from such speculations.

4

The mill at Animo

> Here and there in County Wicklow there are a number of little known places –
> places with curiously melodious names, such as Aughavanna, Glenmalure,
> Annamoe, or Lough Nahanagan – where the people have retained a peculiar
> simplicity, and speak a language in some ways more Elizabethan than the
> English of Connaught, where Irish was used till a much later date. (JMS)

AT THE opening of the twenty-first century, the corpus of Irish heritage is stuffed with annual festive fares. One of Wicklow's least celebrated literary adventures befell Laurence Sterne (1713–1767), the author of *Tristram Shandy* (1760–65) and *A Sentimental Journey* (1768), at a young age. According to a brief 'autobiography', he fell into a mill-race as a child, his death instantly assumed by onlookers who were amazed when he re-emerged more or less unscathed. The incident, which suspiciously resembles one reported of his kinsman Archbishop Richard Sterne of York (?1596–1683), was said to have occurred at Annamoe, while the boy's father was garrisoned at Wicklow town. There is no doubt as to Sterne's association with the village, for his mother's half-sister, Mary Nuttall, was married to the Derrylossary curate, Thomas Fetherston.[1] There were other Irish connections, though the novelist's immediate family is less readily documented than that of John Sterne (1624–1669), founder of the College of Physicians in Dublin, and his son (also John, 1660–1745), a friend of Jonathan Swift and a scholar-bishop.

Among the curious selection of documents which make up the Hatch Papers in the National Library of Ireland, one finds a dossier largely devoted to the accountancy of mill-building on the river – scarcely more than a stream – at Annamoe. Quite why this bunch of grubby dockets should survive is a question worth asking of the collection as a whole. After all, grander projects are less well documented in the surviving archive. For example, work upon the 'mansion house' at Roundwood in which John Hatch set up his daughter Elizabeth and her husband (Francis Synge) following their marriage in 1786 remains unaccounted for. It may be that

The mill at Animo

an explanation for this selectivity among the preserved papers lies in the intimate relations between Hatch and his cousin (Samuel M'Cracken, died 1769) whose name is everywhere in the mill-building accounts. That is to say, the business of choosing what papers were retained was conducted at, or very shortly after, the enterprise to which they relate. On the other hand, the manner in which the Hatch Papers were handed over to the National Library in the mid-twentieth century may itself deserve attention.[2] Between these two explanations one may discern divergent moral imperatives – the consolidation of M'Cracken's identity, the discreet veiling of Synge family history. These are of course ironised 'explanations', for M'Cracken is happily forgotten by the celebrants of Synge dignities.

Hatch's acquisition of an interest in the Roundwood area was largely effected through piecemeal activities conducted by or through his faithful cousin. This was evidently a mutually satisfactory arrangement. The choice of upland Wicklow may be related to the establishment of a Charter School there, for Henry Hatch had been an early subscriber to the Incorporated Society. What little we know of the immediate community into which M'Cracken moved centres on the twenty or so pupils at Templestown and their overseers. The boys of the school had been active in colonising mountain land for farming, and their labour may have featured in John Hatch's calculations. Their company gave the older man some sense of relation with his new surroundings.

Referring to his own purchase of Ballinacor[beg], M'Cracken assured Hatch that he would 'always pray to God to preserve you from your Enemies, give you long life and good health, and prosper all your undertakings'.[3] That was in late 1761. In June 1764, M'Cracken advised that 'something should be done with the river of Animo ... to prevent the mill being taken away in the winter'.[4] The situation was allowed to deteriorate for a futher year, during which the state of the mill – which lay in the townland of Ballinacorbeg – remains unrecorded. Yet we have some twenty documents to consider, covering a few months from late August to mid-November 1765, the period following immediately on John Hatch's marriage to Barbara Synge.[5]

The surviving documentation could be classified under the various trades or crafts involved in the complex operation of (re)building a residential mill in a rural area separated from urban facilities by distances more difficult than lengthy. As M'Cracken and the miller had been in dispute the previous year, and as M'Cracken was proposing to advance his own money, we might deduce that efforts towards reconciliation were afoot.[6] These required specific outlay by M'Cracken, pending repayment by his master in Dublin. The capital city played its part in Annamoe's refurbishment. A Dublin-based glazier, Robert Moore, charged 11s 0d for sixteen and a half foot of 'gleazing' on 6 November. Through the miller (James Foster), James Lafferty (a millwright) was paid £11 16s 5d for ninety-nine days' work – this included 5s 5d for ale. This rate of pay (2s 4d per day) may be compared with the carpenter's 1s 6d, paid to William Wybrants over sixty-five days. From the mason's account, it is possible to deduce the size of the building under (re)construction: 'the front and rare walls 63 feet long Each by 11 feet hy and 2 feet thick'. These were in good order before the end of September.

Goods and the carriage of goods also cost money. At an early stage of the work, Thomas Harrison 'drew for Mr Macraken' timber, an eighteenth-foot shaft and '1 peece of Wheeltimber 16 foot' for a total cost of £4 16s 9d. It is not clear from whence all this material was transported, but payment was levied on quantity – 18s 0d for eighteen-foot shaft, and 16s 0d for the sixteen-foot of wheeltimber. Three hundred and ten bricks were bought from Mr Truel, whose name will recur in the annals of the Synge family – Editha Truell of Clonmannon House, New Rath, marries Francis Synge (the dramatist's uncle) in 1861. Other name-echoes will be repeated in or around the drama itself. In 1765, Thomas Smith worked thirty-eight and a half days of smith's work on the mill project: in the days of JMS's *Well of the Saints* (1905), the local smith was Jim Smith. To conclude the accountancy, labour was paid 4d per day.

The enterprise involved Dublin commercial suppliers, including Benjamin Ball, the College Green ironmonger, and local Wicklow landlords – Lord Powerscourt sold M'Cracken oak. M'Cracken supervised the operation as a whole, rendering his account to John Hatch on 14 November. Thus summarised, the cost amounted to £111 6s 6d, out of which £12 went to the mason, more than £14 to the deal merchant and £11 to Powerscourt's man, Dowse. The sum of £4 12s 0d was paid to Terance Kavanagh for carriage of timber and tiles from Dublin. In this fashion was the miller, James Foster, rehoused in some style, as witnessed by Thomas Hugou on the bill which John Hatch in turn honoured in paying his cousin, M'Cracken, on 22 November 1765. An element of humour may be half-hidden in the mason James Brien's note about 'trials to your generosaty', for M'Cracken only paid him in instalments. Thomas Smith's settlement was witnessed by Mary Salmon, whose name will recur in M'Cracken's final reckoning with the district less than four years later. There is no reference anywhere in these papers to the Stuart brothers who also will play their part in their uncle's last days.

The appearance of Thomas Hugo's name in the spelling 'Hugou' lends some credence to the view that his family were Huguenot in origin. In 1798, the Hugos of Drummin will become notorious for their determined suppression of discontent and opposition. By the middle of the nineteenth century, their property was passing into the hands of very different migrants from France, the wine-merchant Bartons of Bordeaux. Despite its legendary sluggishness, Wicklow land changed hands quite rapidly, and the isolation of the country from the metropolis did not prevent frequent documentation of altered ownership in the Registry of Deeds. John Hatch's initiatives were recorded alongside many others, despite the circuitous manner in which he proceeded.

The mill at Animo

The owner of valuable urban property and member of a Dublin Guild, M'Cracken in his rural seclusion was psychologically attached to the desolate upland rather than the busy mill and fertile valley. In the course of twenty years, he remained a dweller in the mountains, a neighbour of lost children. He complained of loneliness, but he also hugged it to his bosom. An overseer at the rebuilding in Annamoe, and a keeper of other men's accounts, he was less effective in managing his own affairs of body and soul. After his death, several attempts were made formally to record agreements into which he had entered and to set down in writing the terms of these. In December 1769, a memorial was sworn and registered in Dublin, relating to a deed of January 1765. According to this, M'Cracken had indeed promised to give James Foster money to build the mill, but charged 6 per cent on the loan. Thomas Hugou featured as a witness to the retrospectively published agreement.[7]

The soul was to be known through the material world, body through the nervous system. However anachronistically, Sam M'Cracken's death will anticipate the themes of future generations. The wealth of documentation, through which we know pitiful rates of pay and the price of materials, stands in silent contrast to the utter dearth of our understanding in the case of Barbara whose husband faithfully repaid his cousin for his pains at the mill.

5

The state of the roads

Your Uncle John did not care to read books of history, but preferred to read the original letters or records concerned if possible. I remember speaking to him one day in the 'nineties and quoting something I had read in some history, whereupon he replied that the history was probably wrong, and how history was best learned by reading the letters etc. of the time in question. (Samuel Synge, JMS's brother, 3 October 1922, writing to his own daughter)

BY SEPTEMBER 1780, Annamoe Mill was once again 'in a very ruinous condition & likely to fall if not repaired before winter'.[1] So wrote the Revd Ambrose Weekes in a strangely formal note, evidently intended for John Hatch's eyes. The two men had disagreed over the development of roads and, in the late 1790s, Weekes will ally himself with the murderous Thomas Hugo in suppressing rebels and (one strongly suspects) innocents. Yet the new incumbent's arrival in the district in 1765 had been welcomed by the pious melancholic M'Cracken who appears to have sought his advice on occasion.

Weekes had previously been Reader in the parish of Saint Werburgh's, Dublin, an exceedingly modest appointment.[2] In the Wicklow uplands, he succeeded the Revd David Stephens (1696–1765) whose wife, Clothilda Toole, bore a surname as redolent of old Wicklow as her Christian name bespoke new protestantism. Weekes may have married their daughter, though uncertainty about the marriage of a clergyman opens up questions which go beyond the loss of records for the parish of Derrylossary. Weekes's family is difficult to reconstruct: church archives make no reference to a wife, though by 1798 he certainly had a son – James – a yeoman who took part in the attempted murder of his father's Catholic counterpart, Fr Christopher Lowe.[3] A gravestone at Derrylossary commemorates Frances May Weekes, alias Stephens, and also William Sutton Weekes. But, like Barbara Synge and John Hatch, the Revd Ambrose Weekes has not been traced to his lasting resting place. His early days in the parish had been full of promise.

The rebuilding of Annamoe mill in 1765, likewise the prospect of enhancing

The state of the roads

the house at Roundwood as a fit country place for John Hatch and his wife, drew attention to the state of Wicklow's roads. Some material had to be transported from Dublin with a degree of difficulty a new-married and prosperous couple were scarcely to endure in their own comings and goings between town and rural retreat. The improvement and extension of the road system occupied the minds of many in mid-century. Between 1750 and 1770, the landscape of England was transformed by the building of roads on an unprecedented scale. The financing of this huge, discrete undertaking was effected through 'turnpike' trusts, resulting in the appearance on the landscape of 'turnpike gates' at which travellers were obliged to produce tickets, or otherwise to pay for their onward journey.

In Dublin, new thoroughfares doubled as developments in the city's residential expansion. From the south-west corner of Saint Stephen's Green an elegantly curved street was created during the 1770s. Named opportunely after the Viceroy, Harcourt Street greatly added to the housing stock of the Irish capital. According to one recent researcher, the man principally responsible was John Hatch who certainly moved from the Green to a house near the southern end of the new street, which in due course was inherited by one of his Synge sons-in-law. The house in question appears to have been absorbed into the premises of the Erasmus Smith School (1870) which, in some respects, succeeded in the educational mission of the Incorporated Society. Though Harcourt Street framed a splendid view of the Dublin hills (with Wicklow behind them), Hatch's investment there may have distracted him from the development of a rural seat at Roundwood. After the renovations at Annamoe, his building activities in Wicklow were strictly limited.[4]

If the reconstruction of primitive industrial units such as a mill could be reconciled to a traditional view of Nature, road development raised very different issues. Even so radical a figure as Tom Paine protested at 'the artificial chasm filled up by a succession of barriers'. The duty of man, he insisted, was not performed in 'a wilderness of turnpike gates' but involved respect of both God and neighbour.[5] If Paine's reference was substantially to social division, his turnpike metaphor underlined the extent to which technical and economic development reinforced division at the expense of an allegedly primordial harmony. Though Ireland's experience differed from England in many ways, the philosophical and cultural significance of road-building was no less acute. An important contributor to the 'enlightenment discourse' of such improvements was Richard Lovell Edgeworth (1744–1817), father of the novelist Maria Edgeworth (1767–1849) whose *The Absentee* (1812) is partly set in post-Union Wicklow.

From his earliest days in the parish, Weekes promoted a scheme to improve its communications, particularly to build a new stretch of road to cover most of the distance between the mill at Annamoe and Roundwood village. His immediate objective was to avoid a steep gradient on the old road as it skirted the hill at Ballinacorbeg. John Hatch, however, was opposed to any change which would

Settings

have had the effect of downgrading a road which ran close to his house at Roundwood, even though he rarely – if ever – visited it. The difference of opinion was sustained over years, with landlord and parson in confrontation. On 30 July 1785, Hatch replied to Weekes's latest proposal to the effect that 'a little money laid out on the old road would render it a very good one without the great injury to private property that the new one would do'.[6] This exchange occurred when neighbouring landowners were engaged in elaborate improvements, including road building through their lands.

Though Weekes's response retained some interest because of his prolonged familiarity with the terrain, Edward Stephens had no hesitation in the 1930s in coming down on Hatch's side of the dispute. The parson, it seemed to the twentieth-century lawyer, had been 'carried away by the rightness of his case' to the point where he treated the old road 'as if it were an Alpine pass' and expressed himself 'with such force that grammar was subordinated to dramatic vehemence'.[7] The significance of Stephens's account of this trivial dispute is not to be sought in a right answer – apart from other considerations, part of the larger area in question was inundated during the nineteenth century to create a water reservoir for Dublin city. As in a number of other instances, Stephens (who was never a published author, beyond a few brief articles) here takes refuge in polite abuse of one party to an ancient dispute, with a view to establishing the good sense of the other. Other instances of this defence of John Hatch occur in Stephens's manuscript.

The Hatch of history, as distinct from the Hatch redesigned for a progressive account of JMS's pedigree, was no less a man of contradictions than the Revd Weekes. A businessman quietly amassing properties on his own account, he appears to have taken no interest in the lucrative turnpike road at Lissenhall, despite the presence of a tollgate virtually on his door-step.[8] Whatever the reason behind his preference, he chose to operate from Harcourt Street in Dublin rather than exploit either his Wicklow properties or the house near Swords.

In the first *Post-Chaise Companion* (1784), Lissenhall was 'the Seat of Mr Gordon', clear enough evidence that Hatch no longer used it as a residence as he had done in the late 1760s. The second, augmented edition of the *Companion* in 1786 listed Samuel Hatch (and one William Maturin) among the subscribers, but gave no address for either. This pioneering traveller's guide provided itineraries for long-distance journeys, mentioning landmarks and the seats of great persons along the way. It not only 'met a long felt need' but stimulated sight-seeing and so altered notions of scenery and landscape. In the age of colonial nationalism, architectural projects flourished, with attendant improved parklands and gardens. These were not simply private residences, the like of Lissenhall, but residences to which visitors (private, official, and even public) were invited. This traffic in turn demanded improvement in roads.

The state of the roads

In due course, the Synges who inherited from John Hatch will develop their own great good place, though the timing of this (after the Union of 1801) separates them from the golden age of country house-building. When Francis Synge came to erect a Gothic castle at Glenmouth, he was in effect extending a strip of developments southward through the Glen of the Downs, past Mount Kennedy, and linking to an older Hatch/Synge property further inland at Roundwood. General Robert Cunningham's place involved opening up 'the long concealed beauties of the Devil's Glen ...' where 'the river Vartrey falls about an hundred feet, with astonishing fury'. A neighbouring proprietor, Charles Tottenham, 'built a rustic temple, admirably adapted for contemplation, and equally well suited to the gayer purposes of a rural entertainment'.[9] Here was neither public enterprise nor private enlightenment, but an expansion of pleasure outwards from the city towards a still inhospitable countryside.

In his particular account of the Hatch/Weekes conflict, Stephens makes it plain that politics of a kind, and even economic interest, animated their row about a local road. The scale of things in no way rivalled General Cunningham's project. One of Hatch's tenants kept him informed of the parson's activities, partly from self-interest. 'Mr Weekes, evidently feigning ignorance of this, proceeded ... to dispose with subtlety of James Brady's obstruction. "This opposition ... can only arise from a pride of showing his power; or from fear lest good Roads should open the country to strangers who might raise the Price of Land on the old Inhabitants, a species of policy very prevalent among that class."'[10] The notion of tenant power should be read less as an objective account of eighteenth-century class relations, and more as a narrative anticipation of the long-term impact of the French Revolution, Irish insurrection and the decline of landlordism over the coming century.

Even in the travestied version presented by the twentieth-century lawyer, Weekes's argument queried the original arrival of Samuel M'Cracken in the area and the motives of the Hatches in establishing him at Roundwood. After all, they were strangers who sought to raise rents, develop mills and build homes. Yet Stephens's dogged pursuit of the dispute turns it towards greater and imminent changes. Having casually mentioned 'disturbing rumours which circulated among the gossips', he proceeded,

> Interest focussed [sic] round small matters of local concern and rose to excitement when, in the spring of 1789, the tenacious Mr Weekes for the second time presented to the Grand Jury his plan for the new road, and was again defeated.
>
> In summer, however, even in remote places like the Wicklow plateau, news from the continent began to shake the nerve of the landlord class, while the fall of the Bastile [sic] on the 14th July gave new hope to the peasants.[11]

By this time, Weekes had to contend not only with the ageing John Hatch as proprietor of the land in question but also with Francis Synge as occupant of remote Roundwood. The opening up of Wicklow was no longer a matter simply of economic development nor the provision of good roads, but one of personal safety for Mr Hugo and the ladies in his carriage. In due course, political subversion spread along mail-coach routes, while the forces of suppression used the same network in their effort to frustrate the United Irishmen with their talk of liberty, equality and fraternity. These confrontations occurred in the 1790s, and scarcely before 1795. A recent historian of the rebellion has noted how 'even the most conservative and the most radical elements could co-exist in Wicklow prior to the political crisis'. The elements in question were Thomas Hugo and Joseph Holt, and the object of their co-operation was road construction.[12]

The activities of the Wicklow Synges during the revolutionary decade are strangely neglected in their descendant's chronicle: apart from establishing Ambrose Weekes's passion for summary execution of suspected rebels, Stephens has little say about the family's experience of the bloody conflict. There is little reference to Joseph Holt, a protestant rebel of humble origins whom Francis Synge had employed as most favoured henchman, nothing of Isaac Butt's later insinuations of Synge's friendship towards Holt (whose sexual irregularities offended Butt). The road issue, sustained as an apparently parochial row, had highlighted contradictions, some of which at least were best left unspoken. Why did John Hatch never use Roundwood for his own residence nor improve its surrounding amenities? Was there a general economic unviability in the investment he had begun nearly half a century earlier, or was there a specific, personal or familial set of circumstances, which led to the casual treatment of the property?

Weekes was prophetic in one regard. The rebellion was followed by a determined government programme of road building in Wicklow. An immediately post-Union account of the county, sponsored by the Dublin Society, opened with a prompt tribute to the military roads. These were intended to prevent any recurrence of insurrection in mountains scarcely thirty miles from the capital. Robert Fraser approved 'the scientific ability' with which civil and political engineering was to be harmonised. 'This road is to be thirty-six yards wide; for a great part of the extent it will be a dead level, and in no part any sensibile difficulty in the ascent or descent.' In this last detail, the planners indicated that the objective was less to link up pre-existing social collectivities – whether villages or barracks – and more to lay down a vast grid of permanent infantry platforms. Thus the importance of Laragh as a southern terminus lay not in its existing characteristics but in the availability of land to build a block-house in the future.

Despite the acknowledgement of a military rationale, Fraser also saw an economic vision along the road. 'There will be an opening to Enterprize and Capital to speculate in cultivating these at present uninhabited wilds.'[13] The

The state of the roads

contradiction between his accounts of Wicklow's numerous desperados and of its uninhabited virginity forms, as it were, a cross-piece to stabilise the contradictions between military and entrepreneurial priorities. In keeping with the incipient romanticism of these years, the scientific analyst sang a hymn of praise to untainted nature in ancient Glendalough and outlined a scheme for building a new city and a new university amid the mountains and lakes. Again, the military engineers were crucial. 'As the new road will form an immediate communication between this romantic spot, and the city of Dublin, it would more than anything tend to extend civilization and culture into these wilds, if a town was founded in this central spot, and a small fort or garrison, to protect the inhabitants, and the adjacent country.'[14] Nothing of the sort eventuated, and Fraser conceded that the replacement of buildings destroyed during the violence of 1798–1800 might be as much as could be reasonably expected.

The mill/factory at Greenane, which had employed up to three hundred people in a quasi-industrial capacity, was destroyed by rebels in July 1798. No compensation was paid to the proprietor, Henry Allen, allegedly because of his private republican sympathies.[15] If the county's fortunes revived in the nineteenth century, it was not through the reconstruction or modernisation of such 'first revolution' industry. Mining in Wicklow had a discontinuous history reaching back into pre-Christian times, yet its development in the mountains south-west of Annamoe and elsewhere continued to be spasmodic. What the Dublin Society's man pointed to was a more modest pattern of post-insurrectionary reconstruction. 'Near [Glendalough], Mr Hugo, Mr Frizelle, Mr Critchley, and Mr Weeks had made some plantations, and built several houses, which were burnt by the rebels, but I understand they intend soon to rebuild.'[16]

If Roundwood Park fails to intrude on this list of phoenix-like properties, is the reason to be sought in its physical isolation and strategic unimportance or, alternatively, in its owner's ambiguous relation to the conflagration? The Dublin Society's omission of Francis Synge from the roll-call of revolution's victims is complemented by his descendant's silence on Synge's position – even physical whereabouts – during the long turmoil of revolution and bloody repression in Wicklow. Nor was Edward Stephens alone in these historiographical manoeuvres during the 1920s and 1930s. W. B. Yeats was carefully editing the eighteenth century to a somewhat different but related end – the eliciting of an Anglo-Irish Augustan tradition simultaneously independent of brute authority and opposed to popular revolution.

Part II

HATCHED, MATCHED AND DESPATCHED

6

An MP and his wife

On doit des égards aux vivants; on ne doit aux morts que la verité. (Voltaire)

HIS STORY TAKES OFF

IN 1757, John Hatch, still functioning as a subordinate to his father in the agency of the Blundell estates, reported in some detail on a King's County by-election.[1] His ambitions lay beyond business, though they would always rely on business. He does not appear to have been admitted a freeman of Dublin (thereby to gain the franchise) before 1774, perhaps because he regarded his domicile as lying elsewhere – in Swords.[2] Eventually, he was twice elected to the Irish House of Commons, in 1769 and 1783. On the first occasion he appears to have stood in two boroughs, Taghmon (in County Wexford) and Swords (in County Dublin). He chose to sit for the latter having successfully lodged a complaint against the result as first declared. The lengthy business of his contesting the original verdict at Swords can be traced in the Dublin newspapers from the middle of 1768 (when the election actually took place) to Hatch's vindication in December 1769. Polling at Swords had been curtailed by the borough's portrieve who declared the proceedings riotous.[3] Quite why Hatch declined to accept the positive verdict in Taghmon remains unclear: it may be relevant that the borough was controlled by the Hoare (or Hore) family. Henry Hatch had married a Hore widow in 1737.

The wider Hatch family's association with politics at this time can be gauged from two details in the County Louth contests. The verdict in Ardee proved contentious, and when the Ruxton faction gathered to formulate an address to their champions, they met in the house of Thomas Hatch. Earlier in the national proceedings, and further south, a Mr Hatch who kept an inn at Dundalk advertised its convenience for electors travelling to cast their vote. It is quite possible that Thomas Hatch also kept an inn; clearly he was obliging his social superiors by providing premises for their meeting.[4] The Hatches do not appear to have contributed to politics at any higher level before 1769.

An MP and his wife

Before his father's death in 1762, John Hatch either ran into financial difficulties or espied an opportunity for investment which required extra funds. In either case, in conjunction with one James Shiel, he signed a bond for £600, the lender being John Bonham.[5] Both names will recur in Hatch's story, though there is nothing to suggest that the loan went unrepaid. Commencing in 1763, his energies found a more traceable focus as he devoted a portion of them to the agency of the Blundell/Downshire estate at Edenderry, King's County (now Offaly). Opinion as to the nature of this involvement varies, even within the writings of the one historian who has looked into the matter. W. A. Maguire, whose concern is with the economics of estates rather than the character and personality of agents, describes how 'the active management, if you could call it that, was taken over in the early 1760s by ... John Hatch' whose regime is described as 'mininalist'.[6] In the same paper, however, the Downshires' recollection of the Hatch era is quoted to stress the assiduous levying of fees on leases to tenants. What Maguire omits is attention to the agent's other activities, beyond the boundaries of the Edenderry estate, a legitimate omission in the context of a paper focused on absentee landlordism. John Hatch was a thoroughly urban figure, whose country house at Lissenhall in north County Dublin typified a bourgeois cultivation of rural retreats rather than any hereditary principle. Shortly after his marriage, he divested himself of the agricultural lands surrounding the house, leasing close on two hundred acres to Henry Gonne.[7] Later, even the house was set to others.

Back in 1739, Gonne had succeeded his father Thomas as Town Clerk of Dublin. They belonged to a family settled in Ireland since the early seventeenth century, modestly active in Dublin civic affairs, but destined in the age of 'romantic anti-capitalism' to give the world Maud Gonne (1866–1953). Born in Surrey to a British Army officer, the beloved of Yeats will present herself as a 'colon who refuses', the child of Victorian Ireland's oppressors. Less dramatically, she came of old settler (not planter) stock, the agents of emergent business not conquistadors. Her ancestry rubbed shoulders with that of JMS who 'gently hated her' specifically for the lies she told in support of her cause. Perhaps he saw through the shamrogue leafage of her family tree, knowing her roots to have flourished on land once owned by his own great-great-grandfather.[8]

But before John Hatch entered parliament, he entered matrimony on the eve of a 'most dry & warm Summer' with his marriage on 16 May 1765 to Barbara Synge (b. 1731), daughter of Nicholas Synge (bishop of Killaloe, d. 19 January 1771) and his wife Elizabeth Trench (d. 1750). The ceremony was apparently conducted at Lissenhall.[9] As was normal in marriage arrangements at the time, land records document relations between the two families, but in this case the attachment to land differed between the parties, the Synges being part of a clerical and landed interest, and the Hatches being the more commercial and urban-based element. The terms of the marriage settlement reveal a cool even-handedness in the Synge family's treatment of Barbara. In 1762 she had been left a legacy of £500 under the will of her uncle Edward Synge, bishop of Elphin, charged on lands in County Cork; interest had been duly paid to her by her father. Now she was to receive £4,000 outright from her father, to include the legacy.

She was also obliged to 'release acquit and forever discharge all and Every the Lands so charged with the said sum of five hundred pounds and the Interest thereof and also the said Nicholas Lord Bishop of Killaloe his heirs Executors Administrators & assigns and all his Estate Real and personal off and from all claims and demands which she hath made for or upon account of any provision made or intended for her by Settlement or otherwise howsoever'.[10] This strongly suggests a determination on the Synge side to ensure that no further claims could be made by the bride or – more likely – by her husband, in return for which security a lump sum was handed over without the conventional provision of trustees appointed to protect the bride's future interest.

The surviving papers include notes of which the most precise is simply this – 'Mr Hatch proposes that all the above Lands except the unset part of Kilbarry & Haristown [in County Meath] be settled on the first & every other Son in Succession subject to £500 yearly jointure for Miss Synge & subject to a charge of £2,000 to be at his disposal by Deed or Will among the issue ...' In this version, Hatch certainly aims to protect his children against any retention of the wealth by the Synge family. There are yet other versions and notes towards a settlement which, though preserved in the Hatch Papers refer to a man by the initials I (or J) S. These are outlines of a proposal which is deemed unsatisfactory by some third party who has annotated them, pointing out deficiencies of security which would render them unacceptable to the bride's family. It is hardly conceivable that the annotating lawyer is Hatch, commenting on a wholly different marriage settlement. It is scarcely more probable that J. S. is Hatch's lawyer friend, posing the problem in (so to speak) his own name, so as to protect Hatch's identity. There are, however, bearers of these initials among Hatch's acquaintance – James Shiel of the 1757 debt, for example, or Isaac Shiel who emerges later as Hatch's 'private eye'. James Shiel, a merchant from Bride Street, served as one of the city's High Sheriffs.[11]

HER DIGRESSION INTO DEEPER SILENCE

The marriage so altered matters within the Synge family that the father made a new will on 3 or 4 June. In it he recorded the broad terms of the settlement in relation to 'Barbara Synge now Hatch' and proceeded additionally to 'give and bequeath to her the sum of Fifty pounds to buy her mourning' for his funeral. The provision and the size of the sum specified are unremarkable: in the eighteenth century it was not uncommon for minor benefits to be handled in this way. Certainly, the will gives us no cause to think of Nicholas Synge as a harsh man; he

An MP and his wife

commended to his executor's compassion 'the poor blind and maimed woman in Tuam whom I have supported these many years tho' I do not know her Name'. Nevertheless, an air of repressed disapproval or embarrassment surrounds the proceedings.

Amid the paucity of family records, Hatch's diary for 1765 is exasperating in its shorthandedness. In February, we find him travelling with Adam Williams (his attorney) to view land near Navan in County Meath. The weather is noted in some detail though the record is discontinuous and unsystematic. Synges very occasionally feature, though Hatch inscribes the Christian name initial so casually that identification is risky. If the blank page facing the printed calendar for March does indeed record a meeting with 'A. Synge', this can hardly be Alicia Synge (1733–1807) for she was by this date Mrs Joshua Cooper. In this case, A is for Archdeacon, that is Edward Synge (c. 1725–1792), the older brother of Barbara whose will (it may emerge) casts doubt on the one record we have of her death. These finicking considerations are necessary because the diary bears upon the fate of Barbara Synge – if only in its neglect of her and the implication that her brother – and not her father – was the mediator between the Synges and John Hatch.

In the month before his wedding, Hatch was involved in Dublin civic affairs, staying with the Lord Mayor early in April, and later with 'Dr Quin'. Henry Quin was a fashionable doctor and – less predictable in Hatch's circle – an accomplished artist and man of taste. He had married Anne Monck whose family had property in County Wicklow just north of an area in which Hatch was establishing himself through the activities of Cousin M'Cracken.[12] On 8 May – that is, a week before the marriage – B. S. was at Lissenhall. Whether Barbara, or her Bishop father, was inspecting her future home is impossible to determine. A 'Mr Synge' crops up on Saturday 18 May, but things are much clearer in mid-July when 'Arch Synge left town with Boys' – Archdeacon Edward had five sons whom we will encounter in later chapters. If this confirms the Bishop father's absence from the newly married couple's life, it might be said in mitigation that ill health dogged his final years.

The town was Dublin, only twelve kilometres from Lissenhall. To judge from the diary, the Hatches spent most of the time in the city, with Hatch occasionally staying at the Swords residence when his travels took him northwards. On 8 August, he set out for Edenderry with Lord Robert Bertie (part of the Blundell family), and later in the month toured Banbridge, Donaghadee, Dunleer, Lisburn, Newry and other Ulster or Ulster-frontier places. Some time in September, he met Edward Hoare (his brother-in-law) who had been ill. There is, in short, no reference to his wife who was by now pregnant. Such an omission is entirely characteristic of the period, and in itself is innocent.

Nor does the diary of 1765 give any evidence of Hatch's Wicklow investment, unless a near illegible entry for Sunday 20 October – 'R W park' – is taken to refer to Roundwood Park. But as the same entry suggests that he stayed that night with the Garnett family – of Meath – a lengthy excursion southwards becomes doubtful. The diary entry may simply record some decision made about Roundwood, albeit on a Sunday. Certainly Hatch was still based at Lissenhall: two days later he 'Came to town for the winter'. His wife was by now within three months of confinement. During November and December, there are several references to her brother's presence, whose wife (Sophia, née Hutchinson) evidently provided sisterly support. There is even one concentrated reference to 'B^p Kil^{oe}'.

When Nicholas Synge came to add a codicil to his will in 1768, he made no reference to his daughter, Barbara 'now Hatch'.[13] That in itself cannot be taken as evidence of either her exclusion from his thoughts, whether by paternal disapproval or even sterner tribunals. One remarkable feature of the Synge/Hatch marriage is the difficulty – for another moment or two, the impossibility – of establishing beyond doubt when the bride (the more socially elevated partner) died, or where she was buried. The compilers of entries for *The Landed Gentry* and the *Baronetage*, likewise the family genealogist, have long contented themselves with a minimal account of her life. In doing so, they have oddly ignored a terse death notice in Dublin's *Freeman's Journal* of 21–25 April 1767: 'At Stephen's-Green, Mr. [sic] Hatch; wife of John Hatch, Esq.'[14] Quite why this obvious source of information should have been overlooked remains an unfathomable question. Perhaps the most outlandish explanation – we will have to consider it in time – would have it that Barbara Hatch did not in fact die in April 1767. Certainly family chroniclers (like her cousin Dr Edward Synge), if they knew her to be alive (but severely incapacitated) at a later date would wish to leave the matter well alone because, if nothing else, it would reveal the publication of a false death-notice (see p. 11 above). Yet this remains speculation.

It would be transgressing beyond the bounds of plausibility to relate this conundrum of domestic and scholarly neglect to another news item on the same page: '17th [April 1767] In the morning, a new born Infant was found dead, with several Marks of Violence at the Foot of the Steeple of St. Patrick's Cathedral.'[15] However, the two deaths parallel each other in several Dublin newspapers of that week. *The Dublin Mercury* and *Faulkner's Journal* both described Mrs Hatch's death as 'greatly regretted', with the *Mercury* even regarding the place of death as 'her [sic] house'. If it appears gratuitous to associate her with the infant dumped on ecclesiastical ground her father had once trod as Archdeacon of Dublin, it will not be enough simply to argue that such cruelty to children was commonplace. In the first six months of 1765, the *Mercury* reported only one other incident, though doubtless some remained unreported.[16] The mentality of the times accommodated extraordinary public callousness and an exquisite insistence on seclusion in matters of domestic sexuality. So, even though there is no reason to connect the two events recorded by the newspapers in adjacent columns – no reason to connect them in their specificity – they constitute a double image of Georgian mortality.

Barbara's death (if indeed she died) cannot have occurred more than a few weeks after her second daughter's birth, and more likely it occurred within a few days. Yet *nowhere* is Dorothy Hatch's birth recorded: the battered infant corpse at the base of a church wall occupies that vacancy.

This is a line of thought which is not even hypothetical. Yet the issue of Barbara Synge's fate in 1767 (and perhaps after) can only be illuminated if we are prepared to venture beyond the very few known facts of her case. Silence itself can be interrogated. Hatch's humble cousin, Samuel McCracken, wrote to him in February 1769, concluding with the hope that 'this will find you and your Daughters in good health', an expression which implies the absence of a wife and mother.[17] But it does not automatically follow that her absence has been caused by death: other calamities in the eighteenth century could result in the virtual cancellation of a person's existence in what had been his or her most defining and intimate circle. Gross moral offence was perhaps the most common context in which one might be effectively denied by one's family. (But gross moral offence, by its nature, tended to draw attention elsewhere, indeed was often committed exactly to do so.) Extreme physical or mental disablement, incurred suddenly, could lead to the same fate – strokes suffered in childbirth were not uncommon, nor was 'the madwoman in the attic' an original invention of Charlotte Brontë's. It was a trope deployed, rather crudely, in JMS's first extended attempt at play-writing, in a script which undoubtedly alludes to other aspects of Synge family history.

These are melodramatic instances of 'disappearance'. With Barbara and John Hatch, some further details should not be overlooked. It is reasonably well established that the couple's two daughters – Elizabeth and Dorothy – were born in 1766 and 1767. Though no precise date has ever been proposed for Dorothy's birthday, it has been claimed that her sister, Elizabeth, was born on 21 January 1766.[18] While it is odd to be without baptismal details in the case of a bishop's grandchildren, the little we know does tend towards clarification of Mrs Hatch's fate. The date accepted for her elder daughter's birth would fall somewhat less than nine full months (eight months and five days, to be exact) after the marriage. Assuming that the child was legally begotten, we have here a short pregnancy, followed by the commencement of a second within a matter of six months or so, not an infrequent experience for women who resumed sexual activity after childbirth. It is then possible that Barbara died as the consequence of a second short or difficult pregnancy – that might be when Dorothy was born sometime before 21 April 1767. Alternatively, Barbara may have become incapacitated in a manner which behoved her family to avoid reference to her condition. Her brother Edward's will, written in 1792 shortly before his death, will include a plea which bears this latter interpretation. That, however shadowy, is her story.

HISTORY RESUMES

Vir gravis et doctus – solemn and learned man – was the approved type in the Synge family, an ideal which may not have been exemplified in Edward Synge (1726–1792) who in 1765 became John Hatch's brother-in-law. Edward was the last of the eighteenth-century Synges to take holy orders, and he was said to have done so with some reluctance.[19] On 15 February 1752, he married Sophia Helena Maria Hutchinson (1729–1799), daughter of a bishop and sister of a future baronet. The Hutchinsons were to prove a successful late Georgian and nineteenth-century dynasty, but as yet they could not rival the dignity of the Synges.

Edward Synge was one of a numerous family: the printed genealogy places him eldest of nine children. But the order in which these siblings are presented in the family tree is puzzling. Barbara is listed as older but placed as younger than her sister Elizabeth. Among Edward and Sophia's own children, the eldest (another Edward) has his name printed in italic – uniquely in the family tree. Although this document will be of great service in disclosing aspects of the house into which John Hatch married, it is not utterly reliable.[20] Bearing in mind the ultimate concern of *The Silence* with JMS and his generation's anxious interest in pedigree, one should note that the compiler of *The Family of Synge or Sing* (1937) received assistance from two of the dramatist's brothers, and also from Edward Stephens, the nephew who would compile the most extensive dossier of material about JMS.

The uncertainties of the eighteenth century were not unknown to the Synges of the 1890s. Indeed, in 1897 a resident of rural Oxfordshire (Richard Synge Cooper) visited Tuam to repair the grave of Edward Synge (1659–1741), archbishop of Tuam. He found that local (Catholic) people regarded rain, which gathered in the hollow where a monument to the (Protestant) prelate had stood, as holy water.[21] As an example of the confusion associated with the woman whose death notice appeared in April 1767, *Burke's Landed Gentry* of 1912 impossibly stated that 'Francis Synge ... b. 15 April 1761; m. Barbara, dau and co-heir of John Hatch' – perhaps he married his mother.

Confusion may amount to no more than indifference. But changes in sensibility across the decades generate ethical anxiety. It is natural nowadays to be shocked by the treatment meted out two hundred years ago to women and children. It is all the more an obligation on historians to balance their moral and analytical concerns. The great English eighteenth-century philanthropist, John Howard (1726–1790), reported on conditions in a nursery run by the Incorporated Society in premises on the Milltown Road, south of Dublin, in June 1787. 'Here were thirty-three children [under six years old], many of them unhealthy ... I observed an excessive parsimony in linen, soap, and other things necessary for cleanliness and health.' While the Revd John Yeats was rector of Drumcliff in County Sligo, he and Sir Robert Gore-Booth drove for local pupils to be consigned to the Milltown nursery, occasionally encountering stubborn opposition which Yeats commended for its honesty.[22] There is reason to believe that John Hatch may have been involved in the ownership of these premises, which the Society had erected as early as 1773 to augment or replace the York Street premises. When they were later sold, the Kevin Street palace of Bishop Synge was purchased in their stead, ultimately serving as a training school for female teachers. Hatch certainly owned property on the Milltown Road, and through the seneschalship of Saint Sepulchre controlled much of what happened in Kevin Street.[23] His cousin M'Cracken's property in York Street has already been noted, together with the ultimately greater holdings of the Synges.

The materials of the eighteenth century are figured or transfigured in the mentality of the late nineteenth. One awkward but highly relevant example will be found in the play by JMS which revolves round a young Irishman returned from Paris to a decaying Big House where the servant maid is daughter to an inmate of the local asylum, an inmate who is 'a lady' and acknowledged as 'your ladyship'. To acknowledge the general pattern, to trace its process and meditate upon its ironies, is in no sense a capitulation to idealist modes of thought. Walter Benjamin, gathering data for his never completed study of nineteenth-century Paris, asked 'What are phenomena rescued from?' His answer to himself not only addresses the suspicion of antiquarianism – which haunts many a historical inquiry – but also anticipates the cultural politics of today:

> Not only, and not in the main, from the discredit and neglect into which they have fallen, but from the catastrophe represented very often by a certain strain in their dissemination, their 'enshrinement as heritage'. – They are saved through the exhibition of the fissure within them. – There is a tradition that is catastrophe.[24]

The question of evidence, its accidental survival, its deliberate destruction, will be raised again at the end of this long inquiry into the shadow-biography of JMS, the biography – we might say – of what JMS was not. The evidence from the mid-eighteenth century is unquestionably questionable. John Hatch's isolated diary for 1765 carries on its final blank leaf a strange biological note which begins 'Free Martin Twins to Birth Miss Goring sister to Mr Chas Goring 2 male or female Twins lie in one cell in Womb but a male & female are separated by a Membrane. Mr Cs Goring & Sister.' The remainder of the brief note relates to travel and business on Hilsborough's behalf.[25] Apart from one letter recording the death of a grandchild, this is the only personal trace one has of John Hatch (see p. 11 above). The existence of freemartins was a matter of growing veterinary interest in the eighteenth century. Female co-twins with male calves were regarded as sterile and often hermaphroditic in their sexual organisation. Professional medical wisdom appears to have ignored the actual occurrence of human freemartins, while at the same time folk wisdom regarded females of such birth as ill-omened. Hatch's terse and isolated note thus catches an ambiguous theme. It was not until John Howard delivered a paper to the Royal Society in 1779 that even the veterinary questions were scientifically aired. By the middle of the nineteenth century, the 'alleged infecundity of females born co-twins with males' among humans had been challenged on statistical grounds.

Yet the case of Miss Goring remains intriguing simply on the grounds of its attracting Hatch's attention. The Goring family of Traveston Hall, Nenagh (County Tipperary) were implicated in a public scandal when the sister of Mrs Margaret Goring eloped with the castrato singer, Tenducci, apparently in 1766.[26] If twins occurring within Hatch's own family, extended by marriage to Barbara Synge, prompted his diary entry, then one notes Richard and Edward Cooper (whose mother was Alicia Synge, 1733–1807), born in 1763. These seem to have been perfectly ordinary twins.

The births of John Hatch and Barbara Synge's two daughters have been confidently dated, though they remain poorly documented. With this conventional family record remaining inscrutable, other records seem by comparison dull. The Dublin Registry of Deeds records a grant from John Hatch to an Elizabeth Synge, dated 20 February 1771, of lands in County Meath; this was probably Elizabeth Synge (1737–1837), who was Hatch's (late?) wife's sister.[27] The reasons lying behind the transfer of property remain obscure. Nicholas Synge (his father-in-law, her father) had died the previous month. Given the elevated position of the Synges in the Irish Church, and Hatch's own distinction as twice elected to the House of Commons, it is remarkably difficult to establish dates of births and deaths for this generation of Synge's ancestry. The dullness gradually comes to resemble suppression of detail. For John Hatch, we have no birth-date; for his wife, Barbara Synge, no place of burial. *Memorials of the Dead* is a most thorough listing of churchyard inscriptions throughout Ireland, especially attentive to sites where persons of this class might be buried or commemorated, and yet neither Hatch nor his wife can be traced to their graves.

Prosperity was a matter of patching together incomes of diverse kinds. The borough of Swords sold itself to the highest bidder. In ecclesiastial circles, the ancient rural deanery of Swords earned a reputation as 'the Golden Prebend' from its great value in the chapter of Saint Patrick's Cathedral, Dublin.[28] In December 1768, Hatch was appointed by the archbishop of Dublin to the seneschalship of the manor (or liberty) of Saint Sepulchre, to replace George Smyth who had been promoted a baron of the Court of Exchequer.[29] As this office appears to have contributed to the property Hatch in effect left to the Synges, some account of its obscure workings is in order. Liberties were privately governed counties forming part of the system of royal administration. The chief official was the seneschal who reported to the exchequer in the same way that a county sheriff did, and he also presided over the liberty court. By this route Hatch would have participated in the workings of the Prerogative Court through which wills were proven and estates transferred from testator to beneficiary. Apart from these formal proceedings, there was also the income taken for granted by all appointees in the eighteenth century.[30]

Long before Hatch entered public life, the residents and tradesmen of Saint Sepulchre's had petitioned parliament in opposition to the proposed new bridge across the Liffey. They recognised that (what became) Essex Bridge would obstruct the movement of ships up-river and shift the centre of commerce eastwards to their disdvantage. This incident of local politics in 1752 illuminates Hatch's later opposition to more substantial plans to develop the city. What was good for Dublin at large was not necessarily good for the Liberty of Saint Sepulchre's, and what was good for the Liberty was good personally for its seneschal.

The borough close to Hatch's country seat, Swords, was notorious; 'elections in this town afford scenes of the greatest corruption'.[31] With other 'potwalloping' boroughs, it was characterised as 'the very worst species of Representation ... where neither property, nor family connections, nor the good opinion of the neighbourhood, nor any other good species of influence, would weigh against adventurers from Dublin or London with large purses, or backed by any temporary clamour'.[32] While this anonymous description is clearly prejudiced in favour of the eighteenth-century conventions of patronage, there is little in it to dignify JMS's ancestor either as patriot or man of principle. On 27 February 1765, Hatch's scant diary entries recorded social events involving a 'Damer Ball', and a further entry either of 20 May or 20 April – 'Eli: D died of small pox' – may also record his intimate knowledge of Damer family affairs at this period.[33]

During his first parliament (1769–1776), John Hatch was associated with the Ponsonby faction, and was 'probably against Government' on most issues.[34] At the election of 1776, he failed to be returned for Swords, lodged a formal complaint, but subsequently withdrew it. A further complaint was in process in 1777–1778 but failed. While a non-member, Hatch petitioned (unsuccessfully) against a 1778 Bill for the Improvement of Dublin, presumably on the grounds that its provisions conflicted with his own growing interests in the city, or with those of the Liberty over which he presided. As with the issue of roads in Wicklow, he pursued no publicly visible entrepreneurial objective. He continued as agent on the Edenderry estates, and performed similar duties for other landowners. His career mixed business activity on behalf of an aristocratic master, shrewd investment on his own behalf, and the occasional foray into public affairs. He never held political office, though both his predecessors in the seneschalship had become judges. In 1781, his Liberty fell into arrears of £170 in its payments to the County of Dublin.[35]

Though Hatch's activities involved property in Meath and elsewhere, his personal Wicklow involvement (through Samuel M'Cracken) dovetailed with the southern interests of his principal employer. The Hill family of Hillsborough, County Down, were ambitious of rank and dignities, eventually acquiring a marquisate in 1789. In addition to their principal Ulster estates, they held land at Edenderry, County Kildare, and Blessington, County Wicklow. The latter lay close to the area in which Henry Hatch and some of the Hutchinsons had commenced their acquisitions. Arthur Hill (1753–1801, the 2nd marquis) sat in the Irish House of Commons before succeeding his father in 1793 and moving to the upper house. Known by the courtesy title of Lord Kilwarlin, it was primarily he with whom John Hatch dealt in the latter part of the century, together with some female members of the family. Kilwarlin's ward, Catherine Carpenter, married the Scottish poet Walter Scott in the year of Hatch's death.

In the summer of 1782, Samuel Hatch led a party of three on a lengthy English journey, for which he furnished accounts to John Hatch. With Samuel Hatch himself, the travellers were a Mrs Hatch and a Miss Hoare, the last probably a daughter of Elizabeth, John Hatch's only sister. The purpose of the trip – which took them through Holyhead, Chester, Bridgnorth (from whence the Irish Synges had set forth), Shrewsbury, Bristol, Bath – remains obscure. Sam was repaid in almost equal part by John Hatch and Miss Hoare, though his accounts include payments of five guineas to a Mr Hoare (en route) and – among other London extravagances of Mrs Hatch – £3 on '10 yards Brown Lutestring for Nightg[ow]n'.[36]

The first assumption to be drawn from these incidentals is of Samuel Hatch and his wife acting as travelling companions to Miss Hoare. (That he was married can be established beyond reasonable doubt.[37]) Miss Hoare leaves the party before they reach London, this resulting in the couple travelling onwards, having discharged their duty by a young relative by delivering her safely to Bath where Edward Hoare lived. Accounts for these activities are very well documented. For 22 June, Samuel records for John Hatch back home 'Expenses on ourselves in London by your permission ... £11 3s 7d'. And the full statement of account is divided in two parallel parts 'Expended on myself' and 'Expended on Mrs Hatch'. But why should John Hatch finance an expedition for his kinsman and the latter's wife, and why would Samuel Hatch keep separate accounts of his own and his wife's expenditure? Even if Miss Hoare was John Hatch's niece, a resident of Bath returning home after an Irish holiday, the London expenses of her chaperons – including the purchase of female clothing – do not look like the responsibility of a penny-careful businessman.

So a second possibility presents itself. Samuel Hatch, little more than a handyman in his employer's circle, is employed to escort two relatives of John Hatch – his niece and wife. While the theory flies in the face of the 1767 death notices, it does harmonise otherwise puzzling details – John Hatch's paying for female clothing, indeed John Hatch's paying for everything, and then John Hatch's preserving the accounts with his papers. It might be argued that 'Expenses on ourselves' is not the kind of phrase a lowly attorney's clerk would use of himself and his employer's wife, but the distinction is between expenses outlaid directly on members of the travelling party and those incurred through other people – drivers, porters, innkeepers, etc. The unanswerable question would now be: in what condition was Mrs John Hatch during this journey – manifestly an invalid, yet buying lutestring for nightgowns?

Whatever the nature of the trip to Bath and London, it was not politics which detained John Hatch in Dublin. The intermittent pattern of his electoral success kept him out of the House of Commons for the historic debates and decisions of 1782, when the Irish parliament – encouraged by events in America – won a degree of Legislative Independence from Westminister. He was, at the same time, listed among the three 'principal interests' operative in the borough he had earlier represented.[38] In 1783, Hatch was once more elected for Swords (though not without a protest from the defeated). Later that year, he was with the majority which voted against Henry Flood's Volunteer motion for 'the more equal representation of the people in parliament'.[39] Within the specialised context of a legal battle where the mustering of opinion was crucial to success, Hatch took comfort in the thought that 'Irish tenants, like rats, have a great sagacity in discovering an approaching ruin'.[40]

The impression he made on the records of the House was not deep. On 5 November 1783, he was ordered into the custody of the Serjeant at Arms having failed to attend as required. Discharged without a fine two days later, Hatch found himself caught up in procedural antics, which led to his being excused attendance at 'Grattan's Parliament' seven times between late November 1783 and 28 February of the following year. He was only one of a number of MPs who, being disqualified by law from serving on certain Select Committees, were by the House's conventions compelled to attend. This double jeopardy had been eased by a resolution of 6 November 1783, but the result was merely to inscribe Hatch's name as an absentee MP. Though he was voiceless, he was not always voteless: when the Government brought in an extravagant Pensions Bill in March 1787, he was listed as one of the minority who opposed it.[41] Whatever his faults as a parliamentarian, Hatch was no placeman. A year later, together with quite a number of other MPs, he found it expedient to absent himself from the House while balloting to choose a Select Committee was in progress. On 14 February 1788, he was again ordered into the custody of the Serjeant at Arms, and discharged fifteen days later without fines – 'he being sixty Years of Age or upwards'.[42]

The small volume of surviving political correspondence between Kilwarlin and his agent testifies more to his lordship's touchiness than to any substantial alliance or practical co-operation. Undated, Kilwarlin's letters provide no indication of Hatch's objectives as a member of the House of Commons at any given moment. Certain ceremonial occasions can be identified, and the general tenor of Kilwarlin's prejudices emerges:

I am sorry to find, that indisposition had kept you from the House on Friday, by your note of yesterday. The division that took place on that day was not upon the address which gave rise to a torrent of most infamous & illiberal Abuse, but upon a motion [word illegible] of the House to give dignity & proper weight & consequence to our proceedings, & keep up our respectability in the world by the propriety of our conduct & deliberations upon the important question that will come before the House when it resolves itself into a Committee upon the State of the nation. I am very sorry to find that there is so strong a faction in the House as to prevent the execution of such desirable objects. You are very good to me & very flattering to have thought it necessary to write to me a note upon the occasion, & I have not the least doubt that you will use your best endeavours, to prevent our sinking into contempt & derision even in the eyes of him whose favor the Faction is endeavouring to purchase by grossest adulation & unpatriotic means that can possibily be devised.[43]

The setting for this was most probably the Regency crisis of February 1789, when the Whig opposition pressed for an Irish parliamentary address to the Prince of Wales requesting him to assume the powers of regent during his father's mental incapacity. The younger man may indeed have valued Hatch's support, but nothing seems to have persuaded the member for Swords to break his habitual silence. His 'countenanced attendance' was all that could be acknowledged on the occasion of Kilwarlin's performing the ceremonial role of carrying up the address – not on the regency issue – to the king's lord-lieutenant.

John Hatch's two daughters were now well entered upon adulthood. In both cases they ultimately married two Synge brothers, sons of Archdeacon Edward Synge, of Syngefield, Birr), and his wife Sophia Hutchinson. That is to say, Hatch's daughters married their first cousins. In 1786 the elder at the age of twenty, Elizabeth, married Francis Synge (1761–1831, of Roundwood, County Wicklow) who was elected MP for Swords in 1797. One of the few personal glimpses we get of Mrs Elizabeth Synge (née Hatch) comes in the form of her son's 1815 dedication of a book to 'a much lamented mother, to whose early instruction and example, however inadequately valued amidst the follies of youth these tracts are inscribed ...'[44] The piety of this may signal nineteenth-century changes in the family's spiritual outlook more accurately than it records a 1790s upbringing.

At the end of 1789, Hatch was advising Kilwarlin about his lordship's candidature for a seat in County Down, only to discover that the easy victory he predicted had proved hard-won. As far as Swords was concerned, in 1791 the electoral tables were turned with Hatch losing both the election and the familiar complaint which followed. In October 1793, he received 'commands' from his landed employer in relation to Sir Henry Jebb (c. 1750–1811), a notable Dublin surgeon. Hatch felt both sufficiently his own man to refuse, and sufficiently irate about his 'last unfortunate election' to disclose that Jebb had, during the 1791 contest, played 'a very odd prank with the daughter of a relation and friend' of his (Hatch's).[45]

An MP and his wife

Steering a judicious course between dependence on land-agency and over-investment in politics, Hatch had subscribed to the new Royal Canal project in 1789, duly became a director, and sat on an internal committee of inquiry in 1793. The midland Downshire property, however, lay adjacent to the other great navigation development of the day. The Grand Canal, linking Dublin to the River Shannon had opened in 1779; Hatch tried to persuade his employers to relinquish some traditional rights (mainly to bogland) with a view to stimulating building-works, modest industrialisation and local investment. In 1788, he was still hoping that a 'cut' towards the town would be approved 'and then I flatter myself that Edenderry Lands and Ground Rents likewise will not be thought as little of as they now are'.[46] Though the following year did indeed see the canal reach the Downshire property, these prospects proved visionary, wrecked on landlord caution and the general uncertainty of canal development. Quite how Hatch's formal engagement in the Royal Canal Company, and his practical interest in the Grand Canal, were reconciled cannot be established. He resigned his directorship in 1797, but Francis Synge in turn became a director.[47]

John Hatch had married three years after his father's death. The year after his elder daughter married, he sought to resign the Edenderry agency, perhaps intending to hand it over to his son-in-law. But his masters objected, with the result that an ailing man persisted in the business for a further ten years.[48] His poor health raises a question mark after the appearance of his name in yeomanry lists for the year 1796. John Hatch, a captain of infantry in the Liberty of Saint Sepulchre, certainly looks like our man. By the time the list appears in print, Hatch the seneschal was well over seventy.[49] He was, undoubtedly, alert to the changing tide of affairs. In January 1797, he sought instructions about repairs to a barracks, and the following month reported to one of his employers,

> Our Prime Minister came from England last night or this morning and is to open his budget, I hear, this night or tomorrow in the House of Commons, and then we shall know our situation in respect of the vast expense this country has been put to in respect to the late invasion.[50]

The Irish treasury was virtually depleted, while support from London was not generous. The worst, for landlords and supporters of government alike, was yet to come. Hatch personally was increasingly afflicted with ill-health and sought to lay down his responsibilities as agent for the Blundell and Downshire estates. Delays in his furnishing of accounts had been noted from August 1795 onwards. In anticipation of the July/August election of 1797, Hatch opted not to stand but supported his son-in-law Francis Synge who, as a consequence, was able to vote against the Act of Union in 1800.

John Hatch disappeared from public view in 1797. A letter from his dying days indicates weary exasperation with the world. Having demanded keys to a vacant property, he heard to his outrage that a female tenant 'had brought in a Turf man to protect her & her children & now finds that the Protector has left it & that some other people are in possession, by which means the whole town of Portobello will be destroy'd'.⁵¹ Just over a month later, he died, on 22 September. His son-in-law soon found sorting out Hatch's affairs to be a complicated business (see below, pp. 114–115 etc.) There is no reference to Barbara, his wife.

In 1801 his younger daughter, Dorothy (1767–1836), became the second wife of Samuel Synge (1756–1846, who in 1813 became Sir Samuel Synge Hutchinson); they had three children all dying young, before the line was secured with the birth of Francis [Synge] Hutchinson in 1802. They lived in Hatch's Harcourt Street house after his death. In 1807, Francis Synge was still having difficulty with the administration of the estate.⁵² The general division of Hatch's very considerable wealth is traceable in outline through two details. In the 1930s, Lissenhall was in the possession of the Hely-Hutchinsons, kinsmen of Dorothy Hatch's husband. But some of the Hatch papers passed into the hands of those Synges who inherited Glanmore Castle in Wicklow, for example a small rental notebook has a twentieth-century pencil annotation 'from the Hatch Papers Glanmore 1902'.⁵³ These are the kind of primary souces which the 'prentice dramatist preferred over published summary history, according to his cautious yet revealing brother. Here he would have traced the line passing through the marriage of Francis Synge and Elizabeth Hatch, for documentation of its substance was in the library at Glanmore during JMS's occasional sojourns there.

What sort of man John Hatch was remains a question difficult to answer in any detail. Writing on 29 September 1797 to Downshire, Francis Synge sketched a picture of his late father-in-law as worn down by work. A week later, he underscored the theme by regretting that Hatch's employers had not allowed him to retire in 1787, and adding that 'his disposition was much too compassionate for the office of an agent'.⁵⁴ A composite assessment from the Downshire point of view used very different terms. 'As a man of business', Hatch was 'full of professions, bustle, dishonest'.⁵⁵ Certainly, he was secretive and acquisitive, characteristics which were inherited by his son-in-law in the form of complicated property relations rather than personal characteristics. Synge's attempts to administer Hatch's affairs were rudely interrupted by the outbreak of insurrection in Wicklow, where his own portion of the old man's estate lay. The difficulties, both technical and moral, in carrying out the intentions of a man who left no will are illuminated by a brief retrospect on an earlier stage of Hatch/Synge history.

7

Death in the mountains, 1769

They had a habit of writing anonymous letters, and I couldn't stop it. They were at it all the time. They wrote them to one another. (*O'Faolain*)

AT EASTER 1736, the city of Dublin admitted to its roll of freemen a barber named Samuel M'Cracken. The means of his enfranchisement – by Grace Especial – was reserved for two very different types of candidate: dignitaries who were in effect being awarded honorary Freedom of the City, and craftsmen who did not belong to a guild-organised trade.[1] M'Cracken was clearly of the latter type. It would seem, however, that he advanced from the humble service of barbering to the making of perukes. Under the peculiar economy of Ireland in the mid-eighteenth century, a wig-maker (providing he cleaved to the Church of Ireland) might also flourish in the property market. Towards the end of 1743, this particular Dublin peruke-maker set out a house on the south side of York Street to the Reverend Lewis Scoffier. From the surviving records – witnessed by Henry Hatch – it is clear that M'Cracken owned at least three houses at this location. The clientele was respectable, for some years later Alderman Nathaniel Kane took the house beside Scoffier, with Councillor Flood occupying the property on the other side.[2] The Incorporated Society established its first Dublin 'nursery' in the same street.

M'Cracken was not a Dubliner by birth, and his fortunes were closely linked to those of better-educated relatives. About 1750, John Hatch and his 'old cousin' M'Cracken acquired a house at Roundwood, which they held from Luke Gardiner (d. 1755), a tenant of the Temple estate in County Wicklow, also a major administrative figure and entrepreneur. In 1749, M'Cracken had leased the townland of Glassnamullen from the Honourable Jack Temple, a property which he was always to list as separate from the nearby Roundwood holding. No consolidation of the two was ever effected.[3] M'Cracken, it seems, was a northerner like some of the Hatches; he spoke of Kells (in north Meath) as the place he wished to buried, and relatives gave Carrickmacross (in Monaghan) as their home town. These and other actors in the drama soon to play itself out on the side of the Wicklow Mountains hailed from the area now associated with the border between Northern Ireland and the Republic, the north Leinster/Ulster frontier counties of Monaghan and Louth. M'Cracken had no prior connection with County Wicklow, though he took up residence on his own in Roundwood where he lived until his death. Hatch had town houses successively on Saint Stephen's Green and in Harcourt Street, Dublin, which he appears to have preferred to his country place, Lissenhall, in north County Dublin.[4]

His father, Henry Hatch, also employed M'Cracken as a buyer. For example, at Gorey, County Wexford, in 1754, the latter paid £51 7s 1½d for twenty cattle including 'a Red Cow white tale a Hole in the left Ear five years old £2 7s 0'. These pleasing bovine details are more numerous than any confirmed for the human agents involved in the transfer of Roundwood House (later Roundwood Park) to the Synge family. The presence of neighbours named William and Thomas Pollard in the larger Roundwood area reinforces the notion that the Hatches' interest there was linked to Henry Hatch's membership of the Incorporated Society, for Pollards of the same Christian names served as the Society's official carriers. In January 1771, Thomas Pollard was attacked just south of Dublin city while conveying two very young children to the Society's school at Arklow.[5] The reward for such stewardship may have included leases of land further to the north in Wicklow, and by this means an underpopulated district found tenants.

In other regards, a history of M'Cracken's own stewardship can readily be pieced together. By the beginning of 1753, he was setting part of Glassnamullen to Joy Whitmore, for a sugar-loaf rental providing that the latter expended £300 p.a. on improvements to the property. In 1759 he leased a farm to Richard Fleming, Roundwood's innkeeper, the witnesses being John Hatch and Samuel Mercer (master at the nearby Templestown School).[6] These and other transactions indicate a modest programme of development. When a sizeable holding was set to Thomas Manwaring in 1762, its extent (116 acres) was established by reference to a land-survey by Jacob Neville. A pattern of 'networking' can be discerned, the witnesses on this occasion being a Dublin attorney, Adam Williams, and 'Samuel Hatch gent.' who was Williams's clerk.[7]

The following year, legal documentation provides a glimpse of James Stuart of Liverpool, another peruke-maker, son and heir of a Stoneybatter resident in north Dublin.[8] He will prove to be a less helpful participant in a slowly unfolding drama. For, while rent accounts for Glassnamullen refer to monies paid to M'Cracken and a receipt of his dated 9 June 1769, contemporary with this steady management of Hatch's interests in Wicklow, the collector was becoming embroiled in more volatile matters.[9] Advancing in years, M'Cracken had proposed marriage to a great-niece of Henry Hatch's but, if for no other reason than that she was very young, nothing came of the proposal. The girl remains unidentified; another,

Death in the mountains, 1769

apparently of more local background, enters instead, and with lamentable consequences. M'Cracken himself had three nephews – James Stuart, being one of them – who flit through the shadows of his unhappy story; when he sent one of them to Dublin to start in the currier's trade, we can deduce that they were people of no greater social consequence than their uncle.

Nor did M'Cracken possess much more than an approximate literacy. Uncertain in grammar, his surviving letters reflect pronunciation rather than formal correctness. Yet he had a quaint turn of phrase, a transparent piety and devotion to his Hatch relatives. Up on the lonely mountainside, extreme conditions combined with other adversities to trouble the old bachelor's life. At the end of 1761, he referred obscurely to 'the unfortunate house'. After some months of bad weather, he noted with little sense of grievance that 'the winter has been so very severe that it has melted all my Lettuce'. When a change of rector at Derrylossory was imminent, he declared forthrightly, 'I cant like to live when I cannot be instructed to serve God.' M'Cracken saw himself as a servant of others, recalling Henry Hatch as a 'good guairden' [sic] and frequently addressing John Hatch as his 'humble servant to command'.[10]

M'Cracken's role was not simply to hold property on behalf of his relative in Dublin. Early in 1764, while advising Hatch of the need to repair or rebuild the mill at Annamoe, he also moved to acquire more land in the area. In March 1765, he admitted that he was 'looking at every newspaper for the completion of [his cousin's] happiness' – Hatch married Barbara Synge later that year. Newspapers did not circulate easily in these parts, and we can conclude that M'Cracken still travelled occasionally to Wicklow town and even to Dublin. If he was privy to Hatch's marriage plans, it is likely that he was intended to play some role in developing Roundwood as a future country house for the couple, an intention perhaps spoiled by Mrs Hatch's premature death in 1767 or thereafter.

This was a lonely station, though it is now difficult to assess quite what the population of the area was in mid-century. When Richard Mercy of Tinnepark married a Miss Freeman of Tomdaragh in March 1766, she probably left the townland close to Roundwood and joined her husband on the lower, better land. As if to balance matters, a few months later Caleb Smalley of Glasnamullen took the Widow Eadin of Mount Nebo to wife. Humphrey Lloyd and Margaret Burbridge, both of Roundwood, married late in the same year.[11] There was, of course, the little population of the school. There does not appear to have been a great deal of traffic in and out of the establishment. The case of seven-year-old John Broomfield is probably typical. His place of origin being registered as the Wheatsheaf pub in Dublin's Bolton Street, he was sent to Templestown at the end of May 1766. Or consider Anthony Woods: the son of a protestant father and 'papist' mother, he arrived on 23 May 1766, with at least two other boys; ten years later, Woods was apprenticed to a farmer just outside Dublin and – some time later again – died.[12]

Hatched, matched and despatched

Animosities sprang up – then as now – whenever land was at issue. M'Cracken had difficulty in pressing his legal claim to the townland of Ballinacor. A wily miller, who owed rent, tried to plead poverty by covertly selling off his livestock. Pursuing some of this, M'Cracken 'got the cow 15 miles from this ... put her in pound, then seized on the premises a little hay [,] turf and 28 ridges of potatoes about 6 perch long each'.[13] While these activities were part and parcel of the rural economy in eighteenth-century Ireland, M'Cracken was a vulnerable figure, representing a distant superior. Hatch, it seems, did not trouble himself to visit Roundwood.

Consequently, M'Cracken's household in turn became prey to rumour and intimidation. He did not live alone, having at least one servant boy who ran away – 'eloped' was M'Cracken's phrase – in January 1762, wishing that he had enlisted in the king's service while still in Dublin. Later in the same year, it is clear that a female was present. In September, M'Cracken concluded his letter to Hatch, 'Cousen Salmon sends you her good wishes'. On another occasion, 'Cousen Salmon joynes me in love to you'. It is probable that this person was of M'Cracken's own advancing age, for in December 1765 she was 'very bad with her pains'. By this date, the house had already begun to receive unwelcome attentions, and M'Cracken was embroiled in dispute with an invisible, anonymous enemy. 'It must proceed from my taking Ballinacor,' he concluded.[14]

Whatever the motive of his tormentors, the offence complained of was far more intimate than simple land-grabbing. Four years later in August 1769, when M'Cracken fled to John Hatch for protection, he confessed that 'he cou'd never think of returning to his own House, told him of an affair he had with a maid Servant in his house, that the maid Servant married a man in his Neighbourhood who threatened to prosecute him at the assizes'.[15] Yet even in 1765, uncertainty as to the nature of the M'Cracken establishment was discernible. Before Christmas, Hatch had sent a pair of pocket-pistols to his country cousin, who had also requested a holster once owned by Henry Hatch, long the 'guairden and loveing friend'. Acknowledging receipt of the firearms, M'Cracken concluded piously, 'thank God my Friend and me are well. She joines me in wishing you & Mrs Hatch the Comp[limen]ts of the approaching Season.'

Perhaps a more sophisticated letter-writer would have avoided paralleling the newly married couple with 'my Friend and me'; given that there is no reference in the letter to Cousen Salmon, it seems reasonable to deduct that the friend and the cousin were one and the same person. In such a sentiment as 'Cousen Salmon sends you her love and good wishes', M'Cracken conveys to Hatch a strong sense of the attachment which binds all three.[16] The Christmas letter is practically the only external reference to Barbara Synge which has survived.

Despite the need for pistols, M'Cracken retained a degree of humour. Having arrived home suffering from a heavy cold, he joked that he 'ought to thank God' as it kept him safely within doors. He followed his cousin's advice by maintaining his 'former course in keeping good hours', and showed the threatening letter to the parson whom he believed to be 'a very good man'.[17] This latter description strongly suggests that the new parson, Ambrose Weekes, had taken up his post, despite an initial desire to appoint a son of the late David Stephens (curate since 1735) in lieu. Young Stephens had not even been ordained at the time this suggestion was made, a circumstance which provoked M'Cracken to wrath. Weekes's residence in the area, and his subsequent interest in the development of roads, was evidence of better prospects for the Roundwood district. In the late 1790s, these high hopes were to be dashed, and Sam M'Cracken's personal fate in the late 1760s might be read as omens of a wider disaster.

In February 1769, M'Cracken wrote to his prosperous cousin in Dublin, announcing that as 'Mrs Salmon is to lave [sic] me in ten days, I thought it proper to settle affairs between us.' He enclosed a document, 'done to the Best of my good neighbours Judgment', requesting the opinion of Hatch and (if necessary) the assistance of Adam Williams, the Dublin attorney whom Hatch occasionally retained. What M'Cracken was anxious to perfect was 'an Instrument that will be sufficient to Bind both parties'. From this it seems clear that some significant arrangement between him and Mary Salmon was being put in place. M'Cracken's letter proceeded in something like testamentary mode – 'My nephew has left me. As my Intrest [sic] could not provide for him, I am to give him £80: I promised his brother in law the Hatter £50 with my neice, they have a thought to set up together, if that should take place.' On the other hand, he asked Hatch to advance the £50 'untel [sic] May', which suggests a less final set of arrangements than a will.[18] In any case, M'Cracken had made a will several years earlier.

What was the relationship between Samuel M'Cracken and Mary Salmon, both residing in the house at Roundwood? Dated 30 January 1769, the strangely exact agreement which they reached was silent about the cause of their separation. Given M'Cracken's limited powers as a writer, it is not surprising that the 'article' (as it called itself) was witnessed by the Revd Ambrose Weekes and Thomas Hugo; indeed its terminology suggests their active participation:

> This Article made ... between Samuel McCracken of Roundwood in the County of Wicklow Gent: on the one part and Mary Salmon late of Dublin now of Roundwood aforesaid Widow on the other part: Witnesseth that the said Mary Salmon, for and in consideration of the sum of Twenty Pounds Sterling to be paid by the said Samuel McCracken, his heirs and assigns, yearly and every year during the natural Life of the said Mary Salmon, doth hereby assign, give and make over to the said Samuel McCracken, his heirs and Assigns the sum of Ninety-six Pounds, nine shillings and five pence sterling being the full balance of all the cash received by said Samuel McCracken on account of the said Mary Salmon: together with whatever Interest shall now be due thereon: or

due by him on any acct. to the said Mary Salmon ... The said Samuel McCracken and Mary Salmon do hereby bind themselves to each other to sign and perfect any other Instrument to the Purport of the above in case it shall appear necessary to Council learned in the Law.[19]

Though the local dignitaries managed a good imitation of legal jargon, the final sentence reveals how non-professional their talents were. The occasion, we may conclude, was in some way extraordinary; in M'Cracken's mind it may have amounted to a crisis. But Mary Salmon cannot be the maid about whom M'Cracken confessed in August, for the former was a widow (who had aches and pains) whereas the latter had just married and was probably quite young.

Within seven months, M'Cracken was dead, and the consequences required John Hatch to have drawn up a summary of his unfortunate cousin's career. From this essentially strategic document it is possible to extract fundamental dates and events. '1762 May 15 Mr Samuel Macraken of Roundwood in the Co. Wicklow duly made and published his last will ... and thereof appointed John Hatch ... his sole Ex[ecuto]r and ... leaves all his leases to said John Hatch ... This will was left by Mr Macraken in the hands of Mr Duffe [a wig maker in Liffey Street, Dublin] ... together with a letter directed to said John Hatch and dated february 25th 1766 ...' Without any reference to the settlement involving Mary Salmon, the summary proceeds, '1769 Augt 2d He came to town [ie to Dublin] and dined with said John Hatch & on the 4th came to him and complained most grievously of his unfortunate situation, beged [sic] that he (said Hatch) wou'd let him go to Lissenhall & that he wou'd there give him a Garret and let him remain there as he cou'd never think of returning to his own House, told him of an affair he had with a maid Servant in his house, that the maid Servant married a man in his Neighbourhood who threatened to prosecute him at the assizes.'[20]

According to the summary later drawn up for courtroom purposes, Hatch and a friend then advised M'Cracken 'that he shoud [sic] return home the next morning, go to the assizes of Wicklow the tuesday following ...' But, in the event, 'Saturday Augst 5th Mr Macraken went to his lodging in the even: and next morning he called on Mr Hatch between seven and 8 o'clock and about 8 set out for his own house, got home about 11 that night, went to Church next morning, dined at home, read prayers to his family in the Evening went to bed about 9 o'clock and was found Dead on the floor of his bed Chamber next morning with his brains blown about and a Discharged Pistol by his side ...'[21]

Henrik Ibsen could not have asked for more – a brooding landscape, a brooding religion, a discharged gun. But the suicide (if such it was) of M'Cracken did not result in a simple execution of the will in favour of Hatch. An unwitnessed will was discovered, and the proposed beneficiary of this second will (William Stuart, one of the nephews) eventually forged or was believed to have forged a third in the hope of giving effect to the second. A year or two beforehand, a

Death in the mountains, 1769

grocery shop in Francis Street, Dublin, was burgled, the proprietor being named in the papers as William Stuart.[22] There will be evidence to suggest that M'Cracken was the victim of younger urban relatives, who exploited his death and sought to alienate the Roundwood property by force of possession. It was only in February 1774 that Hatch could send his clerk into County Wicklow formally to take possession of Roundwood.[23]

There is evidence to suggest that M'Cracken's death in 1769 had been preceded by at least one earlier threat of suicide. On 25 February 1766, probably while staying with his friend Michael Duff, he had written to another cousin, James Hatch of Kells, County Meath, beginning 'When this comes to your Hand I am no more', asking for decent funeral arrangements to be made, and promising that Counsellor John Hatch 'will send you a token of my love'.[24] No reference to this letter was made in the summary of events later drawn up in connection with John Hatch's defence of his interests in M'Cracken's estate, doubtless because it would have suggested that the deceased had been of unstable mind for years. The letter of 25 February 1766 which was addressed to John Hatch was rather less compromising, if also less coherent:

> 'The Receipt of this will surprize you, as I always liv'd with the thoughts of Death. Dont think this will be any means of it's happening sooner than it pleases God I shod [sic] continue in this troublesome world.'[25]

Nevertheless M'Cracken's determination that he would die is detailed in various ways – the specification of £20 for a nephew Edward Edwards (the hatter) whom the will did not mention, also half a guinea for each horseman who should bear the body to Kells ('or a crown to Dublin'). Other details movingly convey the old man's disappointment – 'I have left an unhappy family in your care, that help'd to embitter my pleasure, yet hope they will merit your friendship ... I have been much displeas'd with some of my Sister's Children, Use your pleasure according to their future deservings.' Elsewhere, a degree of agitation or confusion is evident, as when he records that 'I have order'd Love & Cloaks etc for my Friends ...' Doubtless, M'Cracken intended 'gloves', having been disappointed in love.

8

A battle of wills

THE WILL which M'Cracken had made in 1762 interests us for several reasons, but testamentary effect is not one of them. Proposing to leave his nephew, James Stuart, 'the sum of five shillings sterling and no more', the old man gives every indication of fighting spirit. However, the vellum copy which survives carries marginal notes in his own hand which clearly indicate that this resolution was short-lived – 'Miserable man that I am, who shall deliver me from this body of sin. But thou shall answer for me, o Lord God. Thou that prayest for me, Shall be my Judge.' And again, 'My God, thy will be done, not mine.' At this time, M'Cracken intended to make some provision for the poor, not only by leaving small sums to divided between needy tenants, but also through a bequest of £5 to the charity school at Templestown (Roundwood), and a further £5 to 'the Concordia Society of which I was formerly a member'.

His family emerges in some detail – a sister (Jane Stuart), an uncle Samuel Hatch whose children included a John (these were Kells people.) The many cousins included Elinor Bowles and her brother Thomas Lovett, Joseph and Elizabeth Hatch (whose father was John Hatch of Kells), Charles Hatch, William M'Cracken, and Peter Metge. Only the last-named appears to have broken free from rural obscurity: at least a man of that unusual name was called to the Irish Bar in 1769, becoming one of the Dublin's notable lawyers later in the century.[1] No strong sense of family cohesion is discernible behind the will's little provisions. M'Cracken's household goods, linen, etc., were to be divided equally among his sister, his cousin Mary Salmon and Sarah Edwards who was Mrs Jane Stuart's daughter. There was, by implication, no established house which might be handed on to an heir and successor in the gentlemanly fashion. The original business of wig-making was to be left to Michael Duff of Cope Street, a fellow in the same trade and a friend in whom M'Cracken had confided.

Yet the property was far from negligible – land at Roundwood and Glassnamullen in County Wicklow, houses and chattels in York Street, Dublin, not forgetting a 'seat or Pue' in Saint Andrew's Church. All of this M'Cracken proposed

A battle of wills

to leave to John Hatch of Dublin for his lifetime and then 'unto the first and every son of the Body of the sd. John Hatch my Exctr in tail male lawfully begotten ...' In 1762, Hatch was unmarried, and the phrase just quoted was standard legal idiom. The will, however, proceded to specify who should inherit in the event of Hatch having no male issue, a factor which underlined the limited nature of the bequest. By the time M'Cracken actually died, Hatch had indeed married, but had no sons, and may have had reason to conclude that he was unlikely to beget sons in the future. This first will was dated 15 May 1762.

In the event, it was put aside as having been superseded by later indications of M'Cracken's intentions, including at least one further will. The arrangements set forth in the letters of February 1766 to James Hatch in Kells and John Hatch in Dublin were not activated for more than three years. The provisions of the will referred to were modest but numerous, apart from the leaving of the residue to John Hatch. Hatch's strategy in May 1773 (when a case was evidently heard at Wicklow assizes) was to argue that the practical benefactor of M'Cracken's death 'lives in a very Expensive Manner ... and therefore ... he is lavishing improperly the Effects of the said deceased ...'[2] This may have been a holding action, in which Hatch was not obliged to commit himself to an opinion about the nature of M'Cracken's death and allowing time for investigation of M'Cracken's will or wills.

Given the manner in which his intentions were contested, likewise the ultimate descent of his property to ancestors of JMS, the surviving details of funeral expenses and annuities deserve consideration. Two lists of expenses are preserved in the Hatch Papers, one dated 17 August 1769 and amounting to £55 15s 0d, and the other headed 'Furnished for the Funeral of Mr Samuel McCracken (by his own Order) By James Hatch' amounting to £28 17s 7d.[3] Of the sixteen sums totted up in James Hatch's account, nine relate to mourning clothes, including twenty-three pairs of gloves. The remainder relate principally to churchyard expenses – for example, 6s 6d for 'removing and Fixing Tombs', the same amount for 'Six porters for carrying corpse'. The other account appears to cover expenses incurred in Wicklow or Dublin – the shroud cost £1 10s 0d, 'To the Hearse & Six 4 days £9: 2: 0', and more than £20's worth of fine lawn. A third 'Account of what is Due for my Mourning' appears to relate to a woman's expenses (£5 5s 11½d in all, including a black petticoat), though it is difficult to identify who a female 'chief mourner' might be: M'Cracken was a bachelor, and (as far as one can tell) John Hatch was a widower. Some woman, Kells or Carrickmacross relative, thought it proper to attend his funeral dressed in new weeds. And presented her bill.

The list of beneficiaries is indicative of M'Cracken's financial circumstances at death and his family attachments. The names given below are rearranged alphabetically:

Elinor Bowles	£10
Cove [?] Anuity [sic]	£5
Sarah Edwards D	£10
Char[les] Hatch	£10
Eliza Hatch & Dau[ghte]r	£10
James Hatch	£10
J[onathan?] Hatch	£10
Jos[eph] Hatch	£10
Sam Hatch D	£10
Thomas Lovet	£10
Wm McCracken	£20
Peter Metge	£10
Poor of Kells	£5
Mary Salmon	£20
Fr[ancis] Stoddart	£10
Henry Stuart	£10
James Stuart	5/=
Jane Stuart	£20
Mary Stuart	£50
William Stuart	5/=
Tenants of Glasnamullen	£5
Tenants of Roundwood	£5
Templeton School	£5

In itself this list raises questions, but it is further complicated by the presence (beneath it on the same sheet of paper) of a second list:

Sarah Edwards D	£10
Mary Salmon	£20
Eliza Stuart	£5
Jane Stuart	£20
Mary Stuart	£5
Sam Stuart	£10

Unlike the longer list, these seven provisions are not explicitly termed annuities, and may represent M'Cracken's intention to leave certain sums outright. However, as three of the seven entries exactly replicate the annuities in the first list, there is a strong presumption that the second list should be read as a select version of the first.[4] One striking feature of the shorter list is the predominance of women, the only male beneficiary being Sam Stuart (£10) who is not mentioned in the longer list. This Sam Stuart is probably Samuel Charles Stuart, husband of Mary

A battle of wills

Stuart who, when widowed, will claim her unpaid arrears from John Hatch. A striking reduction in the sum assigned to Mary Stuart (from £50 to £5) also characterises the second list.

The questions then arise as to who was responsible for the selection, and when. Only two answers present themselves – (1) M'Cracken on some second testamentary occasion, later than 1762; (2) John Hatch at the time of his legal battle to acquire M'Cracken's estate more or less *in toto*, that is, between August 1769 and February 1774. It does not seem that there is adequate material to test the handwriting of the documentation, not least because much of what survives is copy (by a clerk) rather than an original from Hatch's pen or M'Cracken's.

Certain probabilities must therefore be weighed. If the will of 1762 (in John Hatch's favour but only for his lifetime) was subject to annuities amounting to more than £250, then its value was severely reduced. The substitution of £70 per annum would represent a very considerable improvement, as far as Hatch was concerned. Hatch was undoubtedly tardy in paying the annuities: we shall see that, as late as April 1778, Widow Stuart was seeking her entitlements, and by the following July, he still had not established payment to Mary Salmon. Fifteen years after the death of his country cousin, Hatch received a semi-literate letter from one Isaac Delemor requesting payment of 'trifling bills', money 'due to me by Mr Samuel Mc Cracking [sic] and Mr Wm Stuard' [sic].[5] Hatch was not quick to meet his obligations, and several of the beneficiaries ended up on skid row.

For the business dragged on into Hatch's first term as an MP, whose own tardiness played its part in these delays. James Hatch of Kells, who had arranged McCracken's funeral in August 1769, inquired for his expenses on 14 February 1770, adding an appeal for 'the token of love' which McCracken had promised more than three years before his death.[6] Circa 1771, John Hatch was receiving quasi-anonymous letters revealing the circumstances in which a will had been forged. These combined a useful degree of circumstantial detail –

> Mr Rooney told me that Edward Rooney's wife & two Labourers were present when the forged will was found behind the Desk which was searched by way of cleaning out the R[oom] previous to an Entertainment given b[y] [Mr] Stewart for the purpose of making public the Discovery under the Pretence of a Ball for the Neighbours and it was so contrived that just as they came in the Discovery should be made.[7]

with atmosphere – 'The country round that part whispered that that [sic] the will was false.'[8] An incomplete list (preserved in the Hatch Papers) of tenants on an unnamed property includes the names of James Stuart, John and Widow Harding, and Edward Rooney, suggesting that Stuart (or Stewart) and Rooney lived close to the scene of the crime and that the 'ball for the Neighbours' was a rural event, rather than one occurring within an urban sphere implied in James Rooney's profession as attorney.⁹ In fact, Edward Rooney had succeeded John Sutton as master in Templestown School in 1766.

At the risk of jeopardising the discrete integrity of several inquiries pursued in the present book, it is tempting to compare the scene of discovery just summarised with a dramatic draft preserved among the Synge papers in Trinity College, Dublin. In the 1890s and after, JMS spent many fruitless months working on a play (sometimes called 'When the Moon Hast Set') for which he devised a denouement involving equally contrived revelations – letters from the past, injunctions against sexual malpractice, a green wedding dress, and (most strikingly) two 'babies dresses' discovered beneath the wedding garment. In this heavily contrived Ibsenite plot, more than the M'Cracken/Hatch legacies are audible from within the family closet.¹⁰

However obscure the setting of the little drama of 1769, the Hatches did not stint expense in arranging M'Cracken's funeral. Given that the instrument of death was very likely a gun provided by Hatch himself, such close attention was only proper. But there is a lapse of time between the stated date of M'Cracken's suicide (Sunday 6 August) and the funeral (?10 or 17 August) which requires comment. No one who took his own life could easily be buried in consecrated ground, and it may have required Hatch's intervention to persuade the church authorities. Where M'Cracken was ultimately interred remains unknown, though distant Kells in County Meath (which he stipulated) is the most likely, if unconfirmed, site. The detail of Hatch's paying for six men to carry the coffin may indicate that no locals were willing to provide that customary service or that the burial did not take place in a locality where the deceased had lived or was known.¹¹ And who were the 'family' to whom M'Cracken had read prayers the evening before his suicide, if indeed suicide it was?

By insisting on public burial, Hatch may not have been attempting to conceal his cousin's act of self-destruction but rather keeping open the possibility of alleging murder. In the event, no charges were ever brought. Instead, there followed the prolonged contest for possession of the property at Roundwood and elsewhere. M'Cracken's will of 1762 may have left all his leases to John Hatch, but the list of annuities drawn up for Hatch would have (if implemented) reduced the value of the estate considerably. The public records indicate that wills (no longer extant) were proven in 1769 and 1771 and, as Hatch ultimately came into possession, it follows that either the will proved on the second occasion favoured him or that he established possession of M'Cracken's estate by other means. Any question of the Stuarts' usurpation of his interest dissolved, likewise any accusation against them, whether of forgery or worse.

Nevertheless, the detection of fraud was rigorously pursued. An undated letter from a Mr Carroll requested a few franks of Hatch, while offering advice about handwriting evidence. It emerged that a Robert Wisdom was 'a subscribing

A battle of wills

witness to a will which the Stewarts pretended Mr Mc Cracken made [shortly] before his death'.¹² Hatch retained the services of Isaac Shiel who appears to have acted almost as a private detective. In February 1770, he gave Hatch a detailed report of premises – evidently in Dublin – where it was suspected a will had been forged. Though he sagaciously used dashes when transcribing names – referring to 'H——n's' when he evidently meant Hatton's, he concluded that, within these premises only James Rooney's quarters were suspect as all others were 'so incumbered' that 'no writing business could have been carried on in either front room or back room'.¹³

There was also that series of anonymous, or near-anonymous, letters reaching Hatch. Three letters from 'R. J.' purported to disclose the mystery of the second will – 'I tell you that Stewarts will is a forged one and that by the means of James rooney Attorney'. This is almost certainly the attorney Rooney of Liffey Street whose wife had died late in 1766. In a letter of 17 July 1771, the correspondent reports how James Rooney failed to persuade Wisdom to give evidence for the Stuarts. Wisdom, also of Liffey Street and (by this date also a widower), was in effect James Rooney's city neighbour.

In the third letter (dated 14 January 1772) the correspondent cites his own brother as declaring that 'there is not a tenant on Roundwood Estate that will pay the Stuarts any rent but one Larence [sic] and he is the only friend they have at present'. Despite these obvious Wicklow affiliations, R. J. reported how he 'was the other night in a public house in High Street [Dublin] and there happened one of Mr Stuarts witnesses as I understood by his discourse, for the man that was with him asked him what he thought of the Suit that was between you and Stuart'. On 1 May 1773, at six in the afternoon, Shiel was visited by 'Mr Jas Rooney & Wm Hutchinson', when James Rooney claimed that the (forged) will was dated 5 August and 'executed' on 14 December 1769, a tale which led to an account of the fortuitous discovery of the document by a labourer named Brady, with Mrs Edward Rooney and others present for the occasion.¹⁴

Quite why 'Wm Hutchinson' was present is unclear, though not his connection (if any) with the family into which Edward Synge (Hatch's brother-in-law) had married in 1753. Family certainly were not be to trusted on principle. A letter from the office of the lawyer Adam Williams, whom John Hatch regularly employed, began 'I really have no just foundations to say that Saml Hatch joyned with the Stuarts ... I only [say?] that from his countenance & sitting with them I rather judged him to be inclined to their camp than otherwise.'¹⁵

Likewise, R. J. defies identification, though his use of words like 'term' (meaning a season of court sittings) might indicate a legal background. Hostile to the Stuarts, he gives no evidence of any northern attachment such as linked the M'Crackens and the wretched Francis Stoddard. The name Jennings surfaces from time to time among Hatch's surviving papers of this period. In May 1774, one Charles Jennings made Hatch aware of promises he (Hatch) had made to reward Robert Wisdom and Jennings for information. Wisdom was in jail in February 1774 'for eight pounds', and Jennings occasionally offered to make himself a legitimate Swords voter, if only Hatch would reward him in the potwalloping manner. It is possible that 'R. J.' was a Jennings, brother to Charles. There is no evidence that Hatch helped Wisdom, who may not have deserved his surname, although it is clear that he did help when James Rooney landed in the Bailiff's confinement during July 1774 (for £12).[16]

Now considerably advanced in fortune, if not fame, Hatch was still entangled in the family affairs of his late cousin. From an account book, we know that he made a payment in March 1777 in relation to the funeral of a Mr M'Cracken (no Christian name specified) and in May a donation for the church at Derrylossary where old Sam M'Cracken worshipped the morning before he died. If these seem too late to be read as settlements of a matter laid to rest in 1769, we must note also that William M'Cracken, living at Stoneybatter in the northern portion of Dublin city 'in a disorderly languishing State of Health', wrote to John Hatch on 7 May 1777 pleading for a speedy outcome in the matter of Samuel M'Cracken's will. A payment was duly made – to a Mrs William M'Cracken – in the same month. Other residents of upland Wicklow bore upon Hatch's purse; in April 1777 he made a payment for the funeral of a Mr Stuart. Right at the end of the year, the suspect kinsman Samuel Hatch noted that members of the Sutton family (associated with the townland of Glassnamullan) had been among the intended beneficiaries; 'Mr M'Cracken perfected a deed of annuity of £12: 0: 0 to the father', but the document fell into Stuart hands.[17] Nor was this the only source of irritation for Hatch; a lawyer wrote on 25 July 1778, demanding payment to his client Mary Salmon, 'legatee of Mr McCracken', and threatening to take out a bill to enforce the claim.[18]

The issue of M'Cracken's will continued to crackle lucratively in the letter baskets of Dublin lawyers. Somebody – almost certainly John Hatch himself – sought counsel's advice in the early part of 1781 about remainders in favour of Samuel and Joseph Hatch. From these provisions, it is clear that M'Cracken had in no way seen himself as simply the Hatches' deputy or dupe, as he may have feared at the time of the original purchase of Glassnamullan. John Hatch's purpose now was to 'acquire an absolute Dominion over said lands'. Unknown counsel's opinion was that Joseph Hatch could not be prevented from so benefiting 'in case John & Saml [Hatch] shall both die without issue'. The lawyer proceeded – in the way lawyers do – to provide reassurance in such measure that it tumbled over and became its own counterfeit – 'I think a purchase from Joseph Hatch of his Contingent Interest in Remr would be safe if Mr McCracken had himself a good title … I presume there is no doubt.'[19]

Of Joseph Hatch nothing further is heard. His cousin, Samuel, who had been employed as a clerk by Adam Williams, the Dublin attorney, appears to have prospered briefly, before overreaching himself. Even before the legal exchanges of 1781, the fate of the brothers Stuart had been exemplary. Of James Stuart little is known, but when application was made to Hatch on behalf of the widowed Mary Stuart (living in Oxford) in April 1778 'for the Arrears of an Annuity under a Will during her late Husband's Life, who died last Novr leaving a numerous family', we have a last sighting of one claimant.[20] James's brother, William, signed a promissory note to the value of £17 10s 0d in December 1775, and this one surviving record of his borrowing was unlikely to have been unique in its day.[21] In any case, William Stuart was in legal trouble by March 1778, if not earlier, and wrote plaintive letters of appeal from sundry Dublin lodgings, one of which (dated 29 August 1778) described his wife's search for accommodation on Miltown Road (10 shillings a week, too much). As a token of his fallen state, he gave his address at 123 The Combe.

Even in extremity, William Stuart did not quite give up his applications to Hatch. More than a year after the attempt to settle near Miltown, he continued to deplore his inability to find a place:

> Surely I would prefer the most indifferent Change to my present Situation – living I may say going on six years in obscurity in a Garret, that one of your meanest servants could scarcely think of occupying. I would have waited on you myself, but since that unhappy affair that was unfortunately set up, still occasions my Shiness [sic]. it really was introduced to me by my own, when I may say safely my mind was unpracticed to vice. But youth, were no protections against the Arts of Cruel men, therefore, fell a victim to those arts at a time of life, when I was as little able to foresee their consequences as to resist the bad attempt. In this unhappy Situation, what could I do. I relied upon the promises of my undoers, which has proved a home step to my utter ruin. Would to God I had courage to leave this life. Surely the change could not be worse than my striving to exist thro' this life in a Sea of trouble. I must say I am now that unfortunate man, that has felt thro' a long Confinement, that bitter Anguish of heart the innocent injured feel. Ah Counclr Hatch. I am truly sensible, I live thro' your Bounty, and on your kind Generosity alone do I depend. And as I have no other friend on earth but you, most earnestly intreat you will picture to yourself my present situation.[22]

Even while it shifts responsibility for the mischief of 1769 on to the shoulders of others, Stuart's final appeal suggests that he had to some degree benefited from Hatch's consideration in the intervening years, insufficient to rescue him from his folly or from Francis Street. He appears to have been the younger brother, not without some gentle education – the Sea of trouble flows from Hamlet's soliloquy – but scarcely a gentleman. One of the striking features of this episode in the protohistory of the Wicklow Synges is the shaky class foundation upon which so much grandeur was later erected – Gothic battlements, Hebrew typefaces, Plymouth Brethrenism, Anglo-Irish drama, for example.

Hatched, matched and despatched

There were lower depths. M'Cracken had a brother-in-law, Francis Stoddard, the widower husband (one must suppose) of a sister other than Jane Stuart. Stoddard was resident in Roundwood by November 1773, three months before John Hatch had been able formally to take possession. At first his demeanour was full of confidence, offering to look after the house and demesne, to prevent depredations.[23] Within less than three years, he was down and out in Kells, 'intirely in a nude Condition ... going from one neighbour's house to another to keep some warmth in my poor decay'd bones'.[24] This decline in his fortunes should not be attributed to Hatch's hardness, at least not exclusively so, for in March 1774 Stoddard expressed a wish to go to his 'Native Burial place' – Ardee, County Louth – for it was his 'ancient place of abode'. Amid these felicitious absurdities, he once again sought Hatch's aid.[25]

By September 1776, John Hatch had installed a semi-literate, Thomas Clarkson, in Roundwood House, who reported on various local figures including 'Corbut, she is a very merry one'. Clarkson evidently had succeeded Stoddard as caretaker. A letter from Samuel Hatch (then in Wicklow town) dated 20 August 1777 strongly indicates that major building work was now under way at Roundwood. Behind these cares of property, there ran a current of impropriety, though it may have emerged relatively late.

An undated letter to one of the Stuarts provides the first evidence of this disturbing theme. Anne Kennedy begged intercedence on her behalf with John Hatch, to establish 'who I was'. Kennedy was not well known to her correspondent. It seems unlikely therefore that she was the maidservant whose husband threatened to prosecute M'Cracken at the assizes in 1769. Yet if she was not, then her insinuations had the effect of doubling the number of younger women in M'Cracken's suspect household. She urged Stuart to consult his own sister, a Mrs Radwell (or Redwill) who 'recollects me very well', and concluded in a touching anticipation of Jacques Derrida, 'I am with All differance your most obedent & humble Servant'.[26]

This is clearly the same person who wrote rather scrappily to Hatch himself 'by the Directions of Mr Stewart'. Some investigation of her identity, legal or moral, had taken place. On an undated slip of paper, she was able to report that Hatch had been pleased to suggest that Stuart should 'have a knowledge of her' and, in conclusion, she apologised for repeated applications to him – but her distress was great. The note was now signed Anne Mc Cracken. Her tempo increased. A letter of c. 9 February 1788 is decidedly less submissive, showing signs of professional advice in its phrasing. In it, Anne Kennedy states that she is the daughter of John Mc Cracken '& had been entertained and acknowledged by Mr McCracken of Roundwood when living & resided with him for some time in his house'. She was 'now a widow & in great distress with two children & my mother but have a brother in Good Circumstances at Lisbon in Portugal'. The implication was that

A battle of wills

Hatch's assistance in paying her fare would relieve him of some anxiety. This she made half explicit in her remark that 'Delicacy forbids me to mention the Degree of affinity subsisting between me & your Honours Family.'[27]

If Kennedy was not the maidservant with whom M'Cracken admitted having an affair, then here is the implication of some second impropriety. And if neither Kennedy nor Salmon was the maidservant, there may have been up to three women residing from time to time in M'Cracken's Roundwood home in a manner which gave rise to local concern. As far as the latter-day administration of the Hatch Papers is concerned, we should note how blithely Edward Stephens reported that M'Cracken had proposed marriage to Henry Hatch's niece, without seeking to identify the young woman by name or by any other description. Was this too an indiscretion or, to be more charitable to M'Cracken whose nerves were not the best, was it an act or proposal open to misunderstanding by salacious neighbours? By her own account, Kennedy could have been M'Cracken's niece.

Evidently her strategem with Hatch worked. On 8 December of the same year one Thomas McCracken, calling himself a 'Soldado de Guardo', wrote from Lisbon to acknowledge kindness shown to his aged mother and his sister (of Carrickmacross, where the Revd Mr Stephens had been born) and describing his involvement in a contraband trade in English velvets.[28] Here at least is further evidence to associate the M'Crackens with a specific area in the north, Carrickmacross being in County Monaghan but virtually on the Louth border with Stoddard's native burial place of Ardee close by.

Whatever Hatch may have done for her, Anne Kennedy (née M'Cracken) did not leave Ireland, at least, did not leave permanently. By 6 July 1793 she was (according to herself) living with the family of a Mrs Browne, of Great George Street and Rutland Square, in north Dublin city. This was a good address, even if she belonged to the below-stairs department. About to depart for the country with the Brownes, she was leaving behind her husband, mother and a child.[29] Once again, Hatch was importuned by one who was a widow with two children in 1788, but five years later had a husband and 'a child' among her dependants. The cryptic point of Kennedy's allusion to her employer might be that Mrs Zacharias Brown had been Mary Hatton, daughter of William Hatton. Departing for the country might even have meant returning to the scene of somebody's crime in County Wicklow. Back in 1765, Brown had written to Samuel M'Cracken demanding a share in any future sale of Ballinacorbeg.[30] When M'Cracken found himself besieged four years later, he was inclined to blame the Hattons and bad feeling about Ballinacorbeg. In 1793 Kennedy was only repeating the demand in a veiled form.

Down at Roundwood, matters had settled somewhat. In place of troublesome northerners, Hatch installed a Dublin alderman and member of the Weavers' Guild as a kind of middleman at Roundwood. Thomas Emerson had been a vigorous performer in metropolitan affairs, who had been implicated in some 'unconstitutional methods' regarding an election and 'the Back Lane Club'. He was elected a High Sheriff in 1766, and became an alderman four years later. As a Commissioner of Police, he was responsible for an area of the city including a workhouse. He and his wife Catherine held a pension of £150 p.a. from the crown.[31] The Roundwood business probably constituted a form of semi-retirement, after an eventful career.

By early summer 1787, Francis Synge (Hatch's son-in-law, the husband of Elizabeth Hatch) was making his presence felt, undertaking to buy small quantities of goods, hay, etc., and generally preparing to take over the house. Hatch's peremptory response to Emerson's inquiries – 'You & I will settle the matter in two minutes' – indicates that the incoming master is perhaps less acute in business than seasoned men of affairs. At the age of eighteen, Synge had been listed to receive a life annuity of £200, the earliest signal of his coming good fortunes.[32] At the beginning of the 1790s, so momentous a decade in Wicklow, Emerson is still in place, sending a sack of English white potatoes from the garden, and reporting slates off the roof due to snow. Mrs Emerson was pleased to know that Hatch might pay a visit. The erstwhile alderman concluded his February 1790 report, with a sentiment which rather bypasses Francis Synge, not to mention his mother-in-law – 'My every Blessing attend you [i.e. Hatch] and your two most Amiable daughters'.

Death, provoked by the unhappy M'Cracken, felt free to intrude among the Hatches and their circle. In May 1792, the two-year-old daughter of Francis Synge was drowned in a small river flowing through the family garden.[33] She had been walking with her older brother and a nurse when the accident occurred, at Syngefield in the midlands. John Hatch, the children's maternal grandfather, abandoned plans to attend a party, instead devoting himself to comforting the distressed mother, 'her near friends being out of town'. From this latter detail, it would appear that Mrs Elizabeth Synge was in Dublin when the accident occurred and not with her child. Writing of all this to Miss Blundell, Hatch apologised for the disruption of his plans and duties, but relied on 'the kind attention you have always been so good to show to my little family'.[34]

Down in Roundwood, the resiliant Thomas Clarkson was finally under pressure to quit, though Hatch's mode of ejectment indicates that his son-in-law would not acquire Roundwood without its attendant chores, 'I have troubled Mr Synge to send to you for a year's Rent ... if you do not pay it to him, I have requested him to Let a person under him to distrain you.'[35] Property imposed its duties, even before the son-in-law could inherit.

The principal source of material for this and the preceding chapter has been an archive compiled at several different historical moments by members of the extended family it chronicles. Some of these were lawyers, including John Hatch himself at the outset, and also Edward Stephens in the mid-twentieth century.

A battle of wills

There is a degree of purposefulness evident in the archive, not least in the calculated preservation of casual material – the anonymous letters – which bolster the case for John Hatch's acquisition of the Wicklow property. By the same token, other kinds of documentation are manifestly absent, not least a convincing copy of Samuel M'Cracken's alleged later will.[36]

Evidence of Hatch's hardness is difficult finally to assess. Numerous claimants to part of M'Cracken's estate were frustrated to the point of abject poverty, yet their own irresponsible conduct cannot be omitted from an explanation of their suffering. In his favour, there is the evidence of 'bailing out' Rooney (a dubious figure, at best) from the bailiff's custody. But negative evidence also abounds even within an archive where a hostile image of the man was not the objective. For example, Samuel Hatch wrote in urgent and abject anxiety one Sunday afternoon in October 1784, 'I am really miserable in my mind, on Account of my Misconduct; and ruined without your protection and Countenance. May God preserve you and yours, ever, is the wish of a most Contrite heart ... I declare I have not one half-guinea for Subsistence[.] Since you withdrew your power of Attny I never received a single shilling, save that of Suttons, sent you by my wife.'[37]

Nor did Hatch reserve severity for kinsmen of low degree. To an improving landlord forebear of C. S. Parnell he wrote plainly in 1783, 'As you have not performed what your L[ea]se of last July imported, I am under the disagreeable Necessity of ordering an Ejectment to be servd next week, as I cannot possibly pay the demands People have on me unless I get in the rents due to me by Persons of Rank & Fortune ...'[38] Beyond the issue of severity there lies the elusive matter of social placement. Were the Hatches 'Persons of Rank', and had they become so through the fortune of the unfortunate M'Cracken and the misfortunes of Rooneys, Stoddards, Stuarts, and Wisdoms? What might be counted as virtuous conduct in such kinship?

9

On debt

It is only by not paying one's bills that one can hope to live in the memory of the commercial classes. (Oscar Wilde)

BUSINESS was not a one-way traffic, even in the supposedly protected milieu of Dublin's protestant merchants and men of affairs. The debt incurred in conjunction with James Shiel was to prove a recurring burden in John Hatch's experience. In 1762, three years before he married, and seven years before Samuel M'Cracken's suicide, Hatch entered into two bonds, one for £2,000 with John Bonham, the other for £200 with M'Cracken.[1] The custom was for the bond to be drawn up in the sum equalling twice the amount actually paid over by the lender, this allowing for an ultimate claim which would, in the event of serious defaulting, cover the lender's risk. Dealings of this kind between the cousins were rare, and M'Cracken appears to have conducted his business in old-fashioned and simple ways.

In contrast, Hatch's borrowing from Bonham recurred at the end of 1777 when he obtained £2,000, and in the interim there were at least six similar transactions, totalling in all to some £8,500, with the decade rounded off in a further loan of £440 obtained from Lundy Foot. The purpose of such large-scale borrowing is unrecorded, and it is possible that investment was Hatch's objective: David La Touche, Dublin's leading banker, was one of the individuals who obliged him. The terms of these loans usually required repayment within three or six months of the sum advanced, plus interest at legal rates.

Clearly, John Hatch's debts are of interest as the preface, so to speak, to his sons-in-law's prosperity. They may also have conditioned the terms of his political career in Dublin. He had been elected to parliament as one of the two members representing Swords, a borough quite distinct from the metropolis, and his success unquestionably cost him money. In the municipal context, it has already been noted that he was elected a guild member no earlier than 1774, the year in which he finally took control of Roundwood. Further advance in the city –

On debt

for example election to the rank of alderman (which presupposed election to the Common Council) – depended on financial security, every successfully elected alderman being proven to possess £2,000 over and above the notional payment of his just debts out of his property.[2] The scrutiny involved in this process could at times give rise to embarrassment.

Not that borrowing on bonds remained hidden from all view. In 1777, there was a particularly heavy run on this form of credit, with Hatch borrowing £6,500 between February and November. It can hardly be a coincidence that, in the Hilary law term of the same year, he was (with others) summoned before the Court of Exchequer by Lord Milltown.[3] These difficulties lay behind the September empowerment of Samuel Hatch to collect his kinsman's rents in Wicklow, the income from which came nowhere close to the borrowings. Even when full beneficial possession of Roundwood had been achieved, the borrowing persisted. Need appears to have arisen sharply in late 1784 and, instead of turning to Dublin's bankers or its helpful individuals, Hatch borrowed £500 from Ann Ruxton of Ardee. As was to happen on more than one occasion, the original debt was never cleared in Hatch's lifetime, Miss Ruxton waiting until June 1802 to get her money. When Alexander Castell lent him £60 in May 1785, the scale of the transaction seemed insignificant, yet the lender ultimately had to seek a court judgement for this and a second bond of £200 in October 1797, that is, a month after Hatch's death. On 26 June 1789, Hatch had signed a bill binding him in the sum of the £200 (to be paid after six months) but 'for the true payment whereof I Bind me & my Heirs, Executors, and Administrators, with legal Interest in the penal sum of Four hundred Pounds'. Whatever happened about earlier loans, Hatch was now entangled in punitive and (it is likely) publicly recorded debt repayment programmes.

Some of the money came from individuals with whom he had professional links. Castell, for example, was registrar of Saint Sepulchre's, while Hatch was seneschal. David and John La Touche, who both advanced money, sat together as the MPs for the borough of Newcastle during the parliament when Hatch represented Swords – both boroughs lying within County Dublin. More locally still, David La Touche and Lundy Foot to whom he had from time to time owed money were part of family networks active in the city's affairs. Content (or otherwise) within the Liberty of Saint Sepulchre, Hatch showed no desire to enter the public life of the larger domain.

Political associations may also have been at work behind the Ruxton loan. Early in the eighteenth century, a John Hatch of Ardee leased land from the Ruxtons who were a powerful faction in that borough's politics. Throughout protracted wrangling between 1768 and 1772, related to the election of John Ruxton to the Commons, the Ardee Hatches supported the Ruxtons in the teeth of much popular opposition. They had done so not only with their votes but also in affidavits to support Ruxton's confirmation as a properly elected MP. In approaching

Ann Ruxton, John Hatch knew of the long-standing alliance between their families, however remote from Ardee he himself had grown.

Other loans drew upon different kinds of connection. When in September 1788 Henry Temple (1739–1802, 2nd viscount Palmerston) agreed to a bond in the curiously precise sum of £1,117 10s 6d, he was lending to a man who had pieced together considerable holdings amid the Temple family's Wicklow property. The following month Hatch borrowed a further £200 from Magdalane Boileau, otherwise unknown, though the cashier to Finlay's Bank in Queen Street was one Solomon Boileau.[4]

Women figured prominently in the list of creditors – Mary Percivall, Ann Ruxton, Isabella Smyth, Ann White – in a manner which reflects the reality of late eighteenth-century patterns of private borrowing. Women's property rights were limited. Widows could expect a better return on such loans than they would get in government securities, and there was the additional satisfaction of knowing that one was investing in some specific scheme or individual. Smyth had a fashionable address in Kildare Street. The others, apart from Ruxton, are less easily placed. Yet John Hatch's loans may, in these cases of female lending, have been negotiated through a business intermediary.

Between November 1789 and May 1790, White advanced £2,000 in cash. In the second of these transactions, the duration of the loan was six months though both parties agreed that an extension of a further six months would be acceptable. The Boileau loan, admittedly small, fell due during this period. Already retribution for his failing to repay had struck Hatch. When Mary Stuart (widow of Samuel Charles Stuart) of Oxford went to the King's Bench to seek payment of £85 arrears in January 1782, the dispute arose out of Hatch's administration of M'Cracken's will rather than from an unpaid debt. But the evidence of financial difficulty may have provoked lenders to demand satisfaction. An indenture dated 17 June 1783 records that Percivall obtained a judgement against Hatch for £1,200.

A man who found himself in these circumstances was open to subtle pressures. When Elizabeth Redwell wrote requesting Hatch's assistance in buying a lease, was she exercising a power which his conduct after 1769 had ironically conferred on less fortunate relatives? Or was she simply appealing for his assistance, one member of the family to another?[5] Attachment and interest may never be as distinguishable as analysts might wish. In the case of Mrs Stuart in Oxford matters were mended, however tardily. In a letter of September 1792 – ten years after the King's Bench application – written from New Inn Hall Lane, she not only acknowledged receipt of money, but mentioned an accident Hatch had evidently suffered. This may refer to the drowning of his granddaughter some four months earlier and, if it does, there is clearly evidence here of surviving good feeling among the contenders of 1769. Alternatively, it may indicate some other misfortune of increasing old age as it afflicted Hatch. The once demanding Mrs Stuart

On debt

now looked forward to him visiting her and her family, an excursion which does not seem to have taken place.⁶

The Oxford case appears to have been exceptional and, long before its happy outcome, retribution kept pace with respectability. On the 1785 Castell-Hatch bond – an agreement between fellow officers of a lucrative church property – there is an endorsement which reads 'October 1797. Judgment entered on this bond & on the annexed bond for £200 as of last Trinity Term 1797 ...' By this stage both registrar and seneschal were dead. Death certainly messed things up, even before it struck Hatch in person. In return for £1,400 formally bonded in May 1791, Gustavus Hume, a County Wicklow landlord and administrator of the affairs of the now dead Ann White, was paid £719 1s 6d in October 1793. White, or her representatives had twice obtained judgements in court against Hatch, a debt of £2,000 being settled in May 1794, and a further £2,000 – subject of a judgement in the Easter law term of 1790 – only being paid to Hume in March 1798. Magdalane Boileau, a spinster, fared no better. By July 1801 when Francis Synge paid £633 to clear two loans in her name to John Hatch, she too was dead.⁷

By far the most embarrassing of these posthumous settlements was one involving Hatch's wife's family. On 25 October 1796, he was given £500 by Elizabeth Synge, a wealthy spinster who ultimately left property in Galway to JMS's father. Miss Synge, however, failed to obtain a receipt for her money; after Hatch's death in September 1797, his unmarried daughter, Dorothy, and her brother-in-law Francis Synge were obliged to deliver a written promise to repay the loan. In death, Hatch was both a man of visible wealth and a hidden burden on his successors.

Part III

THE DEVIL'S GLEN

10

Roundwood and after

> The Mortgager and Mortgagee differ the one from the other, not more in length of purse, than the Jester and Jestee do, in that of memory. (Laurence Sterne, *The Life and Opinions of Tristram Shandy*, chapter 12)

COMPILING his massive biography of JMS in the 1930s, the dramatist's nephew noted the initiative of Jack Temple two hundred years earlier in providing land for a charter school on the Wicklow uplands. The greater financial investment had been made by the Acton family of Kilmacurragh without whom the project might never have got off the ground. Temple's support very likely took the form it did – forty-one acres forever – because the ground in question was poor land. By 1740, the pupils were self-supporting in that they produced enough cloth to cover themselves, in addition to working the land for vegetables, dairy produce and, probably, for meat also. Flax, or seed, was supplied by the Linen Board in Dublin.

Did the idyll of sufficiency gloss a regime of near bondage for these children of Catholic families who were committed to a training in 'the English Spirit of Improvement' and the protestant version of Christianity? Instrumental in directing the little community towards reducing the expenses borne by the Incorporated Society for promoting this particular charter school was 'the Activity and good Management' of David Stephens.[1] His appointment as perpetual curate in the parish of Derrylossary commenced with the opening of the Charter School which represented an early stage of development in this out-of-the-way upland area. Roundwood (previously known as Leitrim) was an unlikely location for a school, remote from any large town where future employers of protestantised servants resided. Yet it was through the Incorporated Society, which regulated the school, that the Hatches and Synges first came in contact with each other and with Wicklow.

Given this very limited degree of exposure to the outer world, what *was* the property at Roundwood for which Samuel M'Cracken had come to grief, and on which figures as different as Francis Stoddard and Alderman Emerson had resided

Roundwood and after

in John Hatch's name? No early drawings have survived; indeed it is easier to recreate the design-book schoolhouse than the eighteenth-century property of JMS's ancestors. Neither have we any charming Victorian cameos of the house as it passed from the Synges to the Guinnesses.[2] The present dwelling (see p. 13 above) has been curiously described in one reference book as

> An early c19 castellated house with turrets and a symmetrical facade. The home of Sean T. O'Kelly, 2nd President of Ireland. Rebuilt on a slightly reduced scale after a fire ca 1957. Now the home of Mr Galen Weston.[3]

This is not very illuminating for students of any period, recent or remote, but it is apt for the house in which silent Barbara Synge never lived. Uncertainty as to the date of a fire in the mid-1950s, when the property belonged to the head of state, maintains a tradition of uncertainty which reaches back two centuries.

A casual memorandum preserved among the Hatch Papers records that 'Mr Brocas' was at Roundwood in 1773, but the date is too early to accommodate any of the artistic members of that family who flourished in the next century.[4] According to some scrappy notes, Edward Rooney claimed to have a lease from James Stuart for 'the Coppice field' (2 acres) at this same time. As for James Stuart himself, his wife is recorded as declaring that he had no lease, never paid rent, and had no receipts to back up any claim he might make. The indications are of exceedingly casual management between M'Cracken's death and Hatch's formal taking possession in 1774. For late 1774, there is still evidence of continuing resistance by William Stuart to be found in an appeal made by a tenant, William Pollard, to Hatch.[5] Another scrap of paper in the surviving Hatch archives records improper late alterations to documents relating to a lease signed by Thomas Pollard and M'Cracken.[6] Pollards with these christian names had served the Incorporated Society as carriers or escorts. Indeed, a William Pollard was acting in this capacity as late as 1790. The Charter School at Templestown had closed in 1776.

Things were gradually tidied up. From 1778, we have 'an Account of the Contents of the Demesne of Roundwood taken by Computation' with details of field-sizes, etc. in acres, roods, and perches:

Slang Meadow & Rabbit Borough hill	20: 0: 0
first Bogg field	4: 0: 0
2nd do.	3: 0: 0
those two are Commonly Called the Bushy fields	
Cows pasture	6: 0: 0
Blackford Meadow	2: 0: 0
Turry [?] field	4: 0: 0

The devil's glen

Brick field	2: 0: 0
Wheat field	7: 0: 0
	48: 0: 0
The above are all Situate on the left hand side of the Great Road.	
Bottoms Well field	3: 0: 0
Cornfield & Bottom	5: 0: 0
Brewhouse Meadow	2: 0: 0
Coppice	4: 0: 0
field above the Coppice	6: 0: 0
Quarry Meadow	5: 0: 0
Upper big field	8: 0: 0
Accorn [sic] field	2: 0: 0
Burk's do. & Old Avenue	2: 0: 0
Pigeonhouse field	1: 2: 0
Cluster Meadow	3: 0: 0
Cowhouse, or Manwaring's Meadow	4: 2: 0
Haggard	0: 2: 0
front Avenue	4: 0: 0
Grave,Yard [sic], Gardens etc	4: 0: 0
	54: 2: 0
	48: 0: 0
	102: 2: 0[7]

These are the appurtenances of a small homely farm, notable only for their inclusion of the graveyard attached to nearby Derrylossary Church where M'Cracken worshipped on the day of his death. No reference is made to Templestown school nearby. The land was poor enough. From 1788, there survives 'an account of the measurement of some Oat and Potatoe [sic] Ground on the lands of Roundwood ... being part of an Estate belonging to John Hatch Esq.'. As the area surveyed by Thomas Smyth (who charged eight shillings and eight pence) amounted only to 8 acres, preservation of the document can be explained in terms of chance as easily as in any other way.[8]

Fashionable life was concentrated in Dublin. On 14 February 1789, Robert Synge and his wife 'were at a party at Mrs French's in Kildare St. the first night of her new furnished Drawing Room'.[9] Apart from Powerscourt near Enniskerry, and a few other accessible country houses, Wicklow had no such social life, nothing remotely like a salon. Its mountainous interior existed in a backwater of time, while Glanmore lay in the future, on the far side of a revolutionary current. There was nothing on the windy eminence of Roundwood to attract inquirers like Sir John Carr who, in 1806, illustrated his *Stranger in Ireland* with an impressive

Roundwood and after

drawing of the daughter-house, Glanmore Castle, at once Gothic and mechanical, masked in young trees further downhill yet with a view to the sea. Samuel Hayes, whom John Hatch badgered for payment in 1783, became the author of *A Practical Treatise on Planting and the Management of Woods and Coppices* (Dublin: Sleater, 1794) and thus the cause of extensive tourism in Wicklow – once the Rebellion was finally suppressed. The displacement of Roundwood by Glanmore resulted from many causes.

Nevertheless, even while John Hatch remained alive, the Synges were establishing themselves at Roundwood. We know from his brother's diary that on 3 June 1787 Francis Synge and his wife went to settle there. The occupancy of Alderman Emerson had become irksome to John Hatch, who took the opportunity to provide his newly married daughter with a rural home. Narrating this crucial development 150 years later, Edward Stephens found it necessary to dwell on certain absurdities in Emerson's proposed terms to renew the lease, rather than comment on the convenience of the outgoing tenant's legal blunder.[10]

Not that Hatch was handing over a single coherently organised estate, in good order and substantial in extent. A note dated 4 August 1790 refers to his leasing to Francis Synge of a fifteen-acre portion of Roundwood (previously held by Richard Fleming, the innkeeper) for thirty-one years commencing 1 May 1786 at a yearly rent of £7 12s 6d.[11] This was but one element of what became Synge's first Wicklow holding, yet it indicates the piecemeal and relatively small-scale nature of the transfer. Hatch had warned his son-in-law against the influence of Weekes, the perpetual curate, who (together with the Emersons) constituted a kind of primitive high society in the district. To Francis Synge 'they appeared ... to have a great deal of the Vicar of Wakefield', and one evening during the handover, Weekeses, Emersons and Synges 'danced six Couple'. The only mystery to be feared in this antic hay is the identity of Mrs Weekes who cannot be traced in the records of the Church in which she was (presumably) married.[12]

Nevertheless, the newcomers were determined to set their own standards for the future, and Francis assured Hatch that he would keep such company at a distance. After all, the Lord Lieutenant on his tour of the kingdom was then staying at Newtownmountkennedy, with John Fitzgibbon (attorney-general) in his retinue. Having scarcely unpacked, the Synges drove down from their moorland home to see the official party. Though Francis was, like Fitzgibbon, a lawyer and a graduate of Trinity College, the distinction between seeing and meeting the grandees is required here. Yet these were circles in which Samuel M'Cracken had never dreamed to move. In the years since his death, Wicklow had certainly developed, not merely in the growing number of elegant houses and landscaped estates but in communications and employment also. At nearby Newtownmountkennedy a stocking and calico manufactury had been established, while mining operations at Avoca were supported by parliamentary grants.

The devil's glen

Synge's interests did not embrace commerce, though he was keen to ensure local valuers did not overprice domestic goods which he and his wife were buying from Emerson. No favours were shown to the newcomers, who reckoned they paid thirty or forty pounds over the odds, for every door lock had its price and even 'the Nigger of the Kitchen Grate' was weighed. Old retainers were dispensed with, Mrs Barny to wait on Mrs Emerson in Dublin and her husband to join the police: Synge was 'on the scent of a man to watch the place'.[13] Wicklow was no Arcadia.

With the alderman dispatched once more to the city, the Synges took up their first Wicklow residence. The following year, their first child (John) was born in Dublin. One further year later, a couple on honeymoon spent some days in the old house with their friends. In addition to the Hatch interest, Sir Francis Hutchinson's property in the area gave the family an opportunity to develop their own holdings. By 1791, Roundwood was being integrated into a pattern of family activity, no longer just a rural outpost or temporary abode. On 11 April Robert Synge (who had business with the Hutchinsons) slept over. Early in June, he and his wife (Margaret Wolfe, a kinswoman of the Lord Kilwarden who would be murdered in 1803) went for a couple of days, accompanied by Dolly Hatch – that is, Dorothy, sister of Mrs Francis Synge, now mistress of Roundwood. The place was clearly within a manageable distance for brief outings from the capital, and the lowland Wicklow roads tolerable.

On 27 June 1791, two of the Roundwood children went down with measles on the same day – John (aged four) was in Dublin, his two-year-old sister Barbara in the Wicklow mansion. She had been named after her maternal grandmother, the Barbara Synge who had married John Hatch in 1765 and of whom little or no trace has been observed since 1767. The growing attachment of the family to Wicklow was demonstrated at the end of 1794 – Francis Synge's sister was married in Derrylossary Church to John Ormsby of Ballygrenane in Limerick, a Captain of Militia. They too passed a few days at Roundwood.[14] It is pretty certain that the house was damaged, if not destroyed, during the 1798 rebellion, for Francis Synge submitted a hefty claim for compensation. What is odd is the silence of family tradition on this point, which can be pursued in due course.

Though we are particularly concerned with the Wicklow Synges, their emergence into the sunlight can only be appreciated against a wider background of family experience. The sons of Archdeacon Edward Synge (1726–1792) – Francis was one of five – had each to find his own way in the world. The eldest, Edward (1753–1818), had begun his education privately under Dr Norris at Drogheda. Having gone up to Trinity College, he transferred his BA from Dublin to Magdalen College, Oxford, in 1776. There he proceeded to take a bachelor's (1783) and, four years later, a doctor's degree, both in divinity. Though he acquired a stay-at-home reputation for maintaining Syngefield in the Irish midlands, it is clear that he continued to visit Oxford quite frequently, presenting a silver bread basket to his old college in 1802.[15]

At the beginning of the 1790s, Robert had a house in Dawson Street: both he and Francis sent their sons to Mr Bonafous's school at Portarlington. The celebrated Huguenot town lay closer to Syngefield than to Dublin, and for a time Robert also kept a house in Portarlington. The scale of this can be judged by the arrangements made for visitors – brother Samuel often slept in the local inn.[16] Though Edward's Syngefield was a substantial two-storey house of seven bays, it makes more sense to see it as one of Maurice Craig's 'classic Irish house of the middle size' rather than some grand fortress of the Anglo-Irish occupier.[17] None of the Synges in this generation were able to live as Bishop Edward of Elphin had done. It was not until after Francis had sorted out the estate of his late father-in-law, John Hatch, that he could embark on building Glanmore Castle.

Nevertheless, prosperity and honour did not shun the family. Ill health persuaded Robert to quit Portarlington in 1797 and move to England. He and his family were in Bristol in 1798 when the Rebellion broke out back home in Ireland. At Clifton – the slave-owners' quarter – the Robert Synges had the Ruxtons for neighbours in the summer of 1799, and the Francis Synges for much of December. By 1800 Robert was overseeing various domestic arrangements for his wife's relatives, including payments to the local apothecary ('well paid for three years attendance on Bess Wolfe'). This was the circle which Maria Edgeworth would satirise in her 1812 novel, *The Absentee*. 'Lady Kilwarden set out from Bath for Abergavanny to drink Goat's Whey.'[18] In 1801 Robert was duly elevated to the baronetcy of the United Kingdom, though the title he took – of Kiltrough – acknowledged his County Meath property. He later lived in Exeter and Tunbridge Wells, dying in London. Quite why he was elevated remains obscure.

Immediately 'post-Union' Ireland has been for too long characterised in terms of a decline in cultural activity and increasing conflict in domestic politics, with the first signs of a renaissance arising in the 1830s. This movement – the argument has run – was rendered more romantically patriotic in the 1840s, only to be eclipsed by the Famine and its consequences until the 1880s when Yeats and his cohorts broke forth into the sunlight. This is a standard cultural nationalist historiography which JMS embraced and, later, his nephew inherited. Edward Stephens, however, introduced some variation on the familiar theme when, in the difficult years of de Valera's first administration, he sought to lay down a synoptic family history. This narrative could comfortably include such Hatches as were essential, and even find room for M'Cracken and the Stuart nephews. But, as it advanced towards JMS's generation, it concentrated solely on a single line of continuity.

Though Robert Synge's departure to England preceded the Union, in a sense it exemplified a gentry deprived of political function by the abolition of the Irish parliament. His brother's prosperity after the Union might have been open to later nationalist suspicion, had Francis also acquired a baronetcy. Stephens pointedly ended his second chapter with the words, 'The vote of Francis Synge was not for sale. He did not leave the Irish Parliament with a title, but, when the doors of the House of Commons closed for the last time, returned to Wicklow as Mr Synge to develop his estate.' If the MP for Swords did not sell his vote, he nonetheless claimed compensation along with hundreds of other 'suffering Loyalists' who had lost property during the Rebellion.[19] The definition of patriotism, implicit in his great-great-grandson's rhetorical tribute, bears little resemblance to the log-jam of interests and prejudices built up *circa* 1798–1800. Furthermore, Stephens was inhibited from investigating how Francis Synge had acquired quite such a valuable portfolio of properties – no indication whether he believed John Hatch had left a will or not, no comment on Hatch's own acquisition of development land south of Saint Patrick's Cathedral.

The ambiguity of Francis Synge's position lay in his having voted anti-unionist while, for thoroughly private reasons, he acquired the wealth suggestive of one who had sold out to government. Stephens transposed this dangerous topic into one more pathetic if not always sympathetic. In his version, Francis Synge developed Glanmore in the style of a *pre*-Union grandee – 'unhappily he undertook this work twenty years too late'. The extravagance of Glanmore thus becomes a matter of anachronism and taste rather than personal folly or anything faintly scented with venality. 'The development of the demesne was work which Francis Synge loved. His expenditure was extravagant but his results were successful. He planted trees carefully chosen to suit different situations, and arranged as to give beautiful combinations of foliage in spring and autumn.' Only after this accomplishment had been written up did Stephens allude vaguely to Francis Synge's 'well secured rents and good building sites' in Dublin. These he had – in a distinctly non-legal term – 'derived [sic] from his father-in-law'.[20]

This verbal hesitation provides a momentary pause in which to note the very substantial and undeniable wealth of Francis Synge in the second decade of the nineteenth century, in contrast to the debt-laden accounts of his father-in-law. Inheritance of the Hatch estate was divided between two Synge brothers as husbands of the co-heiresses. Given the wealth of both brothers, it seems resonable to conclude that Hatch left more than could be tabulated in terms of Wicklow and Meath leases: he left urban development property, some of it at least 'deriving' from Saint Sepulchre's liberty. When the division of the estate was concluding in 1808, Francis Synge issued six cheques to his brother the archdeacon for an amount of just under £5,000. In addition, the Revd Samuel Synge got the town house in Harcourt Street.[21]

A print published in London on 4 June 1806 shows Glanmore Castle in a state of geometric excitement, all tense verticals and accommodating global shadows.

Roundwood and after

The image probably preceded the completion of building on the site, and acts now as a timeless reminder of Francis Synge's impetuous embarking on the aggrandisement of his name. If he looked back to the era of Edward Synge, bishop of Elphin, such opulence had indeed once been theirs. But the author who incorporated the print into his *Stranger in Ireland* unwittingly exposed the instability of the new enterprise. 'The Castle, the seat of Francis Synge Esq., has not yet received the hoary tints of time; some of its battlements were constructing at the time of my visit; but when it is completed, and well coloured by the elements, it will be a fine object.'[22]

If Roundwood came to the Synges through the unsteady, self-cancelling hands of M'Cracken and the determination of his lawyer cousin Hatch, the estate at Glanmore (on lower ground to the east) came into Francis Synge's possession 'partly by purchase and partly under the will of his uncle Sir Francis Hutchinson' who died in 1807.[23] One of the baronet's last contributions to the area had been to build a schoolhouse at Killfee, closer to Glanmore than Roundwood and in effect replacing the old Templestown school. Hatch's wealth contributed to Francis Synge's ability to aggrandise a portion of Wicklow; Hutchinson's adjoining property influenced the choice of site. The romantic 'defile' of The Devil's Glen would serve as a refuge for banditi in 1798 but once that emergency was concluded, it too awaited development, accessible from a large-ish house, then called Glenmouth. According to Edward Stephens, 'at its northern end was a great square of stables and out-houses built on the plan of an artillery barracks for which it may at one time have been used'.[24] This was the site which Francis Synge gothicised with towers at each corner and a crenellated roof, the whole thing set in parkland metamorphosed in successive plantations now of plants, rather than protestants. Mrs Elizabeth Synge (née Hatch) died in 1810, and her widower remarried two years later. His second wife, a widowed Mrs Stewart, bore him a daughter, Frances Dorothy, 'who was the only young person to brighten Glanmore' when his sons by the first marriage were reaching manhood. The phrase just quoted is Edward Stephens's oblique way of saying that John Synge (the dramatist's grandfather) did not regard Glanmore as his home.

Though the position of the resident gentry was uncertain, it did not wholly preclude intellectual enterprise among the younger generation. Francis's elder son married into a family of busy evangelicals, whose concern for the salvation of Catholics bore strange fruit. In 1821, 'Mrs John Synge, Round Wood, Co. Wicklow' served on the committee of the Irish Society for Promoting the Education of the Native Irish Through the Medium of their Own Language (ISPENIMOL).[25] These organisations came to be regarded by Catholic Nationalists (English-speaking, of course) as intrusive, proselytising and patronising. In more neutral terms, one could diagnose an ideological condition in which cultural activity and political conflict were but two sides of the same coin, a condition which Samuel

The devil's glen

Ferguson sought to address from the 1830s onwards but which, in the 1820s, was all too obvious throughout Ireland. One solution involved a recourse to the remote past, to pre-Reformation Ireland, ultimately to a Celtic realm unsullied by Roman or Catholic. Another offered itself through intensely local engagements, whether in archaeology or contemporary good works. A spokesman for the ISPENIMOL allowed that a few Gaelic speakers survived in pre-Famine Wicklow though elsewhere his calculations appear to discount that possibility. At such straws did the conscience-stricken young master of Glanmore clutch.

Though Roundwood was the earliest substantial property which the Synges held in County Wicklow, title to it was a matter of some anxiety. When Francis Synge died in 1831, the resulting legal processes and assessment of assets included no fewer than fifty-two formal searches and inquiries through courts and other agencies. Many of these relate to the Gardiner family, with whom John Hatch had dealings in the middle of the previous century. When a lease of 1736 (Gardiner to George Morgan) was assigned by the latter to Samuel Mc'Cracken on 3 May 1751, the future association of the property with the Synges had been set in motion.[26] By a further lease of 1 May 1753, Luke Gardiner set Roundwood to McCracken once more. However, the circumstances surrounding M'Cracken's death in 1769, and the confusion over his will (or wills) introduced an element of insecurity which persisted. Further difficulties arising at the time of John Hatch's death in 1797 – did he or did he not make a will? – compounded the problem. By a deed of partition, dated 7 April 1807, Hatch's daughters (and their Synge husbands) were rewarded for their bereavement, at least as far as this Wicklow property was concerned. Referring to the totality of formal documentation cited in the course of fifty-two legal searches, a later pencil note reads 'The above original deeds, except McCracken's will [were] sent to J Rawlings [?] by C Hamilton Feb 25 1832.'

The occasion of this inquiry was the death of Francis Synge, and the return to Wicklow of his son, John. A later pencilled annotation indicates that 'Copy of Will of Saml McCracken dated May 15 1762 leaving to John Hatch his cousin Roundwood & other properties' was given to Rawlings (or Rawlin) on 1 March 1832.[27] Though their rights to Roundwood depended in part at least on the legitimacy of M'Cracken's claim, the story of M'Cracken's life and death in Roundwood was not edifying. Yet a schedule of the late Francis Synge's personal properties as valued at Glanmore on 6 January 1832 referred to rents overdue from properties including houses in York Street which, in addition to being the site of a substantial inheritance from John Hatch, had been M'Cracken's field of operation in Dublin before his unfortunate migration into Wicklow. In the same schedule, books were valued at £50, the contents of the cellar at £12 and house linen at a mere £15.[28]

It was left to John Synge, son of Francis Synge and grandson of John Hatch, to give purpose of some sort to the new Gothic castle with its pleasant view to the distant sea. Before he could do so, he had to wander far in spirit. These broader perspectives are examined in later pages, where the theories of the Swiss educationalist, Johan Heinrich Pestalozzi (1746–1827), and the doctrines of the 'Plymouth' Brethren are traced in John Synge's kaleidoscopic mind. These intellectual preoccupations of his deserve our respect precisely because they have never been granted tolerant, let alone sympathetic, consideration in the case of Synge or indeed in any other Irish context.

Along with them, Synge pursued practical interests and economic objectives which have been retrospectively collapsed into an image of Glanmore's master as an eccentric, doomed innovator. There is the evidence of the Ordinance Survey, which mapped this part of Wicklow at the end of the 1830s. In the serene lines of its many sheets, we see a sawmill in position close to a nursery pond, with a boat house on a stretch of water closer to Nuns Cross bridge. To the south stands a ruined church as best it can, with a graveyard by its side: the future and past balanced across a road in the neutral elegance of cartography. Naturally, the pre-Famine commentator takes the positive view:

> In the Glanmore demesne is an extensive and valuable slate quarry, which affords employment to great numbers, and it is to be hoped, will amply remunerate its enterprising and scientific proprietor, Mr. Synge, who has himself planned and made a railway through his demesne, from the slate quarry to Ashford, for the conveyance of slates. A circular saw-mill, which is worked by water, is in constant use, and situate near a chain-bridge which crosses the Vartrey in the demesne. A printing press is also at work, where books have been printed. There is also an extensive garden nursery here, where a great variety of young trees can be purchased. The apparently useless branches of trees, throughout the extensive woods of Glanmore, are collected, and after having been arranged in different sizes by the saw-mill, are shipped at Wicklow harbour for England, for the manufacture of crates.[29]

This is a poignant evocation of single-handed landlord endeavour on the eve of catastrophe. Within less a year, the enterprising and scientific John Synge was dead, and the county faced four years of unprecedented hardship.

Before his career can be taken up, a broader picture of the Synge family and the late eighteenth century is required in which Barbara Synge's name makes an appearance.

22

Her brother's will, 1792

The Lord used to have tea-parties and dances there long ago. (*O'Faolain*)

DURING the seventeenth and eighteenth centuries, the Synges distinguished themselves in the protestant Church of Ireland, achieving its highest dignities. George Synge (1594–1653), bishop of Cork, Cloyne and Ross, was nominated to the archdiocese of Tuam in 1647 but failed to obtain possession due to the state of war in Ireland. His first wife, Anne Edgeworth, had been drowned in 1641 while fleeing the rebellion so dramatically written up later by Sir John Temple. By 1652, George Synge had returned to his native Bridgnorth in Shropshire to die. His brother, Edward (died 1678) successively served as bishop of Limerick and of the united diocese of Cork, Cloyne and Ross. Samuel Synge, one Edward's sons, became Dean of Kildare, married the daughter of an archbishop of Armagh (the primate of all Ireland), and died in 1708 a very wealthy man.

The eighteenth century brought security to these possessions, and with it a dreary perpetuation of favourite Christian names. Edward Synge (1659–1741) was archbishop of the western archdiocese of Tuam from 1716 until his death. His eldest surviving son, Edward (1691–1762), held many offices including a number attached to Saint Patrick's Cathedral in Dublin while Jonathan Swift was dean. Though he assisted Edward in his promotion – to make room for someone he preferred – Swift did not hold a great opinion of him – 'Pox take me ... if I ever thought him worth my Contempt, till I made a bishop of him.'[1] Edward eventually become bishop of Elphin, and left a vivid account of mid-eighteenth-century clerical life in a series of engaging letters to his only surviving child, Alicia. These have recently been published as a testimony to the munificence of an Anglo-Irish prelate, and in this form they testify also to the importance for latter-day commentators of antique dignity in the Synges. Even at the time, of course, one witness could predict of nineteen-year-old Alicia that she 'will be [sic] a vast fortune' having been 'brought up like a princess'.[2]

Her brother's will, 1792

But even on this comfortable cusp, fortune was shortly to begin to turn. Edward's brother Nicholas (1673–1771, bishop of Killaloe from 1745 onwards) was to be 'the fifth and last prelate of the family'.[3] One of Nicholas Synge's children occupies the centre of this narrative – Barbara, who married John Hatch in 1765, only to disappear from view round the time of her second daughter's birth. That another, Edward (1726–1792), husband of Sophia Hutchinson, rose no higher than the rank of archdeacon (Killala) may of course be a tribute to Christian humility or, in a different perspective, to the rival calling of country squire. He had been a major beneficiary of successive family deaths, notably Edward of Elphin's, and he also inherited 'all the land entailed under the will of Samuel Synge, dean of Kildare'.[4] Thus provided for, he lived at Syngefield, an estate near the town of Birr in the midland King's County, whereas his ecclesiastical office attached itself to a cathedral town in north Mayo. Other benefices were granted to him; for example, he was briefly rector of Swords in 1781–1782, during which period he was formally responsible for the spiritual welfare of whoever was living in Lissenhall.

Following his own marriage in 1753, Archdeacon Edward became the father of six children – Edward (1753–1818), Elizabeth (1755–1801), Samuel (1756–1846), George (1757–1806), Robert (1759–1804) and Francis (1761–1831). The girl married an army officer. George settled in the midlands, marrying a County Clare woman (Mary Mac Donnell) whose maternal grandfather was an O'Brien of Dromoland Castle, old Gaelic royalty adapted to the new dispensation. Robert married a Wolfe of Lord Kilwarden's family, and ultimately became a baronet of England. Samuel followed his father into holy orders, rising to the same archdecanal ranking (see chapter 13), and marrying (like his youngest brother Francis) a first cousin, in both cases a daughter of John Hatch and Barbara Synge. The eldest son, Edward, took an Oxford degree, remained unmarried, and inherited Syngefield. He compiled a pedigree of the Irish Synges, and got himself buried at Saint James's, Westminster. An unremarkable chronicle for the times.

The Hutchinsons with whom the Synges had now allied themselves were rising liberal stars in the Anglo-Irish firmament. They also had their roots – to mix metaphors – in the soil of protestant intolerance of Catholicism and fear of Catholic fertility. Archdeacon Hutchinson's wife advised the Incorporated Society in 1787 against any excessive hygiene in managing children at their Longford school. Utilising a common word which would in time bring down Catholic Nationalist wrath on the head of JMS, she declared 'it was impossible to shift the children twice a week, they having only two shifts a-piece'.[5]

Making his will on Saint Patrick's Day 1792, Archdeacon Edward Synge stipulated that he should be buried 'with the greatest privacy either in the Churchyard of Birr very deep in the Earth or with the rest of the family at St Patricks Church [sic] Dublin according to the place I may happen to die'. The downgrading of Ireland's national cathedral, on the day its patron saint is celebrated, may signify

The devil's glen

nothing beyond a solicitor's indifference to ecclesiastical detail, or it may dimly reveal the testator's failing powers. (He died later in the same year.) The document proceeds in conventional fashion, listing such bequests as £4,000 sterling for his 'dear and only daughter Elizabeth' and £1,000 for his 'dear little granddaughter Elizabeth Synge Eldest Daughter of my Son Robert Synge'. To his beloved wife Sophia, he left various extensive properties in Dublin and elsewhere, and much lesser bequests to Charles Synge (£1,000); Francis Synge, third son of George Synge (£1,000); his own son Samuel Synge (gold watch, gold chain and cornelian ring with arms).

Then, following other minor provisions, Edward proceeds with renewed affectionate reference to 'my dear wife the aforesaid Sophia to whom and my dear Daughter I recommend my poor Baba requesting they will make up for my loss to her by every instance of uninterrupted kindness and tenderness'.[6] Here is the first indication of a distress which recurs elsewhere and later in Edward Synge's will. It is possible that 'poor Baba' is a granddaughter – Barbara, daughter of Francis Synge and his wife Elizabeth (née Hatch) who was born on 3 February 1790 and thus was an infant of just two years when the will was drawn up. If this identification could somehow be confirmed, other questions could be laid to rest.

The testator had already referred to a granddaughter, specifying this exact degree of relationship. Why should he omit a similar precision, if he were now alluding to another granddaughter? And why should any relative be mentioned in his will, without a specific benefit being attached? As for the infant Barbara, there is no reason to suppose that she was in any way dependent on her grandfather, nor would she – at so tender an age – feel his 'loss' when he died. Nor is there any explanation of why an infant (whose parents were alive) should be recommended to the care of an ageing widow and an unmarried aunt. The 'uninterrupted' kindness which Edward sought to provide for 'poor Baba' is hardly consistent with the development of a healthy youngster.

The child, however, had been named after her grandmother Barbara Hatch (née Synge) of whom we have heard nothing for many years. Aged now about sixty-one (if alive), this Barbara was the testator's sister, not otherwise mentioned in the will. This latter factor is, of course, wholly consistent with her *not* being still alive. There is, however, no indication of where she might have been buried, despite her father's family's elevated position in the church. And there is also the ambiguous evidence of Sam Hatch's visit to London, which might be read as evidence of Barbara Synge's being alive in 1782. Despite the undeniable evidence of the death notice in 1767 – a detail which escaped the family chroniclers for more than two centuries – there is reason to ask if the archdeacon's will of 1792 did not in fact allude to his sister.

Her disappearance from her husband's traceable papers, likewise the references by Samuel M'Cracken to Hatch and his daughters as though they were wife-and-

Her brother's will, 1792

mother-less, would be consistent with the hypothesis that Barbara Synge had suffered a terrible reversal of health, leading immediately into her virtual eclipse or rustication under the (admittedly) false cover of a death notice. Within this hypothesis, the archdeacon's sister (if alive) would be in need of his widow's kindness and tenderness, for it supposes that she had become incapacitated physically and/or mentally to the point where she could not legally benefit under a will or take responsibility for administering a benefit. It is through her brother's will that we hear the silence of Barbara Synge.

In the light of the archdeacon's will, Samuel Hatch's accounts for a journey undertaken in 1782 earn a second inspection. Why would Samuel Hatch have maintained two categorically separate accounts for himself and his own wife? But if Edward Synge's 1792 will prompts a reconsideration of John Hatch's marital status, the state of health (and ultimate fate) of Mrs John Hatch (née Barbara Synge) become further obscured by the possibility that – having survived two pregnancies in the 1760s – the only subsequent trace of her is to be found in her escort's claims for expenses.

A little additional light may be shed on the matter by examining the circumstances of those to whom the interests of 'poor Baba' were consigned. Both women were assumed to be unattached when the will would be executed, both were resident at Syngefield in the King's County. It was here on 19 May – two months and two days after the will was drawn up – that the infant Barbara drowned while walking in the riverside garden with her nurse and her elder brother. At that date, Edward Synge was still alive. That a granddaughter would stay in the family's seat and yet be omitted from material benefit under her grandfather's will seems unlikely. But if the infant Barbara was congenitally disqualified from such benefit – being, let us suppose for the moment, a Down's Syndrome child – then the archdeacon might well both shelter her under his roof and do no more for her in his will than plead for 'uninterrupted kindness and tenderness'. We have no reason to suspect that young Barbara was anything other than a healthy child – her uncle Robert recorded her death in the matter-of-fact way he recorded everything: certainly he did not deny the incident or the infant.

The archdeacon held property of several kinds, and up to this point in his will, what he had disposed of was 'absolutely my own ... nor am I accountable to any one for any part of it'. There remained property acquired through trusts or by way of marriage settlements with specific clauses for performance. Perhaps there was also entailed property, which might account for the singular absence of the eldest son's name from the will. Though the estate appears to have been substantial, it had to take into account 'just debts'. Yet it was not these but some unspecified burden which prompted the archdeacon to continue, 'I am sorry it does not make a better appearance but my children will I hope do me the justice to recollect that I always shared with them to the last pound [?] or I might have died.' On this

The devil's glen

oddly grim note, he set about 'the division of eight thousand pounds sterling the provision made for my younger children in the settlement entered into on my marriage with Sophia Hutchinson'.

The provisions are unremarkable in themselves.[7] However, 'younger children' again casts into an odd light the non-reference to Edward, the eldest and the presumed heir to his father's estate. In strict terms of inheritance, his interests may have been guaranteed by entail and/or by the Synge/Hutchinson marriage settlement. His father's disinclination to leave him even a ring or watch-chain under the terms of the will might be seen as relegating him to a different league of affection from 'the younger children' – there had never been more than a two-year gap between the births of successive babies. Young Edward Synge's status had already been silently impugned by his mother's brother, Francis Hutchinson (died 18 December 1807, aged about eighty-one), who was created a baronet of Ireland in 1782, with remainder to his younger brother James (c. 1732–1813), and after that to his nephew Samuel Synge.[8] Given that hereditary titles depended on a rationale of marriage and procreation, it was apparently assumed in 1782 (when the remainders were inscribed in the original creation of the baronetcy) that – after the ageing and childless Hutchinson brothers had borne the title – it should pass to their *second-eldest* Synge nephew, Samuel and not to his elder brother, Edward. As neither Samuel nor Edward (nor any of their siblings) was married at this date, there was a deliberate passing over the eldest male to ensure that Samuel inherited the baronetcy by way of special remainder.

Between the creation of the Hutchinson baronetcy and the making of Archdeacon Synge's will ten years later, the family tree had grown. All his sons – except the eldest – had not only married but had been blessed with children. As we have noted, 'my dear little granddaughter Elizabeth Synge Eldest Daughter of my Son Robert Synge' was specifically mentioned in the will. So was Charles, the son of the archdeacon's son, George. Of the other grandchildren, no mention was made: thus excluded was the infant Barbara already referred to and her elder brother John, grandfather of JMS. Excluded also – and more intriguingly – was Frances Synge, daughter of Samuel Synge and Frances Wood (who had died in 1788).

12

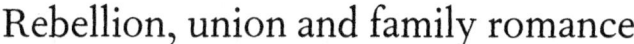

Rebellion, union and family romance

'Then, in Ninety-eight, two so-called Military Roads cut it across and across like a scissors. They were fifty miles long, and straight as rulers. By the way,' he asked suddenly, catching me looking idly out through the window, 'were you ever in County Wicklow?' (*O'Faolain*)

IN MANY ways, the events of 1798 overturned the presumptions of a peaceful century, and the Synge family was no exception to the general pattern. Births in the 1780s and wills made in the early 1790s were subject to grosser and more public events, some of which have become coloured by the passage of time. The decade of the 1790s now possesses a legendary character. No county more powerfully contributed to the legend than Wicklow to which rebellion spread from neighbouring Wexford. A process of complex historical reinterpretation has ebbed and flowed ever since. Elaborate centenary commemorations in 1898 resulted in the intertwining of politics and literature as Yeats saluted Theobald Wolfe Tone and Villiers de l'Isle Adam with left hand and right hand simultaneously. Among the poet's younger associates, JMS was careful to balance these opposing revolutionary and decadent influences, not so much out of innate caution as out of a privileged awareness of their earlier convergence in his family's history. In an article published in 1907, JMS observed that the older people in Wicklow, 'when they meet a wanderer on foot ... stop and talk to him for hours, telling him stories of the Rebellion, or of the fallen angels that ride across the hills ...'[1]

The mountainous district in which Samuel M'Cracken died remained isolated for many years. In the recollections of a barony sub-constable who later distinguished himself as a rebel, a banditti gang from Dublin is described as arriving at Roundwood in 1794, from which they conducted raids on neighbouring houses. Crime by now had political overtones, so it is fitting that Joseph Holt, the tireless pursuer of malefactors, should emerge at the end of the decade as a leader of the insurrection in Wicklow. Of humble birth – he fits what the great American painter Robert Motherwell has called The Homely Protestant – Holt lived from c.

The devil's glen

1782 near Tiglin on a farm acquired through marriage to 'Mrs Long's daughter'. Mrs Long's maiden name had been Manning.[2]

John Hatch died 'suddenly' on 22 September 1797, an elderly and tired man.[3] Within a matter of hours, Henry Stuart offered his services as successor in the Downshire agencies.[4] The tone of the letter suggests that his qualifications should have been familiar to the landlord, as in the case of one who had already been active in the business. In a note dated 29 September, the son-in-law Francis Synge (1761–1831) informed the Marquis of Downshire of Hatch's death; he too offered to take over the role of agent. Stuart, who was part of the M'Cracken family circle in 1769, persisted in his strikingly prompt courtship of Lord Downshire, writing from Pakenham Hall (County Westmeath) in December to keep the question of the agency open.[5]

There were other pressing matters on Francis Synge's mind, which it was appropriate to communicate to Lord Downshire. About Hatch, he wrote that

> I now think my duty to acquaint you that in consequence of his declining to make any will, the total arrangements of his affairs devolves [sic] upon me, on behalf of his two daughters, viz my wife and her sister, and also to assure your lordship that I shall endeavour most zealously to put your accounts (up to the day of his death) in the best order I can, consistent with my total ignorance of the premises and tenants. From Mr Hatch's accuracy and punctuality in money matters (at least till well nigh worn out with age, business and consequent ill health) I have well founded hopes of being able to make out such a statement as may full satisfy your lordship and the ladies who have for so many years honoured him, and his father, with their confidence.[6]

This letter raises several problems. Synge wished to succeed his father-in-law as Downshire's agent but cheerfully admitted total ignorance of the estates. This would hardly seem to describe the person who had surveyed the tenants' emergency needs in the bad winter of 1792/1793. Perhaps the fact that he had the relevant papers in his custody was sufficient to ensure that his wish would be granted, though it seems that by the following year (1798) he had ceased to act in the capacity of agent. His tribute to Hatch's efficiency was qualified by frank admissions that age and other burdens – including business itself – had diminished it in recent years. No explanation was offered as to why so experienced and prosperous a businessman should decline to make a will, with the result that Synge was engrossed in sorting things out well into the new century. The intervening years were tumultous, nowhere more so than in Wicklow where what had been Hatch holdings were consolidated as the Synge estate.

Little more than a week later, Synge wrote again because 'truths (though disagreeable) must sometimes be told'. The image of his father-in-law was now considerably altered for, 'having searched the house [Synge] found only a very few hundred pounds, hardly sufficient to defray the expenses of a private funeral

Rebellion, union and family romance

and to pay off some trifling demands of tradespeople'. Once more stressing his own ignorance of the business, he could find only one defence of Hatch whose 'disposition was much too compassionate for the office of an agent, and [whose] affairs have suffered far more' than those of Downshire and his sisters. Synge's style of writing cannot have inspired instant confidence; he qualified absolute statements and insinuated disturbing modifications of what seemed at first glance reassuring platitudes. Truths must 'sometimes' be told, and the defence of Hatch which he offered was the only one he could urge 'at present'. When he declared that he 'was utterly unacquainted with every part of Mr Hatch's business whether for himself or other people', there remained the possible interpretation that he was acquainted with some part or parts of it.[7]

The coming tumult was now plainly audible. Writing from Bath on 15 March 1798, the widowed Sophie Synge inquired of her son in Dublin: 'What tempts my Friend to be seditious; from the Newspaper I saw, I suspect you have been on your legs ... A long silence now is Death to me, for every day produces terrible News ... hitherto We irish go on as usual. 'tis said the Bishops have had Hints, They had better go home.' The previous summer Francis Synge had been elected MP for the open borough of Swords, partly through the influence of his father-in-law, Hatch. The last Irish parliament opened on 1 January 1798. Evidence of Synge's contribution to the debates of this tumultuous period is slight, though he participated in the debate on Sir Lawrence Parsons's 'State of the Nation' motion on Monday 5 March. It is difficult to see anything but sarcasm in his mother's reference to sedition: Francis Synge was with the huge 'Majority in Favour of Government and the Laws', together with J. C. Beresford, Isaac Corry and Sir Richard Musgrave.[8]

While Mrs Synge's anxious anticipation of trouble was to prove valid, her advice on other matters now sits oddly alongside her son's correspondence with Downshire. In the same letter in which she jokes nervously of sedition, she recommends that Francis Synge 'ought strictly (when you can) to pay every Article mentioned by Mr Hatch, tho' the Legacies may not have yr Approbation'. The clear implication is that John Hatch had made a will, with sufficient provisions to warrant the obligation to pay every one of them, whereas Synge had explicitly told the Marquis that his father-in-law had declined to make one. It is possible that Hatch made a will, but failed to sign it or have it properly witnessed, thus allowing Mrs Synge to refer to legacies intended while her son had no formal basis on which to provide for these. Mrs Synge was no stranger to wills, having been sole executrix of her husband's in 1792/1793 and the author of a nine-page will of her own in 1796 to which she subsequently added a codicil.

Ignorant or otherwise, Synge went about preparing a statement of account for Downshire's estates at Edenderry (King's County) and Dundrum (County Down). On the resulting document, he was described (by himself) as 'administrator of

The devil's glen

John Hatch, Esq.'.[9] With these accounts, he apparently ceased to contribute to the management of the estates, in which connection his role appears to have been largely a retrospective one, pursuing arrears which his father-in-law should have been paid but setting up no permanent system of his own. In June 1798, when permanence itself appeared to be at risk, he wrote to Miss Blundell, the figure with whom Hatch had most amiably correspondence on Edenderry business: 'Should anything befall me during these times it would be great consolation to me that you had an account of even so much as I send … it is impossible for me to compute exactly at present as this unfortunate rebellion (besides some family disasters) has prevented me from having your rent rolls finished.'[10] Loyalists might think the word 'unfortunate' hardly adequate to describe the events of the day.

Blundell, at this point, was staying in Dublin, despite the dangers of rebellion, and it is not clear from what location Synge wrote. Her death in November 1798 may have contributed to the termination of his business links with the family. Though Synge did furnish some kind of statement to Downshire of John Hatch's last efforts, the surviving papers contain no comprehensive account-book comparable to that covering Henry Hatch's agency for the years 1748–1760. The next generation of the Hill family thought Hatch 'full of professions, bustle, dishonest', a man who died 'very rich, much of his wealth having been accumulated out of the estates of absentee proprietors'.[11]

The matter is further complicated by a brief letter from Synge to a barrister, Robert French of Kildare Street, dated 9 June 1799, about 'my Intentions'. While there is insufficient detail to establish precisely what was the subject of Synge's intentions, a note in another hand reads – 'The County of Meath & the lease held under the Vicars Corale of St Patrick – to the eldest – the Vicar Corale – the youngest – all the rest of Mr H: to the eldest.'[12] The simplicity of this statement of provision, albeit derived from a very brief note, stands in marked contrast to Sophie Synge's advice about fulfilling 'every Article' among the 'legacies'. It may be that the letter refers merely to one aspect of the estate. As John Hatch had long been seneschal of Saint Sepulchre's, and thereby involved both in the proving of wills and in the financial affairs of Saint Patrick's Cathedral, it seems reasonable to assume that the letter referred to the division of Hatch's estate between his two daughters. Of these the elder, Elizabeth Hatch, was the wife of Francis Synge.

It is as well to recall the exact details. Elizabeth Hatch (b. 21 January 1766; d. 31 July 1810: buried Glenealy, County Wicklow) had married Francis Synge in 1786. One of the few personal glimpses we get of her comes in her son's dedication of his *Biographical Sketch of the Struggles of Pestalozzi* to one 'to whose early instruction and example, however inadequately valued amidst the follies of youth these tracts are inscribed …' While the filial piety of this is to be applauded in itself and diagnosed as typical of a later generation's spiritual reawakening, a more specific anxiety might be related to the continuing uncertainty as to whether the 'intentions'

Rebellion, union and family romance

were those of Francis Synge trying to administer his intestate father-in-law's affairs, or those of a will (implicit in Sophie Synge's letter) the existence of which had been denied in September 1797. It is of course possible to reconcile denial of the will in September and allusion to its legacies in March – by positing discovery of a document in the intervening six months.

But three difficulties arise, to jeopardise such an explanation. First, Hatch was an experienced man of affairs whose will was unlikely to go missing. Second, Francis Synge categorically stated to Downshire that his father-in-law had declined (not merely neglected) to make a will, phrasing which indicates (or fabricates) deliberation on the old man's part. It is true that a resumé of 'Hatch's accounts, as attempted to be settled in 1802' refers to Synge as 'his executor', but this (like Mrs Sophie Synge's reference to 'legacies') may be an uncalled-for invocation of a term more proper to the administration of a will.[13] For, third, late discovery of a will in this case would have revived memories of the M'Cracken case just one generation earlier. Given that the legal administration of a will is nowhere recorded, we can, I believe, conclude that Synge was handling his late father-in-law's affairs to the best of his own abilities, with minimal guidance in the form of public documentation.

That happy conclusion leaves only one problem – the contradiction between (a) Sophie Synge's comment that the 'legacies' might not have Francis Synge's approval, and (b) Synge's note to French (and its endorsement) to the effect that the bulk of Hatch's estate was to go to 'the eldest', that is, Synge's own wife. In the event, administration of the estate was not completed for another eight or more years, and the final division does not appear to have followed any clear pattern of advantage. For the matter involved more than one inheritrix. Both daughters, and both sons-in-law, did well. It is significant that the younger daughter, Dorothy Hatch (c. 1767–1836), did not marry until 1801, when she became the second wife of Samuel Synge (1756–1846). The involvment of his brother cannot have eased matters for Francis Synge, as it placed him under a kind of scrutiny the Hatch sisters were unlikely to have exercised. As for Dorothy Hatch's motives in marrying the elder Synge, we must await an opportunity to consider his earlier marital career. One factor may be accepted, as a consequence of Dorothy's marriage – her share in the division of the Hatch estate was the more assured for her release from spinsterhood. Though Francis Synge had occupied John Hatch's Harcourt Street house after his death, it was his brother who came into the long-term possession of it.

The delays attendant on the dispersion of the Hatch estate were rudely interrupted by those tumultuous events which threatened both the prosperity already achieved and the vision of great substance yet to come. First-hand evidence of the Synges' attitude towards, or experience of, the rebellion is extremely scarce. What there is deserves and resists analysis. A pocket diary for 1798 contains several pages of summary narrative, principally of events in County Wexford – not Wicklow,

The devil's glen

where they held property.¹⁴ This would suggest that Synge was in Dublin or further afield when news broke, rather than holding the fort at Roundwood.¹⁵ The emphasis falls unmistakably on the cruelties inflicted by the rebels specifically upon protestants, with the massacre at Scullabogue given as an instance. What is striking in the eyes of JMS's readers is the fact of the diary's having been examined by his brother one cold Edwardian Sunday in January 1908. Robert Anthony Synge decided that it had been John Hatch's diary – which is unlikely in that he died several months before the rebellion broke. By a process of elimination, we may conclude that the diarist was Francis Synge, MP.

If the Synges of JMS's generation knew of these papers, what image of the ancestral past did they convey? The few pages of narrative conform to the family's tradition of doughty protestantism which, in those days, involved explicit anti-Catholic animus. The diary as a whole – scarcely used – tells nothing of the day-to-day experiences of the Synge household. While it would be fanciful to conclude that the pages of narrative were deliberately written up after the insurrection to create a record of contemporary interest or concern, it remains true that the diary had been wholly unused for the first four and a half months of the year, having been purchased (one supposes) at the end of 1797. Unless, of course, the undated jottings on the final blank leaf pre-date the summary account of events occurring in May/June.

Here we find the following:

Got from Mr Jo Grey to give to B: Bagl. Harvey Esq if he calls for it –

	One B Note for	3: 8: 3
	One do. for	1: 2: 9
	Silver & sBrass	0: 4: 9
		4:15: 9
Jane Boxols [?] Rect for the Sum of		
		1:13: 8½
	Felim & Hugh's Do.	0: 2: 8½
	Jas Murphy's Do.	0: 2: 8½
	Susy Murphy Do.	0: 1: 7½

together with totallings of the sums listed. Of the names given here one is certainly identifiable. The Wexford landowner, Beauchamp Bagnal Harvey (1762–1798), had been an early member of the United Irishmen, who took command of the rebels in his county, until he was deposed after their reversal in the Battle of Ross (5 June) whereupon he fled to the Saltee Islands, later to be arrested and hanged.¹⁶ The smallness of the sum, to be paid by Synge to Harvey, is matched by the evident haste in which it was assembled, being made up of two bank drafts and miscellaneous coin. The occurrence of the common surname Murphy in the same calculations further suggests that this was not the casual settling of a gentlemanly card-game debt.[17] At some point in the year of rebellion, the year of Harvey's execution, Francis Synge paid the Wexford commander and others less well-born about seven pounds in all, and chose to record this (and little else) in his diary.[18] Less emphatically, one might note that Harvey was arrested with another gentleman-rebel, John Colclough (a Catholic) in 1798: Francis Synge's great-granddaughter married the son of Henry Colclough Stephens in 1884.[19]

Apart from the few cash totals, and thumb-sketches of military action, the only other holograph entry in the diary occurs on the front fly-leaf: it simply directs attention to John Tillotson's sermon on the anniversary of the Gunpowder Plot (1605). His text having been Luke 9: 55–56, the archbishop had said, 'The words thus explained contain this observation, *that a revengeful and cruel and* destructive spirit, is directly contrary to the design and temper of the Gospel, and *not to be executed upon any pretence of zeal for God and religion.*' If we assume that Francis Synge's terse self-direction was written after the cruelties recorded in the little summaries, then a further passage in Tillotson's commemorative sermon deserves quotation. 'I would not be understood to charge every particular person who is, or hath been in the Roman communion, with the guilt of these or the like practices: But I must charge their doctrines and principles with them: I must charge the heads of their church ...'[20] In the circumstances of 1798, the implied analogy between Bagnal Harvey and Guy Fawkes may seem politically strained. But the choice of Tillotson's sermon suggests a liberal response to the 'unfortunate' rebellion, on Synge's part, within a 'reactionary' interpretation of events.

By September 1798, the wider conflict was more or less over, bar a few last-minute retributions. French prisoners of war were being quietly shipped home via Liverpool. A well-placed observer in official circles noted these developments complacently, but went on ungrammatically to note that 'Holt, the commander of the innocents in the mountains of Wicklow, who are said to be in great force, continue their [sic] depredations without interruption.'[21] Indeed, Joseph Holt had quartered his followers in the Devil's Glen virtually on Francis Synge's back-door step. Since his own marriage, the area had been Holt's home territory – until, that is, he had been driven into rebellion through quarrels with Thomas Hugo early in 1798. Though Lord Kingsborough and his North Cork Militia were involved in burning out rebels in the area of Dunran and the Devil's Glen, Francis Synge (Holt's landlord) tolerated the rebel chief, either because he was away from Roundwood and could do nothing about it, or out of fear, or out of some kind of local understanding.[22] Robert Ross's euphemistic term for Holt's men – 'the innocents' – may catch an ambiguity of the times which is now all but irrecoverable.[23]

Synge's wood-ranger, Joseph Thompson, was seized by Holt's rebels in mid-June 1798 and held captive for some time. His offence, however, was not that he was a loyalist or Orangeman, but that he had taken the United Irishmen's oath and

The devil's glen

failed to support their rebellion. Accounts conflict in war, especially in civil war confrontations of a decidedly local kind. Joseph Harding, a tenant of Synge's, had come to blows with friendly neighbours in 1797 but did not denounce them as the sworn rebels they were; they in turn did not molest him a year later. A recent historian has written of 'the intimate nature of the Wicklow rebellion in the politically polarized Roundwood district'. Before the rebels came under pressure from crown forces, they attacked yeomen soldiers who were ploughing in Tomriland: Thomas Hatton escaped, but Robert Freeman (whose fields were being tended) was killed.[24] These family names weave in and out of the more elevated chronicle of Synges and Hatches.

Together with hundreds of Wicklow's 'suffering Loyalists', Synge submitted his claim after the violence had subsided. He gave his address as Harcourt Street, Dublin, though the damage had been sustained at Roundwood. The total sum he sought was £573 16s 8d, for the loss of 'house, horses, furniture and wine'. The size of the claim would suggest that the residence which had come to him from M'Cracken via Hatch had been totally destroyed, and this is consistent with the estimated age of the present house. The Revd Ambrose Weekes, by comparison, was looking for less than £88 for 'Loss of tithes, wine, house', and Weekes is known to have done some rebuilding. Synge's claim was not paid promptly, if indeed it was ever paid. It would be uncharitable to suggest that disappointment – if he went unrewarded – with the authorities on that count affected his attitude to their plans to abolish the parliament he sat in.[25]

Meanwhile the complicated business of Hatch's estate persisted. At some point the 'Diocese of Dublin Benefice of Vicars Choral ... d[id] grant unto the said Francis Synge all that and those the parcels of Ground containing together two acres or thereabouts situate lying and being in Saint Peter's Parish in the County of the City of Dublin whereon are several dwelling houses in York Street and Upper and Lower Mercer Street Dublin in as large and ample a manner as the same were formerly held and enjoyed by John Hatch ...'[26] The property included everything in York Street west of Mercer street, plus at least four houses to the east (nos 17, 31, 45, ?58), plus all the properties in Mercer Street (west side), a very valuable urban possession, adjoining Saint Stephen's Green where Hatch had lived since the 1760s. It would appear that the Vicar's Choral regretted, or at least sought to reverse, this grant some ten or twelve years later.

Synge's position as an MP for Swords put him at a disadvantage in the complex huxtering negotiations which accompanied the Union. Irrespectively of how they voted, members felt that they deserved compensation for the loss they suffered in the abolition of the Irish parliament. But with Swords 'the fixed compensation was, in this case (it being of the class called potwalloping boroughs, and not private property), vested in trustees, for the purpose of educating and apprenticing the children of the humbler classes, without any religious distinction; and a handsome and commodious free school was erected in the town, at an expense of about £2000'.²⁷

Having voted 'patriotically' against the Union in 1800, Synge maintained his efforts to administer the estate of his late father-in-law.²⁸ These efforts are difficult to trace, though the outcome appears to have been fruitful. The problem is complicated not only by the role of Dorothy and Elizabeth Hatch as co-heiresses, but also by the earlier marriage of Francis's brother, Samuel, whose *second* wife was co-heiress. These problems in turn serve to highlight methodological issues in the study of cultural history. What is at stake is the crucial relationship between the historical origins of persons and things (on the one hand) and 'that more intangible historicity of the concepts and categories by which we attempt to understand' them.²⁹

The previous chapter concluded with some details of the Revd Samuel Synge's early domestic life. By marrying into the Wood family, he had set up frontiers with aspects of Irish society to which his forebears had been relative strangers, either by reason of class or creed. The Widmans had served the protestant cause but as mere ensigns in a foot regiment. The Mathews and O'Reillys, for whom one of these Widman/Woods had acted in the matter of a marriage settlement, stood respectably as to class, but also stood very close to old Roman Catholicism. Yet it was not these associations which were to draw unwelcome attention. Mrs Hans Wood had been a sister of the earl of Kingston.

Marriage into the King family was no light undertaking, even at one remove. Beyond controversion, the Revd Samuel Synge's newly acquired kinsman, Robert King (1754–1799, Viscount Kingsborough), shot dead in December 1797 his wife's brother's illegitimate son. Notoriety ran in the family, not always routed through the Ten Commandments, his lordship's mother having been the bastard daughter of Peggy Jordan, his wife having abandoned him.³⁰ The latest scandal involved abduction of a minor, adultery, murder and a strong suspicion of incest. It was fuelled by the colourful detail that the young woman at its heart had been, as a child, under the care of Mary Wollstonecraft (1759–1797) whose novel *Mary* (1788) had drawn on her experiences as a governess in Ireland with the Kingsboroughs. Wollstonecraft herself had died in childbirth on 10 September, but not before marrying the radical philosopher William Godwin.³¹ The militia commander who swept through central east Wicklow was kinsman to one of the Synges, a kinsman with a reputation.

Though Wollstonecraft's death and her widower's response generated their own public turmoil, for the Synges a more intimate concern was the attendance of Major Robert Wood as Kingsborough's 'second' when he exchanged shots with Henry Fitzgerald in Hyde Park in October. Though Wood was publicly declared to be the outraged father's friend, he was also his first cousin. That is to say, he was brother to the first Mrs Samuel Synge.³² Wood's writing a detailed account of the affair in the London newspapers, duly reprinted in the *Hibernian Journal* of 8 October, has been described as part of 'an elaborate scheme to get an official version' of the family conflict before the public. On 8 November, the old earl died; Robert King, now entitled to a trial in the Irish House of Lords, proceeded within weeks to murder Fitzgerald in his bedchamber on 15 December in Kilworth, County Cork. In May 1798, the Lords acquitted King, a matter worthy of comment even in 1890.[33] His lordship died on 17 April 1799, aged forty-five.

The aristocracy Samuel Synge embraced veered closer to the principles of Mazo de la Roche than those of Yeats. Yet from the diary of his brother Robert, it can be established that on 28 May 1788 'Mrs Samuel Synge (nee Wood) [had been] brought to Bed of twins, of whom one died immediately, the other Fanny lived. She died herself June 12th 1788.'[34] This removes the possibility of a bastard, and so highlights a near-century-long allegation (see p. 128 below). One may wonder why no member of the family troubled to correct Burke and lesser genealogical authorities. The decade of revolution was, in certain respects, best left unexamined. But one must also note the suppression of the dead twin, and neglect of Fanny's subsequent history.[35]

This is not simply an obscure instance of fact grubbing. While the Irish protestant community was sufficiently small that it seems in retrospect everyone knew everyone else, and in some cases carnally, the matter of this history is transmitted through powerful censors and other mediatory devices. On the question of familiarity, there is strong evidence to indicate that Samuel Synge's choice of second wife – Dorothy Hatch – was also implicated in Kingsborough circles through her father. In an undated letter – probably written in the early 1790s – Lord Kilwarlin chided John Hatch for giving up 'the exchange of Curacy for your nephew & Mr Lambert. I cannot see why Lambert should hesitate as he would be just as secure of Ld Kingsborough['s] protection from Edenderry'.[36]

Insouciance can explain many wrongful allegations. Impersonal censorship and moral distortion effected by the order in which print is laid out can also be instanced. Samuel Synge's second marriage is treated by the family genealogist in a manner either unsatisfactory or highly suggestive. And whereas the first union took place ten years before John Hatch's death, the second occurred during the period when Francis Synge was seeking to settle his father-in-law's affairs, always bearing in mind that two Hatch daughters were acknowledged as co-heiresses. For the year 1801, or earlier, several major events in the Revd Samuel Synge's life are recorded, though without exact dates. These *may* include (1) the death of a teenage, only (surviving) child, Miss Frances Synge, on some date in 1801, (this controverted by the recent *Peerage*,[37] though accepted by some of its predecessors) and by the family genealogist); (2) the remarriage of her widower father (licence dated 28 February 1801; wedding on 3 March) to his first cousin, Dorothy Hatch. And as (a) the birth of the oldest surviving child[38] of the second marriage is recorded for 18 January 1802, and (b) his sister Sophia was born in 1810, the above list of notable events should – *on the authority of the printed family tree* – include (3) the births of three non-surviving children – Elizabeth, John, and Samuel – in the year of their parents' marriage or earlier.[39]

The last allegation can be dismissed by simple reference again to Mrs Margaret Synge's diary. The births of all Sam and Dolly's children are recorded – Francis Hutchinson (18 January 1802), Elizabeth (23 January 1803), John Hatch (7 June 1805), Samuel (8 June 1807), and Sophia Elizabeth (23 January 1810). To this record should be added the busy deaths – Elizabeth died on 14 or 15 May 1807, and Samuel died of the croup on 12 May 1812. In the case of the other missing or suspect child, the diary for 29 February 1808 is eloquent. 'Got an account of the death of Sams second son John Hatch on the 18th and of his wife's having been delivered of a dead child a few days before.'

Compared to these irresolvable questions of mortality and morality, Francis Synge's dossier is transparent if thin. The death of his mother in January 1799 removed a key witness to his conduct. Neither this, nor John Hatch's death of September 1797, can be identified with 'some family disasters' mentioned by Francis Synge in June 1798, though the deaths of infants might be so described – but none fits Francis's timetable of lament.[40] Sir Francis Hutchinson's death (December 1807) in old age coincided with an apparent initiative in the business of Hatch's posthumous affairs, allowing as it did the two Synge brothers to co-ordinate their benefits.

The previous year, Francis Synge was described as 'administrator of all and singular the good and chattels rights and credits of John Hatch' in an Indenture dated 12 April 1806, relating to land in Meath.[41] No claim is made that he had been appointed executor in any will. One of the great archivist Sir John Ainsworth's reports of manuscript collections in private hands records the survival into the twentieth century of 'Case, with opinion of counsel (Serjeant John Ball) on behalf of Frans. Synge, esq., administrator of John Hatch, esq., deceased'. Dating from c. 1807, this document provides further and formal evidence that Francis Synge was seeking to have Hatch's estate settled, in the absence of a will. If Mrs Sophie Synge accurately alluded to a will in March 1798, she was no longer around to worry about it.

The document of c. 1807 does not appear to have come into the National Library of Ireland with the bulk of the papers held by Edward Stephens, grandson of Henry Colclough Stephens, nephew of JMS and self-appointed biographer.[42] But, from the summary in Report No. 179, we learn that the case at issue, within the larger matter of settling Hatch's affairs, concerned 'a lease made in 1762 by the Prebendary of Swords, with the consent of the Dean of Saint Patrick's and the Archbishop of Dublin, of part of the prebend for 21 years'.[43] Here it might be worth recalling that, among other holdings, the Revd Edward Synge (brother-in-

The devil's glen

law of John Hatch) was briefly rector of Swords in 1781–1782. Amongst other matters of precedent, etc., 'the case' referred to the alleged practice of making such leases in 1637 and 1662, but pointed out that the Archbishop of the day (Charles Agar) was refusing to become party of a lease 'observing that the absurd usage of former Archbishops is no reason for him to continue it, ... and ... that by complying with such an absurd and useless Custom he might hereafter subject himself or his family to some trouble or a law Suit ...'[44]

As with Francis Synge's letter to Robert French in June 1799, this piece of evidence does not tell us much. But it unequivocally confirms that, in the composition of Hatch's wealth, dealings with church property (in some sense) featured to a degree which required expert legal opinion if the estate were to be harvested to the full. Whether the business with the Vicar's Choral (referred to in the letter to French) was linked to the prebendary lease considered by John Ball remains unclear, as does the value of John Hatch's having held the seneschalship of Saint Sepulchre. What is unquestionable is that no evidence of a warm confessional relationship with the church – where evidence would be well documented – emerges for Hatch or his immediate family. Even the plot of sanctified ground in which he was (presumably) buried in September 1797 remains unidentified. Not marble nor gilded monuments commemorate the twice elected Member for Swords. Those who bore his name in his own or earlier generations eschewed holy orders. Of his 'co-heiresses' one (Dorothy) did marry a man of the cloth but not during her father's lifetime. Her husband was so attached to his own name, with its tradition of the *vir gravis et doctus* reaching back to George, bishop of Cloyne (died 1652) that he changed it to Synge-Hutchinson in order to inherit a baronetcy in 1813.[45] Of John Hatch's other son-in-law, little evidence of otherworldliness has been found, apart from the allusion to Archbishop Tillotson.

In 1804, leases on some three hundred and sixty acres at Telltown and Tatestown in County Meath evidently fell in. In the subsequent leasing, Samuel and his wife, Francis Synge and his wife are conjointly listed as the lessors (all having John Hatch's Harcourt Street house as their address) who cannily retained the rights to any mineral deposits on the lands in question. By 1806, Francis and Elizabeth give Glanmore as their address.[46] Indeed, when he finally concluded the 'partition' of John Hatch's Meath estate in 1807, Francis Synge proceeded to aggrandise his 'place' in County Wicklow. The original house, called Glenmouth, was notable for its fine view of the sea to the east. Synge retained the fashionable architect, Francis Johnson, to carry out a thorough transformation of the building. The result, renamed Glanmore Castle, possessed towers at each corner and concealed its roof behind a crenellated parapet. To this neo-Gothic pile, he and his wife moved, leaving remoter Roundwood little used for many years. The estate now stretched for ten miles, including a good deal of open mountain, and an extensive area farmed by tenants whose rents provided an income. The demesne which he personally retained included about three acres at Roundwood, a hill-farm at Tiglin and fifteen hundred acres at Glanmore with pleasure grounds, a deer park and a home farm. His wife had died in July 1810 and was buried in Glenealy, south of the Glanmore estate, in what was later regarded as an exclusively protestant cemetery.[47]

The Vicars Choral of Saint Patrick's unsuccessfully brought a suit against Synge in 1811 specifically relating to leases in York Street, Dublin. Writing on this general issue shortly afterwards, the church historian Monck Mason pointedly referred to the 'shameful abuse, let it happen how it will, that persons, having a life interest only, should be permitted to alienate the property of their successors for a benefit which themselves could only enjoy ... Synge's holding on the south side of Kevin-street, opposite Bride-street, though part of which it is projected to lead a new street to Portobello, was valued, by the foot, at £104: 5s.'[48] Here was urban development potential indeed. In 1814, Francis Synge added to the new opulence of Glanmore a town house of comparable dignity. The magnificent Georgian mansion now known as No. 8 Ely Place was acquired in an area of Dublin where his father-in-law had assembled a valuable portfolio of properties, some undeveloped, others already lucrative. It too would reverberate in the moral annals of the Synges in the mid-twentieth century.[49]

The late Victorian image of the Synges accommodated a sentimental memory of Francis's anti-unionism in 1800, unembarrassed by any recollection of the Hatches or Monck Mason's strictures on the transfer of land in the vicinity of the cathedral. It also carried within it, consciously or otherwise, a distorted account of Samuel's marriages and children. The impact of these misprisions was intensified by the intervening history of the family, its religious and other enthusiasms which bespoke an intensified moral sense, its financial and social decline which hinted at retribution. Francis's son, John Synge (1788–1845), was sent first to Trinity College, Dublin, and then to Magdalen College, Oxford, after which the young man toured in some style on the continent, visiting Portugal, Spain, Italy and Switzerland. The most important event of the tour was John Synge's 1814 meeting with the famous Swiss educationalist, Johann Heinrich Pestalozzi (1746–1827).[50] In 1817, Francis Synge built the church at Nun's Cross, the interior of which is decorated by a later plaque commemorating his son's 'citizenship in heaven'.

By the end of the 1820s, the household at Glanmore was turning inwards, as if in domestic response to the greater convulsions of Daniel O'Connell's campaign for Catholic Emancipation (finally conceded in 1829). Though the widower took widowed Elizabeth Stewart as his second wife, no children ensued. The first marriage had produced two sons, John (already mentioned), and Edward Millington Synge (later rector of Matlock, in Cheshire). Francis Synge was sixty-nine or seventy when he died in 1831, and thus the Nurse Cullin referred to in a servant's letter written in September 1830 was either responsible for the old man's well-

The devil's glen

being, or simply lived within the penumbra of his domestic charity. After Francis Synge's death, John Synge described his father as 'long an invalid & unable to leave [Glanmore].'[51]

While Francis Synge cut quite a figure in developing Glanmore and purchasing Ely House, his situation at death did not wholly confirm a reputation for that Anglo-Irish cultural dignity so beloved of more recent commentators. A 'Schedule of the Personal Properties of the late Francis Synge as Valued at Glanmore Jan 6 1832 for payment of Probate duties' specified items to the total value of £2,959 of which books accounted for only £50 and arrears of rent £560.[52] While the drawing up of such estimates often involved judicious distortion, so as to reduce exposure to taxation, the image of a gentleman's library is difficult to discern amid the grosser possessions. Synge's books, of course, may have been strategically declared to have been already the possession of his heir. Yet a significant cultural change had occurred between the heyday of the last MP for Swords and that of his son, nicknamed 'Pestalozzi'. In short, the change was evangelical revival.

13

Proprieties

IN THE course of his tramping, JMS met a tramp who declared, 'There are two branches of the Synges in the County Wicklow', who then proceeded to recount fragments of folklore in which, for example, a lady used to ride through Roundwood 'on a curious beast' to visit an uncle of hers in Roundwood Park, and who married a Synge and got her weight in gold as a dowry. This can hardly be the elusive Barbara, unheard of since 1767, and so maybe it was her daughter Elizabeth who married Francis Synge, the builder of Glanmore. In this blend of legend, memory and historical detail, no identification of the lucky lady is established. But the tramp spoke the truth in alluding to two Synge establishments in the county.[1] It is with the second, less renowned western branch that we are concerned now.

Born on 22 April 1756, and living until 1 March 1846, Samuel Synge – ultimately the Venerable Sir Samuel Synge-Hutchinson, 3rd Bart. – enjoyed a long and prosperous life. His early domestic life has already come to our notice, especially in so far as it brought his kinsman into Wicklow as the suppressor of rebellion. Samuel married first Frances Wood, the daughter of Hans Wood, of Rosmead, about a mile north-east of Delvin in County Westmeath. Both the family name and the family seat had undergone obscure changes, Wood of an earlier generation having been 'Widman of Hanstown' with all the Germanic vestiges of foreignness which those names conveyed.[2] Rosmead had only been built c. 1780, and so represented a new social accomplishment in its owners.[3] In the early nineteenth century, the house was further dignified by the erection of a triumphal gate taken from nearby Glananea: now only the abducted gate stands and Rosmead is no more. Not even – in Yeats's words for a more memorable eclipse – 'nettles wave upon a shapeless mound'.[4]

According to the *Complete Baronetage*, the marriage licence was dated 6 June 1787: the date of the actual wedding was – a MS annotation in the printed family tree informs us – 12 June. The new Mrs Synge – whose mother was Frances (née King), sister of the first earl of Kingston – died on 12 June 1788, that is, on the first anniversary of her marriage.[5] The published genealogy records the only child of the union, Frances, who died unmarried in 1801 and left property in Meath [recte, Westmeath?] entailed, as having been born on 28 April 1785, that is, more than two years before her parents married. The entail not only deprived the Synges of any benefit from the Wood estate, it also suggests a desire to make special provision for the daughter.[6] The recent *Burke's Irish Families* unblinkingly confirms her bastard status. In the *Peerage and Baronetage*, however, the account of her birth and death evolves from edition to edition with a pleasing concern to legitimise Frances Synge and preserve her to old age. Thus the valedictory edition of the *Peerage* (1999, vol 2, p. 2785) declares that Frances Synge was born on 28 May 1788, and died unmarried on 4 December 1869. This can be confirmed through a death notice appearing in the *Irish Times* some days later.

What should be noted, however, is – first, a sustained public record (for c. 100 years) of illegitimacy in the case of Samuel Synge's first child; second, a primary source (hitherto used only in part) which provides more information. Though this latter will be shown to confirm the later date for the girl's birth, it cannot dispel all the anxiety revealed in her grandmother's will. Archdeacon Edward Synge duly died on 9 October 1792, scarcely six months after making his will. In the interim, his two-year-old granddaughter Barbara had accidentally drowned on 19 May 1792 at Syngefield. What was to prove a grim decade for Ireland as a whole had begun grimly enough for the Synges. Nevertheless, the archdeacon's widow lost no time in having the will proved by 9 February 1793, and the family evidently continued to regard Syngefield as their principal Irish residence. It was in 1795 that Dr Edward (1753–1818), now head of the family, began to assemble notes on his ancestry, and to correspond on this topic with John Blount of Bridgnorth in Shropshire.[7] In domestic terms, this was a poignant moment, mid-way between the death of his father in 1792 and of his mother at the beginning of 1799. It is impossible to say whether his researches had any bearing on the closely policed terms of her will, which she was clearly advised to make now that, as a widow, she held property in her own right.

The moment was also significant in a wider context. Revolutionary ardour alarmed the landed classes and the pillars of ecclesiastical authority. Whether or not there was any additional security – legal or psychological – to be derived from genealogical inquiry, the new master of Syngefield was taking no chances. A craze for heraldry and coats of arms was seizing insolent elements of the commercial classes. 'Certain of our corporate body', a Dublin newspaper reported caustically, 'talk of ancestors as if they had a regular list of them framed and glazed in the family mansion.'[8] Anti-revolutionary politics invoked pedigree even in municipal squabbles. The decade was running out of control.

When Mrs Sophia Synge came to make her own last will and testament in June 1796, the witnesses included Phineas Bury and Windham Quin, both distinguished names in south midlands landed society. She made provision for two servants named Murphy, and left a sum of money to be divided among the meritorious poor of Birr parish. Of course, Sophia was a Hutchinson before she was a Synge, and her blood-kindred were rising stars of late Georgian Ireland. *Noblesse oblige*, no matter how recent the title. Yet her lengthy, careful and repetitious will is haunted by a number of phrases which recur – 'lawfully begotten' (on three occasions), 'lawfully issuing' (four occasions). These can be read as simply the result of tight legal draftsmanship, just as the name of an investment fund is pedantically repeated in full in 'each and every' instance of her making a bequest from it. But 'the legally begotten', like those 'legally issuing' from a marriage, are invoked for reward in unstated contrast with persons conceived outside marriage, whether their extra-marital status relates simply to time (their parents subsequently marrying) or involves a greater disjunction from technical legitimacy. It is therefore a matter of real significance that Mrs Synge invoked the first phrase in relation to just three, and the second in relation to four, of her five sons.[9]

To recap, her children were Edward (1753–1818), Elizabeth (1755–1801), Samuel (1756–1846), George (1757–1806? see appendix below), Robert (1759–1804) and Francis (1761–1831). Only the eldest had not been married by 1796 when Mrs Synge made her will, and Samuel was by then a widower. Edward was over forty, and his bachelor status may have been deemed permanent. Nevertheless, his expectations were virtually guaranteed by the principle of *primo geniture* and – additionally – by the operation of entails which prevented wayward testators from leaving property to whomever they might like. Thus the non-appearance of the phrase 'the Son and Sons of the Body of my said Son [Edward] lawfully begotten' – where parallel phrases naming George, Robert and Francis (but not Samuel) did appear – is at least explicable in terms of Edward's being the eldest of the family (and unlikely ever to marry). Its non-appearance in relation to Samuel – who, additionally, is excluded from clauses about offspring 'lawfully issuing' – is another matter.

All of Sophia Synge's children benefited under the will, together with the husband of her only daughter, the wives of three sons (one other being a bachelor, and yet one other being a widower), and several grandchildren, not to mention lesser beneficiaries. But there is a unique passage in relation to her second son Samuel (the widower), without parallel in her arrangements for others in the family:

> I give and bequeath to my second son Samuel Synge three hundred Pounds Nominal Principal Stock part of the said Stock which I have in the said English funds called Consolidated three per cent Annuities and also two hundred Pounds nominal Principal Stock part of said Stock which I have in the said funds to my Granddaughter ——— Daughter Frances Synge the only Daughter of my said Son Samuel and they may rest assured that my affection and attachment to them is as strong to any other of my Children and GrandChildren. And I would have made greater Provision for them, but that they have been amply

provided for by my most affectionate and fond father Samuel Hutchinson formerly Bishop of Killala. And I give the Picture of my dear Brother Sir Francis Hutchinson Bart which he sent me from Italy unto my said Son Samuel and because [?] my Eldest Son Edward Synge is indebted to me in the Sum of Three Thousand Pounds which is secured to me by three Bonds and Warrants of my said Son Edward and I have not entered Judgment on those Bonds.[10]

Perhaps the first point to clarify is the earlier provision by the bishop of Killala. Samuel Hutchinson had died in 1780, thus any benefit to a grandchild born five years later could only come through a Remainder clause or, generically by means of a Trust. That is to say, the bishop – whose will has not been traced – may have left a bequest for life to Samuel Synge, with a remainder to the latter's child or children, or alternatively, could have appointed trustees in whom the benefit was entrusted until the birth of a qualifying beneficiary. But Frances Synge (born 28 May 1788) cannot have been named in the will. And unless the bishop specified a bequest of this kind to the first-born of Samuel Synge – an unlikely exclusivity – then the benefit would not have been solely Frances Synge's. Nor was Samuel Synge the only grandson whom the testator might have decided to benefit.

There is, therefore, good reason to believe that Sophia's provision for the widower Samuel Synge and his daughter amounted to little more than an alibi for not leaving them anything. The English funds feature in her will principally as a source from which payments would be made to daughters-in-law and grandchildren – sums of £100 nominal value, in most cases. But in the codicil to the will, added in June 1798 when affairs in Ireland stood in a dire state, Mrs Synge bequeathed a further £500 of Stock to Charles and Francis Synge (sons of George Synge); when 'new' property was being disposed of, there was no additional benefit for either Samuel or his daughter.

It is true that Edward, the eldest son, does not emerge from a reading of the will with his reputation unstained. While the principal properties are duly left to him, his mother has gone out of her way publicly to record an unpaid debt, and to divert from his inheritance a family portrait which he might have expected to have acquired with the contents of Syngefield. Such a gesture may have been designed to displease both loser and winner: Samuel, to whom the painting was redirected, may well have seen this as a further mute declaration of where he must look for his future prosperity. Already named in Sir Francis Hutchinson's baronetcy as virtually certain to inherit that dignity, he might as well await the inheritance of Castle Sallagh (in County Wicklow) and the bulk of the baronet's property also. The codicil also adds minor injury to Edward's lot, for in it his mother willed to her daughter Elizabeth 'all the furniture of the Bow Chambers she inhabited in Syngefield and also of the Bow Chamber she inhabited at No. 99 Stephens Green [Dublin] also all the Chintz, Cotton or Calico furniture in said house No. 99 …' These may been negligible diminishments of Edward's inheritance, but they

Proprieties

underline the absence of both the eldest and second eldest son from their mother's final adjustment of her will.

Far more substantial was the redirection of the lands in County Meath. In her will, Sophia Synge had declared that

> Whereas I am intitled under the will of my late dear husband to the reversion in for expectant upon my second Son Samuel Synge without issue male of his Body of and in certain part or parts in the lands of Mornington, Colpe and Kiltrough situate in the County of Meath, now my will is and I so hereby give devise and bequeath the said reversion in this and all my Estate and Interest in the said Lands of Mornington, Colpe and Kiltrough in the County of Meath unto Robert French of the City of Dublin Esquire and his heirs and assins in trust for and to the uses and interests and purposes herein after mentioned expressed and declared of and [word illegible] to the same, that is to say, to the use and [word illegible] of my third Son George Synge ...[11]

There then follows a lengthy series of provisions and precautions – including the repeated emphasis on lawful begetting and lawful issue – whereby three other sons (Robert, Francis and finally Edward, the eldest) are entitled in turn to the inheritance in default. But Samuel nowhere features in this complicated disposal of the Meath lands by his mother.

Other valuable properties lay in County Clare, which had come to the family through its service in the dioceses of Killaloe and Kilfenora. These were left in several lots to Francis, George and Robert Synge, again without any provisions for Edward (who, of course, had already been acknowledged as inheriting Syngefield) or Samuel. Sophia Synge's investments in the funds was evidently substantial, and her disposal of these acknowledged her husband's opinion of various family members:

> Whereas my late dear husband did by his Will bequeath to my granddaughter Elizabeth Synge the Eldest Daughter of my said Son Robert the Sum of one thousand Pounds to be paid to her out of his Stock in the Bank of Ireland which Sum now remains in that fund for her and my said Husband did always recommend my said Granddaughter very particularly to me now on account of such Recommendation and also from my own strong Affection I do give & bequeath to my said GrandDaughter Elizabeth Synge five hundred Pounds nominal Principal Stock part of the Stock which I have in the said English funds called Consolidated three per Cent Annuities. And I give and bequeath to her Sister Sophia Helena Maria Synge the second Daughter of my said Son Robert Synge five hundred Pounds nominal Principal Stock part of the said Stock which I have in the said English funds called Consolidated three per cent Annuities.

Only then did Samuel and his daughter learn of their smaller allocations. There had been no reference to 'poor Baba' who had been so touchingly recommended to the testatrix.

Such documents are not of interest solely for their bequests. They also indicate nuances of family *mores* and practices which are otherwise difficult to document. For example, Archdeacon Edward Synge had begun his will commiting his soul 'in the hand of God, my body when it is beyond a Doubt that I am dead I order to be buried with the greatest privacy ...' Four years later, his widow had been more explicit in her religious faith – 'my soul I commit into the hands of God trusting in the merits of our saviour Jesus Christ for eternal Salvation, my Body I desire may be buried as near my late lord and husband as possible in the same private way he was buried'. The difference may simply represent a woman's sensibility over a masterful cleric's. It may, additionally, indicate a degree of intensified protestant piety, even in one of the worldly Hutchinson clan. Both wills were made in Ireland, both were witnessed by (*inter alia*) John or Jonathan Darby of Leap Castle, King's County. A few years later, the wife of John Darby (1751–1834) gave birth to a son, John Nelson Darby (1800–1882), with whom John Synge collaborated in the founding of what became the Plymouth Brethren.[12]

On 9 December 1798, Sophia Synge suffered severe burns when her clothes were selt alight by a spark as she sat reading in her house at Bath. Three days later, her son Robert and daughter-in-law Peggy (Wolfe) called to see her, returning to Clifton for dinner. From this last detail, the extremity of the injuries caused may perhaps be judged. The old woman lingered into the new year but her death on 24 January 1799 was duly noted in her son Robert's diary.[13] On the last day of the month her wish to be buried at Birr was granted, the body shipped out of the little Avonmouth port of Pill *en route* for the Irish midlands.

The desire to return to Ireland did not take the form of living there in every case. Robert, when he was raised to the baronetcy of the United Kingdom, styled himself Synge of Kiltrough, part of the Meath property his mother had so carefully disposed of, but he died in London and was buried in St James. George remained in King's County, settled at Rathmore with his Mac Donnell wife: their son, Charles, had a distinguished military career during the Peninsular War and subsequently established the Mount Callan branch of the family in County Clare. Sophia's eldest son, Dr Edward, also stayed in King's County, as bachelor master of Syngefield.

Through the several activities of earlier Hatches and Hutchinsons, both Samuel and Francis Synge (sometime MP for Swords) found themselves established in Wicklow. On 3 March 1801, Samuel married for a second time, the bride being his first cousin and his brother's sister-in-law, Dorothy Hatch. But if there was a quickening of evangelical conscience in the rhetoric and terms of Sophia Synge's will, the effects are to be sought less in her ordained sons' lives than in the family of Francis Synge MP. These became the Synges of Glanmore.

Part IV

AFFAIRS WITH THE MOON

JOHN SYNGE 1788–1845

14

How Pestalozzi reached Wicklow

I had sixty schoolchildren on roll when I went there. I had thirty-five when I left. Last year I heard they were reduced to eleven, and five of those were all one family. No wonder the county is full of ruins. You come on them in scores on scores, with, maybe, a tree growing out of the hearth, and the marks of the ridges they ploughed, still there, now smooth with grass. (*O'Faolain*)

TRAVELS IN LATIN EUROPE

JOHN Synge, grandfather of the dramatist, was born in Grafton Street, Dublin, in 1788. His parents were in the process of acquiring the Roundwood property from John Hatch, but continued to regard Syngefield as the family headquarters. When the boy was five-and-a-half years old, he was placed in Mr Bonafous's school at Portarlington, a Huguenot settlement lying between Syngefield and Dublin. By the following summer, if not earlier, the pupils included one Robert French whom John Synge later will meet in Portugal and whose male kinsmen played a major role as advisers on legal matters. By November 1794, Robert Synge had placed his own son in the same school, a respectable preparatory establishment but hardly the forcing ground of aristocracy. The Synges were training their heirs for professional rather than leisured futures.[1]

Having enrolled as an undergraduate at Trinity College, Dublin, on 30 April 1805, he transferred to Magdalen College, Oxford, in 1807, where his uncle Edward had acquired his DD somewhat earlier. His parents spent part of the summer at Buxton in Derbyshire, a town frequented by well-to-do invalids. By 1809, his mother (Elizabeth Synge, née Hatch) was in need of more rigorous medical attention, and she travelled from Dublin to London at the end of February. Husband and son arrived on 14 May, leaving on 7 June with Elizabeth now under the care of Mr Clyne. By mid-August, there was evidently no point in her remaining in the capital. When 'dear Mrs Francis Synge left town on her way home', she was making her last cross-channel journey, to land at Skerries (as the winds determined) on the wrong side of Dublin for Wicklow.[2]

How Pestalozzi reached Wicklow

Little survives to document this phase of the family's history, a circumstance which throws two isolated letters into high relief. During her last London weeks, Mrs Synge wrote from Bryanston Street to John, who was at home in Glanmore. This frank motherly epistle has been preserved alongside a draft letter evidently from the son, addressed at different moments to his father and to his mother, but at yet other moments to 'my father's best friend'. The acknowledged, but scarcely specified, topic was matrimony. As John Synge was then just turned twenty-one, parental approval was important. And as the mature John Synge will be quietly celebrated for pious good works, it is striking that confession (of a sort) took first place in his preliminary announcement.

'[A]n unfortunate business that happened some time since which caused so much uneasiness to you & my mother, was only one of those rash effusions my Conduct has hitherto been so subject to. & the letters it gave rise to were written merely to escape the character of inconsistency & without a thought of ever fulfilling their purport ...' Acknowledging his father's liberality in the past, the youth admitted that 'without your assistance in the way of property I am unfitted for such a step', from which point another gauche change of tack brought him to name his intended bride. 'The object is no other than the amiable Fanny whom I have for three years in silence compared with every person I met ...'[3] At eighteen, it seems, John Synge had met his match. In the event, of course, he will marry Isabella Hamilton as his first wife, and only in the 1830s did he marry (second) Frances Steele, the sister of his brother's wife.

If Mrs Synge's letter was a response to the final version of the draft just quoted, it showed a greater degree of cunning and humane understanding. Initially, young John at Glanmore was reassured about some minor plans involving himself and a friend, possibly William Russell of Magdalen who subsequently took holy orders.[4] Next, a letter from Aunt Dolly – Dorothy Hatch, wife of Archdeacon Samuel Synge [-Hutchinson] – was mentioned, together with remarks about George Synge's son, Francis – 'grown fat as a pig'. As for Charles Synge, even the sight of him disturbed his aunt – 'many & various were the Ideas ... that agitated me not a little'. Her fears arose from a premonition that both nephews would end up in the army; 'what else can they do when they are put into such a line of Acquaintances for I cannot say friends; when they are thrown into the highest most dissipated & Extravagant circles ... without any true & real ballast: ... what can their blinded parents expect but that they will rush forward into whatever line will enable them to pursue those dear but too false phantasms of what is called pleasure'. While the army would continue in its profligate ways for well over a century, the experience of Waterloo was to move many of that generation towards extravagant religion, the second coming of Napoleon prompting thoughts of Armageddon. Among the Synges, Charles stuck to his guns, while John pursued an erratic path.

Of this motherly epistle, the recipient hardly needed to read further, yet

Affairs with the moon

doubtless did so. He was entreated 'to call common Sense & reason, Religion & Duty into Council' and to reflect how unlikely he was to succeed either with [the young woman's name is simply a blank] or her father. 'They have never seen any Steadiness or [sic] Conduct in your Character to give either of them an Opinion of you such as wd warrant the consent or Approbation of either ...'[5] This sounds like the standard maternal response to young love, especially at a time when romantic freedom of choice was constrained by a host of conventions. But was there any reason why the young woman's name could not be repeated in Mrs Synge's otherwise down-to-earth reply to her son? Could 'the amiable Fanny' be Cousin Fanny (daughter of Archdeacon Samuel Synge and his late wife, Frances, née Wood) who was about to celebrate her twenty-first birthday a month later? The familiar practice of marriage between first cousins could not be condemned on principle – after all, John's parents were of this sort – but a second union in two generations was scarcely good form even among the Irish gentry where kissing cousins flourished.

John Synge finished in Oxford without marrying his Fanny or anyone else. His mother's advice had been conveyed amid alarms as to the moral sense of many in the extended family. Charles and Francis, sons of George Synge (one of the 'blinded parents'), had been particular beneficiaries under their grandmother's will; George's brother Samuel was patiently waiting for the death of Sir James Hutchinson (2nd Bart.). The family, seen from a sickbed in a fashionable part of London, appeared to be on the turn into godless ways. Yet Mrs Elizabeth Synge's terms of rebuke and landmarks of virtue were decidedly eighteenth-century – reason and religion sat in council with common sense. If her father had tightened his fist on whichever version of Sam M'Cracken's last will best served the Hatch interest, he had not indulged in pretensions to the aristocratic style.

Her husband, in contrast, was building in Wicklow as no non-clerical Synge had ever dared to do, and reaping a rich reward in Bride Street from property once belonging to Saint Sepulchre. Now her son was displaying the obverse side of this plenty – keen to marry on the basis of passion and to establish a household without personal substance. Second generation prodigality was in danger of destroying her inheritance. Her co-heir sister had not married until after their father John Hatch's death, and then she too married a cousin with great expectations of his own. For Elizabeth the familiar protestant ethic of delayed gratification had an especial importance. If her elder son were to persist in such folly as his ambition to marry some amiable Fanny, then material reserves would be wasted in immaterial display, whether of sexual love or Gothic ornamentation. Before she could worry further, Mrs Synge died on 31 July 1810. She was buried at Glenealy, near but not on her husband's estate, in a grave which I have been unable to locate. Perhaps nothing should be read into the place of interment, as the old graveyard at Killiskey was in poor condition and its successor at Nun's Cross not yet laid out. There

How Pestalozzi reached Wicklow

is something emblematical in the departure of Elizabeth Hatch, Mrs Francis Synge, from this earth. She was only in her mid-forties, yet her attachment to the values of a former age rings ambiguous amid the clamours of anti-revolutionary war.

Revolution had not ended in 1798. When the Revd Richard Wolfe had visited the Robert Synges at Tunbridge Wells in April–May 1803, he carelessly lost a watch-chain and seals, the recovery of which cost his hosts a guinea. Three months later, both the guest and his uncle, Kilwarden, were dead. Yet private hopes revived. In June 1809, Marianne Wolfe (1776–), who had been with her father and cousin when they were murdered, married the son of Dr Shute who had treated Sir Robert for piles. Less complacently, the widow recorded in her diary that she had received a 'letter dated Sept 24 1813 from Dublin that mentioned poor Arthur Wolfe's widow to have got a daughter'.[6] By then, John Synge's mother was three years dead; his father continued active, having embroiled his sister-in-law Peggy in a lawsuit which the Irish Chancellor only resolved in December 1813, remarrying and commencing a second family.

John Synge's graduation from Oxford and his mother's death dominated the year 1810. His Hatch attachments to the city of Dublin were all but vanished, and his father could afford to send him on a wartime version of the Grand Tour. The mood in which young Synge explored the Catholic kingdoms of Portugal and Spain allowed for a degree of cheerful socialising – the opera, several balls and other entertainments. There were also visits to convents and monasteries, hardly evidence of the protestant fears nurtured in so much of Anglo-Ireland. From the frequency with which his name recurs in John Synge's journal, it is clear that Dublin-born Arthur Wellesley was a leading attraction: the future 'iron duke' had entered Madrid in August 1812, and was now busy stimulating Portugal's greater participation in the Iberian campaign against Napoleon. More familiarly, Cousin Charles had been invalided home, arriving in London on 21 September 1812, to recover from a severe thigh wound.

Synge landed at the Portuguese capital on 14 December. Two days later, he 'dined with Marshal Beresford & went at night to the Convent of St Dominick & passed the Evening with Padre Fernando Fortez'. The next evening's dinner was concelebrated with Mrs Jeffreys. On 18 December, the party was ready to enjoy the pleasures of the city, intending to go to the opera 'but by an accident lost our carriage'. The private account of his travels is not extensive, nor does it stray much beyond observations on the scenery, the social life and the comfortably distant effects of the war. Lisbon and Porto earn their place in his notes, with repeated tributes to the countryside, its vineyards and orange groves. On Christmas Eve 1812, he 'went to Mass at the Chapel Royal Campo St Anna where the music was divine'. Then next day the nativity of Christ was duly celebrated at 'a crowded Congregation of Protestants at the Ambassadors' in Lisbon followed by dinner with Robert French, a familiar compatriot through the school at

Portarlington and the elder French's services to the family as legal adviser. Pastimes were various – the performance of a guitar professor, a wretched English play, and a visit to the Irish convent at Belem. 'The Lady Abbess & two sisters we saw all came from Co Galway, the former 36 years in Lisbon.'[7]

By the end of March, Synge and his fellow travellers were in Coimbra, Portugal's ancient university town. Further north, near the cathedral town of Braga, he became absorbed in archaeology. 'These [mile]stones & the Roman Road in its Neighbourhood, together with the remains of a temple of Isis prove the place to have been of great consequence during the Roman occupation of this country.' His journal then continues in a tone which defies classification:

> A temple of Christian Idolatry next attracted our attention N S da Monte a splendid Church & a series of temples in succession as we mounted a long flight of stairs each temple representing a portion of our Saviour's history in figures as large as the life but unfortunately dressed in Modern Portuguese Costume. On our return we visited the Bishop of Braga & being late for another splendid entertainment of our host's he seemed *rudely* hurt; & the rest of the evening was passed in Bourgeois Society of this Place.[8]

There is little here to announce the virtual godfather of Plymouth Brethrenism, though this was to be the role Synge played nearly twenty years later. 'Christian Idolatry' might be a jibe at ostentatious Popery, yet the journal elsewhere is relaxed, even affable, in its description of Catholic churches and ecclesiastics. Though the Braga narrative is not crystal clear, it seems that a prolonged visit to the local bishop delayed the party from reaching their host on time. Who this host was deserves more than a moment's consideration.

If Wellington had inspired Synge to sail from England, the early days in Portugal were supervised by a compatriot of both soldier and traveller. William Carr Beresford (1768–1854) had enjoyed a remarkable career, having entered the military school at Strasburg before the French Revolution, and then fought in the British Army in Canada, Corsica, Egypt, India and South America. After the embarrassment of being taken prisoner in Buenos Aires, he rehabilitated himself through service in the Portuguese army, and it is as Marshal Beresford that he features in the opening pages of John Synge's journal. At home in Ireland, he was better known as the bastard son of the marquis of Waterford.

In the same entourage, the 'Mrs Jeffreys' can safely be identified as Arabella, the widow of James St John Jeffreys (d. 1796), the entrepreneurial owner of Blarney Castle, near Cork. The castle was destroyed by fire in 1799, a factor which may have encouraged both Arabella's travels and her incorporation into a comic ballad, 'The Groves of Blarney', written by the Dublin bookseller, Richard Milliken. She was a sister of the powerful earl of Clare, John Fitzgibbon (1749–1802), whom Synge's parents had driven down to see at Newtownmountkennedy

How Pestalozzi reached Wicklow

when they were first establishing the family name in Wicklow. In the 1780s Fitzgibbon had been attorney-general, his sister Arabella a presumed 'gentry' sponsor of the illegal Whiteboys.⁹ Less rake-hellish Elizabeth, another of the Fitzgibbon girls, had in 1767 married William Beresford, a legitimate member of that family and later archbishop of Tuam. Marianne Jeffreys had married George Frederick Nugent in 1784, who became earl of Westmeath in 1792. The decade in which John Hatch died an obscure commoner of unknown fortune was rich in opportunities.

Compared with these, the Marshal and Mrs Jeffreys walked somewhat on the wild side. Whatever his standing in wartime Portugal, William Carr Beresford was subsequently described by a great military historian as having 'all the scurrility that bad taste and mortified vanity could suggest ... coupled ... with such fulsome adulation of [him]self, that even in a dependent's mouth it would have been sickening'.¹⁰ Beresford's rude behaviour towards his young fellow-countrymen contributed a mite to John Synge's moral education.

This did not spoil the fun immediately available. Having witnessed Spanish dancing 'by one of the Marchioness's sisters whose figure face & manner reminded me of A. G.', John Synge advanced along a beautiful road to Monforte,

> where is a Moorish Castle on a height & close beside it a Convt of St Vicente. We received a billet in the house of Don Ramont Balcarcel whose Lady was very intelligent and civil [and who] showed me all the Curiosities of the Place & gave me introductions both to St Estaban & Orense. In the evening I went to see the College of the Jesuits now a school. A magnificent pile of Building outside, & within [there is] a stone staircase of large dimensions & arched on a peculiar construction [which] demands attention. Also an Image of our Sav. on the Cross of one Stone as large as life where the veins & sandals are natural in the stone ... We passed the Evening in the room of one of the Daughters about 17 who was indisposed & in bed yet joined in the society & was curious in her enquiries about us.¹¹

While his Spanish and Portuguese experiences mixed education with entertainment, observations on farming and young ladies' demeanour, they little prepared John Synge for the latter stage of his European tour. Part of the difficulty in piecing together his development lies in the manner his journal breaks off, perhaps indicating that the amusements of the war zone had concluded in a different spirit. As it is, we might as well imagine him travelling by magic carpet from Portugal to Switzerland, from the occasional company of hardened soldiers to the intimacy of an obscure Alpine academy.

The sketch books which John Synge compiled during his travels provide a few additional details. A view of the Tagus and part of Buenos Aires, dated 23 January 1813, places him in a garret accommodation at no. 19 Rua Sacramenta de Lapa. The motive behind his travels is clear in a subsequent sketch of the grave of Colonel Lake, close to the point where Wellington (then Sir Arthur Wellesley) had first got to grips with the French. By April he was at Oporto, and by May at Compostella. The drawings in the first volume are strong if simple; they grab the landscape with much the same feeling for locality as evinced by the Iron Duke. The month of May initiates a softer and more tentative approach, pictures which are largely undated and untitled to the point where one of them is captioned 'possibly the Estrella Mountains'. The third item in this second album includes a little figure of a man in a hat with sketching-pad: we may be in touch with the artist in embryo. But the next batch of pictures record his Spanish as distinct from Portuguese impressions, nondescript apart from some powerful Toledo scenes.[12]

Asturias, Burgos, San Sebastian, Toledo – a busy itinerary began in August and seems to have occupied Synge until well into 1814, the year of Napoleon's abdication and Wellington's triumphant arrival in Paris (March). The military events are no longer intertwined with the traveller's progress which, strikingly, does not take him into France. The opening (undated) scene in his next album shows 'The Lazaretto & Island of Nisita where Quarantine is performed in the Bay of Naples' strongly suggests that he made his way by sea from Spain to Italy. By the same token, there was no preordained destination in Switzerland. First, Rome and Pompeii claimed his attention, then Bologna and finally the northern lakes. Synge's views of the Eternal City are line drawings, dominated by the dome of Saint Peter's Basilica, while Pompeii appears to have inspired a very limited enthusiasm. By September, however, the magnificent 'chateau' of the Borromeo family on Lake Maggiore had captured his imagination, detaining him just south of the Swiss border. Images of it appear in two albums, including the smaller blue-paper book which was probably used for quick observations on the road.

For the first time, non-landscape material also occurs – a few heads, a woman in traditional dress, studies of sculpture and armour. The isolation of these detailed but contextless drawings invites conjecture, arising as they do in a period (mid-September 1814 onwards) for which no surviving journal provides a commentary. The interest in Borromean properties may have been ignited by a dramatic encounter with the landscape itself. Or it may have involved some awareness of the great Carlo Borromeo (1538–1584), a reforming archbishop of Milan, cardinal and – after his death – saint. In architectural design, liturgy and theology, he had not only played a major role in the Counter-Reformation but influenced later, nineteenth-century religious inquirers in Germany and the United Kingdom.[13] This occurred within a broad phenomenon of spiritual renewal in which Synge participated under what have been generally regarded as local Irish and protestant influences. Nothing suggests a concern with idolatry, whether Christian or Pompeian. The north Italian sketchbook does little to illuminate the artist's mind in the days or weeks prior to his arrival at Pestalozzi's school at Yverdon, though one of the incidental drawings – a hand, holding a small snake as if it were a pen, and with two or three frogs sitting on it – cries out for some explanation.

How Pestalozzi reached Wicklow

These are the images (see p. 15) which John Synge traced before passing over the frontier into what had briefly and recently been the Helvetian Republic.

ENIGMAS AND VOCATIONS

John Synge's short residence in the Alpine valleys did not change the course of history, even in County Wicklow. His experiences, however, touched on many themes which were to arise in Ireland in the decade and a half which followed his return to Ireland, themes which have received scant attention from historians of the nation, and less from Postmodern Theory. In regard to neglect of Synge personally, we have to bear in mind the extent which the child (or rather grandchild) is father to the man – the interests of JMS's early biographers and critics obliged them strictly to limit their account of his paternal grandfather. The prophet whom John Synge chose to follow in 1814 only compounded the problem.

Johann Heinrich Pestalozzi (1746–1827) is not a name which springs to the minds even of those who deplore Harry Lime's slander on Swiss culture. Yet the educationalist of Yverdon more than once attracted the attention of Walter Benjamin as he assembled his never-finished 'Arcades Project', that study of nineteenth-century Paris which was intended to abolish schisms between philosophy and excavation, history and materialism. It is in keeping with Benjamin's fondness of marginalia, of justified obscurity, and of a theological stratum within his heterodox Marxism, that he should share Pestalozzi with John Synge of Glanmore, of whose creativity little now survives but a sundial in a New York apartment. Time's revenge, perhaps.

Benjamin associated Pestalozzi with Charles Fourier (1772–1837), the French social theorist who advocated a reform of society based on co-operatives. It was not that Fourier approved of Pestalozzi, at least not for long. Benjamin records the matter as a passing, yet significant, moment in the (or not-to-be) history of Paris:

> In *Le Nouveau Monde industriel*, Fourier's rancor against Pestalozzi is very evident. He says he took up Pestalozzi's 'intuitive method' in his *Traité de l'association domestique-agricole* of 1822 because of the great success it had had with the public. Lacking such popular success, it would have created an unfavorable impression on its readers. Of Yverdon he recounts, at best, tales of scandal calculated to prove that institutions of harmony cannot be introduced with impunity into civilization.[14]

In a more skeletal outline of themes for the project, Benjamin juxtaposed 'Fourier's archaic idyll: the child of nature as consumer' with 'Pestalozzi's modern utopia: the bourgeois as producer'. Later, in the same sketches, he lists Pestalozzi (between Jean Paul and Fourier) after the phrase – 'Materialist tendencies in the bourgeoisie'.[15] This is not a line of development in which we will find John Synge following. Nevertheless, Benjamin's occasional comments help to distinguish the phases and passing fancies of Synge's intellectual development, especially in relation to his commitment to education. In his essay on Goethe, Benjamin had attributed some of the most significant changes of emphasis occurring in the second of the Wilhelm Meister novels to a programme of reading which included the Sage of Yverdon. In the *Wander Years* (he argued), it is typical 'that farming is held to be obligatory, whereas instruction in the dead languages goes unmentioned. The "humanists" of *Wilhelm Meister's Apprenticeship* have all turned into artisans: Wilhelm is a surgeon, Jarno a mining engineer, Philine a seamstress. Goethe took over the idea of vocational education from Pestalozzi.'[16] In Synge's case the dead languages come to life, even in remotest County Wicklow.

In the decisive change of intellectual focus between Goethe's two Wilhelm Meister novels, one can read a concentrated and contradictory account of Enlightenment and its fate in post-revolutionary Europe. Neglected themes become audible here. For, closer to home (if the concept is viable for this period), there is a parallel shift in the fiction of Maria Edgeworth (1767–1849) between the coded classico-utilitarianism of her *Ennui* (1804) and the professionalism approvingly – and apprehensively – explored in *Patronage* (1814). Edgeworth's literary influence will prove to be unexpectedly diverse, even Gothic. In life, the Edgeworths proved not averse to the benefits of Lord Grey's patronage a few years after the novel's completion.[17] The treatment of revolution in the two works is exemplary, however. That is, the earlier presents local insurrectionary violence as a pretext through which the *ennui*sed and Anglicised landlord will duly discover an unsuspected local (but conservative) identity, while the later secretes the already-effected influence of covert insurrection in the ability of a 'great minister of state' or 'European statesman' to act as an autonomous human subject, as his own master. In *Ennui* (and more subtly in *The Absentee*, 1812), a form of enlightened conversion is narrated, with suitable modifications and admonitory disclaimers; in *Patronage*, professional training for what Max Weber will term secular vocation is earnestly, but not always convincingly recommended.

While the Synges have remained the focal point for discussion of Pestalozzi's Irish influence, there was earlier interest among the protean Edgeworths. A family party touring in Europe during the brief peace of 1803 visited Paris where Pestalozzi was staying as a representative of the Helvetic Republic, a Napoleonic creation. Mrs Frances Anne Edgeworth despatched home an account of Maria and her father listening to the Swiss educationalist for two hours, an event which signifies the nature of Edgeworth *père*'s political contacts as well as his daughter's involvement in pedagogic inquiry.[18]

The Synges of this period are the unsung non-heroes of Edgeworthian fiction, neither aristocrats nor bourgeois. Like Mrs Raffarty in *The Absentee*, Francis Synge (MP) builds a Gothic home in County Wicklow and – like Mrs Raffarty's prototype in 'real life' – shuffles between worldly ostentation and investment in the life to come. In Francis Synge's son John (of whom we treat in this chapter) – one of the youngest beneficiaries under Sophia Synge's will – a visit to the *welthistorische* battlefields of the Peninsula was combined with a sojourn at Yverdon. Contradiction had been rife during these tumultuous years, with R. L. Edgeworth (1744–1817) voting against the Union alongside Francis Synge, the one basing his decision on ethics rather than politics, and the other keeping his counsel as secret as his bank account. Who could find heroes in this age of flagrant compromise?[19]

But if Fourier had been disappointed in Pestalozzi's adaptability to another's cause, Benjamin could privately laud the Switzer's dogged spirit. Describing 'brief episodes of writing and reading' at the beginning of the 1930s, Benjamin reported how he had come across 'one of the most splendid and moving *documents humains* ... the life of Pestalozzi as seen through the eyes of people who knew him personally. It is surely difficult to speak about bourgeois education without calling this physiogamy to mind. I was told that almost nothing of it is evident in his famous pedagogical novels; on the contrary, everything about it is evident in his personal impact and his misfortune – he compared himself to Job at the end of his life.'[20] It is no accident that the recipient of this tribute was living in Palestine at the time, for a right understanding of Jewish history and the harmonious relationship of Judaism and Christianity lay at the heart of much that links Pestalozzi, his religious preoccupations and the Messianic-Marxist Benjamin.

Much that Pestalozzi advocated and practised has come down to the present through the better-known Friedrich Fröbel (1782–1852) who worked at Yverdon from 1808 to 1810. Child-centred education is now virtually a cliché. In the latter half of the eighteenth century, however, such notions were regarded as the dangerous legacy of Jean-Jacques Rousseau (1712–1778) and his belief that everything was good when it left the Creator's hands, whereas everything degenerated in the hands of man. In the case of Pestalozzi, the social and political context in which he grew up – that of Zurich – is at least as important as any externally acquired philosophical system. Swiss democracy had attrified into an oligarchy of powerful families who, with the Zwinglian church, imposed a rigid code of behaviour in thought, word and deed. One feature of Swiss society in the middle of the eighteenth century strikingly resembled that of Ireland; 'the country people were not even interested in the improvement of the land, for an increase in production would have meant higher dues to their landlords'.[21]

Rather than stress the influence of Rousseau and his *soi-disant* rallying cry, 'Back to Nature!', Kate Silber has discerned an unlikely alliance of religious Pietism and philosophical Enlightenment as the moving force in these circles. These are positions which overlap at certain points in Irish intellectual life also. And, in an aside which would have pleased Benjamin, she notes the growth of cotton manufacture as an economic factor, for it shifted attention towards the potential value of land and so away from the traditional merchant activities which underwrote Swiss prosperity.

Literature played an important mediating role in these negotiations between economics and religion. It was English periodicals such as Addision's *Spectator* which provided a model for Zurich's 'Moral Weeklies'. In the contest between continental and English influences, the latter won out. If the visiting German poet, F. G. Klopstock (1724–1803) wrote an ode celebrating Lake Zurich, and elsewhere imitated Milton's protestant epics, his Pietistic training allowed for a more open acknowledgement of human nature, the pleasures of female company, than the church of his hosts permitted. The cults of *Sturm-und-Drang* and of Sentimentalism caught on in Swiss writing, just as Physiocrat doctrines challenged established Mercantalist practices. Nature, in various senses of the word, unsettled Cultivation.

The particular social conjunction in which his family found themselves is also an active factor in the development of (Johann) Heinrich Pestalozzi's ideas. Of Italian origins, they possessed the right of election to Zurich's city council, but had not for generations taken any active part in politics. His mother's family included several doctors and surgeons, but they were of rural stock and possessed no civic rights. To complete a pattern of disadvantage, Johann Baptist Pestalozzi (an unsuccessful surgeon turned modest town clerk) died when his son was only five years old. Though women in the boy's early life were devoted and loving, he grew up in lonely seclusion from other children, a factor partly resulting from economic difficulties at odds with the family's inherited status. Only in the village where his grandfather was pastor did he find a sense of community, which also prompted questions about the contrast between town and country, rich and poor, nature and artifice.

Pestalozzi became known for the series of educational establishments which he set up at Gut Neuhof, Burgdorf, and from 1804 to 1825 at Yverdon. He wrote and published fictional and didactic works, interested himself in philosophical, political and psychological matters, but never constructed a system of his own. The extent of his moral radicalism can be judged from his sympathetic attitude to the 'fallen woman' issue. An unmarried mother, even an infanticide, deserved to be considered as a victim and not as a malefactor.[22] *Lienhard und Gertrud. Ein Buch für das Volk* (1781) began as a novel – much of it in dialogue – about a woman whose drunken husband has got into debt. The social plot – which transmits her complaint above the estate steward to the landowner who in due course unmasks the corrupt steward – resembles Maria Edgeworth's fiction in several regards. Pestalozzi's subsequent additions to the book reduced its literary qualities while extending its sociological range. As an educationalist, he was significant in stressing the role of the mother, encouraging the innate abilities of children (including disadvantaged children), and developing methods of teaching and learning which were not coercive or mechanical. His reputation spread less through channels of formal communication such as book publication or lecturing than through the testimony of those who had met him.

Fichte as well as Goethe acknowledged a debt to him. At the end of the nineteenth century, professional educators and others (including J. A. Green) reopened the debate about Pestalozzi's contribution to the science of teaching. Nor was the family lost without trace. In the year of JMS's departure from Paris, the Société des Étudiants Protestants recorded the admission of Carl Pestalozzi. By 1903, Synge is very unlikely to have had any lingering connection with the group to which he had affiliated on first arrival in the French capital, yet the occurrence of a distinguished and unusual Swiss name doubtless caused a ripple among the still-faithful membership.

VARIETIES OF PROGRESSIVE UNIONISM

All of this may indicate the aptness of the older John Synge's discovery of Pestalozzi. Yet quite how he became interested is difficult now to establish, for the (surviving) journals which he kept on his continental tour break off before he arrives at Yverdon late in 1814. Certainly there were earlier and sustained links between Ireland and the Swiss reforming educational institutes. In Paris during April 1820, Maria Edgeworth 'talked much at dinner of Pestalozzi and German literature'. When they met a few months later in Switzerland, each recognised the other from 1803: he was 'the same wild-looking black monkey sort of german [sic] whom we saw at Mme Gautier's'. She also acknowledged how aged and infirm he had become. 'He does not gesticulate now or struggle to explain with arms, legs, chin, jaws and eyebrows as he used to do.'[23] John Synge's conversion was to a master in the declining phase of his career.

The Lecky family was also in contact and, through an intermediary, the Dublin doctor Charles Edward Henry Orpen (1791–1856).[24] While Orpen became a medical philanthropist of considerable reputation in his own right, the elevated if now forgotten figure of John Vesey (1771–1855, 2nd viscount de Vesci) was more influential at the outset. Living at Abbeyleix, and serving as lord lieutenant of Queen's County, de Vesci had for not-too-distant neighbours the Synges of Syngefield (King's County) and the Leckys of New Garden and Shrule Castle, County Carlow.[25] These were very different from the rackety upper-class Irish of the Marshall Beresford and Mrs Jeffreys type: these were middle-class in sensibility if not in economic or social practice. Among British pioneers of the Pestalozzian system was Charles Mayo (1792–1846), sometime headmaster of Bridgnorth Grammar School, who owed his initiation to John Synge, a descendent of the Bridgnorth Synges. In the published text of a public tribute to Pestalozzi delivered in London, Mayo in his opening words invoked John Synge ('The Irish Traveller') – though not by name.[26] Synge was participating in a broader reform of manners among some Irish landowners, ironically handicapped by the very lateness of his father's adoption of eighteenth-century extravagance.

Pestalozzian ideas enjoyed a limited but undeniable success in the United Kingdom.[27] The social experiments of Robert Owen at New Lanark in Scotland provided a context of educational reform in which the Switzer's ideas might be received. When Owen travelled to Dublin in 1823, he expended a great deal on publishing accounts of his public meetings, together with an illustration (see p. 14 above) of what an Irish 'New Lanark' might look like. His allies included Lord Cloncurry – a former United Irishman – and among his assailants was the Revd Robert Daly (1783–1872), sometime teacher at Abbeyleix who would soon feature in County Wicklow experiments of a more spiritual kind.[28]

William Allen (1770–1843), a London Quaker and scientist, had been a partner with Owen and Jeremy Bentham in the New Lanark community, while also playing an important role in the campaign to abolish slavery throughout the British Empire. In his religious capacity, he frequently visited annual meetings of Irish Friends. Two extreme tensions underlay these developments. One existed between those reformers (like Owen) who were atheistic and those (like Pestalozzi himself, and the Quaker Allen) for whom religious sensibility was an important component of human nature. Though there was probably no direct correlation between them, this fundamental 'aporia' was complicated by another: that distinguishing universalist from localist tendencies. Herein lay seeds of future disputations between revolutionaries and reformers generally. In the immediate circumstances of the second and third decades of the nineteenth century, the localist tendency led to seemingly divergent practices: Pestalozzian schools in one area were established to educate the poor, while in other instances the children of the wealthy were specifically targeted. The potential for trouble is well apprehended in the experience of an English teacher who borrowed materials from John Synge. The governors of his school complained that 'these children are to be servants to our sons one of these days, and they must not be cleverer than their masters'.[29]

De Vesci inaugurated an estate school for children of the well-to-do – including his own children – and subscribed generously to Pestalozzi's poor-schools in Switzerland. In Kildare Street, Dublin, a school said to have been run along Pestalozzian lines was opened in 1811, with remarkably broad support from the contentious denominations of Irish Christianity. Its prime mover was the Quaker, Samuel Bewley. When Allen travelled to Dublin in the spring of 1820, his hosts included the Pims and Bewleys – stalwarts of the Irish Quaker community – but also William Harding, with whom he dined on 28 April.[30] Allen's interests were extraordinarily diverse, and took in Russian education, Irish poverty, the Royal Society (of which he was a Fellow) and anti-slavery everywhere.

Orpen concentrated on the education of deaf-mutes previously regarded as mentally defective if not downright heathen. Commencing with a modest establishment in 1816, he went on to build up what became in time the National Institute for the Education of the Deaf and Dumb, at Glasnevin in north Dublin.

How Pestalozzi reached Wicklow

Taking his mission across the Irish Sea, he opened a school for 'the sons of the higher ranks of society' near Birkenhead, under the guidance of a former pupil of Pestalozzi's who had also taught in the de Vesci school. In a later and more reflective phase of activity, Orpen published *Pestalozzi's System of Domestic Education* (Dublin, 1829) in four parts. A short biography of the Irish pioneer appeared from the pen of Sheridan Le Fanu's mother in 1860.

From all of this it might seem that an enlightened reform of Irish education was genuinely possible, and actively attempted, in the early part of the nineteenth century. Mrs Le Fanu could even report that Orpen had overseen the introduction of the Pestalozzian method 'in no long time into almost every infant school'.[31] A memoir of those stirring times, published during JMS's life, described extensive friction in the countryside, 'education was set up against education, school against school, teacher against teacher; and the whole intellect of the country was made the prize for contending hosts. The war raged long and loudly, and in some places the spiritual brought the fleshly arm to its aid. Teachers were sometimes burnt out of their schools by nightly marauders; flourishing Kildare Place colonies were in a moment annihilated by a single anathema from the Popish altar.' The author of these words was Thomas Wyse (1791–1862), a Jesuit-and-Trinity-educated Catholic of liberal opinions who married a niece of the Emperor Napoleon. His son, the minor poet William Charles Bonaparte Wyse (1826–1892), was attracted by the Félibres, descendants of the Troubadours, learnt their dialect and thus anticipated Ezra Pound by a long chalk.[32]

If these latter details reveal unexpected cultural and social diversity within the familiar model of Catholic cabin and Protestant Ascendancy, by the same token uninterrupted enlightenment was far from the case. In Ireland, education was becoming a central issue in politics with – from the 1830s onwards – the Catholic Church and the state lining up on opposing sides, both determined to exercise dominance in the shaping of young Irish minds, especially among the lower orders. Consequently, the endeavours of John Synge to introduce continental ideas cut little ice with the insular mammoths. In particular, his taking up residence in Wicklow complicated an already daunting task. Roundwood Park was an isolated mountain lodge by comparison with the well-watered, cultivated mid-land Abbeyleix demesne of de Vesci or the amenities of Orpen's suburban institute at Clairmont.

In County Clare, on the Western seaboard, another branch of the Synges was weathering the Atlantic gales with sustained faith in the protestantism of winds which had dispersed the Spanish Armada more than two centuries earlier. Edward Synge of Carhue was a zealous proselytiser prepared to evict tenants who did not respond positively to his new protestant schools, his free distribution of bibles and other aggressive challenges to the traditional religious practices of the area.[33] In theological terms, Edward and his Wicklow-based cousin probably saw eye-to-eye, but it is likely that the milder regime at Glanmore owned something to the influence of Pestalozzi. It is wrong to deduce extensive conclusions from isolated instances. Both Synge of Carhue's mother and sister-in-law were relatives of the liberal Sir Edward O'Brien of Drumoland whose son, William Smith O'Brien (1803–1864), would shortly cross the frontier from liberalism into outright rebellion.

Measured against the political correctness of a more recent century, the objectives and expressive language of this circle ring an alarm bell of disturbing familiarity. In 1834 the future rebel took part in a dinner party at Allen's London home where the 'great opening for usefulness now at Zacetecas, in Mexico' was discussed by the company who noted also that 'liberal institutions would be admitted'.[34] Maria Edgeworth wrote to Allen in January 1827 to wish him well in his Irish endeavours. The daughter of radical R. L. Edgeworth expressed herself in suitably guarded terms, saying that 'colonization at home, would be preferable to colonization abroad, if it can be carried into effect, because it would, in the first place, save all the risk, expense, and suffering of emigration, and would in the next place, secure to the home country the benefits of increased and improved cultivation and civilization'.[35] The key term here was not 'colonization' (in which she was merely citing Allen himself) but 'home'. In distinction from Mexico, Ireland was part of 'the home country' just like New Lanark, Royal Ascot and the slums of Saint Giles in London. But within the United Kingdom, Ireland was not so obviously part of 'the home country' as Lanark, Ascot, Saint Giles, etc. It awaited the benefits of civilisation through the establishment of such colonies as those envisaged by Allen, the Kildare Place Society, and other moral entrepreneurs like Orpen and Synge.

This was not wholly a territorial issue, as Edgeworth indicated: she advised Allen that he needed 'a more intimate knowledge of the habits of the peasantry of Ireland, than a *first* visit to this country could afford'. Switzerland featured in her argument about class and cultivation:

> Your *dairy plans* for instance, which have succeeded so well in Switzerland, would not do in this country, at least, not without a century's experiments. Paddy would *fall* to disputing with the *dairyman*, would go to law with him for his share of the *common* cow's milk, or for her *trespassing*, or he would pledge his eighth or sixteenth part of *her* for his rent, or his bottle of whisky, and the cow would be pounded and re-*pledged*, and *re*-pounded and bailed and *canted*; and things impossible for you to foresee, perhaps impossible for your English imagination to conceive, would happen to the cow and the dairyman.[36]

Not just territory, or even that impudent aspirant (nation), but class and language are introduced here by Edgeworth's evasive yet penetrating letter. In psychological terms, her mimicry of Paddy's accent (and apparently inconsistent stress pattern) signals the difficulty she has in accounting for the distance or difference existing between them. In sociological terms, the distance cannot be reconciled simply by application of the novelist's art. Since the writing of *Castle Rackrent* in the dying (and killing) days of the eighteenth century, an insurgent discourse has become audible, with a nation as its potential object. Edgeworth may speak of her 'poor dear countrymen' but she warns the English Quaker that 'they would be always making out a short cut, not a royal road, but a bog-road to their own *by-*objects'. Within the Union, Edgeworth and Allen coexist in every kind of mutual understanding, despite their different attitudes towards religion or capital punishment or whatever. But within Ireland, Edgeworth and Paddy occupy divergent spheres. She may understand him, at least to her own dissatisfaction, but she can no longer control him.

The background to John Synge's initiatives in education and theology is to be written up in terms of these painful and protracted adjustments, taking place over a quarter of a century or more. From the ethical anti-unionism of R. L. Edgeworth in 1800 through the increasingly defensive course of Maria Edgeworth's long career as estate-manager and commentator on public events, there emerge varieties of pro-unionism, stated or unstated. What Allen and Owen were proposing might be viewed as progressive or liberal unionism, that is, a policy of accepting the constitution of the United Kingdom as the basis for social reform. In their Irish operations, this required a powerful commitment to religious toleration, in practice supporting Catholic Emancipation and opposing the privileges of the Established Church in education as elsewhere. Among the Irish figures themselves, one might now make new distinctions which would align John Synge (also Orpen, etc.) with the progressive unionists, while tending to assign Maria Edgeworth to the conservative camp.[37] Meanwhile, the Synges of Carhue were routinely condemned in the House of Commons as examples of bigoted landlordism.[38]

This is neither the time nor place to regiment these suggestions into a typology, class-list or ideological directory, though the pursuit of Hatch/Synge history is clearly affected by altered views of what constituted progressive or conservative thought. The clearest demonstration of this thesis follows in a later chapter, when John Synge's involvement with the Plymouth Brethren is examined. In that context, we will note the long career of G. V. Wigram (1805–1879), a prime mover among the early Brethren who lived to be a nuisance to the young Charles Stewart Parnell. More particularly, we might note that Wigram confessed he 'never knew the gospel till, at nineteeen [he] spent a long and tiring day on the field of Waterloo in June 1824'.[39] Virtually uninterrupted war, from 1792 until 1815, locked Britain into the very process of defining and defending reaction, with the outbreak of Irish insurrection in 1798 and again in 1803 acting as catalysts for repression and the extension of state power. If this is the great period of Romanticism, any reassessment of its cultural history requires the closest attention to religious sensibility – Chateaubriand in France, Schleiermacher in Germany, Coleridge and Wilberforce in England.

Affairs with the moon

PEOPLE OF THE BOOKLET

These colossi of Metropolitan Europe had no counterpart on the island of Ireland. From an earlier generation Edmund Burke, long resident in England and dying in 1797, might be singled out as the harbinger of a Romanticism coloured by his distinctive sympathy with Irish Catholicism. But Burke was gone by 1800, gone even from the great debate on Union.[40] And whereas the second generation Romantics flourished while print technology advanced in sophistication and range of distribution, in Ireland the book trade had gone into sudden decline. This resulted less from the impact of insurrection and more from the eclipse of the Irish parliament in which John Hatch and Francis Synge had sat.

In John Synge's largest effort to float Pestalozzi on the choppy tide of Irish public opinion, a lengthy portion of the text is given over to the post-revolutionary condition of Switzerland. A heterodox but fervent native of protestant Zurich, in 1798 Pestalozzi had found himself obliged to work in a predominantly Catholic canton devasted by war. At Stanz he saw how 'houses and fields lay in ashes' while he pursued his educational and social objectives 'unbefriended, unassisted, but by the odious authority of an unpopular magistracy'.[41] These conditions might as well be Irish, in some montage of violence in 1798 and social engineering in the 1820s or 1830s. The alienation of the teacher from his patria, the conflict between native and revolutionary loyalties, and the unmistakeable contrast between secular and spiritual authority – these were aspects of Pestalozzi's predicament to which Synge (it seems) instinctively responded. Arriving at the Yverdon establishment in the autumn of 1814, having gone to Europe 'to watch the war' and dine with monsters, he stayed three months and underwent what can only be termed a conversion. It remains an unchronicled experience, whether from modesty or carelessness or the editorial impact of mildew no one can say. Nevertheless, within a year Synge published *A Biographical Sketch of the Struggles of Pestalozzi*, running to 116 pages, under the pseudonymous description 'An Irish Traveller'.

It was a frankly 'amateur' production, in every sense of the term. Footnotes threatened to overwhelm the narrative just as the editor's enthusiasm threatened to obliterate his message. Very early in the text, a note breaks off to explain how he

> wishes to add his conviction of the imperfect orthography of these tracts in many instances; but hopes his anxiety to put his countrymen as soon as possible in possession of thoughts, which appeared to him so likely to assist their present strenuous excertions for the improvement of the lower classes, will plead in excuse of the errors of style, and the too frequent recurrence of foreign idioms in the translation, which would require much time and repeated correction before they could be thoroughly expunged.[42]

Given that the *Sketch* itself is made up of two or three lengthy excerpts from Pestalozzi's letters and little more, these asides represent the author or (as Synge

How Pestalozzi reached Wicklow

preferred to style himself) the Editor. Such modesty is in keeping with the apologetic tone of the note just quoted, its anxiety and urgency, and its admission of an imperfect return to its native language. In this latter context, the issue as to who the Editor's countrymen may be takes on more significance than the phrase otherwise warrants. Styling himself an *Irish* traveller, he also refers to a recent publication by 'our countrywoman Miss Hamilton' about Pestalozzi. Elizabeth Hamilton (1758–1816) was the Scottish author of *The Cottagers of Glenburnie* (1808) and other improving fictions. In referring to her as he does, Synge may simply be reassimilating himself into English by emphasising their shared language or, at a somewhat deeper level, he may be underlining the union (existing only since 1801) of Ireland with Scotland and England.

As against this, he was perhaps simply buttressing his first essay in publication by reference to a well-known and established author. Whatever the motive in regard to the passing acknowledgement of Miss Hamilton, buttressing of his position, even of his identity, does on examination emerge as a constant concern in the *Sketch*. The dedication to Elizabeth Synge (née Hatch), who had died two years before the Editor had set out on his continental tour, addresses 'a much lamented mother, to whose early instruction and example, however inadequately valued amidst the follies of youth these tracts are inscribed …' In this detail, Synge reinscribes in his own personal history a cardinal tenet of Pestalozzi's outlook – the priority of the mother in nurturing a child's character and abilities, even, as in this case, a dead mother. Like others who sought to recommend Pestalozzi in the English-speaking world, Synge was 'anxious to express his conviction, that the Bible is, and ever has been, the guide of every thought of Pestalozzi'.[43]

He admitted to being an enthusiast whose friends complained in advance of publication about his excessive repetition of the term 'relations' derived from Pestalozzi's scheme for teaching mathematics. Two years after the *Sketch*, Synge turned his mind precisely to this aspect of the master's work, issuing *The Relation and Description of Forms According to the Principles of Pestalozzi*. Complete with folding plates, the book (amounting as yet only to Part One of the whole) ran to more than two hundred pages. Again, it was published in Dublin (as the *Sketch* had been) but the print-work had been carried out at Roundwood in County Wicklow. The book itself is printed on poor quality paper, and the press-work is not of professional quality. The proof-reading of a very repetitive yet subtly varying text must have taxed the patience and dedication of Synge and his printer, George P. Bull. The plates additionally indicate much painstaking labour on copper with the etcher's pen. The village of Roundwood did not become a print-shop overnight.[44]

In 1817, when John Synge made his second contribution to the Irish Pestalozzi movement, he was a bachelor of less than thirty. The following year he married Isabella Hamilton – no relative of the Scottish novelist – described by the family

Affairs with the moon

historian as a young heiress 'who brought a fine property into settlement'. Mrs Synge's grandfather, Hugh Hamilton (1729–1805), was bishop of Ossory for the seven years before his death: his predecessor, Thomas O'Beirne, had been an active propagandist on behalf of the Union: both men were 'serious' Bible Christians whose Ossory Clerical Association (centred on Kilkenny) played a major role in moving the Church of Ireland after 1800 towards fervent evangelicalism.[45] Isabella's father (the layman Alexander Hamilton) and uncle (the reverend George Hamilton of Killermogh) were active in the Hibernian Church Missionary Society, founded in 1814.[46] This was the Society for which Samuel Synge (1867–1951), the dramatist's brother, became in 1896 the first minister specifically ordained for missionary work overseas. The gap of seventy years between the Society's foundation and its deliberate preparation for overseas missions is only one indicator of its preoccupation with the home front and the attempt to convert Irish Catholics. Young John Synge, coming under the influence of such a family, encountered a religious tradition very different from the recent Synge pattern of worldly archdeacons. A mathematician of near-genius, Hugh Hamilton wrote in Latin on conic sections, was elected a Fellow of the Royal Society and helped to found the Royal Irish Academy. If he resembled earlier generations of Synges in his combination of scholarship and protestant piety, his evangelicalism was more combative than the creed of the Synge prelates. In his children's generation, interfaith relations flared up into sustained and vigorous animosity.

Marriage did not extinguish John Synge's passion for Pestalozzi. Between 1817 and 1819, and with Bull's technical assistance, he published a further four books, adaptations of the Switzer's method. Each of these was substantial in numbers of pages, though frail in its amateur stitching. Initially, distribution was sought through a combination of friendly booksellers in Dublin and a philanthropic organisation; the fourth of these publications was issued more conventionally under the imprint of the Grafton Street bookseller, R. M. Tims.[47]

The participation of Tims was a harbinger of things to come. By religious attachment a member of Dublin's Independent congregation, the bookseller associated with several of the city's spiritually reawakened souls who would shortly find their way into the Brethren movement. At a time when publishing booksellers attached to the Establishment were numerous, Synge nonetheless chose a follower of the old style Independent, William Cooper, whose Plunkett Street chapel was a rebuke to the Church of Ireland. In 1828, while he was living in England, Synge nevertheless ensured that the latest of his Pestalozzian manuals was made available to the Irish public through the same outlet.[48]

The location of a printing press in Roundwood and the desire to cultivate a market in Dublin did not combine to make commercial sense. Behind these arrangements lay Synge's evident preference for rural living whenever he was in Ireland. His printer, Bull, may have had a different view for, by 1825 when Synge

How Pestalozzi reached Wicklow

issued a second edition of *Pestalozzi's Intuitive Relations of Numbers* (Part 1), he used a young Dublin printer (Goodwin) in combination with Tims's retail outlet. Five years later, Bull's name appears on *Laws and Ordinances of the Orange Institution of Ireland* (Dublin: printed by George P. Bull, 40, South Great George's Street, 1830. 24pp.). Between 1819 and 1830, the temperature of Irish debate had risen to the point where exotic (if admirable) educational schemes melted from public view. Synge's parting from Bull occurred during the period when the Revd J. N. Darby was exercising an increasing influence on Wicklow's evangelicals. And Darby, who would later become leader of the Plymouth Brethren, was adamantly opposed to 'political protestantism' as organised through the Orange Order. Even in the little world of printed manuals, major ideological divisions could be felt.

The couple lived for nine interrupted years at Roundwood, made over to John Synge by his father who had by now brought Glanmore Castle to gorgeous completion. Landlordism on this scale brought responsibilities or excited public expectations. In 1817 Francis Synge built a church at Nun's Cross to replace an older and dilapidated one at Killiskey graveyard, and to complement the school house erected by Sir Francis Hutchinson ten years earlier. His daughter-in-law Isabella became active in the Irish Society for Promoting the Education of the Native Irish through the Medium of their Own Language. As a mark of changing times, the Irish Society (as it liked to be called) blamed the old Incorporated Society for neglecting the vernacular of those whom it had sought to proselytise. Meanwhile, Isabella's husband gradually earned the sobriquet 'Pestalozzi' – not calculated to reassure in an age increasingly sensitive to Irish 'identity'.[49] Opportunities presented themselves to the Synges: the Charter School at Templestown (Roundwood) had not long survived Samuel M'Cracken, and it seemed right to 'revive' it under the auspices of new developments in education and religious practice. But it was the Kilfee building, erected as recently as 1807, which put a roof over the new enterprise, thus associating the Pestalozzi experiment less with the bleak mountainside and more with the Gothic parkland of Glanmore.

The school at Kilfee, also known as Nun's Cross (after a family called Nunn), appears to have housed a printing press though only one item can be confidently assigned to it. *Hymns for Cottage Worship* ('printed at the Nunscross Press, Co. Wicklow') has no title-page nor is the authorship of any of the hymns given. Some of the most celebrated are included – 'When I survey the wondrous cross' (no. 3) and 'Guide us O thou great Jehovah' (no. 43), etc. – but many are undistinguished to a high degree. For example, no. 33 – 'Not all the blood of beasts,/ On Jewish altars slain,/ Could give the guilty conscience peace,/ Or wash away the stain'. Like Bull's earliest printing for John Synge, *Hymns for Cottage Worship* (a far smaller book, a mere chapbook) is paginated in three sequences; perhaps each of the three was distributed separately. The second sequence is devoted to

'Hymns for Children', evidence of the continuing commitment to instruction of the young. The 'Advent Hymns' which make up the final sequence are, without exception, closer to millennarian songs than to the pre-Christmas hymnology familiar from official collections:

> The night is wearing fast away,
> A streak of light is dawning;
> Sweet harbinger of that bright day,
> The fair Millenial [sic] morning.[50]

This is closer to the prophetic strain of evangelical protestantism pursued by the Scottish Edward Irving (1792–1834) than to the Church of Ireland. Irving associated with dissident evangelicals in Dublin and Wicklow, including those – with John Synge's assistance – who later became famous as the Plymouth Brethren. These were lively times, indeed the Second Coming was an annual expectation. Despite growing excitement about an Irish reformation, it was difficult wholly to suppress the suspicion that only a pale and puny imitation of the great sixteenth-century upheavals of Wittenberg and Geneva was now due. The Bible, expounded at length in all its prophetic and ethical power, was still the Good Book, but it was increasingly surrounded by a cloud of chapbooks, pamphlets and leaflets, a host of witnesses who obscured what they sought to venerate and commend.

A dizzying succession of enthusiasms, which carried John Synge from Oxford to the Alps and back to the Devil's Glen, roughly coincided with his courtship and first marriage. There is, however, a parallel record of continuity. Before Isabella died in February 1830, she bore him seven children. Perhaps because the couple moved between Ireland and England, exact details of birth-dates are difficult to establish. Two of the boys became ordained clergymen, but the eldest and youngest were to be of more significance in JMS's life. Francis (died 1878) acquired Glanmore and was forced to lose Roundwood after 'Pestalozzi' Synge's death in 1845. His younger brother, John Hatch Synge (1824–1872) became the dramatist's father in 1871. The shadowy figure who had left such uncertainty behind him in 1797 was being woven into the fabric of Synge Christian names in the 1820s.

Though it would be difficult to imagine two 'patron saints' more contrasting than Sir John Temple and Heinrich Pestalozzi, to the emergent Catholic Irish nation there was all too much continuity between Cromwellian confiscation and evangelical fervour. The experience of teachers supported by the Kildare Place Society, already quoted, is only one indication of the turbulence breaking out all over Ireland – but especially the southern half – throughout the decade. Agricultural prices were depressed after the conclusion of the Napoleonic wars, and social unrest in the countryside masked itself violently under the name Captain Rock. Daniel O'Connell's campaign for Catholic Emancipation (conceded in 1829) was waged through parish gatherings which, in the eyes of a besieged protestant establishment, were indistinguishable from the mob. The bitter legacies of 1798 and the broken promises of 1800–1801 were ensuring that an increasingly sectarian polarisation in Irish politics did not lack historical resonance.

Apart from neighbouring Wexford, no southern county could match Wicklow in the annals of insurrection and retribution. Counties Antrim, Down and Armagh had also 'risen' in 1798, but Ulster was already diverging from the rest of Ireland in its economic and social life. The part of Wicklow to which newly married John Synge retired c. 1820 was still an anomaly as it had been in M'Cracken and Hatch's day, but it was a different anomaly. New roads linked it to the capital, and new villas decorated its northern horizons, the country houses of bankers and other *arrivistes*. Early Christian remains attracted artists of Romantic inspiration, but no major development – whether of the kind proposed by Robert Fraser or by Robert Owen – invigorated post-Union Wicklow. The high proportion of non-Catholics continued to distinguish it from counties lying to the west, the mountains protected its eccentic integrity. Much later, the railways, advancing in the wake of the Great Famine, would glance along the Wicklow coast like a shaft of iron light thrust at its neo-medieval gloom.

Architecturally, Francis Synge had already made his own contribution to the gothicising of the county at Glanmore. At much the same time, nearby Ballycurry House was rebuilt by the same architect, Francis Johnston, though in a conventional Irish Georgian style. There were older houses in the district, including Rossanagh to the south-east of Ashford village, and Altidore Castle near Kilpeddar. These and other grand residences have intriguing histories, as do later Victorian buildings such as the Casement house at Cronroe (due south of Ashford) and the gingerbread cottage-mansion of Luggala north of Roundwood. None quite matches the obscurity of Roundwood Park.

Between the mid-1790s (when Alderman Emerson was evidently still in residence) and 1820 (when John Synge took his bride there), the house which had been built or renovated for John Hatch had been eclipsed by Francis Synge's development at Glanmore. That it should have become home to the first printing press in the county, and host to a Pestalozzian academy, could not have been predicted by Samuel M'Cracken and his scarcely literate successors. Yet, in a more liberally comparative view, the uncultivated Switzer whose language Maria Edgeworth found unsatisfactorily mixed may have been closer in social experience to the lonely suicide of Roundwood than he was to the pedagogues of Edgeworthstown.

Like does not always follow from like. The 'conversion' at Yverdon might have been impossible without the Iberian adventures and the Borromean sublime. If Synge was destined to go home and (after some time) participate in the virtual founding of a new protestant denomination, it may have been his positive and relaxed encounter with continental Catholicism which provided the necessary release from inherited prejudices. From his unlikely vantage point, he undertook not only to educate the young but also to revitalise the church of his day. He was not alone in these undertakings, even among the Wicklow mountains. Nor did the congeries of sermons, teaching aids and tracts, which piled up on his table go unnoticed. Before examining the Synge family's contribution to the Brethren movement, we might consider how the area in which he took up permanent abode featured in contemporary fiction less reasonable than Maria Edgeworth's. In short, we should ask if the Irish Traveller was kin to Melmoth the Wanderer.

15

Melmoth the stay-at-home

As the sexual union of horse and donkey produces two different hybrids, the mule and the hinny, so the mixture of historical writing and free invention gives rise to different products which, under the common designation of historical novel, sometimes want to be appreciated as history, sometimes as novel. (Sigmund Freud)

Like most wanderers, he fears death more than others, because he has seen many shadowy or splendid places where he has had no time to live, and has lived in other places long enough to feel in breaking from them a share of the desolation which is completed in death. (JMS on Pierre Loti, 1903)

UP TO this point, *The Silence* has developed along basically accumulative lines. Research has unearthed much that had never seemed relevant to those concerned exclusively with the Synge side of JMS's inheritance. The point in the dramatist's evolution where the Hatch/M'Cracken history is reactivated is – if Euclid can forgive the solecism – a long one, the composition and revision of 'When the Moon Has Set'. A rudimentary argument connecting the events of 1769 and the plot of this irritating playscript was made in *Fool of the Family*, where the underlying dynamic of JMS's apprenticeship was identified as the desire to rewrite, or more exactly un-write Ibsen's 'Ghosts' as a means of dealing with unwelcome family news from the past. Quite independent of the biography, the latter-day Irish dramatist Frank McGuinness discovered strong echoes of Ibsen's 'Rosmersholm' in the same 'prentice work of JMS.[1]

While a digression on the immature work of JMS may seem scandalously unchronological, the reflexive nature of his period's historical consciousness renders it exemplary. According to a woman whom he loved, he was 'immensely proud' that his grandfather had voted against the Union. Proud perhaps, but inaccurate, for it was his great-grandfather who cast his vote against government, government having refused to pay the compensation he claimed as a loyalist of doubtful loyalties.[2] The era of the United Irishmen, 'bold Robert Emmet', and war with Napoleon was a costume-box from which to pick a heritage, an identity or a mask. After his release from prison in 1897, Oscar Wilde adopted the nom-de-plume Sebastian Melmoth, the second element of which he took from a famous novel, *Melmoth the Wanderer* (1820) written by one whom Wilde liked to claim as a relative.

The decades surrounding the Union stimulated a good deal of popular literature on Irish themes, much of it now forgotten. In London, the Minerva Press issued novels which linked insurrectionary and Gothic themes. At a more sophisticated level, William Godwin's *Caleb Williams* (1794) investigated how the plot of vengeful pursuit illuminated political relations between Britain and Ireland.[3] When Maria Edgeworth published her first Irish novel in 1800, its title – *Castle Rackrent* – at once echoed the castles of Horace Walpole and Mrs Radcliffe and mocked the pretensions of Irish country-house builders. But the great moment of convergence between Gothic and Irish anxieties was achieved in *Melmoth*, by which the prolific Charles Robert Maturin (1780–1824) is remembered. If Irish Romanticism had no counterpart to the religious romanticism of Chateaubriand and Schleiermacher, it produced Maturin instead, of whom Coleridge was symptomatically jealous.

Divided into four books, *Melmoth* is a construction of stories set in exotic places and covering a period of one hundred and fifty years. The titular hero had struck an occult bargain with the Devil and, in return for extended life, must constantly seek a fellow human being so wretched as to take over the Wanderer's side of the bargain. Thus the dominant narratives involve an English madhouse, a Spanish monastery under the Inquisition, Asiatic barbarism, and so forth. The 'quest' is an inversion of the Arthurian (later Wagnerian) Holy Grail legend: indeed Maturin's novel is placed midway between the medieval and the proto-fascist, and its modification of the Wandering Jew motif is profoundly ambiguous.

As its editor in the Oxford English Novels series conceded, the apparently unimportant opening scenes in Wicklow are 'among the most interesting ... in their details of life and customs in those outlandish parts'.[4] In order to appreciate this *centrality of the marginal* (as I would want to call it) an allegorical reading of the fiction as a whole is required in the historicist manner recommended and exemplified in Fredric Jameson's *The Political Unconscious* (1981). It is no less important to note that a new edition of the novel, with a long introduction by Wilde's friend, Robert Ross, became available to JMS in 1892.

The text opens:

> In the autumn of 1816, John Melmoth, a student in Trinity College, Dublin, quitted it to attend a dying uncle on whom his hopes for independence chiefly rested ... The beauty of the country through which he travelled (it was the county Wicklow) could not prevent his mind from dwelling on many painful thoughts, some borrowed from the past, and more from the future.[5]

Melmoth the stay-at-home

He is dropped by the mail coach 'near the Lodge (the name of old Melmoth's seat)' and makes his way – like innumerable orphans in fiction and film – towards the unwelcoming home of a reluctant benefactor. The Lodge has its own lodge, with 'an adjacent cabin', and gradually the approach to old Melmoth's seat is made by way of 'the miry road which had once been the approach'. These slippages of terminology aptly preface the reader's arrival at the 'house itself' which 'stood strongly defined even amid the darkness of the evening sky; for there were neither wings, or offices, or shrubbery or tree, to shade or support it, and soften its strong harsh outline'. Once inside the house, young John is in the numerous company of his uncle's servants and followers, who are eating sumptuously in the enforced absence of the old, dying miser. Pre-eminent among these is 'a withered Sybil', ambiguously linked socially to 'his honour's kitchen, or the cottar's hut', and whose powers are so comprehensive that 'if there were no lives to be shortened, there were fortunes to be told'. Through this figure, compounded of Greek mythological traces and snatches of Gaelic folklore, a theme of prophecy is established at the outset of the many narratives in *Melmoth the Wanderer*.

If we take the Oxford editor's hint, and treat the Wicklow of Maturin's masterpiece as its substantive (but repressed or undeclared) subject, then the narratives which intervene may be regarded as dreams stimulated in the young inheritor by the outlandish surroundings in which he finds himself reading an obscure manuscript. Rather than see Maturin's successive chapters and books as a transcript of what young Melmoth reads, we should regard them as a counter-script arising out of the specific person and place. One figure for that alternative text is, as I have suggested, the dream – if by dream is meant something comprehensive enough to include both the biblical and the psychoanalytical types. Prophetic dreams such as those interpreted by Joseph in Egypt were not only familiar to Maturin in his professional capacity, they constituted a model for the prophetic form of evangelicalism which was coming into prominence in Irish protestantism. *The Interpretation of Dreams* (1899) presents a different account, preferring childhood sexuality (and the past) to the prophets' futurity as the site of dream-reality: as Freud's often stated respect for the Old Testament dream-seers indicates, the two approaches are complementary. They differ crucially, however, in that the psychoanalyst is generally available to see patients and invokes a science with general validity, while the Jacobs and Isaiahs only arose when the spirit moved them. A question often asked in the Ireland of Maturin's time was – will the spirit move anyone today, here?

The confused signals of *Melmoth*'s opening pages do not only connote social decline (to be consummated in the future), they can readily be seen as testifying to the mixed origins of the house (a past still pregnant). While family honour prefers a monofilament pedigree, a comprehensive history must admit the marriages of financial convenience (if not the caretaker administrations) as well as the unbroken

Affairs with the moon

line of titular inheritors. In the case of Roundwood Park, we saw the semi-literate Stoddart cohabit with Alderman Emerson, Ann Kennedy taunt John Hatch on questions of delicacy while Hatch in turn warns Francis Synge against the Weekes's company. Out of such alliances, temporary unions and suspended antagonisms was Anglo-Ireland born, not in the pages of Burke's *Landed Gentry*.

Maturin's opening *mise-en-scène* allows for this coming together, partly through the theme of soothsaying and partly by focusing on the kitchen where the labour which supports ostentation is plainly visible and where the social hierarchy stands on its head. The succeeding paragraphs detail the lavish if mannerless feast to be consumed below stairs – the salted salmon and slink-veal both derive (as Maturin's own note admits) from Maria Edgeworth's *The Absentee*. This was one of her tales of fashionable (that is, contemporary) life, published and set just four years earlier than the present action, and set (in part, and with adjustments) in the Wicklow villa of Mrs La Touche. Huguenots long settled in Ireland, the family were bankers (as John Hatch had reason to know) and evangelical philanthropists: James Digges La Touche (1788–1826) promoted Pestalozzi's educational theories in Ireland and worked with John 'Pestalozzi' Synge in the Irish Society. Their assortment of names is a microcosm of that wider world in which the great issues of salvation and enlightenment, democracy and reaction were being worked out. Maturin's Gothic thriller opens in rural Ireland, only to move (in time as well as space) to Restoration London; Edgeworth's improving fable opens in contemporary London, only to move to rural Irish houses where Herodotus and the Scythians are points of learned reference.

But – back to the kitchen, the Sybil and the slink-veal. 'Finally, there were lobsters and *fried* turbot enough to justify what the author of the tale asserts, "suo periculo," that when his great grandfather, the Dean of Kilalla, hired servants at the deanery, they stipulated that they should not be required to eat turbot or lobster more than twice a-week.' All of this carnivalesque is woven from material which partly arises from the ongoing scene in the Lodge kitchen and which partly belongs to literary or historical allusion. The effect – repeated throughout the novel – is to break down distinctions between presence and absence, present and past, the actual and the textual. A prophetess rightly stands amid the scene as its representative figure.

If the novelist's allusion to his ancestor, Peter Maturin (dean of Kilalla from 1724 to 1741), would have struck Jane Austen as improper in a literary artist, it serves several important purposes in this most un-Austenesque novel. First, it establishes a *kind* of authority for the author himself, who had prefaced the novel with remarks identifying one of his own sermons as the source of its basic plot and bemoaning the inadequacy of his clerical profession to support him. It provides the clergyman-novelist with an ancestor, also a clergyman, and thus points to the long-established Huguenot tradition within the Church of Ireland. But it also

Melmoth the stay-at-home

tends to align this ancestor with a kind of sumptuary excess – however reluctantly inherited from his predecessor in the Killala deanery – now associated with the house of Melmoth in dissolution and the imminent unveiling of that family's ancestry and its spiritual excess.

While the early emergence of a subversive, jacobin, or even satanic, aspect of the novelist's imaginative procedures is worthy of note, the local or Killala aspect deserves a little more attention. The see of Killala lies on the western seaboard – hence Grant's confusion, perhaps, about the geography of the opening chapters – within the archdiocese of Tuam. If Peter Maturin had ministered there as dean in the 1720s and 1730s, his archbishop throughout was Edward Synge (1659–1741). (Indeed the two men died in the same year.) Killala was not short of notables at its own humbler level – Samuel Hutchinson had been bishop until his death in 1780, and his son-in-law Edward Synge (1726–1792) became archdeacon. In 1798 the French landed at Killala in support of the United Irishmen (including those of Wicklow), and an important account of the invasion was published by the then dean, Joseph Stock.

Maturin's novel will linger long in the grip of the Spanish Inquisition, an example of tyranny, cruelty and religious persecution most Anglophone protestants found irresistible. It diverts itself, however, on a number of occasions to cite more local and recent Irish episodes as verifications of the exotic past. Within the Wicklow-theory of this novel, the footnotes constitute moments of half-waking from the dream (Restoration mad-house, Inquisition, etc.) into a local and mundane reality which serves only to confirm the dream as valid and (perhaps) to send young Melmoth back to his exotic manuscript.

These episode/notations included the murder of the antiquarian clergyman William Hamilton in Donegal and the better known killing (by Robert Emmet's followers in 1803) of Arthur Wolfe, viscount Kilwarden.[6] Dr Hamilton was not a relative of the family into which John soon-to-be-'Pestalozzi' Synge would marry, but Kilwarden was closely related to Robert Synge's wife. In the parish of Clondevaddock, Hamilton was succeeded in 1797 by the Revd Henry Maturin (died 1842): it was a living in the gift of Trinity College, and so the translation of a Maturin might be read fictionalised in the early pages of C. R. Maturin's novel. By these even-handed confessions of non-connection and connection, we can raise the issue of *Melmoth*'s bearing upon the Synges of County Wicklow.

There is no intention to suggest that Maturin's rambling Gothic fiction is a *roman-à-clef*. Apart from any other consideration, nothing so orderly could be devised in, or extrapolated from, a narrative which is strongest in recounting emotion and weakest in explaining how one event leads to another. This last-mentioned characteristic is well illustrated when young Melmoth witnesses a shipwreck on the Wicklow coast, in the heat of which he also observes a sinister, isolated figure standing aloof on the rocks. The next morning after sleep (which

Affairs with the moon

may have included dreams of this 'event'), young Melmoth wonders if anyone apart from himself survived the shipwreck – of which, of course, he had been a mere spectator, like the sinister figure (his Faustian ancestor). Shipwrecks on the south-east coast of Ireland were not uncommon, though Wexford is more frequently reported in this connection than Wicklow. An anonymous poem, published in 1830, saluted the county with dogged, iambic respect:

> Wicklow! whose wave reposing bosom seems
> But made for shipwrecked souls or airy dreams.[7]

In more reliably topographical terms, there are high rocky outcrops – Arklow Head, Wicklow Head, Bray Head, not to mention The Grey Stones – upon which a ship might founder within the county's boundaries. The location of Glanmore Castle was approved by the Synges precisely because it afforded a view of the sublime coastline between Arklow and Wicklow Heads. In terms of the contemporary English novel, it may be at least as relevant to point to shipwrecks or dangerous landings which feature at the opening of Edgeworth's *Patronage* and Frances Burney's *The Wanderer* (both 1814).

Certainly, Glanmore cannot be an original for The Lodge. It was built too recently and far too obviously in the Gothic style. Given that it was renamed from the generally accepted Glenmouth, it smacked too readily of Gothic Revival in its satanic aspect, for the glen in question was the Devil's Glen (the haunt of Joseph Holt in 1798 and after). Philology aside, it was also, for the time being, too prosperous: Old Melmoth, far from being the oldest Melmoth, lived in something simpler, meaner, older, without attached out-offices or 'wings'. But it is a long – and wrong – leap to assume that, because Roundwood was simpler, meaner, more ruinous (after 1798) and older than Glanmore, it automatically becomes a candidate for the distinction of ghosting Melmoth's Lodge. Nowhere plays that part. Utopia.

There is, however, one awkward bibliographical detail. As we have seen, John 'Pestalozzi' Synge's devotion to the cause of progressive education led him to establish a printing press up on the bleak mountain where M'Cracken had killed himself, where Hatch had imposed his ownership, and sundry tenants had struggled to write their names in the soil while older claims persisted. In the relatively extensive life of this rustic enterprise, nothing except educational piety and no author but Pestalozzi had ever darkened paper at Roundwood. Except in one case. In 1818, a Miss E. M. Maturin published (posthumously) a small duodecimo volume called *Letters to a Friend* and giving Roundwood as its place of publication. The biography of the Revd Charles Robert Maturin has yet to be written and, to judge from the work of earlier commentators, the material is not extensive, certainly not adequate to identify the author of these *Letters*. Nor have the Synge/Hatch papers – extensive but known to be incomplete – alluded to

Melmoth the stay-at-home

anyone of that distinctive name. An obituarist referred to the novelist exercising 'his eccentricities [in] the romantic solitudes of Wicklow', but went no further.[8] Thus what the cultural historian is left with is a bleakly unique detail – a few leaves of earnest correspondence – which does nothing but link the family of *Melmoth*'s author to the printing press of John 'Pestalozzi' Synge.

There are further hidden connections, however. In his diary for 1799 Sir Robert Synge recorded that an 'uncle Maturin' of his wife Margaret (née Wolfe, died 1838) had died. Years later, his widow completed the record – 'my poor aunt Maturin was released from her long sufferings'.[9] The Wolfes' relationship with the Maturins was touchingly evidenced in the will of Margaret Synge's father for, among the smaller benefits, he left £600 to Peter Maturin. Margaret Synge was the daughter of Theobald Wolfe (1710–1784), kinsman of both the republican Theobald Wolfe Tone (d. 1798) and of Arthur Wolfe, Lord Kilwarden (1738–1803) who enters *Melmoth* in a footnote. Robert and Peggy Synge were naturally attached to her Wolfe relatives, he acting in 1791 as a witness to the will of Arthur Wolfe (then the Irish Attorney-General) whose wife Anne Ruxton (d. 1804) was in turn related to the Edgeworths. Back in 1641, Mrs Ann Synge (née Edgeworth) was drowned while trying to escape with her children from the Irish rebels.

These patterns of nominal return are the very stuff of *Melmoth the Wanderer*, which begins and ends with its hero in close proximity to his remote ancestor and namesake. Wolfe and Maturin ... Wolfe and Synge ... Synge and Edgeworth ... Maturin quoting Edgeworth ... So the waves of family names ebb and flow through fiction and non-fiction alike. *Melmoth* might be read in conjunction with Godwin's *Mandeville* (1817), a novel of predominantly English setting which nonetheless takes off from an episode in the same execrable Irish rebellion profitably written up by Sir John Temple. Whereas the English radical dissenter advances his plot along a line of narrative development, the Irish Huguenot clergyman repeatedly stresses the synchronicity of discrete experiences, or the identity of experiences pertaining to discrete individuals. Thus in Volume Three – when the action relates to the Spanish Inquisition – footnotes parallel fatal incidents in the Ireland of 1797 and 1803, the first befalling the Dr Hamilton who will be succeeded in his parish by the novelist's brother, and the second befalling Arthur Wolfe whose uncle had eased the lot of Maturin relatives. Another pattern of recurring names.

Is this anything more than coxcomb self-centredness? In strictly verbal terms, the name-parallels are plainly evident, whereas the family relationships are invisible to most readers. The verbal detail is, however, closely linked to the notion of seeing or reading. Apostrophising on a mangled victim of the Spanish mob, Maturin's narrator-within-narrator declares, 'Had Spain mortgaged all her reliques from Madrid to Monserrat, from the Pyrennees to Gibraltar, she could not have have recovered the paring of a nail to canonize.' In the next paragraph, the same narrator admits that, as witness to this butchery, he found himself involuntarily screaming the screams of the victim – 'offering worlds in imagination to be able to remove from the window, yet feeling as if every shriek I uttered was as a nail that fastened me to it'. This is still contained within the Spaniard's Tale but, after a few paragraphs, the same words, images and situations recur in a footnote describing the murder of Arthur Wolfe:

> In the year 1803, when Emmett's insurrection broke out in Dublin – (*the* fact from which this account is drawn was related to me by an eye-witness) – Lord Kilwarden, in passing through Thomas Street, was dragged from his carriage, and murdered in the most horrid manner. Pike after pike was thrust through his body, till at last he was nailed to a door, and called out to his murderers to 'put him out of his pain.' At this moment, a shoemaker, who lodged in the garret of an opposite house, was drawn to the window by the horrible cries he heard. He stood at the window, gasping with horror, his wife attempting vainly to drag him away. He saw the last blow struck – he heard the last groan uttered, as the sufferer cried, 'put me out of pain,' while sixty pikes were thrusting at him. The man stood at his window as if nailed to it: and when dragged from it, became – an *idiot for life*.[10]

There is plenty here to remind a reader hostile to Gothic fiction of its reliance on repetition and accumulated horror – too many thrusting pikes, too many windows. But Maturin's procedures involve a degree of word play uncharacteristic of the literary school to which he is generally assigned. The first 'nail' is human bone, or to be more exact, modified epidermis (skin). The second is, of course, the verb to nail, as when an object is affixed to another by means of metal rods sharpened at one end and with a retaining head at the other. The virtually unstated linked between these two usages is, in *Melmoth the Wanderer*, the nailing of Christ to the cross. The sanctity of the 'modified epidermis' is established through (botched) theological concepts of canonisation and through indistinct echoes of Boccaccio's stories about relics of the saints, the holy cross and even the annunciatory angel. The Spanish mob's victim being a Jew, the risk of supreme blasphemy hangs low over these passages.

In the light of this analysis of *Melmoth*'s opening pages and occasional footnotes, it makes more sense to read the serial-substance of the principal narratives, *not* as accounts from the past, illustrative of the lost soul's desperate search for a sufferer more wretched than himself, but as prophecy. Perhaps before leaping to such a conclusion, one might observe that the novel's Spain of the Inquisition (through which most of its narratives and sub-narratives are channelled) can be read allegorically as the Peninsular War. Ever since the dying falls of Edmund Burke's condemnation of Protestant Ascendancy, there was a framework of rhetorical mirrors in which Irish affairs and those of the Napoleonic polity could be used one to interpret the other. The sacrifice of Arthur Wolfe now is redeemed

Melmoth the stay-at-home

in the victory of Arthur Wellesley, flowers both of what later will be celebrated as the Protestant Ascendancy.

The battlefield of Waterloo bred converts to evangelical Christianity in Ireland. Despite keeping company with Marshal Beresford, and attending closely to the Borromean shrines, John Synge too was a delayed beneficiary. By the time he was fully engaged with Dublin's protestant printers, Maturin was dead. Commencing his literary career as a romantic nationalist, the novelist had steadily been driven into religious controversy. His *Sermons* of 1819 provided a 'text' (in the preacher's sense) for his famous novel of the following year. But *Women; or, Pour et Contre* (1818) had already satirised evangelical circles in contemporary Dublin, and his final novel, *The Albigenses* (1824), dealt with the late medieval Cathar heresy in southern France. *Five Sermons on the Errors of the Roman Catholic Church* summarised his theological position at more than satisfactory length.

Though Maturin died on 30 October 1824, his reputation did not evaporate overnight. A French translation of *Melmoth* had appeared in 1821, a London stage version in three acts was produced in 1823. Balzac wrote a sequel in 1835 at a time when, in Ireland, the Gothic torch had been taken up by Maturin's fellow-Huguenot, Sheridan Le Fanu. It is too easy to assume that John Synge of Glanmore remained oblivious to the masterpiece of 1820. For early nineteenth-century readers of his class, fiction and religious anxiety, literature and history were not marked off from each other with sharp boundaries. Le Fanu's father, the Dean of Emly, had a small library of shockers among his multi-volumed ecclesiological treatises. Strict literary boundaries have been imposed by a later thought-police than the Victorian clergy.

When Sigmund Freud spoke of the different hybrids which result from the conjunction of historical writing and free invention, he was nervously introducing the essay which later became famous as *Moses and Monotheism* (1939). In its earlier form, it was described by him as a historical novel. Writing in the 1930s, Freud had good reason to worry about the classification of this highly innovative work, for its ultimate proposition assailed the very basis of Jewish thought and historiography. Freud sought to show that Moses was not a Jew, but an Egyptian.

In terms of theory, what Freud was attempting to transcend was 'the gulf between individual and group psychology'. He was far from satisfied that he had succeeded in any general sense, and continued to regard with distrust any notion of a 'collective' unconscious.[11] While his treatment of non-archaic material is minimal, Freud allows himself to instance three nineteenth-century European figures who, like Moses, belong socially or politically to one group while their name suggests another. The German-language poet, Adelbert von Chamisso, was 'French by birth', the French Emperor Napoleon was 'of Italian extraction', and the British Prime Minister Benjamin Disraeli was Italian Jewish.

These recent instances do not go far towards reassuring anyone who feels that

Freudian theories of ancient heroism can illuminate latter-day political or cultural history. For the moment, it is sufficient to say that the issue of *origins* lies at the heart of the matter. The hero is not so much distinguished by his strength or cunning, his bravery or wisdom – though something like this he must possess as a licence to practise heroism. He is distinguished *from* those for whom he is a hero by having different origins, the difference being at once apparent and denied. This latter contradiction implicates others – a people venerate their hero but also reject or even kill him; the hero returns both to liberate and to punish his people.

I want very concisely to summarise how *Melmoth the Wanderer* impinges on the history of the Hatch/Synge family, the history of Wicklow, and the reflexive historical consciousness of JMS's generation. At one obvious level, the novel has a hero – of the Faustian type. At another, it presents a satirical account of domestic squalor. The common denominator in these two aspects of Maturin's composition is Old Melmoth. The historical framework is provided (however implausibly) by the Sybil – 'The first of the Melmoths, she says, who settled in Ireland, was an officer in Cromwell's army, who obtained a grant of lands, the confiscated property of an Irish family attached to the royal cause. The elder brother of this man was one who had travelled abroad, and resided so long on the Continent, that his family had lost all recollection of him.'[12] This introduces the 'the curse of Cromwell' motif so familiar in Irish folklore.[13] Strictly examined, this parallels (and does not identify) the confiscator Melmoth with a quite separate other Melmoth who is the bargainer with Satan. The novel insinuates the proposition that there may be a worse evil than expropriation of Irish land from its traditional possessors, but that worse evil must be figured as an *elder* brother, that is, one whose primogenitural authority cannot be denied. Historically, younger brothers were likely adventurers – in Virgina, Ireland, India. Theologically, authority at home retains divine approval through the laying on of hands, bishop upon monarch.

The distinction also functions as a contamination. That is, the expropriator might as well be a bargainer with Satan, and indeed by the metonymic processes of folklore is regarded as such. Ironically, this leads to the suppression in the text of any reference to Cromwellian outrages which are, however, signalled negatively through the madness of the Restoration. A restored king is blessed with a divine right which has suffered interruption. But such readings do not occur in the text, they require a reader, and the act of reading involves an exchange between two parties. JMS, reading *Melmoth* in Robert Ross's edition, may in one capacity have achieved aesthetic detachment and imaginative engagement in the manner approved by Coleridge. But in another capacity, he cannot have failed to recognise the Lodge as being of the same general class as the Roundwood in which his own grandfather lived, nor can he have ignored general resemblances between young Melmoth's inherited situation and his own. His own relationship with his family's Wicklow property placed an uncle centrally (Francis II of Glanmore) who died when JMS was a boy. And his one attempt to dramatise family history turns on a nephew inheriting (like John Melmoth) from an uncle who leaves manuscripts for a legacy.

Rather than pursue these resemblances through a tabulation of facts in the external world, it is more valuable to consider the reflexive role of literature. The crucial text is JMS's long-germinating and unsatisfactory play, 'When the Moon Has Set'. That this was embarked upon as a rewriting of Ibsen's 'Ghosts', with a view to reversing implications of inherited guilt (at once sexual, denominational and fiscal) seems to be already proven. Frank McGuinness's contribution to this discussion of JMS's debt to Ibsen has been to invoke 'Rosmersholm' which, unwittingly, also draws in *Melmoth the Wanderer*. What all three of these precursor-texts share is the theme of the living who retain their dead relatives, a theme which successfuly demands to be rewritten in terms of the dead controlling their living kin.[14]

The symptom of this unhealthy relationship is melodramatically presented in Ibsen's 'Ghosts' as syphilis; in 'Rosmersholm' it is insanity in one party and incest in another. These are original offences in the sense that, with or through them, a phantasmal account of origins is propagated. Freud, when he came to comment on 'Rosmersholm' noted how common was the motif of a girl's phantasy of replacing her employer's wife. The play's tragic dimension, he argued, derives from the supplementary circumstance that the heroine's daydream had been preceded by a correspondent reality which enacted incest with her father. It is this (unadmitted) guilt and not the acknowledged attempt to eliminate Mrs Rosmer which really drives Rebecca West to take her own life alongside John Rosmer. Here, in different but no less grave terms, is the same transfer which has been observed in *Melmoth the Wanderer*, the transfer of odium from the Cromwellian ancestor to the Satanic elder brother of whom no one had any recollection.

The growing burden of a violent ancestry, regarded as the origin of a newly emerging 'Anglo-Irish' social constituency, can be measured in this lateral displacement in Maturin's Gothic novel of 1820. More extensively, it informs the fiction of Sheridan Le Fanu. But to pursue this theme into the period of the Irish Literary revival, we must resume our inquiry into the course of John Synge's career and its impact on his family.

16

In Darby's field

You are demanding that, at the cock-crow of the state, I shall betray the ideal for which I have lived. (Henrik Ibsen)[1]

THE 1820s in Ireland are remembered principally for the Catholic Emancipation Act of 1829. Daniel O'Connell's long campaign in that cause nurtured a widespread and deep-rooted sense of social disruption, but the Liberator was not alone in contributing to it. The millennialist vocabulary of some who opposed Emancipation threatened to escalate an essentially political matter to the level of Holy War. As we have seen, educational discussion and reform fell victim to the mood of the times. If the economic repercussions of peace – established after Waterloo – depressed agriculture and damaged Irish trade, the failure of any programme of progressive Unionism to emerge completed a circle of disappointment. By the time Emancipation was finally conceded, its beneficiaries had been extensively alienated from a political settlement less than thirty years in existence.

Sectarian violence had a long history in Ireland, but the 1820s saw the growth of outrages of another kind. The desecration of the chapel in Ardee suggests a new vulgarity in the insult and a new insecurity among the perpetrators. Catholic clergy were quick to identify William Magee, archbishop of Dublin in the Established Church, as a leading culprit. Magee's visitation charge of 1822 – in layman's terms, instructions to his clergy – launched the confrontational attitudes of what became known variously as the Second Reformation or the Irish Reformation.

John Synge's fourth son, Edward, was born early in March 1826 in England. By April 1828, Roundwood was empty, not merely of pupils and Synges but even of furniture. 'Pestalozzi' wrote to his children (who were settled into Buckridge in Devon), describing the solitary appearance of the place and expressing the hope that 'some person will be found soon to go and live there'.[2] It is recorded that migration to the English south coast was prompted by Mrs Synge's ill-health. Certainly, she died in 1830. Less acceptable is the claim that John Synge travelled

In Darby's field

so as to find (or keep in touch with) fellow believers in the doctrines of what will later become the Plymouth Brethren. The crucial development inside that movement – separation from the State Church – effectively took place in Ireland, not England, when 'the saints' decided that a non-ordained layman could administer holy communion. The Irish Sea did not divide but united these immovable seceders.

The power which divided the Red Sea in Moses' time might yet bind those divided by the Irish Sea under the Union. John Synge's household would be a testing ground. While living near Teignmouth, Synge had employed as a tutor to his children Henry Craik (1805–1866), who had already performed the same task for Exeter-based A. N. Groves. As the young man's diary shows, his duties were by no means restricted to instruction of his employer's sons. While still in Exeter, he was spending up to eight hours a day on 'Greek Roots for Mr. Synge' and devoting the rest of his time to 'the Scriptures etc.'. These labours are an early indication of Synge's concern with the teaching of classical languages, contrary to the preferences of his first mentor, J. H. Pestalozzi. By August 1829, however, the tutor was fully engaged – 'Morning at Genesis with Mr. Synge. Forenoon, as usual, with my pupils. Spent the afternoon in my study, and had a long and happy solitary walk. Evening engaged with Homer, and Greek Testament translations for Mr. Synge.'[3] Craik's attachment at this juncture was the local Baptist Church, and it is a mark of Synge's evangelical liberalism that one so far from being 'Church' should be entrusted with the education of his sons.

Still in his early twenties, Craik was confident he could spiritually classify 'all those that generally attend our ministry in any part of the day' and mark up a list 'according to what condition we consider them to be in – converted, inquiring, doubting, or dead'. In the midst of this assessment, he was also paying court to Miss Mary Anderson, a local woman of compatible views. His work as a tutor was evidently rewarding for, on Friday of the week in question, he spent 'till 2 as usual, only more than usual pleasure with my dear boys'. How many of John Synge's offspring came under his tutelage remains a question difficult to answer exactly.

The authorised family tree is not entirely clear about their birth-dates. The eldest, another Francis (1819–1878), was familiar at least by name to the very young JMS, for 'Uncle Francis' inherited (or, rather, repurchased) Glanmore in the wake of the Great Famine. He was born on 11 April 1819, and thus was ten when Henry Craik became the family tutor. For the next boy, Alexander Hamilton Synge, the genealogist provides no date of birth though it is likely he arrived in 1821. There was also Edward – again entered without a birth-date, though he can be assigned to 1826, and finally (so to speak) John Hatch Synge, for whom a date of 10 June 1824 is provided.[4] Pedantry on the question of John Hatch Synge's age may be forgiven on two counts – first, as he was baptised in memory of his grandfather (the silent MP), he testifies to a degree of confidence in that ancestry as a wholly proper one; second, if he was instructed by Craik (the future

Plymouth Brother) then the material legacy in turn transmitted to his own household should be further considered in the light of such instruction.

Even if John Hatch Synge was born in 1823 (as some evidence suggests) rather than 1824, he may not have come under Craik's influence as early as 1829. By the end of that year, tutor and employer were absorbed in a *Principia Herbraica* on which the younger man might labour 'between seven and eight hours' in a day while nonetheless praying His Heavenly Father to make this 'a week of prayer'. The conflict between activity and reflection was one Craik noted acutely within the emergent group of 'saints', for he had observed a difference between his own inclinations and those of George Anderson, his future brother-in-law – 'he fitted for activity, and I for contemplation'. The conflicting occupations of fallen man, he trusted 'will be united in the rest of heaven'.[5]

The relationship between master and employee was scarcely any clearer. Craik recorded time spent correcting the proofs of the *Principia*, but Synge's contribution to the work cannot be estimated. That their partnership was designed to be temporary is manifest in Craik's attempts to enlist himself for overseas activity with the Baptist Missionary Society. When, on 7 December 1829, he wrote 'Mr. Synge and Francis Synge', the implication is that the master was no longer at Teignmouth but probably back in Ireland. The second of his addressees was almost certainly Francis [Synge-] Hutchinson (1802–1833), the son of Archdeacon Samuel Synge and Dorothy Hatch. Nevertheless, Craik could not rely on his employer's approval of a rapid departure for India – after all, there was still work to be done. And so, on the last day of January 1830, he 'enjoyed some meltings of heart, and prayed that Mr. Synge's heart might be inclined for my immediate entrance upon missionary work'.[6] The desired approval depended on completion of the Hebrew project before Synge's return at the end of February. In April 1830, the two men were working together again, and in the event Craik differed with the Baptists about the preparations necessary for work abroad. The following year, he published *Principia Hebraica; or, an Easy Introduction to the Hebrew Language: exhibiting, in twenty-four tables, the interpretation of all the Hebrew and Chaldee words, both primitives and derivatives, contained in the Old Testament Scriptures*. According to his later associates among the Brethren, the book was published 'at the expense of John Synge Esq.' whose any other contribution to it is passed over in silence.[7] As with the uncertainty about Craik's contribution to little John Hatch Synge's education, these lacunae affect our appreciation of life at Glanmore in the 1830s and 1840s when JMS's father was growing up.

In April 1831, Craik forsook Buckridge House for the local Baptists, though the break was hardly schismatic. John Synge's wife was by now dead and the family entering into a new existence. One reason behind Craik's choice lay in his eventual conviction that there was no scriptural authority for infant baptism: this certainly confirms his difference from 'Church' but not necessarily from John

In Darby's field

Synge whose own children remain elusive among the parish registers of Devon and Dublin. We must assume that those of his sons who entered Holy Orders had been duly baptised, but the record of John Hatch Synge still remains largely blank.

One phase of Synge's life had closed with the death of Isabella Hamilton in February 1830. Whether or not her poor health had encouraged his English Riviera exile, the future lay in County Wicklow. The death of his father Francis Synge (sometime MP) in 1831 added further weight to the argument. A letter to the family governess acknowledged that social responsibility must draw him to Glanmore – 'indeed, were I disposed to cast it all behind my back, justice to others would oblige me for some time to labour at it'.[8] And whether or not Frances Steele (whom he married, very promptly, in 1832) was the amiable Fanny of 1809 is now probably beyond resolution. In marrying his brother's wife's sister, he followed a family pattern in which extended prior acquaintance was normal.

Like her predecessor, the second Mrs Synge brought seven children to birth.[9] Concerning these the family tree has little to say – Samuel (died s.p.), Richard (died in Australia aged 39 in 1874, having married and begotten children), Isabella (married and bore children), Robert Daly (joined 90th Regiment, died s.p. at Lucknow in 1857), Henry (also a soldier and colonel of the Egyptian Gendarmarie; ransomed for £15,000 when captured at Salonika, died 1883), Frances Mary (born 16 April 1842 at Glanmore, married an English clergyman in 1869, died at Cheltenham in 1883), and finally George (born 1842, died 1926, no further details). Second families have a difficult role in life, often usurping the physical space of survivors from the first, yet never displacing them in terms of entail or seniority. John Hatch Synge, the dramatist's father, grew up in Glanmore as these half-brothers and sisters came successively into the world. The existence – in legal documentation – of an otherwise untraceable Thomas Synge will be considered in chapter 18.

Colonel Synge of Salonika hit the discreet headlines of *The Times* and other papers in the 1870s, when the British Government was forced to negotiate with 'brigands' and pay a large ransom for his release. Otherwise there was no recurrence of the distinction which had marked the family during its Irish ecclesiastical eighteenth-century heyday. The less renowned of the two soldiers derived his Christian names from Robert Daly (1783–1872) who, having long served as rector of Powerscourt (County Wicklow), became bishop of Cashel in 1843. In this fashion, John Synge and his second wife signalled their continuing attachment to the Church of Ireland at a time when secession was in the air.

Synge's activities in the 1820s embraced educational and religious initiatives, the results communicated to the public through his own printing press. Although he displayed reluctance to take up his Wicklow cross on the death of his father, but cultivated an intense domesticity at Buckridge House, his interests were part and parcel of a broader movement. There is no doubt that many participants in the

Second (or Irish) reformation regarded their cause as a progressive one, even if the foe adopted the language both of democratic reform and Catholic reconciliation with the state. The millenarian expectations of some among the evangelical protestants was matched by widespread belief in the Prophecies of Pastorini among the Catholic populace. Ironically, these latter were a folk-version of speculations about the Revelation of Saint John the Divine, originally propagated in England in the 1770s.[10]

Through histories of the Kildare Place Society and the opposition its schools encountered, it is tempting to regard the period as demonstrating once again the binary structure of Irish conflict – between protestant and Catholic. In practice, both 'parties' were far from homogeneous in their words or deeds. Catholicism did not connote nationalism to the extent which would characterise the latter third of the nineteenth century (and after); what's more, within the Catholic Church liberal and conservative elements were discernible. The energetic James Warren Doyle (1786–1834), who was Catholic bishop of Kildare and Leighlin from 1819, encapsulated in his own life much that was paradoxical in Irish ideological strife. His reputation, and the ecumenical values associated with him, pervades *An Irish Utopia* (1906), one of the minor works of Wicklow literature to be considered near the close of the present book.

Doyle came from a family with both Catholic and protestant wings. An Augustinian friar, he was educated at the University of Coimbra from which vantage point he observed the war against Napoleon until, in 1813, he returned to a series of professorships at the seminary in Carlow. Philosophically, he found no problem in combining acceptance of the British constitution, founded on Lockean principles, with his obligations as a Catholic priest in Ireland. While in Portugal, he had served as a volunteer under Wellesley, and assisted in conveying diplomatic papers in 1808. Doyle, who had witnessed violence in 1798, was a lifelong opponent of revolution in any form, a dedicated reformer of his own diocese and an articulate critic of the Establishment, religious and administrative, in Ireland.

The Church of Ireland in those days sported a numerous episopacy amongst whom frugal living did not command wide support. By 1840, it would have its ermine wings clipped, and by 1870 its status as the Established Church completely annihilated. But in the 1820s, everything seemed redeemable. While protestant missionary societies worked relentlessly for the conversion of Catholics, Archbishop Magee of Dublin could question the political reliability of such converts. It was this apparent prioritising of worldly considerations (security of the United Kingdom) over spiritual ones (bringing souls to the Heavenly Kingdom) which so outraged the curate in Powerscourt parish that he launched upon a path which led him to become the leader of the early 'Darbyites' as the Christian Brethren (their presently preferred designation) were called.

The formal origins of the Brethren lie in Dublin University and in the County

In Darby's field

of Wicklow; they can be dated for convenience to a conference held in September 1833 at Powerscourt House in Wicklow, chaired by John Synge, as a sympathetic local landlord. Sir Samuel Synge Hutchinson's son, Francis Synge Hutchinson (1802–1833), accommodated the urban equivalent of the Powerscourt meetings at his home on Fitzwilliam Square. Thus the Brethren emerged out of the Church of Ireland under the guidance of two first cousins – John 'Pestalozzi' Synge and Francis Synge Hutchinson, whose fathers had married John Hatch's daughters. In formal terms, the Synges stayed within the Church, while following the defection with sympathy.

The intellectual or spiritual origins of the Brethren include the Irvingite movement, the Moravian Church, pietism, and even the late medieval followers of Thomas à Kempis. Their affinity to the *ancienne dissidence* of Switzerland is also noteworthy.[11] But of more immediate concern here is the principle of anti-territoriality upon which they agreed at their foundation in the 1830s and which (with modifications) holds true for them today. The evangelical breakfasts at Fitzwilliam Square had resulted in the bold decision that an ordained minister or priest was not essential to the celebration of Holy Communion, that any layman might break bread and invite others to join in the sacrament. With this anti-clericalism, there came in time the practice (if not actually a theory) of anti-territorialism, that is, the organisation of religious life without reference to such entities as the parish, circuit, or the district.

In developmental terms, there was initially no break with the Established Church – meetings were, so to speak, additional to normal services. But with the Brethren gradually forced into a separate organisation, their denial of a priestly role highlighted the absence among them of any parsonage or presbytery, that is, the residence or dedicated private property which contributed to the distinctive life of the local church leader. In turn, the right of any layman to take the initiative (if moved by grace) in worship became an ecclesiology, a theory of the Church stressing its non-identification with any earthly institution. It was a spiritual fellowship of believers (or 'saints'), requiring no territorial divisions or hierarchies of office.

In local eyes these abstract principles might appear as little more than eccentric practices. John Synge's travels backwards and forwards across the Irish Sea led to the introduction of several new ways of doing things on the Glanmore Estate. During the mid-1830s, he was active in using print for the purposes of domestic instruction. One memoir of the time directly links this earnest educational endeavour with religious inquiry and renewal. In the words of the Revd R. S. Brooke, the master of Glanmore was 'a skilled Hebraist [who] had written for the use of his sons, an excellent grammar of that language, which he had himself drawn up, and printed in his house, possessing a press and a font of Hebrew types, and working the sheets off himself'.[12] In fact, the book exists in two quite different forms – one a large folio-sized 'teaching aid' for classroom use, and the other a standard-sized textbook intended for the instructor rather than the instructed. This latter distinction, however, was not sustained in Synge's pedagogy. The lengthy title perhaps stressed too many objectives, but the isolated superiority of a teacher was not among them – *An Easy Introduction to the Hebrew Language on the Principles of Pestalozzi; Intended to Enable Parents and Teachers who Consider the Original of the Word of God the Most Suitable Object of Early Instruction To Acquire it Themselves in the Act of Teaching.*[13] The method of instruction which allowed the teacher to admit to his pupils his own limited knowledge of the subject they studied together was one Synge had observed at Iverdun – as he styled Pestalozzi's establishment. Though the Swiss master's example is cited on several occasions in the prefatory material, other influences are also acknowledged, including R. L. Edgeworth. Early in his introductory remarks, Synge had confessed that he had been induced to inquire 'whether his duty as a Christian parent did not demand of him to make the change' from prioritising the classics to introducing Hebrew. However indirectly, this shift of emphasis leaned towards a recognition of vernaculars, and hence of Gaelic. Dedicated to domestic education, *An Easy Introduction* also admitted to broader ambitions, notably the conversion of latter-day Jews to Christianity through their ancient language.[14] Here Synge touched on a distinctive aspect of Brethren theology.

From the same witness, it is established that the book was never published in the commercial sense, and thus represented yet another instance of what might be termed 'progressive retreat'. Keen to ensure the best means of educating children – and naturally commencing with his own – Synge went to the trouble of writing a book and simultaneously limited its distribution to his own circle. What is striking is the use of print rather than mere manuscript circulation: there is a seizing upon technology (admittedly limited and scarcely 'industrial' in scale) and then a rural seclusion which balances or cancels the progressive thrust. Synge's printing is emblematic of his outlook in general. This factor is particularly evident in the folio version of *An Easy Introduction*, which includes twenty-four tables of Hebrew roots, scrupulously orders these in reverse (as one reads Hebrew from right to left), and places a title-page at what Westerners would regard as the back of the book. The mental discipline and energy required for the production of such a book – normally undertaken only by a university press such as Oxford's – was immense. Even if the task had been shared with Barnett at the time of initial publication in 1831, it still testified to Synge's total commitment of mind and body to a programme of education in which religious, linguistic, pedagogic and domestic conventions were overturned, renewed and (in a strict sense) revolutionised. If, as R. S. Brooke strongly implied, the whole operation was at some point in the early 1830s crated and transported across the Irish sea from Devon to Wicklow, then dedication is seen to veer towards benign fanaticism.

In Darby's field

The vestiges of Synge's endeavour survive in pathetic confusion. The Library at Trinity College, Dublin, possesses a larger folder (Papyrus Case 43) of related Glanmore 'publications', nearly seventy large printed leaves, teaching material including spelling lists, instructive tales, geographical data, etc. Most of these were printed by Thomas Collins at Glanmore. *Reading Lessons from the Instructor The Three Kingdoms of Nature* ran to at least seventeen items of which ten survive. These were written by John Synge c. 1835.[15] The role of God the Creator is stressed occasionally, but the tendency of the work is to disclose the enormous variety of nature. This leads sometimes to rather odd announcements. For example, 'Fish have no voice, and no external organs of hearing; yet a few, as the tunny, and the ling, utter slight sounds; a species of gurnard has a note like the cuckoo ...' (Lesson 8). Some of the spelling lessons were 'Printed for R. M. Tims ...' which indicates a degree of commercial ambition. Two items were the work of 'Barnett, Printer, Teignmouth', and these use a chain border which reappears in the Glanmore printings, further evidence of the transfer of type and ornaments from Devon.

While all of this reads now as the admirable industry of a concerned parent, in the Irish context of the 1820s and 1830s, the fanaticism may not have seemed so benign. George Bull, a minor figure among Dublin printers, had been involved in Synge's first venture into good works, responsible for setting up the Pestalozzi manuals at Roundwood. His subsequent appearance as the printer of Orange Order material cannot be taken as any indication of his former employer's political allegiance, but the recurrence of R. M. Tims among Dublin booksellers offering Synge's educational material for sale is almost as indicative of support for bible-and-church attitudes.

Recognising himself as essentially an indoor evangelist and a thinker, Synge had persuaded an Englishman to join him in 1832. William Graeme Rhind (1794–1863) was born in Gillingham in Kent, the son of a naval doctor. After experience at sea, the young man betook himself to Cambridge where he mixed with a circle including several converted Jews.[16] The style of evangelicalism which he and John Synge embraced was decidedly sympathetic to Judaism, and Rhind's undergraduate experience contributed to his friend's more scholarly interest in the Hebrew language. Together with his wife and two children, Rhind took up residence at the mouth of the Devil's Glen, and spent the best part of seven years in Clorah Cottage. His task was to act as 'moral agent' on the Synge estate, in imitation of the example set on the larger and more prosperous Powerscourt estate to the north. Spiritual and material objectives were speedily identified; these involved religious exhortation and bible reading on his part, requiring in turn a commitment to cottage industry on the part of the local people generally.

In some respects, the mixture was as before, when the Incorporated Society ran Templestown School with a view to inculcating biblical protestantism and thrift among the few inhabitants of upland Wicklow. But in the century after 1735, too much had altered for the formula to be swallowed without difficulty. The population had increased considerably and, though no one could predict the crisis, Ireland stood on the brink of Famine. In step with this increase had gone a radical shift in popular attitudes towards authority, whether of church or state. Since 1829, Catholics were permitted to sit in parliament, while church building flourished in the aftermath of Emancipation. The bitter conflicts of the 1820s on the issue of education had led to the establishment of a Board of Commissioners for National Education in 1831. While John Synge was setting up his Pestalozzian system indoors at Glanmore, his friend Rhind was obliged to preach among cottagers less remote from bureaucratic state initiative and popular religious renewal.

If it were possible to isolate Rhind's initiatives from these wider developments, then they would deserve high commendation. His priority was 'to give, as much as possible, employment to those in health'. His second objective – 'to administer to the sick, both by medicine and other necessities' – reveals the evangelical motivation underlying the first. While he successfully promoted knitting, spinning and weaving among seventy families on Synge's estate, even the material benefits did not automatically accrue to the workers. Rhind's own cloak and travelling bag were made of painted linen prepared under his supervision; likewise his daughter wore stockings knitted by cottagers. His own account of this mini-economy quickly reveals its limited character:

> often times I am made their savings bank, until their earnings reach seven or eight shillings, for a little pig etc. Thus, also the shops are aided; the shoemaker, a poor Protestant man, and true Christian, is also aided; and the great wheel goes round easier and better: for although I do not oblige them to take their earnings out in clothing, yet nine-tenths prefer it. If they are sick, I visit them; and if in need, I aid them; and during the confinement of mothers of families, if my funds admit of it, I give them extra aid – not in money (this, as much as possible, I avoid), but in flannels, baby clothes, etc.[17]

Rhind's system was never designed to generate independence among Synge's tenants and, in so far as they became self-sufficient in clothing, they also covered the moral agent and his family in homespun.

The administration of medicine likewise involved a degree of benefit returning to the agent himself. Synge allowed Rhind funds 'sufficient entirely to support a weekly general dispensary, and also one of daily call' at Clorah Cottage. Not only does this suggest that the moral agent doubled up as valetudinarian, the unfolding account of medical provision on the Glanmore Estate also casts him in the role of amateur doctor and vet. It is true that he relied on 'the physicians of the two neighbouring towns, distant five miles each', who attended *gratis* to any cases Rhind sent to them and admitted the patients to hospital where necesary. However, he personally vaccinated children, while 'the poor people for miles around entertained a high opinion of the "doctor's" skill, and not unfrequently have their hearts been rejoiced at seeing their cow, or the pig, which they feared would die, perfectly restored under the skilful treatment of "his honour"'.[18]

Shortly after his arrival, Rhind encountered the devastating effects of cholera in Wicklow. According to his loyal biographer, he alone was prepared to enter the home of a dying victim, while the terrified family clustered round the door. Such an incident would have stood the newcomer in good stead, even if he had refused to take a proffered glass of whiskey as protection. Though courage was recognised, motives might still be suspect in the eyes of a populace for whom biblical protestantism was decidedly the commitment of a minority. Some time round 1835, Rhind was severely burnt when the children's bedroom at Clorah caught fire. Though the nurse had already rescued her charges, their father impetuously 'grasped the now ignited bed in his arms, scarcely knowing what he did, and ... in a few hours he lay blind and deaf, his hands and face a mass of blisters, at the hospitable dwelling of his friend Mr. Synge'. Such crises reveal a great deal about the circle in which the father (John Hatch Synge) and favourite aunts of the future dramatist JMS were growing up. While Rhind's panic is understandable to any parent, the accepted explanation of the event is not – in that very week, Rhind had neglected to maintain an annual 'abstinence from all pleasant food' and so regarded his suffering as 'the Lord's voice to him in consequence'.[19] Superstition amongs the tenantry met its match in the superstition of their instructors.

The Synges' urban property endured throughout these country excitements. In June 1836, John Synge leased premises on the north side of Hatch Street in Dublin to a builder named Samuel Roberts. The development of such possessions underwrote the expense of spiritual devotion, and John Synge's sons, Alexander Hamilton Synge and John Hatch Synge greatly expanded the family's leasings to Roberts in the 1860s as each sought to buttress a professional salary with the fruits of inherited real estate.[20] Holy living in the world became increasingly perilous, at least if gentry status was to be preserved in tandem with piety. The contribution of the Brethren was to rewrite the terms in which a professionalised clergy was to be considered and the terms also in which land related to church.

Rhind left Ireland in 1838, having decided that conscience would not permit him to take holy orders. He cleaved to the Brethren, to which commitment his friendship with John Synge and Lady Powerscourt formed no barrier. Yet, like Synge, he did not quit the Church in any public act. Before departing, he addressed himself at length to the local people in a handbill which we may assume was printed at Glanmore on John Synge's press. In this he stressed the paradoxical attitude towards good works which characterised the new evangelicalism. 'If you are saved, it is not your works, but the blood of Jesus Christ that must save you, and the Holy Ghost who must teach you; and if he does, he will make you *holy* men, women, and children, delighting in good works.'[21] This last concession was to have important consequences for the Brethren when famine hit Ireland a decade later, for it marked them off from the 'soupers' who provided nourishment but on condition that the beneficiary conform to protestantism.

Back in Britain, the moral agent had a different story to tell. Answering questions in 1844 from a man named O'Byrne who was compiling a biographical dictionary of naval officers, Rhind declared that he 'was paid off in March 1816 & since then have been unemployed'.[22] Did missionary work in Wicklow count as something higher than employment? Was Rhind a liar and a humbug? The climate within and surrounding Glanmore did not encourage clarity of thought. The catalogue of Synge Papers in Trinity College Library describes as a mystical experience an incident which befell the master of Glanmore and his youngest son in May 1839. On the endpaper of his sketchbook, the father jotted down a brief report of what happened, 'Thursday night a Minute or two before 11 oclock Jack and I felt our room shake distinctly three times. He was in bed & I was standing in the middle of the Room.' While this seems too banal to be mystical, there can be little doubt that the three vibrations were read by Synge as a Trinitarian sign, and he continued his account by recalling how 'the Sunday before we had remarked a curious ring round the Sun'.[23]

In the church which his father had built, John Synge's clerical friends erected a plaque to commemorate his 'real humility and genuine faith'. The gesture at once confirmed his attachment to the religious Establishment and signified a need to proclaim this as if in defiance of contrary evidence. His affections had been fixed on things above, 'thus affording to all who knew him the surest evidence of being found in his lot amongst the blessed'. The grammar of this commemoration mirrors the lingering uncertainty of Synge's ultimate affiliation – how could the proper focus of *his* affections afford to others any indication of their own lot? The citation concludes, however, with an emphasis on the last things, 'the coming of the lord of glory for which he looked and waited daily'.[24]

The previous ten years had been dominated by hopes which required no institutional support, a factor which emphasised the radical aspect of Brethren attitudes towards earthly authority. The split of 1848 resulting in the conflict between Open and Exclusive Brethren was articulated by J. N. Darby in the words, 'You have received those enemies of the faith, and have partaken of their evil deeds.'[25] These events took place within a longer process of development in which Darby's authority was expressed less through charisma and increasingly through an insistence on tradition (i.e., his own teaching). The Darbyist Exclusive Brethren themselves split in 1879, allegedly because it was discovered that a member of the Ryde meeting had married his deceased wife's sister. Further schism broke out after Darby's death in 1882, and in 1908 the Tunbridge Wells meeting split into 'Strange' and 'anti-Strange' factions, their names deriving from the member whose behaviour had caused the difficulty.[26]

In Darby's field

It is all too easy to dismiss the conduct of Brethren as so much pie-in the-sky, humbug, or whatever other sweetmeat fails to take your fancy. The discovery that Major Webber Gardiner and his wife (the former Mrs Francis Synge, née Editha Truell) held investments in the Indianapolis Brewery is depressing, given their rigorous Exclusivism in religion, homeopathic allegiances in medicine and evangelical attitude towards alcohol.[27] Nor is Mrs Gardiner's refusal to submit to a British doctor's examination for the purposes of completing a Life Insurance policy wholly consistent with her subscription to J. N. Darby's rigour. Gardiner's illness – whatever afflicted the poor man – required him to stand up while eating his meals, which he did by placing his food on a drum-like device raised above the table – or even sideboard, when the non-Exclusive were present on suffrance. But these are human beings no more prone to self-contradiction than the average Fellow of All Souls or nun of Kenmare.

The split between 'open' and 'exclusive' parties within the Brethren, occurring in the late 1840s, should not be written off merely as further evidence of the fissiparous tendency of all sects, nor – though this is a less absolute plea – as the consequence of Darby's autocratic personality. Though the ground shared by Catholics and Brethren (as they came to be known) in the early 1830s has been noted, there issued from a (briefly) common experience roads which led in divergent directions. Metaphors of ground and road seem apt because landownership, as the nineteenth century's nervous image of realty, aspired to reality. While binary sectarianism flourished in Irish politics, an egalitarianism of the possessors emerged alongside: in this context, the anti-territorialism of the Brethren remained a radical feature, at least until 1848, with some benefit to the non-possessors or dispossessed in the Famine years.

The split, when it came, was lost to most eyes amid the larger events commencing in 1848 – the defeat of Chartism, the four-year survival of the second French Republic and the defeat of Hungary in a long war against Austria and Russia. By this point, the saints had ceased to have any meaningful attachment to Ireland as their *fons et origo*: they were Plymouth Brethren in Britain, Darbyistes in France and Switzerland. The split occurred in the continental context of revolution and counter-revolution. French protestants generally found the altered political situation required a careful response, both as to their relations with the state and with each other. The suffragan pastor of the Reformed (i.e. Calvinist) Church in Paris caught a specific line of thought in *The Way of Patience Better than that of Secession*.[28] While the internal situation in France was highly complex – and beyond the competence of this writer – what is significant for debates in the 1890s involving J. M. Synge's Paris acquaintance is the appearance of such reflections in English-language London publications.

Darby, for his part, attended to the Francophone world with far greater assiduity. Pamphlets flew from his pen with all the confidence of Holy Writ itself, their title pages proclaiming simultaneous publication in Geneva, Lausanne, Montpellier, Nîmes, Paris, Vevey.[29] Unlike the Irish experience, French protestantism in the sixteenth century had sprung from indigenous sources; despite his association with Geneva, John Calvin (1509–1564) was born in northern France and studied in Paris. In the words of one authority, Calvin's writing 'helped to adapt the construction of the French sentence to argument as distinct from narrative'.[30] The wars of religion (1562–1598) were, in a pure sense, civil conflicts with the rival parties equally 'French' in any modern nationalist sense. If there was an 'alien' element it was Catherine de' Medici, Italian mother of two successive Catholic kings. The protestant victor, Henry of Navarre, became a Catholic and ascended the throne as Henry IV (the first Bourbon king). In 1598, he issued the Edict of Nantes protecting the religious liberties of Huguenots (or Francophone Calvinists.)

This relatively ancient history was, of course, to be throughly interrogated in the light of subsequent events. Opponents of the Revolution in 1789, which unseated the Bourbons, believed it to have been prompted by international conspiracies of Freemasons and Illuminati, with whom all the non-Catholic French might be guiltily associated. In the course of the nineteenth century, the identification of Catholicism with French nationalism was intensified through the growth of an explicitly secular revolutionary movement, and by the 1890s Charles Maurras' Action Française could target a protestant family such as the Monods as a network of foreign influence, hostile to the true France.

In this developing context, exclusive Darbyisme after 1848 inverted the radicalism of the movement's origins, based upon a rigid interpretation of II Corinthians 6: 17.[31] Marx, if he thought about it at all, would not have been surprised. The aftermath of 1848 was to be bourgeois reaction and the abandonment of the proletariat to their potent but isolated position as revolutionary vanguard. An anonymous attack directed at Darby's Irish followers in 1872 rhetorically inquired 'Is it true that "exclusivism" is to the assemblies and meetings of Christians what the House of Commons is to different London clubs?' The context of this specifically political analogy was the post-Establishment moment, whose memorable objective 'Home Rule' was the coinage of a churchman. The pamphleteer went further in tracing his analogy, accusing Darby's right-hand man, William Kelly (1821–1906), of falling into 'the Roman Catholic error'. If Darbysism was still radical at the time of J. M. Synge's birth, it was by the same token hierarchical, a spiritual tyranny.[32]

After the split of 1848/1849, the 'open' response among Brethren was hardly less reactionary, as the movement settled into being one sect amongst many in Britain and Ireland. But, in Ireland at least, separation did not exclude simultaneous participation in larger religious projects – parish activities of the Established Church and interdenominational missions – perhaps as a consequence of the

In Darby's field

trauma of Famine. To be sure, the next great evangelical tumult – the Ulster revival of 1859 – occurred in an industrialising zone and tended to confirm the opium theory of Marx.[33] But in time, the more fluid attitude of Irish Open Brethren – with whom the Synge family maintained open doors – converged with a broader and far more important current of thought in the late nineteenth century. This saw the growth – or restart – of pan-protestant 'Christian socialism', in which evangelical concern for the soul and philanthropic endeavours to assist the hard-pressed body merged in 'city missions'.[34] The protestant Paris, to which JMS travelled on New Year's Day 1895, was home to the alma mater of John Calvin and the location of new bodies such as Société des Étudiants Protestantes. Synge joined the latter, and its wider cultural significance demands attention.

In tracing this sudden effusion of local piety and its unexpectedly global repercussions – global and obscure – we lost sight of the charismatic founder. Yet it may be that his image has returned to the locality through a dramatic and ironic transfer from the theological to the cultural which is our underlying concern. John Nelson Darby (1800–1882) had been the youngest son of an Irish landlord with merchant interests in London who in 1823 inherited the family seat at Leap, in County Offaly, and took up residence. His son had already graduated from Trinity College in 1819, and was expected to follow a career at the bar. But, even before he had graduated, he was in touch with Robert Daly: his sister, Susannah Darby, had married Edward Pennefather, a distinguished lawyer whose County Wicklow home lay close to Robert Daly's parish of Enniskerry. The spring of 1823 had seen Daly contend in Dublin with Robert Owen, and the two men shared a sense of urgency with regard to politico-religious issues. Later, Darby described the years 1819–1827 as a time when 'universal sorrow and sin pressed upon my spirit'.[35] Significantly, the experience persisted while he served as curate to Daly, attending to an upland portion of the parish. Yet he was regarded at the same time as a man of boundless capacity. His brother-in-law thought he might 'reduce the legal chaos to order', while the perpetual curacy he occupied for a few years seems to have been carved from neighbouring parishes exactly to accommodate him. A school already stood in that desolate place, a dividend perhaps from Daly's earlier involvement with De Vesci as a governor of the Abbeyleix Pestalozzian experiment.[36]

Enniskerry was dominated by the Wingfield estate, which in turn existed under the sway of Theodosia (1800–1836), the second wife of the 5th Viscount Powerscourt. Her ladyship came from the Howard family, and thus the household constituted an alliance of Wicklow landlords given to religious enthusiasm. Although they had begun in amity, the late 1820s witnessed a struggle between Daly and Darby, between Establishment and secession. This was all the more fierce for its taking place within a church claiming a hegemonic entitlement to the loyalty – also the tithes – of rich and poor alike. If Darby's church at Calary stood on the northern edge of an extensive bog, with the neat estate village of Enniskerry reassuringly close, then John Synge's half-abandoned Roundwood Park stood at the southern end, with gothic Glanmore below it among the trees.

The setting is not unlike the Jutlandish landscape within which Søren Kierkegaaard will rise up in protest against Hegelian system a decade later. And if Theodosia and Daly have not as individuals left their mark on the nineteenth century, through Darby they participated in a drama which has gone round the world, a drama to which Synge closely attended. There are formal, even processional movements to be observed. When Darby transferred his loyalty from the law to the church, he was only undertaking the first stage of a metamorphosis which would take years to complete. Indeed, this professional manoeuvre scarcely counted: the second 'stage' would constitute for him the sole but total transformation, compared to which ordination had been but a poor substitute.

For an account of this Damascus-near-Delgany, we turn to a curiously English and sceptical source. In an autobiography of 1850, Frank Newman (1805–1897), brother of the cardinal, left a brief but moving testimony of the time he spent in Ireland following his election (1826) as a Fellow of Balliol College. He passed fifteen months as private tutor to Edward Pennefather in whose household he made the acquaintance of Darby, a kinsman of his host. This occurred before Darby had broken with the Established Church, and when he was still labouring among the few faithful of Calary, on the edge of the Wicklow Mountains:

> A fallen cheek, a bloodshot eye, crippled limbs resting on crutches, a seldom shaven beard, a shabby suit of clothes and a generally neglected person ... Every evening he sallied forth to teach in the cabins, and roving far and wide over mountain and amid bogs, was seldom home before midnight. By such exertions his strength was undermined, and he so suffered in his limbs that not lameness only, but yet more serious results were feared. He did not fast on purpose, but his long walks through wild country and indigent people inflicted on him much severe deprivation: moreover, he ate whatever food offered itself, – food unpalatable and often indigestible to him, his whole frame might have vied in emaciation with a monk of La Trappe.
>
> Such a phenomenon intensely excited the poor Romanists, who looked on him as a genuine 'saint' of the ancient breed.[37]

Before Newman's death in 1897, he had been an active writer on a variety of political and social issues, having contributed to the development of University Hall, part of the network of lodgings and other accommodation in which JMS himself stayed when visiting London. Whether JMS read *Phases of Faith* – much reprinted – scarcely matters, for memories of Darby's appearance doubtless survived in other quarters, including folklore in Wicklow. As Eric Hobsbawm has observed in timely fashion, folk-history is an unsatisfactory model in many instances, but it can open up a reflexive possibility in otherwise leaden accounts of the past.[38] The proposition – that the Saint in JMS's 'The Well of the Saints' (1905) owes something to the founder of the Brethren – gains a material and historical dimension through the continuing availability of Newman's account. It also carries within it a cargo of local and domestic significances.

While Darby despised the opportunism of his Church on the issue of Catholic admission to parliament, he preached in a context which was hostile to 'Rome'. He was only part of a wider protestant movement directed towards the conversion of Irish Catholics. While the Irish Reformation of the 1820s had been principally based in County Cavan, Wicklow felt its impact and aspired to follow. The Newcastle Baronial Reformation Society was founded at Newtownmountkennedy in February 1827; recorded conversions – not numerous – including at least two at Nun's Cross within six months. At the outset, on Sunday 25 February, a Catholic schoolmaster and his wife 'conformed' somewhere in the Newcastle Society's territory. Later in 1827, Darby resigned his curacy and moved towards what would become – with John Synge's not uncritical assistance – the Brethren.

The Saint of the play miraculously restores the sight of Martin Doul and his wife, Mary, both of whom are beggars ironically devoted to the making of rushlights. It would be a crude reduction to regard Darby as the 'original' of a dramatic character, or *The Christian Examiner* as JMS's source for the Douls. Yet 'blindness' was a commonly used term for the spiritual condition in which 'the poor Romanists' were said to exist by Irish evangelicals of Mrs Kathleen Synge's generation and later. These theological animosities carried manifest evidence of class conflict, not because something called 'the Protestant Ascendancy' exercised political, economic and social power over a largely Catholic populace, but – a quite different matter – because the idea of Ascendancy emerged as a recognition (semi-conscious, at best) that such power was impermanent, contested, and subject to a more complex and dynamic class conflict.[39] This aspect of the larger movement of social forces in Ireland during the nineteenth century is not remote from the action of the play. When Martin Doul receives his sight, instead of being advanced into the company of those who have cured him he is compelled to work at the village forge.

Part V

LITERATURE AT NURSE

17

John Hatch, a country doctor

Mr Hugo's Mountains are Poisoned, and all Persons are hereby Cautioned not to take Dogs thereon.[1]

AMONG the Hatches entered on the rolls of Dublin's eighteenth-century freemen, John Hatch MP did not feature. He was of course without male issue, yet when one bearing both his Christian and surname turns up in County Wicklow early in the next century it is worth inquiring what his relationship with the progenitor of Synges may have been. After all, John 'Pestalozzi' Synge had consciously chosen to christen his third son John Hatch in 1824, and the boy was growing up at Glanmore when a Dr John Hatch came to practise medicine nearby. Theirs was a privileged and comfortable world, though it included differences like any other. There is no evidence that Dr John Hatch ever crossed the threshold of Glanmore, even in the late 1860s when a recurrence of cholera in the area led to the relaxation of 'social distance' among all those struggling to control the outbreak. But we have yet to trace this younger John Hatch's arrival into the county.

Relationship is a delicate issue. Though it was scarcely any worse than London and its 'charter'd streets', Dublin at the end of the eighteenth century dispersed large numbers of embarrassing children through the agency of its Foundling Hospital and, beyond that, through schools where – it was certainly alleged – the names of infants were changed or invented along lines of crude metonymy. (John Field was found in the field, etc.) The counties of Dublin, Wicklow and Carlow were extensively used to settle the unfortunate products of the system.

In the early 1790s, the House of Commons set up a Committee of Enquiry into the management of the Foundling Hospital. In its report of April 1792, a detailed analysis of one Wicklow district (Dunlavin) provided grim statistics. According to records, 469 children were at nurse here on the Wicklow/Kildare/Dublin border. Of these only sixty-five could be reliably traced. More than twice this number were frankly declared to be dead. Seven were said to be with strolling

John Hatch, a country doctor

beggars, two hundred and one with nurses (i.e. surrogate mothers) elsewhere. Of the remaining sixty or so, nothing was known.[2] The resulting report fell stillborn upon the table of the House. More than sixty years later, the legend of these practices – by no means extinct – would echo through the memoirs and manifestos of a newly emergent middle class, Catholic rather than Protestant. In 1867 Fanny Taylor, Protestant English born but converted to the faith of Ireland's majority, cited an unnamed priest on the subject of the Charter Schools. 'Names are changed so that [the children] may have no communication with their [Catholic] parents, and after a little time they are transferred to another parish that the isolation may be the more complete.'[3]

Doubtless this is a synthetic judgement, merging elements which are true in one case or at one time with others which relate to different places or dates. The animosity on both sides cannot be explained away. Yet underlying these stubborn historical themes was another which few if any wished to voice – the doubled existences of the foundlings and the coerced converts, the restlessness of mind and body in these trained mimics of presumed identity. The covert influence of institutions ran like water underground, beneath the grosser, superficial powers of magnates and legal systems. Such unease might outlive revolution itself.

Dunlavin is infamous for the massacre of villagers by loyalist militia in 1798, just six years after the tally of missing infants. The place lies somewhat off an old main road running from Dublin, down the west boundary of County Wicklow, towards Carlow. The immediate vicinity is rich in prehistoric stone monuments, pre-Reformation Christian ruins, and the evidence of seventeenth-century turmoil and settlement. The notable landlord's residence (Tynte Park) was built as late as 1820, further evidence of restored 'normalcy' in a disturbed district. In other ways, Dunlavin's landscape in the nineteenth century protected it from the overt influence of a not too distant capital city. Having endured its world-historical moment, the village slipped off the frontiers of significance into a new rural obscurity. In mid-century, the railway took another route. A tiny outpost of the barony of Upper Talbotstown, its immediate parochial neighbour is Rathsallagh, where the Very Revd Sir Samuel Synge Hutchinson, Bart., had a country seat, Castle Sallagh.

Inside the ecclesiastical structures of the Church of Ireland, Dunlavin had greater distinction through its prebendal stall in Saint Patrick's, where the incumbent sat as a member of the cathedral chapter. In his early days, Jonathan Swift occupied the Dunlavin seat. The second John Hatch appears in the parish's Vestry Minutes for 1 April 1823. He subscribed to a fund to erect a stove in the church in 1824.[4] By late 1824, he is referred to as Dr Hatch. He took part in a parochial Visitation held in Saint Patrick's Cathedral on 25 September 1828. By this date, he is serving as a church warden, and does so again in 1836. If the eighteenth-century Hatches eschewed holy orders, this nineteenth-century kinsman behaved like a model layman, a pillar of his rural parish.

Literature at nurse

The future doctor was born on 20 July 1796, the son of Jeremiah Hatch and his wife Ann (née Hatch). His parents wedded when they were both aged forty or so. Only their maturity in years prevents a recent chronicler from proposing a degree of irregularity in the marriage, which consisted of a civil ceremony followed some time later (on 20 August 1793) of a second *in facie ecclesiae*. They were of course blood-kindred, and suspicion is further increased by their declaring (falsely) that they were Dublin residents at the time they married. Their children were the first of the Ardee family to enjoy university education. In 1820, John (their third son) married Mary Harriet, daughter of Simeon Freeman, who may also have been an Ardee man, though the name Freeman had long been associated with an area of Wicklow into which Dr John Hatch subsequently moved. Freemans had lived at Tomdaragh and Tomriland at least from the mid-eighteenth century, in close proximity to the M'Cracken lands which became part of the Glanmore-Roundwood estate.

Of Dr Hatch's own family, the following can be traced in the parish records: Jeremiah Simeon, born 11 March 1828, baptised 23 March 1828. Mary Harriott [sic], born 1 July 1832, baptised 19 October 1832; Jeremiah Anthony, born 13 November 1834, baptised 16 November 1834. However, Father Mac Iomhair lists two further names – Anna Maria and Jane – while omitting any reference to Jeremiah Simeon and Mary Harriet.[5] As we shall see, an older boy – named after his uncle, the ill-visaged William Hatch of Ardee Castle – had been born in Dublin.

Though his native Ardee was an early sponsor of the local dispensary system, Dr Hatch never had any links with it, preferring Wicklow to which he had moved for reasons now inscrutable.[6] He was not an applicant for the Ardee appointment in 1827, when it fell vacant, choosing to remain in Dunlavin. It seems clear that he moved across country to the Laragh area in mid-east Wicklow during the middle years of the century. A modest increase in income and the desire to secure a larger practice combined to motivate the change. By August 1834, he had been left by Dame Hannah Tynte Caldwell a plot of ground in Dunlavin previously the site of an old playhouse. He was to have use of the property for sixty years, provided he built a house for which she had left specifications; if he omitted to build, the land was his for just twenty-one years. The profit rent he derived from the house duly built was £12 p.a., suggesting a very modest increase of professional comfort for the village doctor. The intention of Dame Hannah's bequest was to assist a man with a young family, whose background did not provide the necessary support.

Opportunities for additional income were rare enough. At its first meeting of 1850, Rathdrum Poor Law Union added Dr Hatch to its list of recognised vaccinators (for the Glendalough and Roundwood area) to be paid a shilling for every successful case. This benefit, it might be noted, came his way five years after his putative kinsman and sometime chair of the Union, John Synge, had died.[7] These changes at Glanmore may have assisted the doctor in settling into mid-Wicklow.

John Hatch, a country doctor

By the time of Griffith's Valuations of c. 1853, no Hatch was registered in Dunlavin, but John Hatch held one acre (house, out-offices and a garden) from Thomas J. Barton in the townland of Laragh East, which lies on the road to Annamoe. In 'When the Moon Has Set', JMS's never-completed-never-abandoned dramatic inquiry into Big House origins, a doctor hovers off-stage, assisting a proprietor to die, carrying the incriminating photograph which might prove a guilty liaison between master and maidservant, a doctor who helpfully lived closer to the town than Kilgreine and who could not quite be accommodated into the house and its uneasy class-consciousness, a messenger of the gods as these died.

A grim, simple, latter-day or imitation structure, Laragh Castle dated from the aftermath of the 1798 rebellion. It stands behind Saint John's Church in the village, and is approached by an avenue graced with a stone arch built of the granite which characterises the house itself. Here for years, Dr Hatch dwelt in relative comfort as a tenant. In May 1858, his eldest son died in India, and a commemorative plaque was erected in the new church close by, recording William Thomas Hatch's birth in Dublin thirty-two years earlier.[8]

Dr Hatch served as medical officer for the Annamoe Dispensary District, and registrar of births, marriages and deaths, from 1845 till 1870. If Griffith's Valuation lists him as a ratepayer in Laragh East, Thom's Directory has him in Rathdrum as late as 1884 (which, as we will see, is impossible). One medical directory of the mid-nineteenth century confirms the identity of the Ardee man and the Annamoe doctor, adding for good measure that he was 'sixteen years superintendent Dunlavin [County Wicklow] District Disp.'. Father Mac Iomhair, drawing on papers preserved in an Ardee solicitor's office, suggests that Dr Hatch retired to his native place in 1870, succeeding his late brother as master of the Castle. Certainly, he was proposed to attend the first post-Disestablishment synod as Ardee parish's fourth representative.

Moving early in his career from Dunlavin to Laragh, Hatch appears to have succeeded Dr Charles Frizell of Castle Kevin who practiced medicine at Annamoe at the beginning of the 1840s. But Hatch's office-holding was not without some interruption. In 1844, the 'Medical Officer of Dispenary of Annamoe and Luganure Mines' was Edward Henry Harding MD, whom Hatch finally replaced the following year. If W. G. Rhind – John 'Pestalozzi' Synge's moral agent at Glanmore – relied on the Annamoe dispensary in the 1830s, the doctor in question was almost certainly Frizell, a landed gentleman of the area. Frizell/Harding/Hatch – this succession of country doctors (to whom we might add Samuel Manning, medical officer at Rathdrum Workhouse) provides a list of names which weave in and out of JMS's life-story, for a Manning was the third co-proprietor (with Synge's brother-in-law, Harry Stephens, and Margaret Huxley) of the Elpis Nursing Home in Dublin where the dramatist died in March 1909.

The Luganure lead mines were named after a geological 'lode' rather than a (surface) place; they had been operated by the Mining Company of Ireland (who also ran Ballycorus near Dublin to smelt ore from Wicklow) in extensive lands south and west of Lough Nahanagan. The company held these lands since 1824 on a lease from the archdiocese of Dublin.[9] The provision of a dispensary doctor for so small an area as Annamoe made sense if the officer served the mining community also. Luganure upped and downed during the 1840s, a portent of unimaginable prosperity one moment, and then an example of Ireland's complex 'waste land' as contemporary charities expressed it. Wicklow mining generally went into decline from 1870 or earlier.

The best known of these mines – the copper workings at Avoca – drew in labour from England and Wales, and operated at a level of internal organisation which made them the equivalent of a separate industrial community.[10] Luganure was a more local operation. Nevertheless, the mines there constitute a quite different concentration of labour from the age-old mill at Annamoe. Apart from the more explicitly industrial nature of the enterprise, and its reliance on a market far removed from east Wicklow, by the middle of the nineteenth century local denominational allegiances were evident in a way untraceable for M'Cracken's neighbours eighty years earlier. John Gower, temporary occupant of Roundwood Park in the early 1840s, worried about the risk of conflict between local Orangemen and the miners.[11] In the civil parish of Derrylossary, the single townland of Brockagh contained some one hundred and fifty households, including the village of Laragh. In excess of fifty houses, together with a crushing mill and forge, were owned by the Mining Company. If we take a conservative estimate of four persons to each miner's home, then this mining community amounted to more than six hundred in this one specific area. With the mines employing men who lived beyond the confines of Brockagh, and the doctor's clients including people quite unattached to the mines, it is clear that Hatch now served a large and various population. It differed markedly from the sequestered meadows, prehistoric stone circles and gentle hills round Dunlavin. In the early days of Hatch's appointment as dispensary doctor to the mines, Brockagh typified impermanent industrial settlement, devoid of the facilities customary in even the least developed village, 'neither public houses nor grocers in it nor any public road except an old bridle path for the accommodation of the inhabitants'. The discovery in 1874 of an unknown woman's corpse in a turf bank, with a rope still round her neck, encapsulates the violation of custom and nature which the mines represented in the eyes of many.[12] Many, for this reason, closed their eyes to the actuality, preferring to invent a pastoral world which JMS in due course challenged in 'In the Shadow of the Glen' (1903) and 'The Well of the Saints' (1905).

Nevertheless, the testimony of JMS on this issue is contradictory. A fragmentary note gathered by his editor into a composite article describes how 'at the end of the Upper Lake at Glendalough one is quite shut off from the part that has been spoiled by civilization, and when one fishes there from dusk to midnight a feeling of isolation creeps over one that it would be hard to pass'.[13] This is almost certainly an early instance of JMS writing about the Wicklow landscape, and his satiric intention may have been to contrast civilisation (the ruined monastery beloved by tourists) with an isolation which includes nature and the ruins of miners' cottages. For the end of Glendalough's Upper Lake is the location of more than a score of such cottages, which were less ruined and more numerous in his day than they are now.

Satiric or selective, JMS was well aware of the changes overtaking the Wicklow landscape in the half-century before his birth. While the presence of 'R. C.' chapels on the new Ordnance Survey maps bore testimony to the actuality of Catholic allegiance in the populace, a list of the Brockagh miners is far from conclusive in indicating personal allegiance. Given the order they were perceived by the recording angels of bureaucracy to live in – that is, side by side, without reference to familial ties or generation, without relation, textureless text – here they are:

> Matthew Hennessy, James Humphrey, Matthew Doyle, Michael Cullen, Patrick Doyle, Michael Douglas, Charles Byrne, George Reid, Thomas Pitts, John Woodburn, James Donnelly, James Ryan, John Murray, John Lyons, James Mourne, Andrew Cullen, Andrew Cullen Jnr., John Moorehead, Francis McGrath, Andrew Valentine, Thomas Watters, Maria Kavanagh, Edward Cuddy, Patrick Kavanagh, James Devlin, James Kirwan, James M'Grath, Daniel Ryan, James M'Donald, Samuel Long, Abraham Davis, Leonard M'Ginn, William Grafton, Bryan Donnelly.

These men – with one woman, almost certainly a widowed mother of mining sons – held property with an annual rateable valuation of between five shillings and £1 10s 0d on lease from the company. Another group of fourteen or fifteen houses were rated between ten and five shillings. Elsewhere, off the map (so to speak), were the casual labourers, virtually camp-site men. The mines were not limited to Brockagh; the Company held seventeen acres from Thomas W. Hugo in Seven Churches (or Camadery) townland. Here the head-lessor was again the Archbishop of Dublin, from whom it held property rated at £500, on which an ore-crushing mill had been established. The alchemy of Celtic Christianity now turned land into lead.

Whether as financial investment or territorial ornamentation, Francis Synge of Glanmore planted more than forty-five thousand trees on his estate in the year ending November 1862, with the bulk of these – scotch fir, larch, oak, Spanish chestnut, ash and alder – concentrated on the lands of Clorah where William Rhind had practised amateur medicine twenty-five years earlier. What's more he swore a formal statement to this effect, evidently for the benefit of his Tottenham neighbours. In December 1863, the Revd A. H. Synge and John Hatch Synge

(JMS's father) – the younger brothers who had inherited the Hatch Street properties – leased nos 5 to 12 to the builder Samuel Roberts.[14] Not all changes to property use were so public as crushing-mills and afforestation, nor were all properties as grand as Hatch Street. Somewhere on the outer branches of the family tree, there were mere sparrows. We may pause to note that a Memorial 1847: 8: 198 indicates that Dr Hatch conveyed to James Cuthbertson of Dorset Street, Dublin, a plot of land at Dunlavan [sic], County Wicklow. Cuthbertson, a fellow doctor, had married Hatch's younger sister, Rose-Ann. The property in question was almost certainly the former playhouse site, for the latter is specifically mentioned in Memorial 1858: 28: 70. No recollection of such a playhouse exists today among local historians.

Why Dr Hatch should have felt free to trade in a property for which he had only a fixed term interest is probably revealed in a series of transactions earlier in the decade. In August 1840, a certain Albert William Browne had (in London) insured his own life for £1,000, and assigned the policy the following month to Hatch. By a bond of April 1841, Hatch bound himself to Cuthbertson in the penal sum of £471 1s 0d, and assigned the Browne insurance policy to his brother-in-law as additional collateral security. Hatch at some point borrowed a further £100, and together with one William Cooke, became bound again to Cuthbertson. On this last named bond, Cuthbertson obtaind two judgements in the Michaelmas term of 1846. The transfer of Dame Hannah Tynte Caldwell's legacy, which followed in less than a year, evidently satisfied the demands made in these judgements, even though there was now less than fifty years to run on Hatch's lease to the old playhouse site.[15]

All of this powerfully symbolises the life of quiet desperation which a Victorian Irish rural doctor led, behind the castellation of his home and the avenue he rode his horse up each evening. The cholera crisis of 1866 saw Hatch claim a quarter's additional salary of £22 from the Rathdrum Poor Law Guardians. Private difficulties were also amenable to adjustment. Despite the imposing legal apparatus by which Cuthbertson bound Hatch, informal agreements drew the sting from their dealings. When the countryman paid interest on his loans, the cityman reduced the interest rate levied on the outstanding principal. Cuthbertson also declined to call in this money in advance of Browne's death (by which Hatch would ultimately benefit). But in return, the Dunlavin site appears to have been transferred to the 'soi-disant Turf-man', William Hatch of Ardee Castle, who was better able to pay his brother's interest-debt. The saga only concluded when Cuthbertson died and his widow, Rose-Ann Hatch, was paid the outstanding balance in July 1871. By then, her brother the doctor was well over seventy and in semi-retirement. He died on 30 October 1874.

In all of this, there is no reference to John Hatch, the silent MP and great-great-grandfather of the dramatist (born 1871). Difficulty does not rise in tracing the obscure rural doctor's family, but in pushing back beyond one generation of the MP's. Yet as Dr Hatch dealt with his metropolitan kin, vestiges of the old M'Cracken/Hatch acquisitions surfaced in Victorian records. A memorial drawn up in 1837 and signed by hundreds of residents in the baronies of Shillelagh and Ballinacor South included a Samuel Hatch of Ballagh.[16] Joseph Hatch of West Arran Street, Dublin (and his wife) is named in Memorial 1863: 2: 109 in connection with property at Carrarasticks, Ballinacor, where the sorry tale of 1769 had some of its origins. West Arran Street was a mere passage between Smithfield Markets and the quays. Joseph Hatch was a packing case manufacturer, with premises in Cook Street.

The Dublin in which Cuthbertson practised medicine was subject to economic and social change no less than the mining community down in Wicklow. Dorset Street, where Cuthbertson lived at two successive addresses before moving out to salubrious Booterstown Avenue in 1865, was in decline as a residential area. In 1880, the future proletarian dramatist, Sean O'Casey, will be born there. Dedication to medicine, in the case of both Cuthbertson and the second John Hatch, elevated them above their milieu. Despite the efforts of the elder John Hatch in the eighteenth century, and the extravagance of his sons-in-law, the later Victorians – Hatches and Synges alike – prospered through the lucrative but demanding professions – engineering, law and medicine. When their paths cross once more, the Hatch in question was John Anthony Freeman Hatch (1867–1931), grandson of Annamoe's Dr Hatch. He was a pupil in the Rathmines School with the elder Synge boys, and served in the RAMC during the Great War. Later still c. 1929, Laragh Castle, where Dr Hatch had lived throughout his long career, was bought by Maud Gonne for her daughter Iseult and son-in-law the novelist Francis Stuart. It served as a point of rendezvous for a Nazi agent during Iseult's suzerainty.

18

Windfalls

The Greens and Ryders and Pughs, and the rest of them, were soldiers who long ago trickled down into the houses of the poor. Intermarried there, and became poor themselves as a result. (*O'Faolain*)

SOCIAL change in upland Wicklow can be documented in many ways. The brief career of Thomas Lynch (1844–1887) serves as a background to the shadowy movements of Synges and near-Synges. Lynch was not a native of Wicklow but, after ordination in the Catholic diocese of Dublin, he was appointed curate in Roundwood in 1873 when he commenced energetically to build a new chapel. The area was much changed in the aftermath of the Famine, and the old mastership at Roundwood Park had disappeared. When Lynch was moved by his superiors to west Wicklow, he found himself stationed in what was known as 'Orange Donard'. His renewed commitment to church building led to a breakdown in his health, c. 1880, after which he was cared for by his family outside the county. Poignant though Father Lynch's story is, it indicates the direction in which southern Irish society was moving, even before the excitements of the Home Rule agitation and the rise of Parnell.[1] There were Synges still occupying big houses on both sides of the Wicklow Mountains; in addition, however, one finds less easily accommodated figures bearing the name.

TOM SYNGE OF TOMRILAND, c. 1850

Evidence for the life of Thomas Synge derives – exclusively, for the moment – from Sir Richard Griffith's 'valuations' of Irish land carried out in the 1850s. He features as the lessor to various tenants of about 154 acres in the townland of Tiglin South, immediately adjacent to the demesne at Glanmore Castle, in the parish of Killiskey to which the family had contributed much by way of religious service in John 'Pestalozzi' Synge's time. Little more is known of him, except that in the townland of Tomriland further south, this Thomas Synge held fifty-three acres (a house, out-offices and land) which was in practice occupied by 'Big' Peter Mooney as tenant.

Leased land of more than two hundred acres brought in an income, but hardly a genteel one. While it was not unusual to find lessors featuring as lessees of a property owned by a neighbour, the striking feature of the Valuations' account of Thomas Synge is his presence as absence. He leases to humbler tenants, but is nowhere an occupier whether of fee simple land or land held on a lease. In figurative language, he plays the role of preposition rather than proper name, a transferee, a relationship, scarcely an identity. Nor can he be assimilated to the older and notorious ranks of eighteenth-century absentees. For Thomas Synge is absent from more than his possession, he is absent from his own genealogy.

If this human being truly existed – born, schooled, directed to find a living, finding that living and mixing with his neighbours and making friends, eating, worshipping his Maker (at least on Sundays), marrying perhaps and/or having children – then the one source of information is scandalously reductive. The fullness implicit in the word 'life' is mocked. The inevitable richness of his parentage – mother, father, ancestral line, relations of many possible kinds – has all been shrunken into a single name. At this point, Thomas Synge functions – we can hardly repeat the word 'exists' – somewhere between a datum of ancient sociology and the image of Wodwo, the last man, the wild man of the woods.

Unrelated in the family annals, Tom – as I shall call him, for I suspect a degree of familiarity, even in his failure to register socially – fits into a pattern more drably factual and statistical than these romantic notions authorise. If he leased his fifty-three acres to 'Big' Peter Mooney, this contract is matched almost to the nearest rood or perch by another, in the same townland of Tomriland. By this second lease, 'Little' Peter Mooney held a similar farm from Francis Synge, of whose identity we are in no doubt. The parallel of two leases between the two Peter Mooneys and two Synges – one of them the Master of Glanmore, the other missed somehow from other records – frames the holding of enigmatic Thomas Synge.

But, thanks to Sir Richard's enumerators, Thomas Synge occupies another 'somewhere', named perhaps more exactly than its lessor – Tomriland. This part of County Wicklow is best known as the summer base of JMS at the time when he was writing 'In the Shadow of the Glen'. Defined in this way, Tomriland was a modest but sturdy farmhouse whose long-term occupants were the Coleman family, members of the Church of Ireland. At the time of John 'Pestalozzi' Synge's inheritance of the family estates, an 'Outline of new Arrangement of Receipts & Payments' lists rents totalling £4,095, of which Roundwood brought in £599 and Tomriland £562.[2] Between 1832 and 1903, the term (or sign) Tomriland signified different social and economic realities, and this in several distinct regards. For it is not enough simply to argue that the value of Irish land had declined for the great proprietors in the course of the nineteenth century, or even to point to altering demographic conditions, distributions of residence, size of household, etc. What one is attending to is the multivalency of the linguistic sign within a broad social discourse, so that even at the same moment Tomriland signifies:

1. a territory, a named tract of land perhaps open to man and beast, certainly to birds of the air;
2. a legal possession of some specifed human being(s), with rights and limitations defined as to extent and usage;
3. a domicile for organised human life, involving relations of blood and service, custom and payment, seasonally altering diets and daily habits, birth, copulation, and death;
4. a locus defined or apprehended from outside, by the stranger or visitor who has never been in Tomriland before, or even by the reader who may never reach that elusive crossroads of signs.

Thomas Synge of Tomriland does not feature in any of the great charts which make up *The Family of Synge or Sing* (1937). Yet it can be established that the townland was still part of the Glanmore estate in the days when the widow of Francis Synge (1819–1878) was in possession. Together with her husband, Major Theodore Webber Gardiner, Mrs Editha Gardiner held the castle during a prolonged period when males of the Synge family were, for one reason or another, removed from the scene of residential landlordism. The Gardiners were Exclusive Brethren, but that in itself did not distance them from the descendents of John 'Pestalozzi' Synge. And though Mrs Gardiner had only been a Synge by marriage, her parental home was Clonmannon, which lay a short distance to the south-east of Glanmore: her maiden name was Truell, which had featured on the 1765 accounts for the building of Annamoe mill.

These intimacies and continuities do not conceal the irony of a Synge occupying lesser Tomriland while a Mrs Gardiner maintained Glanmore as best she could. In the 1880s, Tomriland crossroads had been the spot chosen by the Gardiners' evicting agent – a brother of JMS's – to muster his adequate forces for the ejectment of Hugh Carey and two sisters from their cottage at Aghowle. In this instance, continuity can be better established for named tenants than named landlords, for in a 'rental of Ballycullen & Aghoule as taken from tenants' receipts Jan 5 1832', the first on the list is Mat Carey, holding 32 acres.[3] By the later date, Thomas Synge of Tomriland had almost certainly gone from the area though not – it would seem – to the local churchyard. Though his greater identity deserves attention, one should not miss the maintenance of the landlord role, in this case through Mrs Gardiner's use of her late husband's nephew in his professional capacity.

We are still left with a very threadbare biography of Thomas Synge. Even if his place of burial, and maybe date of death, were to be established together with

Windfalls

some account of his (say) quite unremarkable ownership of Tomriland over a score of years or more, he would remain a datum. To discern his greater identity, we may have to have recourse to forms of analysis more appropriate to allegory than to empirical research. Within the longer historical context invoked and generated precisely by the genealogists who exclude him, it is his Christian name which deserves attention. Thomas was not traditional among the male Synges, as Edward, Francis, George and Samuel were. The female pattern was wont to vary more frequently, for each marriage brought in a name which might be perpetuated in a daughter or a niece. Indeed the relatively conservative way Synges named their children is highlighted in two outer branches or twigs of the family tree which perhaps intertwine here in Tomriland.

From an earlier chapter it will be remembered that Samuel Synge and his wife, Dorothy (née Hatch) had three children who are recorded as dying young. The deaths of all three at a young age caused great grief to the parents, being a multiple loss of a kind not known in the family since 1641 when a number of Synge children were drowned with their mother in flight from the rebels. Indeed such is the grief one must imagine that it seems more charitable to suggest that the parents' marriage in 1801 – some months after another (step)-daughter's death also – proceeded on a happier basis. Instead of all three being cut off, some at least were merely written off: that is, Elizabeth, John and Samuel Synge of that generation did not all die in infancy or childhood, but some of them lived to have their own children, unrecorded.

Here, in theory, is a branch of the family tree to which Thomas Synge of Tomriland might now be reattached. By 1887, no adult male of the name Synge or Hatch was registered to vote in either the East Wicklow or West Wicklow parliamentary constituencies. The descendents of two MPs had disappeared from the electoral rolls of the county. Across the northern boundary with Dublin, Sir Edward Synge Hutchinson resided at Palermo, though he owned Wicklow property in the townlands of Gibbstown, Kelshamore and Rustyduff. Rather than vote in the rural division of Knockanarrigan, he registered his franchise in the town of Bray.

MISS SYNGE-HUTCHINSON, d. 1869

By far the longest living of those eighteenth-century Synges, children of the archdeacon, was Samuel who reached the same ecclesiastical rank but eclipsed it on the secular side by becoming a baronet in 1813. He had been born in 1756, married twice, and outlived his only son, to die finally at the age of ninety in the second year of the Great Famine. One of his young relatives, Caroline (1818–1862, daughter of Col. Charles Synge, of Mount Callan) described him in her private journal as an old lion who was 'deaf and dead [and] selfish as to those about him and their enjoyments'.[4]

The leonine Sir Samuel made a will on 8 May 1843, which he found necessary to augment with a codicil the next day, adding a further codicil a week later and a third codicil the following year.⁵ His second wife (Dolly Hatch, who died in 1836) had given birth to six children, one of whom was dead at birth (1808). Only two survived early childhood. These were Francis Hutchinson Synge (born 1802) and Sophia Elizabeth Synge (born 1810). By 1843, the first of these was himself dead, and the other a widow. However, while these fatalities simplified the octogenarian archdeacon in disposing of his property, he still had a daughter alive, the child of his first wife (Frances Wood, died 1788).

Sir Samuel's will is of interest in confirming the transmission to the Synges of valuable properties which had been acquired by John Hatch, particularly through his office as seneschal of Saint Sepulchre's. In fact, the will's description of the town house in Harcourt Street goes to the trouble of locating it in 'the Liberty of St. Sepulchre, County of Dublin'. In addition there was part of a farm also in Saint Sepulchre's, described as 'lately purchased from the archbishop of Dublin, the Ecclesiastical Commissioners, and Thomas N. Needham Esq.', a transaction which we may regard as extending or consolidating a lease Hatch had originally acquired. The same interpretation applies to lands of the prebend of Swords, lands at Castlefarm and part of Newtown near Swords and – with a modification – to 'lands of Seatown (leased from the Archbishop of Dublin for three lives)'.⁶

In addition, there was the house (Palermo, known to Caroline as 'that fearful den') in south County Dublin, together with other lands and tenements in Old Connaught and Little Bray; lands and tithes at Colpe, Mornington and Kiltrough in County Meath, a £4,000 mortgage on Tatestown in the same county, lands and premises in what is now County Offaly, with a few scattered bits and pieces on the Dublin road to Swords and in Dublin itself. Sir Samuel's estate (which also included substantial investments) was a great inheritance, but it still resembled John Hatch's of 1797 in that it had not been transfigured into 'a great good place'. Despite the baronetcy, Samuel Synge was a bourgeois accumulator and not a hereditary lord of the manor.

The bulk of this portfolio was to go to Fanny (Frances, born 1788), the elder of his two surviving children. Trustees were appointed to hold the lands and tithes in Meath for her use during her life, and thereafter for the use of Sir Samuel's grandson. They also were empowered to hold Bank of England stock in order to pay the dividends to her and her heirs. Furniture, books, pictures, plate, and 'all wines in the cellar' at Palermo were to be hers outright. In relation to Palermo, however, Fanny was to inherit it on condition that she pay £5,000 within five years of her father's death to his nephew, Francis Hely Hutchinson. Having made various provisions for his other daughter, for sundry lesser relatives and servants, Sir Samuel left the residue to Fanny.

Twenty-four hours later, he added the first of three codicils which modified this generous settlement. Extensive properties in Dublin and Meath (with the Offaly fragments) are now to be held in trust for the younger daughter, Sophia Elizabeth, widow of Coote Hely Hutchinson. The most significant implication of this alteration removed the Harcourt Street house from the 'residual' provisions of the will proper, that is, from the portion ultimately going to Fanny. She, however, was to be allowed to occupy the Dublin house for seven years after her father's death and to acquire its linen as part of the furnishings generally left to her. The second major provision of the codicil of 9 May 1843 authorised Sophia Elizabeth to raise a mortgage on the Dublin properties in order to continue improving the lands 'for building'. In short, the codicil greatly benefited the younger daughter at the expense of the elder, while also indicating the entrepreneurial value of Dublin land.

The second codicil, dated 17 May, sought to control what its predecessor had ordained. If Harcourt Street was to sold or leased, it should be under conditions which would prevent the house being used for 'any noisy or offensive trade or business'. Building, development, the entrepreneuring spirit, such forces were endorsed but – as we say nowadays – NIMBY (not in my back yard). Of greater interest is the final codicil of 28 June 1844. In it Sir Samuel requested that all his descendents renounce their claims upon £4,000 of stock held in trust under the terms of the first baronet's will. He went further than requesting this, making provision that anyone not making the required sacrifice would forfeit every legacy benefiting them in the will. The objective of this cumbersome mechanism would appear to have been the augmentation of what residue would go to Fanny Synge.

The surviving daughter of Samuel and his first wife, Frances (née Wood), Fanny was fifty-six years of age when the final adjustment to her father's will was made. She was evidently unmarried, and so unlikely to have heirs of her body. There was, however, no bar upon her marrying even at middle age. Sir Samuel's provision for her was in turn generous, damagingly qualified, and once again positive. But nowhere in the evolving text of his testamentary arrangements was the prospect of Fanny's marrying actively considered, by – for example – protecting her inheritance from the depredations of a husband.

IN THE WHITWORTH HOSPITAL, 1885

As against this profusion of data, consider the bare essentials conveyed in Entry 368 in the register of deaths recorded for Dublin City North (No. 3 district) for 1885. On 24 April, at the Whitworth Hospital expired Francis Synge formerly of Chapel Lane, a married labourer of sixty-two years. The cause of death was given as cardiac arrest, the informant as Mary Reilly who was evidently a resident at the hospital. She made her mark, being unable to sign her name. By a displeasing irony, the hospital had been designed by the same architect who built Gothic Glanmore Castle for a different Francis Synge. The Whitworth, named after an early nineteenth-century viceroy, was a hospital within the larger institutional framework of the Dublin House of Industry, still basically a haven for vagrants.[7]

Less than a year later, in another part of North Dublin, Mrs Eliza Synge (an eighty-five-year-old widow) died at 27 Great Britain Street (now Parnell Street) of asthenia, that is, general debility or diminution of vital powers. The informant was Phoebe M. Doyle, listed as the occupier of the same address, though a half-completed and then cancelled note suggests that she had been 'in attend[ance]' rather than residing with Mrs Synge. Who were these all too ordinary Dubliners, bearing a less than common surname? As the young Samuel Synge, brother of JMS, began his medical studies in Trinity College, what did he know of obscure deaths off the page of the family bible? Mrs Eliza Synge had not been born into the purple of bishops and baronets, but who had her husband been? Do these two records chart the departure of a couple, somehow ill-matched in age, certainly ill-provided for. Both were buried in Mount Jerome Cemetery, a predominantly protestant institution of the dead. How close was Francis Synge (labourer) to Francis Synge (MP)?

Only in the case of Julia Synge, sister of the dramatist's father, can one trace a marriage which even approximated to this declension of class. After she died in 1890, her seagoing fisherman husband, John Angus MacLeod, became an inmate of Lady Matheson's House for Sailors, at Stornoway in the Outer Hebrides, distant from his nervously proud in-laws. But Dublin landlordism carried within its many mansions the inevitability of contact with the soiled. When the lease of nos 33–36 York Street was renewed in June 1875, solemnly reciting an indenture 'bearing date the thirtieth day of April one thousand seven hundred and ninety nine and expressed to be made between Francis Synge administrator of all and singular the goods and chattels rights and credits of John Hatch Esquire deceased and Elizabeth Synge otherwise Hatch his wife and Dorothea Hatch of Harcourt Street aforesaid spinster', were the inhabitants of those houses closer in mode of living to Mrs Eliza Synge of Great Britain Street than to the lessors?[8] The family's urban property was sliding down the social scale, ultimately to be requisitioned under legislation of a new state. In 1881, the young Sam Synge sold pigeons in the vicinity of Saint Patrick's Cathedral, and his dramatist-brother (more careful in his recollections) lingered among the squabbling slum-children after he had listened to Bach's Saint Matthew Passion a few years later.[9] The world of O'Casey lay implicit in the world of the Synges – but off-stage.

19

Workhouse insurgency

> To thee I owe my glorious faith,
> More precious far than life,
> Which gives me courage to sustain
> The combat and the strife.[1]

THE CONDITION of Wicklow throughout the nineteenth century can only be reconstructed through the histories of activities, economies, houses, individuals, institutions, which appear remote from each other in kind. Lacking any strong county town, overshadowed by Dublin and yet difficult of access, it experienced neglect and local development in a peculiarly sharp manner. Nor was its entire population settled. Writing of post-Famine conditions, the social historian Eva Ó Cathaoir has valuably synthesised economic and cultural perspectives:

> Migrant labourers, discharged soldiers, the homeless and the occasional eccentric continued to be treated with distrust when admitted to the workhouses during the second half of the nineteenth century. They began to feature as 'tramps' and 'casuals', having been previously ignored, and were still among the denizens of the Wicklow poorhouses in the twentieth century, when they caught the literary imagination of J. M. Synge.[2]

In fact, JMS's interest in the tramps of Wicklow pre-dates the twentieth century, a point less compelling than the relevance of Ms Ó Cathaoir's larger argument to the topic of the playwright's first attempts at drama. The history of the workhouse or 'Union' lies behind his literary enterprise as a whole. It also provides a means of connecting the early activities of John 'Pestalozzi' Synge with the more celebrated achievements of his grandson.

Originally, responsibility for poor law in Ireland was vested in the English Poor Law Commission. It was only in 1847 that a separate commission was established. Before that date, five poor law unions were devised to cover County Wicklow and some parts of adjacent counties. Rathdrum Union, which included the electoral divisions of Killiskey and Roundwood where the Synges were still notables in the land, was established on 30 October 1839. The departure of John Synge's moral agent the previous year may have been determined in part by the growth of state facilities for the relief of the poor. The Union building stood (till 1970) just outside Rathdrum, a place with which the Synges had maintained little contact in previous decades. Social engineering shifted the balance among Wicklow's small towns in pre-Famine years. Built to accommodate up to six hundred inmates, the Union was formally opened in March 1842.

A meeting of the Board of Guardians had been held as early as 5 November 1839. Ten of these were ex-officio, by virtue of their status as large landowners in the county. Their number included John Synge of Glanmore and John Parnell of Avondale; the first chairman was Col. Thomas Acton MP. The ensuing sixty years would see massive social change in Ireland, to which the list of Guardians testifies at every stage. The Famine of 1845–1849 placed a wholly unpredicted burden on the poor law and landlord systems alike. Some Rathdrum guardians, who were particularly active between 1869 and 1873, joined the Wicklow Tenants Association, and called for land reform. They also displayed support for Home Rule, a movement to which Synge's own class had given encouragement first through Isaac Butt's and later Charles Stewart Parnell's leadership.[3] In 1899, a landlord (Col. Charles Tottenham) still took the chair at Rathdrum Guardians' meetings, but the composition of the Board had altered remarkably. The name of Synge no longer featured, and the only vestige of Glanmore's lost grandeur was to be traced through William Coleman of Tomriland, a former tenant of the family.

At the outset, John Synge of Glanmore was to the fore in overseeing the affairs of the Union, frequently acting as chairman in the years 1840–1844. Together with William Kemmis of Ballinacor, in 1842 he moved to insure its property 'in the oldest established office' that would offer competitive terms. This reliance on long-established business experience can be too easily contrasted with Synge's adventurous religious ideas, though his remaining within the Established Church was at least as significant as his endorsement of Brethren ideas. When in February 1844, the Board of Guardians discussed tenders for replacing the Union's laundry floor, it chose a contractor but stipulated 'the flagging substituted to be brought from Mr Synge's quarry'. A few months later, Synge proposed a motion roundly condemning the Master's proselytism among the inmates, following a complaint from the Catholic chaplain, Fr James McKenna. In short, as a guardian of Rathdrum's poor, John Synge proved to be diligent, practical and even-handed. His death on the eve of the Great Famine deprived the Union of a valuable overseer, and the resultant deterioration in standards of record-keeping is evident even before the failure of the potato drove unprecedented numbers through its ugly gates.[4]

Workhouse insurgency

Between 1839 and the end of the century, the workhouses or 'unions' of Ireland were home to many of the most wretched of her people. In the first year of operation, Rathdrum's administrators admitted (or supervised the birth of) 767 persons. On 1 January 1843, 323 remained, the rest dying or being discharged. At the height of the Famine, the numbers were running at twice this level. Time did not assuage suffering. In the year following JMS's birth in April 1871, 3,248 souls sought relief through Rathdrum Union, 2,000 of these being inmates at some point or other. In 1892, when JMS came of age, just under 2,000 admissions were registered, with more than 1,200 claiming outdoor relief. Nor did the new century ease the problem. In 1907, the year of 'The Playboy of the Western World', Rathdrum Union alone accepted over 6,000 applicants for relief, indoor or outdoor. These boring statistics should serve to qualify the romantic notions which buzz round discussion of JMS's tramps and vagabonds, including notions indulged by the dramatist himself.

'The Union' was more than a staging post in the lives of Wicklow's poor, it also drew attention to the moral and medical state of the surrouding countryside. The quality of staff at Rathdrum was not exceptionally high. After the first two and a half years, the Guardians had replaced its clerk, and twice replaced the master and cook. In 1849, a collector named O'Rourke made off with £400 of the Union's funds. To put this in perspective, compare the salaries of skilled employees. Teachers were paid £15 p.a., and sometimes found their living quarters uncomfortably close to the cells of lunatic inmates: the sum had to be doubled in 1848 to attract suitable applicants. In December 1847, Ann Williams, the Rathdrum matron, gave birth to an illegitimate child in the poorhouse, and was obliged to resign after a number of paupers confined in the Union succeeded in smuggling the infant to the outside world. The Poor Law Commissioners' letter of inquiry strongly suggested that moral laxity had not been restricted to one individual, for they wrote 'requesting to be informed of the result of the investigation ... into the conduct of the Master, Matron, Porter, and Schoolmistress'.[5] In addition to proselytism, and an implied part in the matron's disgrace, the master was also accused of bringing goods into the Union without authorisation and then damaging them in 'an aggravation of the offence'.

These abuses decreased as the century advanced though jobbery persisted, with the Flower and Manning families having extensive dynasties of petty power. Isaac Flower (master from March 1850 to 1899) married the new matron's daughter (Mary Ogilvy) who succeeded her in that office. A younger Flower served at both Rathdrum and Rathdown unions in the county.[6] Mannings served as both guardians and officials at Rathdrum, and in April 1848 a Mrs Manning was paid £1 16s 0d for mantua-making. The family also held numerous powerful offices in the town; for example, Ralph Manning was appointed process-server in 1866, in which year Joseph Manning was charged with unlawful possession of a gun while resisting arrest. Later, in 1881, James Manning was a commissioner for oaths, William Manning Clerk of the Court, and Bernard Manning registrar at the workhouse.[7] This petty oligarchy, while it may have irritated the Catholic majority in the surrounding area, more significantly represented the gathering eclipse of landlord power. The Synges never controlled a town in the manner the Ruxtons had managed Ardee.

Dr Manning permitted the use of stimulants (that is, porter) by ailing inmates in the 1860s. Incensed by a series of thefts in the workhouse, Flower took to the roads of Wicklow, and eventually tracked down a gang led by a former inmate, John Sutton, who had doubled up as lunatic keeper in the poorhouse. When his charge died, Sutton stripped the body and decamped in the clothes. He was convicted in 1869, and served two terms in Wicklow Jail. A pathetic figure, he became thoroughly institutionalised, dividing his time between prison and workhouse. After these excitements, an inspection in 1876 declared Rathdrum to be in 'excellent order' despite its practice of assigning only one bed to every two men.[8]

Throughout the century, admission to the Union affected quite distinctive grades of people, beginning with the downright destitute. In immediate post-Famine years, however, the typical inmate at Rathdrum was healthy and able-bodied, though administrative disorder also throve. Francis Synge was a guardian in December 1849 when a drunken assistant master named Doran tried to rally the Union's paupers to his cause.[9] Illness and social stigma were factors propelling members of the community into dependence. Admission to the Union became a stigma in itself, and conditions inside did not favour good health. For a three-week period in late 1852, the one hundred healthy inmates of Rathdrum included thirty children of inmates, six deserted children, one person over sixty-five years of age, and seven unmarried mothers (with seven babies.) Among the twenty others who were not healthy, two were classified as idiots, and three as 'infirm'. On 1 January 1854, more than half of the 121 women in the Union were the mothers of eighty-nine illegitimate children.[10] For a variety of reasons, the institution became associated with immorality, especially immoral conduct in which sexuality and/or intellectual deficiencies were implicated.

Because of its close proximity to the capital, and the smallness of its own towns, Wicklow became both a dumping ground for Dublin's problems – especially 'foundlings' – and a breeding ground for patients deprived of local professional care. The county of Wicklow long suffered from its inclusion in the catchment area of Dublin's main public hospital for the insane. Officially the Richmond Asylum (1814), under the name Grangegorman this grim urban institution additionally catered for anyone unfortunate enough to be referred by the authorities in Wicklow. Its reputation lingered well into the second half of the twentieth century as a gulag of lost reason. Overcrowing in Grangegorman led to the improper use of Wicklow Jail as a lunatic asylum. Unions such as that at Rathdrum were also expected to house disturbed patients, in conditions which exacerbated the problem instead of easing it.

Illegitimacy, fears of incest or (at the other extreme) social 'miscegenation' led to Wicklow's gaining a reputation as 'the bastard farm of Ireland'. Given that many of the resulting problems were assigned to the poorhouse, the county's ill-managed Unions became in effect the breeding ground for scores of 'identity crises'. Problems arising from family monopolies have already been noted, and these carried with them a distinct air of sectarian privilege. The kind of 'duty work' satirised by Maria Edgeworth as early as 1800, and exploited by W. R. Rhind even in the 1830s, was maintained by Isaac Flower in the late 1850s: inmates at Rathdrum were expected to stitch a patchwork quilt for the master, while also embroidering dresses for the matron (his wife) and the schoolmistress.[11]

Whereas the oppression complained of in Edgeworth's *Castle Rackrent* took place in an unfettered realm of landlord-and-tenant relations, Flower's regime was one which was neither social nor penal, though it was perhaps both. While the country suffered increasing depopulation, and the Unions even assisted by organising migration to America, conditions inside became increasingly congested, both physically and psychically. In the twenty years to 1862, at least eighteen instances of sectarian controversy illuminated the minutes of the Rathdrum Guardians, though less than 10 per cent of the inmates were protestant. In 1870, a three-year-old orphan died in a fire when his grandmother (officially charged to mind him) was at Mass and the ward attendant (his aunt) was inexplicably absent. Coercion and collusion did not always take such affable forms: officials intercepted letters from the outside world in the hope of identifying the fathers of illegitimate children and obtaining maintenance orders.[12]

The prominence of the workhouse highlighted the tensions existent between human sexuality and family organisation. Poverty and illness were inclined to strike at a household (or evicted family) rather than just an individual. Yet when people went to the Union, males were separated from females in keeping with the principle of 'minimum relief' – conditions inside were to be sufficiently harsh to discourage loafers and scroungers! This assault on the moral unity of husband and wife was intensified by the character of many among the single individuals admitted to segregated wards – habitually drunken men, or women known to have been 'loose'. It was consistent with the general Victorian perspective on sexual morality that women should feature in the bad publicity which grew up around the institution of the workhouse. Bastards tended to have mothers, rarely fathers. The wife of a Guardian, Elizabeth Smith of West Wicklow, heartily concurred with a poor woman's preference of life with her children in a ditch rather than 'the wickedness of the poorhouse'.[13] In due course, the Land War brought into the workhouses a class of respectable tenantry which served to sharpen their internal politics.

Yet even before this explicit shift in the relation between the institution and national politics, the contradictory inner world of the Unions encouraged sexual strife. The Rathdrum matron's own bastard has already been noted. The master of Loughlinstown disappeared in 1853, only to be traced to a Dublin brothel. Illicit relations between segregated inmates, between staff and inmates, between adults and children all feature in the minutes of County Wicklow's five Unions. The treatment of mental illness was generally very poor, but weighed most oppressively on women. A Shillelagh inmate killed her baby in 1878. In 1883, overcrowding drove one deranged woman to kill the second occupant of her cell. By this date, the proportion of women among inmates classed as lunatics was consistently high – seven out of thirteen in Baltinglass, twenty-four out of thirty-five in Naas, fifty-six out of eighty in Rathdown, a striking twenty out of twenty-six in Rathdrum, seven out of ten in Shillelagh.[14]

The condition of women, and the increased politicisation of the workhouses generally, bore very directly on the Wicklow scene. Before the Famine, the Guardians might declare 'that in future should any charge for insubordination be brought against Susan Costello' she was to be 'forthwith discharged from the House'.[15] These boardroom edicts were not destined to remain local secrets. Asenath Nicholson, an American woman travelling in Ireland in the 1840s, singled out Rathdrum poorhouse for comment in her book, *The Bible in Ireland* (1847). Sexual politics ran through the entire fabric of the work- (or poor-) houses in a way which JMS would nervously recognise at the end of the nineteenth century. Women only became eligible to sit on the boards of guardians in 1896. At the beginning of the twentieth century, Lady Meath – wife of a substantial Wicklow landowner – specifically criticised the manner in which epileptic patients were housed among paupers and lunatics, a practice echoing that of the Incorporated Schools. Maud Gonne, a different kind of critic, visited Loughlinstown Union in 1899. But, at mid-century, the role of women in ameliorating the condition of inmates already involved a new religious and social group in Victorian Ireland – the nuns.

The growth of religious orders for women is part of the post-Emancipation history of the Irish Catholic Church. Prevented from celebrating the sacraments, nuns were active in nursing, teaching, the relief of the poor and, of course, in meditation. When cholera returned to Wicklow in late 1866, it struck the town of Arklow (part of the Rathdrum catchment area) with particular virulence. Although poverty was not an inevitable feature of those stricken, the poorhouses and workhouses seemed at first glance to provide accommodation on the scale necessary to deal with the crisis. However, reluctance to enter these stigmatised institutions was stubborn and widespread. As a result, Catholic priests invited the Order of the Sisters of Mercy to care for patients in their own homes.[16] The Rathdrum Union appointed Jane Elliott in October at £20 p.a., plus accommodation. Irrespective of what happened to this nurse of unchallengeably protestant credentials, in practice two nuns – Sisters Julia and Marcella – attended the sick near Ashford, a growing village on the main road east of the Synges' Glanmore estate. They were paid £1 per week for four weeks, having promised to work longer if necessary. A Miss Murdock in the neighbourhood was reimbursed from public funds for their lodgings and other expenses. The Board of Guardians, on which John 'Pestalozzi' Synge' had sat as of right, duly noted in their minutes this role of Catholic religious in handling the local (and indeed national) crisis.[17] Somewhere, W. G. Rhind of the Brethren was turning in his grave.

The arrival of nuns under the shadow of Glanmore's Gothic turrets symbolises a modest and yet momentous shift in power. No Synges were publicly linked to the Ashford Dispensary during the cholera crisis, though it is likely that Miss Murdock was a member of the Synge household. Francis Synge, who had been active earlier as a Justice of the Peace, seems to have been unavailable during the later part of the year, perhaps due to his own ill-health or travel outside the district. The role of the Big House as protector of the weakest amongs its tenants had little structural durability and – in the case of the Synge properties – a brief history, at best. The Actons had built Kilmacurragh (near Rathdrum) in 1697, a fitting monument to the Williamite victory of that decade; the next generation or two had been active in promoting the Chartered School at Templestown in the 1730s and after. Compared with these, the forebears of JMS were newcomers in Wicklow, whose major initiatives were synchonised with crisis for their class – 1798, the Union, Catholic Emancipation, the Famine. By the time Francis Synge (sometime MP) was giving evidence of pious and philanthropic endeavour, Glanmore's financial base was already shaky and its authority among the general populace challenged by a variety of political and religious changes. The family's penchant for an evangelicalism bordering on the Darbyite rendered it eccentric to the self-celebrated Anglo-Irish tradition. That tradition was Low Church, but it was Church. When similar families had patronised the Brethren, they had done so either from a stronger base – Lady Powerscourt, the earl of Carrick, and others of that class – or from a more modest and sustainable style of living. Edith Truell of neighbouring Clonmannon, who married a later Francis Synge in 1861 and became mistress of Glanmore, was of the latter kind, at least by birth if not always by practice. It was an unconscious achievement of John 'Pestalozzi' Synge to transform his father's dynastic ambition into minority and transitory values. In Marxist terms (however remote these might seem) quantity had indeed become quality; but the scale of things which had reduced just their value was being infused with the peculiar instant-eternal of dispensationalism. The Rathdrum workhouse, over which Synges and Actons had presided, now became a forum of dispute and (sotto voce) accusation. The nuns' unspoken prescription was socio-historical – the days of landlord patronage are over, especially for those landlords who employed Craiks and Rhinds.

Something close to farce occurred in 1886 in the neighbouring county of Wexford. When tenants on the Marquess of Ely's estate at Fethard were evicted for non-payment of rent, they took refuge in the workhouse. In doing so, they forced local ratepayers (notably the landlords) to pay for their maintenance. Being (they insisted) respectable inmates, they retained their own clothing and ate in family groups. William O'Brien's *United Ireland* published a drawing of 'The Ward of Honor [sic], New Ross Workhouse' with three nuns serving at table. The American spelling silently pointed to the greater audience of this local drama.[18]

Respectable inmates, however, disrupted the miserable existence of regular inmates, creating hierarchies of privilege and publicity. One ward of destitute women at New Ross stripped themselves naked and challenged the police to intervene. At this point the nationalist press lost interest. Several of JMS's mature plays, however, revel in female insurrectionary tactics, but only after his first attempt to write for the stage – 'When the Moon Has Set' – had placed nuns at the heart of a Big House not far from Rathdrum. The Marquis of Ely's ancestors had built No. 8 Ely Place, Dublin, acquired by Francis Synge in a burst of post-Union extravangance, and the house remained in Synge ownership until the 1940s, when JMS's brother Samuel was party to its ultimate disposal.

By the end of the nineteenth century, the workhouse at Loughlinstown had been taken over by the Poor Servants of the Mother of God, an order founded by Fanny Taylor (1832–1900, in religion Mother Mary Magdalen). Rathdrum, a loyalist stronghold in 1798, held out till 1922. Among Mother Mary's numerous Irish Jesuit friends was Father Matthew Russell who published some of JMS's early poems.[19]

Part VI

CONCERNING J. M. SYNGE
(1871–1909)

20

Madness and local government

> In Wicklow, as in the rest of Ireland, the union, though it is a home of refuge for the tramps and tinkers, is looked on with supreme horror by the peasants. The madhouse, which they know better, is less dreaded. (JMS)

IT HAS been JMS's misfortune to be identified in the public mind with two or three renowned works – 'The Aran Islands', 'The Playboy', 'Riders to the Sea'. The aesthetic and popular success of these has obscured both the merits of some other published texts – 'The Well of the Saints', also the essays about Wicklow – and the value of much writing which remained unpublished for long after his death in 1909. In particular, the play known as 'When the Moon Has Set' has bothered admirers of the dramatist, even after it was admitted to the *Collected Works* of 1962–1968 in a conflate one-act version. Publication of a two-act version in 1982 has led to some more considered analysis of it, less as a dramatic accomplishment, more as a mediating text between life and art.

As a prologue to considering the play, we could do worse than choose a passage from one of JMS's Wicklow essays in which he quotes at length a woman whom he knew and whom he encountered in 'a lonely public house near Rathnew':

> 'Ah, your honour,' she said, 'I hear you're going off in a short time to Dublin, or to France, and maybe we won't be in the place at all when you come back. There's no fences on the bit of farm I have, the way I'm destroyed running. The calves do be straying, and the geese do be straying, and the hens do be straying, and I'm destroyed running after them. We've no man in the place since himself died in the winter ... My brother Michael has come back to his own place after being seven years in the Richmond Asylum; but what can you ask of him, and he with a long family of his own? And, indeed, it's a wonder he ever came back when it was a fine time he had in the asylum.'
>
> She saw my movement of surprise, and went on: -
>
> 'There was a son of my own, as fine a lad as you'd see in the county ... Well, he was a keeper in a kind of private asylum, I think they call it, and when

Michael was taken bad, he went to see him, and didn't he know the keepers that were in charge of him, and, indeed, he was always a quiet man that would give no trouble. After the first three years he was free in the place, and he walking about like a gentleman, doing any light work he'd find agreeable.'

Part of this may be treated as social manoeuvring on the woman's part with a view to demonstrating her ability to overcome misfortune. There is also an undeniable ease of address between the widow and the young gentleman she converses with in a pub-cum-grocery, as if his association with France broke down what might otherwise be the barriers between her cottage and his summer residence at Castle Kevin. But the essay, as JMS eventually published it, records his walking up the long hill from Laragh to Sugar Loaf Mountain till, 'towards the top of the hill I passed through a narrow gap with high rocks on one side of it and fir trees above them, and a handful of jagged sky filled with extraordinarily brilliant stars'. This is not a factual account of walking or cycling, as indeed the details of constricted access reveal: it is a textual path towards family and psychic history:

> In a few moments I passed out on the brow of the hill that runs behind the Devil's Glen, and smelt the fragrance of the bogs. I mounted again. There was not light enough to show the mountains round me, and the earth seemed to have dwindled away into a mere platform where an astrologer might watch. Among these emotions of the night one cannot wonder that the madhouse is so often named in Wicklow.[1]

JMS's most extended investigation of this social condition was conducted through the many versions of 'When the Moon Has Set'. The play's hero is Columb Sweeny, a priggish young man whose career path – the term seems apt – strongly resembles that of the immature dramatist. Columb has returned from France, while in 'The People of the Glens', the essayist is about to depart thence. The women of the play are of greater interest. They include two nuns, one of whom remains off-stage while the other (Sister Eileen) becomes emotionally involved with the prig, despite being his cousin. No real dramatic role is assigned to the off-stage nun (Sister Dora), giving rise to the suspicion that the two derive in some fashion from the two Infirmarian Sisters who assisted the Ashford Dispensary during the cholera epidemic of 1866. The other notable character is Bride, a maid in the Sweeny house, through whom a complex earlier generation of Costellos, Kavanaghs and Sweenys is implicated. Through these the Union finds a place in the stilted dialogue. Describing her parents to the young Columb Sweeny, Bride says: 'He's a very innocent poor man, God help him, but my mother is like a lady. I'm told they do called her "your ladyship" below in the Asylum.'[2]

Asylum is identifiable with Union, and cuts through the euphemisms conventionally employed. Like Michael Dara in 'In the Shadow of the Glen' Bride is inclined to recommend the institution. Her mother is 'there a good bit now, but they say she doesn't be lonesome in it at all, there do be so many coming in from all the houses in the country'. The implication here is of applicants to the Union from a better class of person than was generally associated with it. A convergence of Bride's class and Columb's, in the unlikely common ground of Rathdrum Union, is further revealed in details of her uncle, her mother's brother, Stephen:

> He's a Costello from an old Castilian family, and it's fine people they were, and it's no lie I'm telling you. For my mother was a big tall woman herself, and I had an aunt that's dead, who was the finest girl, I've heard them say, you'ld find in the whole world. She was reared with the nuns (*looking at him with a curious expression*) and maybe you've heard his honour speak of her, God rest his soul.

From this and other broad hints a pre-history can be deduced. The elder Columb Sweeny (whose death is expected from the outset, and duly occurs) had an affair with Bride's now dead aunt, a Costello by name. This woman's sister spends much of her time in the Union where she is (according to her husband) 'as comfortable as any lady in England, France or Germany, walking round in the Asylum with fine shoes on her feet'.[3] Her brother, however, is 'the maddest man ... left walking in the world'; that is, though insane he is not confined to the Asylum/Union. This Stephen Costello 'has sworn his Bible oath he'll shoot the next heir, cousin or descendent of his honour, God rest his soul, who comes down into the place'.

Basically, the historical plot is constructed through a series of displacements, with the Union acting as a shunting-yard. The proposition, that Costello is a Castilian name of high degree, repeats a widespread Irish popular belief of the period (and later) about the former noble standing of families now in low circumstances. But the Castilian origin is nonsense.[4] We know that a semi-literate James Costello died in 1901 between Roundwood and Annamoe, and that Mrs Synge attended the funeral at Derrylossary church. This Costello evidently lived as a dependent of the Booth family in Laragh House. The cause of death was 'general debility', further evidence that he was likely to have been in the Union or to have feared being sent there. James Costello's relationship to the local gentry remains inscrutable, though members of the Archer, Barton and Synge families were present at his burial.[5]

Apart from the curiously positive account of the Union provided by several of its characters, 'When the Moon Has Set' is noteworthy for three other, interconnecting features: i) echoes of Hatch family history; ii) accounts of degeneration and madness; iii) anticipations of JMS's mature drama.

Sweeny Senior has left a will and a letter to his heir, 'in a box between the library windows', together with a drawing of a girl. While some of this material is acted upon as soon as Sweeny Junior receives it, there is delay in opening the box. This can be compared to the discovery of a second will after Samuel M'Cracken's death because, in Sweeny Senior's box, are rings and a dress for a woman he had hoped to marry. But 'she was poor. She died afterwards, and her brother became crazy. He would have shot me but some vow restrained him. He thought I had wronged her'.[6] This brings together two features of M'Cracken's confession to John Hatch and the Stuarts' attempt to frustrate Hatch's inheritance. However, in Sweeny Senior's letter (just quoted), the heir is abjured, 'You will not love a woman it is not lawful to love.' This suggests that the old man's offence had not merely crossed class boundaries but violated some stricter code of legal prohibition. As far as the play is concerned, no such possibility is discernible because there is no suggestion that Miss Costello was either related to Sweeny or already married: her avenger is her brother. In the case of 1769, there was both M'Cracken's proposal to marry a niece of his cousin Henry Hatch, and the threats of an outraged husband to sue M'Cracken at Wicklow Assizes for an offence against someone we presume to be another woman (not Hatch's niece).

One dramatically redundant detail in the play proposes that Stephen Costello and his sister whom Sweeny Senior wished to marry were twins – 'that would account for the resemblance' between the prisoner who has been photographed in prison before his trial and the drawing found among the dead man's effects. The comparison of images is a conflation of historical distinctions. Here the imposition of visual record-keeping on prisoners, a distinctly nineteenth-century bureaucratic procedure, is brought side by side with an essentially private keepsake valorisation of portraits, however sketchy. In the unnecessary specification of twins, we also have the basic features of those freemartin births in which John Hatch had concerned himself in the year of his marriage, or somewhat later – a double birth, one male and one female.

When Stephen Costello shoots Sweeny Junior in the play, he is tried 'down at the town ... down at the assizes'. Though convicted, Costello is put 'into a kind of a Criminal Asylum for the rest of his life'. Given that he has already been described as 'the maddest man left walking the world', one wonders why his ladylike sister and not Stephen has been confined in the Union. Apart from the crude requirement that he must be free if he is to take revenge, there is the more significant consequence of his being JMS's first tramp. Bride's comments on her mother's Castilian dignities goes some way towards meeting JMS's own observations that the younger or artistic sons of well-to-do families come to resemble tramps, in their combination of independence and poverty. No examples from the life are cited in support of this theory, though Victorian Wicklow certainly knew of one case when a man described as tramp-painter murdered a young woman in Delgany by whom he was infatuated. After the trial, he was confined to an asylum though the *Wicklow News-Letter* declared 'We must confess that the evidence of his insanity was extremely slight, and the jury that tried him believed he was perfectly sane.'[7] Leniency among the authorities, and the fact that the convict's name was the unusual one of Wigwell, strongly suggests that he did indeed come from a higher rank of society than that usually associated with tramping. Madness was a matter of judgement, in this case imposed by a legal authority to save a man from the gallows.

Wigwell may have lingered in the county's memory, but he is unlikely to have contributed anything to the making of Stephen Costello. What his case illustrates is the arbitrary nature of insanity as an institutional category. This is certainly a preoccupation in the play. On the night his uncle dies, Columb Sweeny has encountered 'a queer man talking to himself under some trees', and supposes he is 'almost mad'.[8] Bride starts at the announcment of this encounter (we are to suppose later that she recognises *her* uncle in this description) though Sister Eileen (a relative stranger) announces that 'there are many people about here who are not sane'. The discussion of the Asylum/Union then follows. A letter arrives from Columb which prompts a comparison of his Paris experiences with Ireland. To Sister Eileen, he declares 'in this life of Ireland, men go mad every hour and you do not ask them to change ... Madness is caused by the killing out or exaggeration of some part of the personality, and life here has been withered away by men that are held up in contrast to the French till we are more degenerate than they are'.[9] Spotting a man outside in the trees, Columb exclaimed 'It is the avenging lunatic.' It was.

Columb's theory of Irish degeneracy is resumed in the second act, when he writes in reply to his friend in Paris. He attributes it to 'old-fashioned Irish conservatism and morality' and characterises it as melancholic. 'Everyone seemed to be taking his friends to the asylum or bringing them back from it.'[10] Amidst these difficulties, Columb is keen to assert an aesthetic theory which is mixed up with versions of evolution. 'A man is sterile when he is beautiful, and withered when he produces.' If this means anything, it suggests that men remain sexually inactive (chaste) while they retain their physical beauty. He continues, 'This illness has brought me a relapse into puberty, I have the envy I used to have of the wild plants that crush and strangle each other in a cold rage of growth.' Puberty, if approached by way of a relapse, involves a reverse or reduction of sexual potency, a condition difficult to reconcile with his wish to marry his cousin, though it may mutely reveal something of his attitude towards Bride, the servant in his uncle's household. Columb, of course, has not been ill; to be precise, he has suffered shoulder wounds in Stephen's attack, as a result of which he cannot write with his right hand. This disability necessitates Sister Eileen's remaining in the house, and so assisting in the discovery of the wedding dress, the letter and the injunction to love lawfully. Against all the odds, Sister Eileen agrees to wed her cousin, Columb, 'in the Name of the Summer, and The Sun, and the Whole World'. Perhaps a deciding factor is her discovery that Bride is pregnant, for the logic of displacement from one character on to another underpins both the *non sequiturs* of Columb's theorising and the social ranking of Sweenys, Costellos and Kavanaghs.

Madness and local government

Decadence, degeneration, madness – these were by no means monopolies of the Wicklow or Irish gentry. Late nineteenth-century Europe was anxiously agog at the evidences of decline, evidently the counterpart of social evolution along neo-Darwinian lines. It is the great theme of Max Nordau's *Entartung* (1893), though in more subtle forms it had been analysed by Ibsen and Nietzsche long before the *fin de siècle*. As a mind capable of reading beyond the syllabus approved by his insular cultural training, the young JMS was inevitably exposed to its allure and its pessimistic diagnosis. What is striking in the play known as 'When the Moon Has Set' is his palpable if also unclear merger of philosophical (largely aesthetic) analysis and historical excavation. Neither is rigorous, each endeavour being potentially at risk should the other succeed.

Let us first take the inquiry into family history. Both at the level of specific exposure of details from his own ancestry, and at the theoretical level of accounting for origin, succession and perpetuation generally – Columb's exposition is held in check, lest too much of the record should render unnecessary or inadequate the philosophical-aesthetic analysis. Conversely, his theories of art as it relates to emotion (including sexual feeling) cannot be pushed too far, lest they suddenly confirm what is still merely implicit in the family closet. In terms of plot, the only resolution is marriage within the family.

How this bears on Synge history, and the self-consciousness of JMS's generation, will never be exactly measured. How it bears on the mature drama which he published and saw produced will also remain a matter of dispute. In the latter connection, 'When the Moon Has Set' clearly reveals his early experiments with Wicklow dialect through the voices of Bride, Mrs Byrne and Pat Kavanagh who match in number characters drawn from the householder's background. Even when a character appears to be self-contained, family affiliation emerges to draw him or her into a compact. The crucial off-stage figures of Stephen Costello, his sister in the Asylum, and his other (dead) sister not only constitute the largest family grouping, they imply guilty associations between the two families at an earlier date. What is more or less admitted is that Sweeny Senior loved the now dead Miss Costello and in doing so gave mortal offence, though nothing came of their planned-for wedding. What is not admitted, though its outline can just about be inferred, is that Sweeny was the father of Bride, her mother having been banished to the Asylum, and a dead sister invoked as a 'blind'.

Two textual sources can be mobilised to give point to this inferred scandal in the Sweeny family. One relates to the photograph of Stephen Costello referred to in the two-act version of 'When the Moon Has Set'. This object, an icon of Victorian bureaucracy and institutionalisation, is not produced on stage although, by the very nature of its technology, copies could be distributed to every police-barracks or magistrate's big house in the county. It is only alluded to on one occasion, and in this regard it could be assimilated into the dozens of other passing references to works of art (by Chopin, Rodin, Rousseau, Rubens, etc.). No doubt a mug-shot taken for the Royal Irish Constabulary might feel out of place in such company, yet it is never given any kind of status as a truth-statement in counterdistinction from its existence as image. Indeed, the photograph stands in instead of a full account of Costello's trial. It has been shown to Sister Eileen by the local doctor (Burke by name) when he dropped in with news of the trial. With insufficient time to tell of the trial 'fully', he substituted the image. In the nun's words, 'he took me out to the door when he was going away, and showed me a photograph that had been taken in the prison'. The image of Stephen never enters the big house at Kilgreine, just as Stephen himself remained outside even when he shot the new 'master'.

The substitution of Stephen's image for an account of Stephen's trial not only avoids any extended account of the links binding Sweenys and Costellos, it also – as the play treats it – draws attention to that suppression. Yet suppression goes further – the image cannot be brought across the threshold. It is possible to argue that Kilgreine is still in mourning (with the curtains drawn) and so the photograph must be examined at the doorway. Nothing of this crepitude prevents Eileen and Columb examining drawings, pictures and documents (included aged documents). The non-introduction of Stephen Costello's image closes down any further inquiry into his madness, his purpose, his relationship with the Sweeny family, his origins. New technology functions to preserve the old regime from scrutiny.

Nevertheless, when Columb and Eileen briefly discuss the photograph, uncertainty of reference or representation or comparison results. To some extent this itself results from JMS's incompetence as a writer for the stage, his unsureness of touch. He composes the plot from within a consciousness of family history which is at once pervasive as air and wholly contrived: it is the consciousness of the oxygen tent. Maybe the setting derives from Ibsen, influence is less important than manifest intention. In the 'old family library' where the action takes place in both acts or scenes, 'a large portrait' hangs over the fireplace: its subject is never specified but the audience is allowed to assume that Columb Sweeny Senior is therein portrayed. This is one of the details which prompted Frank McGuinness to see affinity between 'When the Moon Has Set' and 'Rosmersholm'.

In the first act, the picture is explicitly alluded to when Sister Eileen makes an effort to calculate the dead master's age. The effort does not make things clearer, because the words spoken leave the audience still to decide whether the figures whom Columb and she mention ' ... he was not more than thirty five ... He must have been about fifty ...' are disposed so as to establish the remoteness in time of some other event ('my grand Aunt's funeral') which has no dramatic significance whatsoever.[11] While all this is going on, the audience is always present not only hearing but also seeing, looking at and (if it is properly attentive) actively watching the portrait over the fireplace. It is a focal point of the drama, an image of the man under discussion, an image held at some unspecific moment in time, his age.

Madness and local government

In the second act of JMS's play, when the elder Sweeny has been replaced by his nephew-namesake, the picture is still in place. Under its gaze, a kind of orgy of images takes place. The younger Columb Sweeny and Sister Eileen – for whom orgy lies beyond the play's closure – discuss two images which the audience cannot possibly see, the pocket-book drawing of Miss Costello long ago (which may have been the work, Eileen earlier suggested, of Columb Sweeny Senior), and the now familiar photograph of Stephen Costello, her brother. Twin images, twins, She and He.

For the second source which can be mobilised to illuminate family scandal, we turn to the composite text of 'When the Moon Has Set' prepared by Ann Saddlemyer for the third volume of the *Collected Works* (1968). The inclusion of any version of this play was a brave endeavour at the time, when Edward Stephens's widow was still alive, likewise other members of the Synge family in the same generation. If JMS's inept gesture towards photography in his first play might be rehabilitated by pointing to the way in which its role is adapted towards preservation of family honour, the alternative text which Saddlemyer edited introduces far more dangerous material.

This is a one-act version, assembled from several manuscripts. The setting is the same old 'country house', though there is some suggestion that its location is not isolated. For example, when the drawing of blinds is suggested Sister Eileen remarks that 'the people will think it strange' and refers to to windows 'next the lane'. The social status of the house appears identical in all versions, but here – in these one acters – there is greater encroachment from the town, from some local community which is distanced in the phrase 'the people' even as it implicitly concedes their authority.

As if to compensate for this growth in external representativeness in the people outside, the *dramatis personae* of the one-act version admits fewer of their number within the house. The two-acter has Mrs Byrne, Bride (the maid) and Pat Kavanagh (her father); Stephen Costello comes near enough to fire through the window, while his sister and a more distant figure named Murphy are also alluded to. The one-acter retains Bride, but also brings Mary Costello directly into the action. Her admission is ostentatiously prefaced by the portrait which, in this version, represents the woman whom Colm Sweeny Senior had loved, rather than Sweeny himself. Once the subject of the picture has been identified by Bride as the woman of Castilian origin long confined to the Asylum, Colm takes it down and places it in a corner. There is no photograph, for there is no latter-day criminal, and there is no doctor.

The concentration of the short play results in a rapid and cheerful *denouément*, but it fails to convince psychologically or dramatically. The sudden eruption of Mary Costello into 'the family library' suggests a disturbance in the archives, a blemish carved (however long ago) on the family tree. Her instant concentration on a bureau – *'sees that one of the drawers is open and pounces on it'* – leads promptly to the discovery of two rings, some white linen and a silk dress. Alerted to the fact that the elder Sweeny has died, she pronounces:

> I was afeard it was my little children (*she looks up to COLM, and speak piteously*) – for I was never married your honour, and have no children I do be thinking it's alive they must be if I never had them itself ... (*Raising her voice to a plaintive cry.*) I do see them sometimes when my head's bad and I do be falling into my sleep ... There are five children, five children that wanted to live. God help them, if the nuns and the priests with them had let me be (*swaying herself with anguish*) ...'[12]

In a matter of moments, the nun Sister Eileen (a distant cousin of Colm's) has decided to marry him in a quasi-pagan ceremony. Quite apart from the theatrical inadequacy of this conversion, the material of Mary Costello's uncertain history makes for compelling study.

While the action replays the business of M'Cracken's bureau being moved and suspect documents 'discovered', the absence of a will from the one-act version of 'When the Moon Has Set' distances it from the events of 1769. In turn, however, this feature of the short play draws attention to the unexamined will in the two-act version. JMS never finalised the text, so that conflicts, overlapppings and omissions characterise the piece as we move from one set of manuscripts to another in a process not unlike that of the characters themselves. The Asylum and its context of distinctly nineteenth-century social malaise looms larger in the one-acter because of Mary Costello's presence on stage which, ironically, vindicates Bride's account of 'the great lot were coming in from all the houses in the country, and herself as well off as any lady in England, France or Germany'. Here, on stage, is a former Asylum-inmate standing in the Big House, holding the dress in which she was intended to marry, talking to young persons who might have been her relatives by marriage, persons who study her portrait in the library where it has acted as her substitute.

The inner contraction of the play is summarised in the children which Mary Costello has borne and not borne. Superficially, her long reference to these is the evidence of her madness, the rightness of her detention in the Asylum. Yet, when Colm had been walking close to the graveyard where his uncle is to be buried, and had lost his way, it was Mary Costello who gave him reliable directions. In a line which rings out with a simplicity the play elsewhere lacks, 'I went wrong coming home, and this woman put me right.' Indeed, despite its preachy awkwardness, the most convincing aspect of 'When the Moon Has Set' is its author's proto-feminism: 'I am not a woman and I cannot judge of all your feelings, yet I know that you have a profound impulse for what is peculiar to women.'[13]

With Mary Costello occupying centre-stage, the play expands and contracts in implied historical time, sometimes emphasising immediate social agencies and instruments such as nursing nuns, the Asylum and telegraphs, sometimes echoing eighteenth-century scandals of illicit love and pistol-shot at Roundwood. In keeping with this restlessness, the play offers too many accounts of why the elder Sweeny and Mary Costello did not marry. She was socially beneath him, as Bride explains while contradicting this with accounts of Castilian dignity preserved even in the Asylum. He did not believe in God, as Sister Eileen protests, on the eve of her own apostasy. According to the document left for his heir, she was (by implied parallel) a woman 'it is not lawful to love'. And there is Mary's own cryptic remark 'There's great marrying in the world but it's late we were surely', which hints that marriage did indeed take place but insufficiently early to be acceptable.[14] Here the relics of that ceremony take on an ambiguous appearance, for the linen which is found with the rings and the dress is, in one version at least, explicitly called 'baby linen'.[15]

The most extensive comparison of this disturbing play to its author's mature work is to be found in Mary King's account of JMS's last and unfinished work, 'Deirdre of the Sorrows' (1909).[16] Central to her analysis was the perceived concern of each play with a ruling class in crisis and terminal decline. More generally, of course, 'When the Moon Has Set' can be regarded as JMS's preliminary experiments with Wicklow dialect as used principally here by Mrs Byrne. The family name, Byrne, is very common in Wicklow, and it is not surprising to find it occurring in 'When the Moon Has Set', 'The Tinker's Wedding' and 'The Well of the Saints'. Less expected, however, is an echo of Mrs Byrne in 'Riders to the Sea', Synge's first published play, set on the western seaboard and with a cast who never aspire to surnames. Ann Saddlemyer noted this inscription of the prentice work into what is often regarded as the playright's most finished text, when she edited the plays in the 1960s.

But it is no longer necessary to argue that 'like Wilde, Synge was loath to give up a useful phrase ...'[17] In an early draft of 'When the Moon Has Set', the young servant laments her dead father in words which will later become old Maurya's in 'Riders to the Sea' – 'I'm destroyed entirely; but what good is in it. We must be satisfied, and what man at all can be living forever.' Posed thus as a question, Bride/Maurya's words hint at a religious answer couched in terms of immortality, and between the two plays where they appear there is an undoubted movement away from the transcendental (whether of God the Son, or God the Sun) towards a stoical-secular acceptance of death's inevitability and finality. Saddlemyer's concern to treat such transcriptions from 'When the Moon Has Set' into the mature plays concludes with a comprehensive relating of Mary Costello with both the earliest one-act and the unfinished three-act tragedies:

> In the final draft Mary Costello repeats Maurya again in her defiance of the priests: '... for it's little the like of them, I was saying, know about women or

the seven sorrows of the earth', and predicts Deirdre's actions: 'There's great marrying in the world but it's late we were surely, and let yourselves not be the same.'[18]

These are telling citations, but their implication goes well beyond the notion of Synge as an economic re-user of disgarded material. Perhaps the deeper presence of 'When the Moon Has Set' in the mature plays can be traced through a parallel which Saddlemyer did not cite. The canonical moment occurs in 'Riders to the Sea' before Maurya learns of her final bereavement:

> I've had a husband, and a husband's father, and six sons in this house – six fine men, though it was a hard birth I had with every one of them and they coming to the world – and some of them were found and some of them were not found, but they're gone now the lot of them.[19]

In its anticipation of her last son's death, and in its uncanny rationalisation of death in a primitive economy, this passage surely recalls Mary Costello's most enigmatic words in 'When the Moon Has Set':

> And a long rest behind him, why would that trouble me now? I was afeard it was my little children for if I was never married your honour, and have no children I do be thinking it's alive they must be if I never had them itself ... There are five children, five children that wanted to live ...[20]

Despite the contrived derangement of the character's words, and the ostentatious differences of circumstance, one wonders if this is not the moment when the silence of Barbara Synge was finally broken.

21

Instituting 'The Playboy'

> Once, when midnight smote the air
> Eunuchs ran through Hell and met
> On every crowded street to stare ... (W.B. Yeats)

THE DRAMA for which JMS is celebrated occupies a space apparently uncluttered by the factors discussed in the previous chapter. Island, lonely glen, crossroads-side, western shoreline – setting preserves an elemental quality even when the action takes place within doors. A political context for this contrast surrounds the Local Government Act of 1898, a measure of constructive unionism (as the phrase now has it) timed to coincide with the centenary of the United Irishmen's insurrection. Away went grand juries and poor law boards; in came elected county councils. The franchise for important areas of local government included women for the first time, and the overall effect was to eradicate the patriarchal system whereby John 'Pestalozzi' Synge had a birthright to rule over the inmates of Rathdrum Union.

If the conservative operations of memory protected many from the implications of change, in Synge's work dialogue busily unsettles vestigial-primeval Ireland, with a schedule of institutions, licences, organisations and public bodies. The most thoroughly unsettled of the plays is the last, 'The Playboy of the Western World'. It is set, according to Pegeen Mike, in an area to which 'the mad Mulrannies were driven from California and they lost in their wits'. Here she fears 'the thousand militia – bad cess to them! – walking idle through the land'. Her father's pub is no reincarnation of the Shakespearean inn or Chaucer's Tabard. It functions thanks to recent legislation for – as Michael James explains – the words 'Licensed for the Sale of Beer and Spirits, to be Consumed on the Premises' are written in white letters above the door.

The official practice of licensing runs through the play almost as if it were the counter-motif to the 'shifts' which caused the riot. When Christy finally admits boastfully that he killed his poor father, he adds quickly, 'I never used weapons.

I've no license, and I'm a law-fearing man.' This comic detail is strangely echoed, stilled and returned to an earlier moment in the play when Pegeen inquires, 'You never hanged him, the way Jimmy Farrell hanged his dog from the licence, and had it screeching and wriggling three hours at the butt of a string, and himself swearing it was a dead dog, and the peelers swearing it had life?' From being a word on a noticeboard, through being a written permission, the licence has now become a solid object – solid enough to bear the weight of an animal, to be a gallows.

A marginal note should be added at this point, to clarify the object of Pegeen's rhetorical question. To the average theatregoer, accustomed to Irish dramatic hyperbole, she surely invokes some legendary figure (Cromwell, or Billy Buck, the Ragman) in the district, whose awful deeds are more often spoken of than verified. But, no. Jimmy Farrell is on stage, no further away from Pegeen than Christy is. There is no missing Jimmy. A striking number of the men in 'The Playboy' are described in the stage directions as fat, but Jimmy is more particularly 'fat and amorous'. He is the one who stiffened the licence into a gibbet, whose dispute with the 'peelers' revolves unresolvably on the question of whether or when the dog was dead. Protestant Elizabethans ritually hanged a *d-o-g* to mock the hanged *g-o-d* whom Catholics displayed on their crucifixes. Jimmy Farrell is close to the bone, for all his amorous fat.

The institutional reference insists on resurfacing in the play's tweedy texture, like a stitch which cannot be dropped. Christy initially presents his father as a strong farmer, though the *dramatis personae* has him 'a squatter'. The play nimbly shifts from contemporary reference to recent history, invoking land wars which have ended, resentments and anxieties which persist. At the end of Act One, the playboy who slew his da speaks of him as a man who had been 'locked in the asylums for battering peelers or assaulting men'. The asylums will recur though less frequently than the police who, as 'peelers', have been the pervasive institutional presence of the first act. The second act gets off to a clear start, with little mention of anything beyond Christy's growing confidence. But when Pegeen mentions an execution she has read about in the newspaper, the jargon of circuit-court judges, juries and peelers wells up. Behind this, the ease with which Pegeen has access to newspapers, without having to buy one, exemplifies how thoroughly the organs of middle-class opinion have pervaded even this allegedly remote place. While the implied map features Ballina, Belturbet, Castlebar and Crossmolina – notable towns in County Mayo – there is also reference to a wider dispersion. Christy fears being 'drawn to the cities where you'd hear a voice kissing', the Widow Quin mentions the Sligo boat as a means of escape and Shawn Keogh knows that even Kilmainham Jail (in Dublin) would fail to constrain the playboy.

Pervasive agencies play hide-and-seek with formally delineated characters. Constraint is invoked as an antonym for unbridled action, lack of control. The

Instituting 'The Playboy'

sudden appearance of Old Mahon, deflating Christy in the eyes of the Widow, is accompanied by accusations of madness. Christy, it seems, had been regarded back home as 'the looney of Mahon's' while, to discredit the resurrected father, the Widow is prepared to 'swear he's a maniac', adding for good measure that she 'could take an oath I seen him raving on the sands to-day'.

Nothing of this is to be taken seriously: it is all part of the extravagant discussion of actions which are never implemented, the gallous story as proclaimed by all and sundry. The bravado of language, and ornamental grotesquerie of image, should not detract from the particular nuances of the dialogue. Though none of the plays lacks distinguishing traces of modernised, commercial society, 'The Playboy' is especially rich in casual, yet revealing gestures towards the enormous nineteenth-century engine of control. The gutsy brilliance of its comedy, the acccuracy of its tragic momentum are not diminished by an acknowledgement that it is a play of post–1890s Ireland written by one who, in fear and trembling, had brought Ibsen to bear on his own domestic inheritance.

Act Three opens with fat Jimmy Farrell alluding to bankrupcy, the law on self-incrimination, museums in Dublin, the Liverpool boat, and much more. The Widow Quin and Old Mahon enter, and with them the theme of lunacy and violence. The vocabulary of these high jinks deserves close scrutiny, even cross-examination. Jimmy 'knew a party was kicked in the head by a red mare, and he went killing horses a great while, till he eat the insides of a clock and died after'. This is great fun for the audience, not all of whom pause to note Jimmy's legalistic, courtroom term ('a party') for a man. Christy's off-stage triumph in the races provokes Old Mahon to recognise his 'wandering son' in pride and anger, but a draft of September 1904 shows the hero 'being elected county councillor' while standing (for election?) on a table.[1] These two instances exemplify the thorough penetration of 'the western world' by administrative jargon, and the new local government arrangements, even as JMS tries to cancel it in comic business.

Normality also is invoked as a smokescreen. The Widow tries to set up an alternative identity for the playboy as 'a man is going to make a marriage with the daughter of this house, a place with fine trade, with a licence, and with poteen too'. The opulence of her vision – legal and illegal spirits from the same brimming bowl – is too much for Old Mahon, who wonders if it is not 'in a crazy-house for females' that he has landed. If the new county council has been written out by the dramatist himself, his most mischevous character has responded with licensing laws, his overthrown father with asylums and unions. The emerging reality of the third act is repeatedly challenged by allegations or anticipations of madness, defined with reference to bureaucratic control. In one form or another the word is uttered a dozen times, with its various synonyms (crazy, fool, idiot, etc.) adding at least a score of emphatic diagnoses in confirmation.

These are not pure reiterations of a classical theme in which madness is the partner of poetry or love. Nevertheless, when Jimmy Farrell recalls 'a party was kicked in the head by a red mare, and he went killing horses a great while', he half echoes Sophocles, whose Ajax had slaughtered whole herds of sheep, mistaking them for treacherous kinsmen. In the play, it is Tecmessa, the demented hero's wife, who finds a way to 'speak a thing that appalls my speech', to recall 'an accident Awful as death'.[2] For Synge, dramatic form itself is the voice which can articulate silence.

To be sure, madness is associated with drunkenness here, though not with anything remotely Bacchic. When Old Mahon contradicts himself in claiming that he 'never went mad to this day', he proceeds with memories of being 'not three weeks' – that is, not more than three weeks – 'with the Limerick girls drinking myself silly and parlatic'. If idiom allows 'paralytic' as a Jovial synonym for 'drunk ... speechless ... footless ... ', parlatic also approaches General Paralysis of the Insane, a favourite late Victorian diagnosis for various terminal states, including that of tertiary syphilitic infection. Madness in the language of 'The Playboy' is – to borrow from Foucault – socially constructed. Indeed, it is strangely reflexive. Old Mahon admits that, on some previous occasion he had been 'a terrible and fearful case ... screeching in a straightened waistcoat, with seven doctors writing out my sayings in a printed book'. The book, evidently scripted in advance, is both the source and outcome of his ravings. And in acknowledgement that this condition has descended on him once more in what he suspects to be 'a crazy-house' he resolves to 'be going to the union beyond, and there'll be a welcome before me ...'.

As we have seen in a detailed account of Rathdrum, the Union became the focal point for myriad lamentations, visions and retributions in nineteenth-century Ireland. In the year of 'The Playboy', Rathdrum took in 6,000 supplicants who, in way or another, were of the same cloth as Old Mahon in his confusion. If the play's one reference to the Union is a climactic moment, reached through a series of repeated soundings of related themes, and then transformed through Christy's assertion of a power over his father which in effect redirects the older man from ignominy, similar explorations had occurred already with 'In the Shadow of the Glen' (1903). The earlier, Wicklow-set play has its idiomatic links with the West of 'The Playboy', with Dublin's madhouse serving as a point of interchange.

Introducing himself to Nora Burke, the Tramp of the one-act play avers that 'if myself was easily afeard, I'm telling you, it's long ago I'd have been locked into the Richmond Asylum ...' – that is, the Dublin mental hospital which served Wicklow in the absence of any county provision. The unease pervading Nora's cabin arises less from her sham-dead husband, her would-be lover, or even the nervous Tramp, but undeniably from the absent Patch Darcy, 'the man [who] went queer in his head the year that's gone' and who had been 'mad dying' before he was eaten by crows.

Instituting 'The Playboy'

In life, Patch Darcy had been celebrated locally for his ability to move through his herds of sheep, noticing the absence of any stray, being the very antithesis of frenzied Ajax. Yet Darcy, himself astray in the play, is suspected of dalliance with the young married woman. Though an original-in-life has been established, at least with respect to the manner of his death, there is no reason to believe that the actual John Winterbottom engaged in any romantic liaison. On the contrary, his career seems to have been pathetic in every regard, bodily and mentally.[3] This being the case, the suspicion harboured by Dan Burke beneath his temporary shroud may derive from an 1895 trial of nine people for murder. In newspaper accounts of the trial JMS could have read of a woman variously suspected of being possessed by the fairies or being too friendly with a passing trader (see below in chapter 22). Traditionally regarded as an appropriation of Ibsen's 'A Doll's House' for Irish purposes, 'In the Shadow of the Glen' should also be seen as a dramatic rewriting of Bridget Cleary's dreadful fate.

But before Nora can be redeemed, she admits her offences with many passing men, and her sham husband rises wrathfully from his bier to banish her and her lacklustre lover to the roads. The Tramp protests while Michael Dara (the lover) says timidly, 'There's a fine Union below in Rathdrum' – perhaps the only Wicklowman, not sitting on the Board of Guardians, to hold that view. Yet in a play which JMS never released for production on the stage, a similar view is expounded, this time by a Wicklow woman.

22

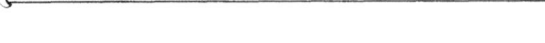

A county in romance

AFTER a severe winter, a married woman of twenty-six was progressively burnt to death in her home near Mullinahone, Tipperary. The torment was inflicted during March 1895, the perpetrators being the woman's husband, her father and several neighbours including women. This was not an act of marquis-de-Sadism, drunken or otherwise. The humble and inexperienced torturers of Bridget Cleary were attempting to drive the fairies out of her body by suspending it/her on the cast-iron grate while a fire burnt below. The matter was widely reported when charges were brought. If this was an isolated incident it derived, however, from widespread belief in a supernatural realm hostile to humankind.[1] Such was the credal system which so impressed W. B. Yeats and Lady Gregory who found in it an alternative to the modernising, levelling tendencies of the age.

Mrs Cleary's tragic death occurred many miles from the suburban Dublin of JMS and his protective family, and as many miles from the county from which they still took their social definition, despite several decades of exclusion from 'the Big House' of Glanmore. Nevertheless, the trial of nine persons at Clonmel courthouse attracted the attention of the press throughout Ireland and Britain: the young E. F. Benson wrote an article for *The Nineteenth Century*.[2] But even contemporary history of this kind slides towards oblivion and may find peace there until some kindred occurrence stirs the memory. In 1907, when the Abbey Theatre erupted during the first performances of 'The Playboy of the Western World', a trainee doctor taunted the rioters with the cry, 'What about Mullinahone and the witch burning?'[3]

This was a penetrating attack on popular rectitude. James Lynchahaun – who 'bit the yellow lady's nostril on the northern shore' and so entered the heroic gossip of Synge's masterpiece – had been in jail with Michael Cleary and the other seedy sinners from Ballyvadlea.[4] Their sexually charged crimes of perverted violence testified to the existence of a sub-world completely inadmissable among the shopkeepers, clerks and strong farmers who were busily constructing a visible regime of Irish-Catholic propriety and bourgeois rectitude, gradually to replace the older order of protestant and landlord dominance. The cottage in which a wife was tortured to death was not the mud-walled protuberance from antique dung and dust imaged in *Punch* and other mockeries of post-Famine Ireland. It was a slate-roofed labourer's abode built only a few years earlier, a model residence of its kind, the product of enlightened local government. In one of its rooms stood a Singer sewing-machine at which Mrs Cleary – almost certainly convent-educated – worked with skill as a dressmaker-milliner.[5]

While the Tipperary prisoners of 1895 were treated leniently by the courts, on the basis that their intentions were not criminal, a counter-intuition was advanced in 1960 by Hubert Butler. Before her persecution, Bridget Cleary had begun to walk the roads whenever a travelling dealer in eggs was in the area. 'When the story was all told in the Clonmel Court House the eggman was only mentioned once and never again by judge, jury, witnesses or prisoners. For all the relevance he appeared to have to the story he and his cart might well have been swallowed up into the fairy mound. Yet these oblique and tender-hearted people had a habit of hiding their thoughts from themselves, and perhaps they sometimes thrust upon the fairies their guilt for desires and jealousies whose crudities they shrank from facing.'[6] In Butler's obliquely stated analysis, the accused may well have committed murder in response to Bridget's violation of sexual custom, while half-believing they were exorcising fairies. Far from registering some triumph of secular reason over superstition it was difficult, in Butler's sombrely understated conclusion, to think 'that the fairies suffered any serious set-back by the happenings at Ballvadlea'.

Closer to the event, and on the occasion of a different outrage, it would appear to have been the view of young Dr Daniel Sheehan in 1907. By shouting out the name of Bridget Cleary's home town (in effect) during the 'Playboy' riots, he drew attention to guilty precedents for the steady burning of Christy Mahon's leg by his new neighbours. Dragged towards the fire by his self-appointed protectors, Christy is an involuntary mimic of Bridget, role-reversing to disclose Pegeen Mike as mistress of all torment:

> SHAWN: I'm afeard of him. [*To Pegeen*] Lift a lighted sod will you and scorch his leg.
> PEGEEN: [*Blowing the fire with a bellows*] Leave go now young fellow or I'll scorch your shins.
> CHRISTY: You're blowing for to torture me? [*His voice rising and growing stronger*] That's your kind, is it? Then let the lot of you be wary, for if I've to face the gallows I'll have a gay march down, I tell you, and shed the blood of some of you before I die.

And a moment later,

> SHAWN: [*shrieking*]. My leg's bit on me! He's the like of a mad dog …[7]

Concerning J. M. Synge

Sedulously ignoring these disclosures of communal savagery and vampiric retaliation, the Abbey Theatre audience focused instead on Christy's indelicate vocabulary. And while the rioters deplored references to Pegeen Mike's underwear, Dr Sheehan re-excavated the submerged distopia, to point out behaviour which had previously characterised those who now disguised their own sexual anxieties. If the rioters wished to identify themselves by virtue of their rejection of Christy, they did so by accepting their part in the burning of Bridget Cleary, the biting of Mrs Macdonnell. It is not likely that Sheehan's obscure argument was appreciated on the occasion, but at least one journalist thought it worth recording.[8]

Referring to an inquest held upon Bridget Cleary's body in 1895, and the subsequent trial of her husband and others, Angela Bourke has identified Social Darwinism as the underlying ideological discourse.[9] By implication, the people amongst whom depraved conduct had been detected existed at the bottom of some evolutionary scale. If one account of Mrs Cleary's suffering placed her in the native oral tradition of fairies and potions and cures, others invoked Hottentots and witch-burning, that is, savage or pre-modern points of reference. Nevertheless, the story never quite went away. Just seven years later, the rumpus inspired by 'The Playboy of the Western World' led (as we have noted) to at least one coded reference to the earlier Tipperary events. Nor was Sheehan alone in its diagnosis. When Patrick Kenny came to defend Synge's plays, he shrewdly invoked the Darwinian paradigm by inverting it: Shawneen Keogh was half-idiot but Pegeen tolerates the prospect of him as a husband 'in all his unfitness' because

> all the fit ones have fled ... He remains because of his cowardice and idiocy in a region where fear is the first of the virtues, and where the survival of the unfittest is the established law of life ... We see in him how the Irish race die out in Ireland, filling the lunatic asylums more full from a declining population, and selecting for continuance in the future the human specimens most calculated to bring the race lower and lower ... 'Shaneen' accepts terror as the regular condition of his existence.[10]

Perhaps for his critique of Irish society 'Pat' was simply adopting the lexicon of madness employed by Old Mahon in the play, but the prompt and positive manner in which JMS replied in the following day's paper strongly suggests prior agreement, and even collusion, between playwright and correspondent. Less than a week later, 'Pat' chaired the debate organised by W. B. Yeats with a view to airing rival arguments and (simultaneously) vindicating the Abbey. If both dramatist and chairman were influenced by contemporary Darwinism, their conclusions led to a diagnosis of degeneration rather than underdevelopment. Ireland had, in some critical psychic zone, ceased to function, or had started alarmingly to 'dysfunction'.

Given the choice – and few of us are given it – one should always attend to the distopia before pursuing whatever utopias survive that scrutiny. Irish cultural

A county in romance

conditions encouraged the polarising of anxieties, dreams and schemes along a resented binary division. Protestant missionaries worked for an island converted from ineradicable Catholicism to reformed homogeneity; nationalists preached a gospel of political inclusiveness which ignored the new stubbornness of protestant-unionism. Victims of rural squalor longed for the amenities of urban life – street lights and privacy. Victims of urban alienation dreamt of communal warmth and some vague unity of experience. These sketchy utopias and distopias were not interchangeable, but it was possible to imagine a machine which would match discontent to its satisfaction, would match but never meet these needs. 'The Land of Heart's Desire', Yeats called it, but it rarely answered to others. In the nineteenth century, English literature had pondered these matters to some effect. The original *Utopia* (1516) of Sir Thomas More had – with little attention to ambivalence – provided a description for the social experiments of Robert Owen (1771–1858) and others which in 1872 were satirised by Samuel Butler in *Erewhon* – that is Nowhere reversed.[11]

While Bridget Cleary fell ill, was diagnosed as being a changeling, and then slowly killed, JMS was commencing his studies in decadent Paris. Privately, even covertly, he was at work on his first extended attempt at a play, one in which death has taken possession of the Big House, which nevertheless remains prey to intrusion by mad Mary Costello or her vengeful brother. Though 'When the Moon Has Set' might have been explained away by reference to Wilkie Collins and the sensational fiction of forty years earlier, no one has ever been confident enough to expose it as just such a work of imitation – a Woman in Green. Instead, the play's various scripts remained out of view for seventy years, its anxieties about children who were never born, about twins, about nobility in the County Asylum carefully protected.

Instead, JMS became famous almost overnight in October 1903 with a one-act play set in a rural cottage where a young woman, given to talking and walking with a passing young man, abandons her husband for a tramp who celebrates the traditional power of old-fashioned sewing. 'There's great safety in a needle, lady of the house – I'd be putting a little stitch here and there in my old coat, the time I'll be praying for his soul, and it going up naked to the saints of God.'[12] The play makes no reference to Tipperary, nor is there any reason why it should. But other reasons, or rationalisations, for its Wicklow setting deserve attention. No Singer disturbed the life of Glenmalure, for the mines which had supported its once substantial population had collapsed close on twenty years before such technology and temptation was offered to the weaker sex. Yet it is exactly that vestigial or peripheral location – close to Dublin, primitively rural, post-industrial, leased from a once-established church – which energises JMS's Wicklow. When he writes about the oppression of the hills, the motivating emotion is not political but agoraphobic. That is, the infinite spaces of a Victorian provincial Nature are transformed into a psychic congestion which replicates but almost obliterates the nearby city.

Frederic Jameson – innocent of any concern with JMS – has suggested that the twentieth-century fear of urban concentration can be traced back through an 'older ideologically far more transparent, nineteenth-century terror of the mob ... (Scott, Manzoni, and Dickens offer rich dramatizations) but whose real credentials for menace are to be found in the great revolutionary "days' of 1789–94'.[13] One has only to adjust the dates by a few years to see how closely and locally this analysis fits the inheritance of the Hatches and Synges. Indeed, the earlier episodes of Hatch encroachment on upland Wicklow during the 1740s and after uniquely coloured Roundwood with urban features – the Charter School, M'Cracken's will and its discussion in Dublin pubs, Alderman Emerson, the printing of Miss Maturin's posthumous *Letters*. The Synge interest in Wicklow was – to reverse a classical trope – *urbs in rure*, shot through with the peculiar solitude of the metropolis.

Browsers in Dublin second-hand bookshops are familiar with John H. Edge's *An Irish Utopia*, first published in 1906 and much reprinted in the decade following. Its setting in the same Wicklow landscape as 'In the Shadow of the Glen' has given Edge's book a certain cachet among bibliophiles, who are less likely to know the book which prompted it – Brian MacDermot's *Leigh of Lara'* (1899). Neither deserves much attention, if aesthetic merit is the sole criterion, and yet the two together raise issues of considerable importance for literary critics and historians of the Irish book trade as well as inquirers into Synge family history. Both authors were lawyers by profession, Edge being more readily traced because he published legal material as well as the book under discussion. Both books were distributed in London by Simpkin, Marshall & Co., run-of-the-mill publishers with a penchant for popular religious material. The principal issuing publisher in each case was Dublin-based – but here the parallels divide. While Edge's *Irish Utopia* was published by Hodges, Figgis & Co., a company of stolidly protestant character, MacDermot's *Leigh of Lara'* came from the house of M. H. Gill, an older firm which had steadily become identified with Catholic and nationalist sympathies.

These distinctly provincial bookseller/publishers typified the Irish book trade in the years before Maunsell & Co., the Cuala Press, and other specialised outlets were called forth by the Literary Revival of Lady Gregory, JMS and Yeats. Their literary productions were decidedly middle-of-the-road, unadventurous in theme and technique. Yet in their thorough-going obscurity, they are examples of what we have come to identify in literature as the political unconscious. The two books under examination resume their parallel relationship when plot is considered: each tells a tale of personal romance and mistaken identity, ending happily. Each is set – and here we reveal the motive behind our attention to them – in the area of Wicklow which surrounds Laragh village. The choice of setting is dictated in

A county in romance

each case by the narrator's origins — a son of the district, drawing on personal memory — and there is every evidence that this narrative perspective simply reproduces the author's. MacDermot, implying that he was raised a Catholic whereas most of his characters cleave (loosely) to the Church of Ireland, recalled that 'we lads used to know that it was Christmas Day if we saw James Mahon from the Seven Churches cross the bridge and walk solemnly and slowly up the rise towards the church'.[14] Elsewhere in his opening pages, he referred to the Edge family home, though John H. Edge will, in successive editions of *An Irish Utopia* trace a more diversified history of his ancestors' residence near Laragh and further afield.

While these ostentatious orientations of the author towards his setting provide a plausible explanation of the books' concentration on a single Wicklow valley, other factors deserve attention. In his 1906 preface Edge, for example, recommends Black's *Guide* and Murray's *Handbook* to Wicklow, signalling that the burgeoning travel literature of the day constituted a backcloth against which he cast his series of fictional and historic images. The novel is to be contextualised with reference to tourism, parties from Dublin, bicycling holidays and other recreational matters. Not that these intrude in either book which, in the manner of nineteenth-century fiction generally, is in each case ostentatiously set in the past. However, round the time that MacDermot and Edge were preparing their tales of Laragh and Knockrath, the young JMS was observing the impact of visitors on the neighbouring village of Annamoe:

> All the afternoon the peasants who have laboured all the week among the sweet scents of the earth stand in rows upon the bridge and watch the procession of riotous women and young men that drives wildly to the city. The smell of the limes is blown across them, every moment some exquisite change in the light upon the hills fills the stream with beauty yet these peasants stand with delated [sic] nostrils and pursed lips sucking delirium from the pageants of disease. Man is not fashioned as are the swine and stars.[15]

While JMS was acutely sensitive to issues of pollution and decadence, especially as these affected a rural economy over which his family no longer exercised any influence, the writing lawyers merely excluded from their fictions whatever latter-day unpleasantness might detract from their moral histories: as with all lawyers, their clients are innocent. On the general issue of setting, it is worth adding that Shaw's 'John Bull's Other Island' (1904) happily inverts many of the platitudes built into the work of MacDermot/Edge, while JMS's 'The Well of the Saints' (1905) establishes its own ironic perspective by invoking a vaguely historical epoch of 'one or more centuries ago'. All four 'village-dramas' exemplify in various ways the tonalities and tensions of Edwardian Ireland, though MacDermot published while the Dear Old Queen was yet alive.

The central story of his 'romance of a Wicklow vale' revolves round Charles

Leigh who, at the opening of the novel, is staying with Mrs Leigh and a child in the hotel at Glendalough. Even when the Leighs rent Laragh Castle on a permanent basis, they occupy separate quarters, a detail which does not prevent local gossips from deploring Charles Leigh's attentions to young Nora Mortimer, daughter of a local Big House. In the end, Charles emerges as Mrs Leigh's brother-in-law (not husband), and in this way propriety is shown never to have been endangered. But the conclusion is only reached after some tedious confusion about brothers, a bout of gentlemanly fist-fighting and recourse to America. Charles marries Nora, and Mrs Leigh's rightful husband is restored. Nothing in the plot is worth a second moment's thought.

Instead, the fiction dis-places facts and actualities which remain traceable in *Leigh of Lara'*. There is the house in which the Leighs will live: this is introduced as 'a veritable walled-in castle':

> When it was built, for what purpose it was walled round, I never could clearly ascertain. But there it was with a turreted front and single tower, and with outer walls embrasured at the angles, enclosing about two acres of land and standing about ten or eleven feet high. It may have owed its origin to the turbulent times of '98 – it did not look older than that date – and soldiers may have been actually stationed in it. From the roof there was to be obtained a magnificent view of the surrounding scenery. The wooded hills of Derrybawn stood right in front across the valley on the other side of the village, extending to the right in the precipitous side of Lugduff, which frowned down into the deep waters of the Upper lake, with St. Kevin's bed excavated in the almost perpendicular cliff. Further on to the right the view was shortened somewhat by the intervention of a hill called Brockagh, covered with little farm cottages nestling amongst trees and land with infinite difficulty cultivated almost up to the very top of its sloping side. Truly a delightful prospect and admirably chosen from a scenic point of view, but why in the wide world it was selected for military or strategic purposes this deponent knoweth not.[16]

This, without ambiguity, is the Laragh Castle occupied at diferent times by Dr John Hatch and Francis Stuart. Its role (or, strictly speaking, that of Lara [sic] Castle in Brian MacDermot's little fiction is partly to accommodate the awkwardly intrusive Leigh family, a role which could not be assigned to more thoroughly domestic residences in the area without implicating identifiable local families. In addition, Lara Castle exemplifies and excludes the element of tourism and scenery-appreciation so nervously deplored by JMS in his notebook: that is, Lara Castle is ornamental rather than strategic, and its only recorded merit appears to be the magnificent view it commands [sic] over the surrounding scenery. The area on view notably includes Brockagh whose miners and their cabins have been replaced by 'little farm cottages nestling amongst trees'. Here, however, ambiguity suddenly erupts from out the political unconscious.

A county in romance

If we emphasise MacDermot's punctuation by adding an additional word for clarity, then Brockagh was 'covered with little farm cottages nestling amongst trees and [with] land with infinite difficulty cultivated almost up to the very top …' But, to say that a hill was covered with land is a tautology, little modified by mental adjustment to say that it was covered with cultivated land. The ambiguity moves round the close proximity of 'nestling' and 'difficulty', for the former is a cliché suggesting easeful assimilation. If we repunctuate MacDermot's sentence (adding a comma after 'trees') to state that the view from Lara Castle was shortened by Brockagh and also by 'land with infinite difficulty cultivated …' then the view is drastically divided into two zones, one tonally reassuring (cottages that nestle) and another tonally more exacting (land cultivated to the highest level, but with infinite difficulty). The mining operations have not only gone underground to the point of increased invisibility, but surface agriculture has been split into two separate zones, one of cosy habitation and the other of dehumanised cultivation. This passage, however nit-picking the analysis, reveals much of the novel's function as a narrative redistribution of local interests, powers and values.

After this account of the view from its roof, readers were informed that 'for a considerable time, before the events which I am about to narrate took place, the castle was tenanted by two old maiden ladies, with the curate of the large parish of Derralossary as their lodger. But one of them died in the early part of this year, and two months afterwards the other followed … So the curate found it necessary to surrender the Castle to a new tenant, who had purchased all the goods and chattels of the old ladies …' All of this appears to be beside the point, as neither the curate nor his hostesses will enter the tale. But, when Charles Leigh fells Mr Burton of Drummin, and Nora Mortimer falls into a consequential swoon, the victims are treated by Dr Hatch, 'that much abused practitioner'.[17] These two sudden introductions of the local doctor's name return us to other inquiries, by which we had established that the historical John Hatch MD (1796–1874) had lived in Laragh Castle as a tenant of Thomas Barton of Drummin. Taking fiction and history together, the reader of *Leigh of Lara* finds that Dr Hatch both is and is not a resident of the Castle, that the proprietor of Drummin is Barton/Burton. A key to these parochial aporias might be found in a prejudice held by Mrs Mortimer in the novel – 'To her the arrival of new tenants at such a place as Laragh Castle was an event of no importance whatever. People who were contented to take up their abode in such a poor dwelling-place could not possibly, as so she would argue, be of much consequence, and the idea of calling on them never once occurred to her.'[18] In terms of class, the Castle is ambiguous at its own uncertain social level as the Brockagh cottages nestling on an infinitely difficult terrain. Not that the novelist-narrator leaves us in the dark about his own prejudices: 'the Foozels of Castlekeen' are his reworking of the Frizells of Castlekevin.

This decidedly limp social criticism should not be taken as proof positive of the book's unimportance. There had been a family named Frizell who lived in the house so named, but the Land War (1879–1882) had persuaded them to flee: from 1892 JMS's mother rented Castlekevin as a summer residence. There the future author of 'The Playboy of the Western World' briefly resumed a species of intimacy with the county where his uncle had been High Sheriff. When we read in *Leigh of Lara'* that Mrs Mortimer knew that 'Foozel sat on the bench of magistrates with her husband at Rathdrum petty sessions, and there was a young family at Castlekeen with whom it might have beneficial for her children to associate', we may pass over the sentence in silence. Yet these allusions to county affairs complicate the issue of the plot's location in time, just as Dr Hatch's presence is complicated by the placing of others – the two maiden ladies with the curate, and then the Leighs – in the Castle where he in fact resided. This displacement of Hatch effectively generates an elasticity in time within which it is possible to regard 'a young family at Castlekeen' as referring to the Synges, for the text is oddly careful not to specify that Foozel/Frizell was the family's name.

If this matters one whit, the reason is to be found in the novel's attitude towards violence. The exchange of gentlemanly blows between Charles Leigh and Lara''s outraged heads-of-household does not amount to much. And right at the beginning of the novel, there had been a casual reference to Luganure miners – 'many a time I have seen two of them in deadly encounter with the fists outside the door of the solitary inn ...'[19] The pastoralising of Brockagh had apparently disposed of all these disruptive figures, to leave the field clear for a romantic and well-born hero and heroine. But when the misunderstandings have been tidied up, and Leigh's brother (Hugh) is able to join his wife at the Castle, the district experiences what can only be called 'the return of the repressed':

> The miners came from Luganure, the men of Brockagh, of Glenmackanass, of Ballard, and of Annamoe, and discussed the tidings that the real husband had arrived at last at the Castle ... and drank his health and the health of all the inmates of the Castle ... Mrs Murphy did a roaring trade that evening, and the police also had a busy time. For there were isolated fights between individuals, just to keep themselves in tune; and finally the great faction fight of the Johnsons and Quinns was renewed, and many a shillelagh drank blood that night to celebrate Hugh's return ...[20]

The nervous condescension of the finale manifestly fails to disguise the potential for organised social insurgency in this Wicklow 'vale'. The Leighs have no hereditary association with Lara'; indeed ownership of the not-very-venerable Castle is never stated and its occupants, from the nameless old ladies to Leigh ('a wealthy Englishman who was coming over to reside there'), are without exception tenants.

The local workforce turns out to welcome a chieftain of decidedly non-traditional character, but the violence which follows indicates that the deception or delusion will not be maintained for long. Even if there is an element of *roman-à-*

clef about *Leigh of Lara'*, alluding by a sly redistribution of names and places to actual families in the district, the latent moral of MacDermot's romance relates to issues of discontinuity, impermanence and intrusion in an enfeebled gentry class. It is in this light that it bears upon the family history of JMS.

Apart from the early notes on Annamoe, he had little to record of village life in Wicklow, preferring the hills and roadsides, the tramps, tinkers and frequenters of fairs and races. Both MacDermot and the author of those notes were alert to the changes affecting life in the county, the one responding with a sentimentally contrived allegory of 'restoration', the other with an excessive apprehension of decadence, disease and disorder. Their accounts of Laragh and Annamoe respectively diverge from anything which might be taken as objective. Village life was less responsive to romantic resolution than MacDermot suggested, less vulnerable to epidemics of urban pollution than the future dramatist feared.

Yet the possibilities of violence reached well beyond the brawls of Brockagh miners: What the story of a Tipperary vale tells us relates sexual to textual repression. Read in the light of witch-burning, MacDermot's harmless novel seems less decent, less scenic than its artless narrative suggests. One flattering literary context in which *Leigh of Lara'* might be briefly situated is that defined by Thomas Hardy's fiction, the disturbed rural communities of Eustacia Vye, Jude Fawley and Tess Durbeyfield. If the talent displayed by the Irish lawyer scarcely justifies the comparison, it may nonetheless reveal telling points – the libido is in the detail. Just as it is significant that Bridget Cleary was unconsciously suspected of liaison with specifically an eggman – a trader in fertility, at one remove – so the initial violence of miners outside Lara's solitary inn bespeaks a wider, more pervasive disturbance. This in turn can be stated by way of contradiction: the submergence of Brockagh's miners beneath trees which nestle cottages *is* the subversion it attempts to conceal. The dead woman in a Brockagh ditch of 1870 is also buried and discovered, just as that date marks Dr Hatch's departure from the district, his departure from a Castle (contemporaneous with Glanmore Castle) the novel insists others successively lived in. Bridget Cleary was not the only victim of Victorian Ireland's sexually mischarged violence, nor was the realm of fairy utterly separate from the subterranean existence of miners and their molls.

Amid all this discreet landscaping of mines and murders, MacDermot's novel comes close to calling a spade a loy. The episode in which young Charles Leigh rises up against the local paterfamilias may have nothing of the symbolic force innate in Christy Mahon's assaults upon his father, but it does represent the lowest point of nominal disguise in the book. Burton is too close to Barton to escape unchallenged. If the Leighs are fictional characters deemed unimportant interlopers by the haughty Mrs Mortimer of Derrybawn, the Bartons had very recently played that role in real life, certainly as interlopers, though their importance remained to be assessed. The property at Drummin had been purchased after

Concerning J. M. Synge

Hugh Barton, of the Bordeaux wine exporting company Barton & Guestier, acquired a large fortune, with which he purchased an estate at Straffan in County Kildare, and his third son, Thomas [Johnson] Barton (1802–1864) displaced the Hugos in Wicklow. In fact both Derrybawn and Drummin had been Hugo properties – the former acquired by the Bookey family – and thus the plot of *Leigh of Lara*' can be read as a romance of property written in an age of increasing propriety.[21] The book does not merely record the assimilation of newcomers (in the Leighs), it seeks to effect it on behalf of those families who displaced the Hugos. Nor were the Bartons the last of the intruders; one of the Barton girls married the English scholar, Robert Caesar Childers, and thus introduced and propagated another 'blow-in' family. Given the subsequent politics of their son, it may even have been prescient of the fictitious Mrs Mortimer to deplore the arrival of the young Englishman in Lara Castle.

By comparison, *An Irish Utopia* is a sophisticated affair, not least because it occasionally abandons the pretence of literature and affects a historical or spiritual purpose. Edge found this possible through his support for 'the unity of Christendom' in the name of which he introduced as a fictional character, James Warren Doyle (1786–1834), the Catholic bishop of Kildare and Leighlin. Doyle, or JLK as he was generally known, had served as a volunteer with Wellesley during the Peninsular Wars, and later worked for the reform of his diocese as well as the defence of his Church. In the early pages of Edge's 'novel' a humbler Catholic cleric, Father O'Toole, is invited to baptise the twin sons of Michael Corbet, a Wicklow landowner of Cromwellian descent, in the absence of their parson-uncle. This absentee protestant cleric had been rescued from a town riot in Dublin by one of the rioters, Ambrose Malet, an Orangeman. With the latter, Edge introduces the Christian name of an earlier and actual cleric in the area, Ambrose Weekes, who had distinguished himself in suppressing rebellion in 1798.

From these and other details it becomes clear that, while *An Irish Utopia* is no *roman-à-clef*, it rearranges facts, memories and names to construct a parable of reality. For example, the surname Manning which we have found to be pervasive in the records of Rathdrum occurs in the novel in the person of Lady Violet Manning, 'a fine-looking, handsome English girl, with masses of golden hair' (p. 14). Externally, we may note the death of an actual Ambrose Manning in Rathdrum aged 27 in 1857. But, within five chapters of the fiction, Lady Violet has married Mr Malet, to the grief of her aristocratic Irish relations. Then the Famine sets in, bringing ruin to upland parts of Wicklow where small holdings had been perilously established during the boom years of the Napoleonic wars. With this prolonged misfortune, class differences emerge between Malet and his titled landlord, while family memories of Cromwellian camaraderie are evoked to forge a substitute alliance in the face of popular murmuring.

These rival responses to the Famine give an unstated meaning to the question

A county in romance

of twins. In the author's desired views of things, protestantism and Catholicism might prove to be twins, equal in dignity, co-heirs to the Christian gospel, closest of allies. This religious utopia is paralleled by another – less explicit, perhaps – in which Edge supports the Union between Great Britain and Ireland, wishing that 'the clamour for Home Rule [had] died out as it did in Scotland'.[22] But relations between the two islands had not only been soured by the Irish experience of Famine, they had been unbalanced by the larger island's discovery (or, rather, mobilisation) of mineral and industrial resources. This last theme intrudes into the lives and destinies of the Corbet twins, for George seeks to boost himself as a suitor by announcing that he will inherit newly discovered coal seams in Dartmoor. Further in praise of his nuptial attractions, he boasts that he can prove himself the elder of the two twins, thus disinheriting his brother Stephen who is (you've guessed it) the more likeable, learned and charitable of the two. Among the other predictable incidents in the twins' subplot is the disappearance of church records.

Slight though it is, *An Irish Utopia* could be read as a fictionalised Wicklow response to the publication of a report on economic relations under the Union. Among those most excited by this apparent admission of gross overtaxation of Ireland was historical novelist, Standish O'Grady, who issued *All Ireland* in response.[23] The nominal compiler, Hugh Culling Eardley Childers (1827–1896), had been chancellor of the exchequer under Gladstone. It was his brother, the orientalist scholar Robert Caesar Childers (1838–1876), who had married Anna Mary Barton, daughter of Thomas Johnson Barton. The Bartons' money had been made in the French wine trade, and Hugh Barton who re-established the family in Ireland simultaneously acquired the Château Langoa near Bordeaux. This remote detail may be refracted through the otherwise puzzling inclusion in *An Irish Utopia* of a Château Dijon, 'built after the plan of an Italian mansion early in the eighteenth century' with 'a grand view of the whole of Glenmalure'.[24] Here indeed is utopia – apart from the financial ruin it almost precipitated on its founder. In east County Wicklow, Italianate architecture is best known in Powerscourt, and certainly there is no such house commanding a view of Glenmalure. When Thomas Barton did build at Drummin in 1838, his Tudor-Gothic front transformed the much smaller Hugo residence, and with these changes came a change of name – to Glendalough House. Further Gothic additions were made in the early 1880s when the children of R. C. Childers took up residence with their Barton uncle.

In due course, that generation – Robert Childers Barton (1881–1975) and Robert Erskine Childers (1870–1922) – would break decisively from their inherited traditions, moving from the disillusioned Unionism of O'Grady to the far end of the political spectrum. Together with others like David Robinson they would constitute Gentry Republicanism, a distinctive Wicklow component in Irish political culture. The warring twins in *Finnegans Wake* (1939) owe a small debt to George and Stephen Corbet, for Joyce's motific initials HCE both repeat those of the reforming chancellor, and declare (Haveth Childers Everywhere) the resurrection of his republican nephew executed by former comrades in the Civil War.

This is to look ahead, but not to look much further than is discerned in JMS's last play, 'Deirdre of the Sorrows' (1909). The extent to which writing in the Irish *fin de siècle* proved prophetic in its concern with violence and epochal change is only matched by the diplomacy with which most of its writers attributed responsibility for this turbulence to others. W. B. Yeats, chief among the prophets, foresaw a battle between civilisations hardly caricatured in such formulations as Growth or Manufacture, Tradition Against Modernity, Faery Versus Factory. Angela Bourke, in her account of Bridget Cleary's death, pays attention to the role of one man – Jack Dunne – whose lore of herbal medicine and traditional cures was vast. This old knowledge, she argues, contributed to his neighbour's horrific death because it lay 'in fields whose creditworthiness had all but disappeared. The expertise in negotiating the web of fairy-lore which would have been his symbolic capital in an oral culture had become next to worthless as literacy became general.'[25]

In this acute analysis, the juxtaposition of 'fields' and 'capital' where both are 'symbolic' tells us much of the presuppositions underlining even advanced commentary on the transitions of late nineteenth-century Ireland. For while the well-known farming unit of enclosed land can be equated 'symbolically' with areas of expertise – fields of endeavour, etc. – there was a thoroughly non-symbolic capital setting to work elsewhere in Ireland with increasing force.

The province of Ulster and the city of Belfast seemed to monopolise industry, progress and – by a happy coincidence – sectarian strife. But the upsurge of unionist feeling in the early 1880s had to a large measure marked off Ulster from the rest of Ireland even to the point where it was possible, in some mouths at least, to speak of Ireland as if the factories of the Lagan Valley did not exist. In this context, the Ulster setting of 'Deirdre' was unsettling. Other areas to the south had known industrialisation, though never on the scale now expanding round Belfast: there was mining in County Kilkenny, for example. Milling had its own concentrations of employment, involving complex transport, housing and maintenance arrangements: but the local mill was generally treated as the end of an agricultural process rather than a dynamic stage in a wider social and economic pattern.[26]

Cities such as Cork, Limerick and Galway had their own distinctive motions, in which the port played a significant role. Among the counties Wicklow occupied perhaps a unique position, adjacent to the metropolis and its port, yet self-contained geographically and culturally. It had known prolonged and savage conflict in 1798, yet its gentry were generally on better terms with their tenants than in some more peaceable counties. It suffered less than its neighbours during the Famine, and later supported a considerable itinerant population. Yet Wicklow had no general hospital worthy of the name, while its reputation for madness deputised for any active provision in that regard. Its mining operations took place in a curiously inward fashion, and did not lead to the development of an export business within the county. Indeed, Victorian and Edwardian Wicklow had no town bigger than a small English midlands village.[27] Instead, it manifested startling juxtapositions of wilderness and modest 'georgian' architecture rarely extending beyond a single building, an isolated country house. Here urbanity flourished without urban concentration, urban facilities. Such a house was the obverse of that city-haunted Glenmalure in which the drama of Nora Bourke was played out.

Perhaps it is sentimental to invoke the Campagna or the hills south of Rome. Yet the actual home of Lord Edward Fitzgerald, which lay between Wicklow and the city of Dublin was Frascati and the fictional Wicklow residence of Edgeworth's Mrs Raffarty Tusculum. These were raw properties in the early nineteenth century, and only in the long course of Victoria's mellowing, opiate reign did they assimilate into the landscape. The 'Big House' tradition of fiction contributed to this process, largely by demonising other areas of the country. Following hard on the heels of Famine, the Land War did not pass over Wicklow in biblical fashion. But the influence of Charles Stewart Parnell, and the liberal practice of the Earl Fitzwilliam further south in the county, moderated the impact of agrarian unrest. This inheritance allowed for the nervous utopian component in the fictions of Brian MacDermot and John H. Edge; Wicklow, unlike the so-called 'congested districts' of the far west, was still visible through rose-coloured spectacles.

It is therefore all the more remarkable that JMS should set his most disturbing drama amid 'the many lovely vales of beautiful Wicklow'.[28] Perhaps 'When the Moon has Set' failed to get off the ground as an actable play but that failure in part at least resulted from its remaining faithful to the grounds upon which it was based. Its several versions reveal the author's difficulties in absorbing fragmentary ancestral matter into a contemporary social fabric which bore striking evidence of widespread malaise. Dramatic time, as implicit in this scenario, is luridly highlighted as The Past and The Present, the moment of offence and the period of revelation or consequence. Between these, external time locates the expulsion (or was it exodus?) of the Synges from Glanmore; dramatic time allows for a diplomatic interval between the two acts. The alternative readings of that movement suggest guilt (and subsequent expulsion from the Garden of Ireland, as Wicklow is sometimes termed) or rescue from servitude with a Promised Land just out of sight. In either perspective, Utopia of a christianised kind plays its part.

For obvious reasons, it is customary now to locate JMS and his celebrated plays in the context designed later by W. B. Yeats. The plays are recognised as part of the Abbey Theatre tradition, with 'In the Shadow of the Glen' taking its place alongside Yeats's 'On Baile's Strand' or Lady Gregory's 'Spreading the News'. But, if we recognise the continuity between JMS's attempts at drama before he made Yeats's acquaintance and the plays which made him famous, we also see how his Wicklow writings challenge a local tradition now largely forgotten. Though he manifestly transcended the boundaries set by Boucicault in the theatre, and even more thoroughly the discretions insisted upon by MacDermot and Edge in their incidental fictions, JMS retained a striking relationship with the landscape of Wicklow and its social history. The discontinuous chronicle of his own family, especially of those branches which did not bear the name of Synge, can be tapped on rare occasions in *Leigh of Lara'* when Dr Hatch is invoked and (less obviously) in *An Irish Utopia* when names such as Ambrose and Manning recall associates of Francis Synge and his son, John 'Pestalozzi' Synge, together with the Castle Kevin in which JMS spent thoughtful holidays.

23

The wounded dramatist takes a bow

Dvanov went outside in fear of the punishment to come, hatless and in his socks, saw the dangerous unanswering night, and dashed off through the village into his own distance. (Andrei Platonov)

THOUGH JMS never wrote an autobiography, this omission did not prevent his editors from constructing one. In the opening paragraphs of their synthetic memoir, the playwright elevates music as the supreme art – a commonplace observation at the end of the nineteenth century. The argument, however, is fraught with difficulty. 'The emotions which pass through us have neither end nor beginning,' he had written somewhere in a notebook, suggesting that the individual life is only a staging post in some larger cosmic process ('the sequence of existence'). Having thus acknowledged the insignificance and powerlessness of any single, partial life, he proceeded to insist that 'the laws of the world are in harmony'. In their different ways, these two positions can be read as residues of a conventional Christianity, rather desperately piled against the world's alien vastness and indifference, not to mention the absence of any higher or further reality. The example of heroic art is evoked – Michelangelo and Beethoven – as reassurance that individual insight and overcoming may be possible. Then JMS is quoted by his busy editor as writing:

> I do not think biography – even autobiography – can give this revelation. But while the thoughts and deeds of a lifetime are impersonal and concrete – might have been done by anyone – art is the expression of the essential or abstract beauty of the person.[1]

So severe a doctrine can best be understood as a resistance on the part of a man scarcely embarked upon adult life; fittingly, these words recur in the two-act version of 'When the Moon Has Set' where they feature as part of a work-in-progress sketched only in the rough by the character Columb. Once again words are recycled, but on this occasion their successive roles are not exclusively dramatic. They participate in an interrelated definition and diffusion of identity, in which denial and dramatisation are equally active.

This feature of the untidy state in which the JMS literary archive survived is, paradoxically, its most unifying characteristic. Or, rather, it is highly suggestive of the hermeneutical procedures which his work has been conspicuously denied by critical friend and adoring foe alike. The tendency to elevate 'The Playboy of the Western World' as his achievement of genius has thrived largely because it suited the needs of quite different parties; it is the unanimous opinion of irreconcilable elements. Were the plays and other texts to be approached in a way which regarded the meaning of each as inseparable from the meaning of the whole corpus, then very different verdicts might be passed. For then, the object of study or regard would not be a single item but rather a relationship between texts. Instead of seeing 'Riders to the Sea' as a miraculous incarnation of classic tragedy within the twentieth century, such an approach would acknowledge the play's borrowings from 'When the Moon Has Set' and from the writings of Asenath Nicholson – to go no further.[2] These would no longer have the status of mere borrowings but would both take on, and uncover, new meanings. The incorporation of 'When the Moon Has Set' into the field where interpretation of JMS can meaningfully take place is not a New Critical judgement. It releases the canonical plays from a peasant-mythic double bind in which – despite much fine endeavour – they have been locked ever since Yeats's appropriation of JMS to his cause. The objections of George O'Brien to the space accorded 'When the Moon Has Set' in *Fool* may have been answered in the foregoing pages.[3] If so, the means by which this has occurred is the according of more attention to this dramatically insignificant work.

O'Brien invokes Jean-Paul Sartre and his biography of Flaubert. In a preface to his vast final work, Sartre had identified in a letter what he took as the alluring problem at the heart of his subject. In 1864 Flaubert had written, 'It is by the sheer force of work that I am able to silence my innate melancholy. But the old nature often reappears, the old nature that no one knows, the deep, always hidden wound.'[4] Can a wound be innate, Sartre wonders, in the way his predecessor implies? The origins of this heartfelt grumble lie deep in European consciousness. The Greek myths told of the incurable wound suffered by Philoctetes, when he accidentally struck himself with one of the arrows given him by his dying friend Hercules. So offensive was the smell of this wound that the hero was banished from the Greek armies, though the bow he had also inherited from Hercules was the essential weapon if Troy was ever to be taken. Myths are by nature ambiguous, their heroes rarely without blemish. Noble Ulysses had been responsible for the shabby treatment of Philoctetes, while the accident which befell the latter resulted from his betrayal of Hercules' last resting place. In any case, Troy fell and Western History commenced with the founding of Rome by descendants of the survivors. In a saga of dishonour, myth and truth contend for the honours.

The wounded dramatist takes a bow

Flaubert's deep, always hidden wound was probed at length by Sartre, who devoted almost a thousand pages to the novelist's childhood and family relations. It is a psychoanalytical investigation whose compelling power is augmented by the richness of material – thirteen volumes of correspondence, for a start – left behind by Flaubert and published by dedicated editors. The story of JMS is very different, especially in these material considerations. It is well known that his papers were decimated by the family in the aftermath of his death in March 1909. Several decimations probably took place, even as late as the 1920s. Quite why these brutal excisions were made is unclear. His brother Edward was something of a philistine and a pious low Evangelical. A nephew known as Hutchie, who worked intermittently on a Life of his uncle, eventually went mad but not before he destroyed some correspondence. To complicate matters, there were also fictive, or largely fictive, papers issued to the public. In 1932, the playwright's brother, the Reverend Dr Samuel Synge, published *Letters to My Daughter; Memories of John Millington Synge*. By 1996, however, it was tacitly admitted by the family that no originals for these had ever existed, and that the Archdeacon had invented the texts as a way of communicating fact to the public and 'to dispel speculation & rumours'.[5] To what always hidden wound in JMS might these rumours of the later 1920s have referred, if any?

It is advisable first to consider the anxieties which might have stricken his family, as distinct from those of JMS himself. Leanings towards Roman Catholicism or political radicalism would have disturbed the Synges, and indeed his courtship of Molly Allgood and friendship with nationalists like Stephen MacKenna had tested their tolerance. But there was no serious personal commitment to these strange gods, beyond the open-mindedness of a man finding release from inherited prejudice. Ill health posed greater problems for both the man himself and his immediate family. Cancer was at the time a scarcely mentionable terror, and the particular cancer of which JMS was a victim – Hodgkin's disease – had the added disadvantage of resembling syphilis in some of its manifestations. Here indeed was good reason why his family took pains to dispel speculation and rumour, openly by publishing anodyne and fabricated evidence, and covertly (perhaps) by destroying actual evidence. The hidden wound was surgical, the bandages hardly hidden at all.

This line of inquiry does little justice to the distress registered by JMS in a short note entitled 'Under Ether' which his cautious relatives and executors included in the four-volume *Works* of 1910. An examination of the surviving typescript reveals that the text had been severely cut before publication though it remains impossible to tell whether the author himself or some other had been responsible. Paper suffers wounds more hidden than those of the flesh, and archives are occasionally purged of rank dressings.

One explanation of the family's rattled nerves was proposed recently – JMS may have been homosexual.⁶ This is, of course, a 'diagnosis' almost impossible to refute once it has been uttered, not least because habits of (hetero-)sexual continence have become suspect in the intervening century. The only evidence which might be interpreted in this way is to be found in correspondence between JMS and a Breton friend, Henri Lebeau. Lebeau's written English accommodated an emotional intensity some might regard as typically Gallic; beyond this, there is a certain awkwardness in his response to news of JMS's engagement to Molly Allgood, balanced on the other side of the relationship by the Irish dramatist's dogged reluctance to share a room with Lebeau while holidaying together. In the event, there was no such holiday as the need for surgery prevented JMS from travelling. Given that Lebeau's letters survive (or at least some of them) in the Synge Papers, the family cannot have harboured serious fears of what they would have regarded as gross immorality.⁷

The proposal of homosexuality should perhaps be considered further, even at the risk of taking it into the realm of Orwellian nu-speak. JMS repeatedly proposed marriage to a childhood sweetheart, Cherrie Matheson, who differed profoundly from him on religious and (hence) moral issues. Later, he maintained a lengthy relationship (culminating in formal betrothal) with Molly whose *petit bourgeois* and Catholic background constituted a barrier to her acceptance among the Synges. Perhaps these two sustained emotional commitments can be re-jigged as diversionary activity, much in the way that Senator Joe McCarthy saw everything as evidence of covert communism. Accordingly, the incompatibilities of belief or social status become JMS's subconscious choices which simultaneously advertised heterosexuality while blocking consummation. No refutation can outwit these self-verifying arguments. Only at the end of exhaustive contemplation of non-evidence, can one conclude that no love which cannot speak its name inhabits the hidden wound of JMS.

On the basis of the work published in his lifetime, no wound cries out for identification. But as soon as the *Works* of 1910 are postulated, argument ensues. The Synge family, however, are more inclined to admit journalistic material about the pathology of a newly emergent Ireland than Yeats is, while both parties are tacitly agreed that 'When the Moon Has Set' does not deserve the light of day in any of its several versions. Its survival beyond 1910 remains a mystery. What is disputed between Yeats and the Synge family is history itself which, on the one hand, may be treated through attention to immediate social conditions or, on the other, through the substitution of myth. While it is difficult to see Edward and Robert Synge as radical reformers or even philanthropists, they do accept a moral obligation to note social distress even if they semi-consciously attribute it to the 'darkness' of popular Catholicism. In contrast, Yeats simultaneously begins to abandon that concern and to substitute in its place a hard doctrine of beggar and nobleman, each required as the eternal complement to the other.

The wounded dramatist takes a bow

JMS, we know, took a direct interest in history, especially of the county of which he was not (quite) a native. His clerical brother testified to the dramatist's preference for history as mediated through contemporary letters and other documents rather than through synoptic chronicles written after the event. His brother-in-law, Harry Stephens, strove to administer surviving portions of the Synge estate as it had come down to Mrs Synge and her children. The library at Glanmore Castle housed bits – perhaps more than bits – of the Hatch archive, which took the story of the Synges back to a period prior to their arrival in Wicklow. In those days, the Synges graced the Church, though not without hostile comment from – amongst others – Dean Swift. In those days, the Synges possessed land, though not without the embarrassment of poor relatives.

This is the history related here, with fewer bishops and peers than previously displayed. Yet to record a history and to epitomise a body of drama falls short of establishing the nature of the relationship between them. Years ago the New Criticism, which we have virtually forgotten, denied that any such relationship was significant, *aesthetically*. At about the same time, versions of Marxism propounded a determination of superstructure by economic base, of the literature by the history (fully understood). These rival approaches have cancelled each other, with the ironic effect of perpetuating their worst features and obscuring what was valuable in each. Escape from the base-and-superstructure model, for which we owe Raymond Williams a greater debt than has ever been paid, led all too quickly into career cynicism.

For all that feminists may applaud her partial recovery in these pages, I read the postmodern dismissal of literary history *tout court* as the condition of Barbara Synge. Philosophically to appreciate her, we can hardly do better than examine broad changes in literary practice occurring within her own lifetime. And in preference to some immediate and negotiable shift of Irish sensibility – with all its alluring promises of reconciliation – let us take G. E. Lessing's *Laocoön* (1766) as a point of reference, the archaic past as the backdrop for our reflections.

While the essay is renowned for its careful discrimination between the plastic and the verbal arts – duly echoed in the 'Proteus' episode of Joyce's *Ulysses* – in fact the opening theme is the representation of pain. In this connection, Philoctetes once again is the exemplary figure. But the contradictions of myth are precisely what the modern imagination appreciates in it. According to Homer and others, the great archer was abandoned on the island of Lemnos by the Greek army, because his wounded foot smelled so foul. 'The laments, the cries, the wild curses with which his anger filled the camp and interrupted all the sacrifices and the sacred rites resounded no less terribly through the desert island …' As Flaubert and Joyce indirectly indicate, we are no longer content with this analysis which, *en passant*, Lessing was demolishing. Either Philoctetes was banished because he stank or because he shrieked: for the German, the two cannot be merged. And it is no longer true to say that cries in a crowded camp are heard equally on a deserted beach. (Why has Stephen Dedalus come out from the military installation of his temporary home to pace alone on Sandymount Strand?) In the classic period, Sophocles may not have bothered about these distinctions but 'we more refined Europeans of a wiser, later age know better how to govern our mouths and our eyes'.[8] This is not only a matter of stage convention, it affected behaviour in such unscripted performances as warfare itself, while also permeating intimate relations between the sexes. Michel Foucault saw the evolution of soldiering in the eighteenth century as crucially linked to the substitution of 'an inapt body' for 'a lively, alert manner, an erect head, a taut stomach', etc.[9] Notions of 'manliness' in the avoidance of evident emotion go hand in hand with this.

It scarcely needs to be said that this code of the stiff upper lip progressed in the Victorian Age, to reach its epitome in the Edwardian prelude to Mons and Passchendale, in step with the increasing mechanisation of the fighting man. In local terms, the Synges – those of Wicklow, at least – eschewed the military profession just as they renewed a 'religion of the heart' which itself contained elements of rigid discipline and suburban rectititude. A now-discredited but tenacious psychology fatally located woman at its inaccessible centre. For this reason, Barbara Synge, rather than John Hatch MP or the Reverend Sir Samuel Synge Hutchinson, is the significant forebear of JMS. Knowing so little, we may assign her to the type of Tecmessa, foremost (and hence forgotten) among women who are told that silence is their role, their ideal contribution to human culture. In the manner of mythology, Ajax's wife is not just better known than an obscure eighteenth-century Irish daughter and mother; we know too much of Tecmessa, we know her contradictions. Her assigned role is silence because her eloquence moved Ajax to tears, the consequence of his order (her submission) is his suicide.

Nothing in this remotely proposes Sam M'Cracken as the Ajax of Roundwood: no Joycean parallelism is implied. But JMS knew of M'Cracken and his cousin John Hatch, knew of Hatch's marriage, and the lady drawn in opulence through the Wicklow countryside – knew of all this both as family history and as popular folklore. Its distinguishing feature was pain, in mind and body. M'Cracken suffered and took his own life. The inmates of Rathdrum Union suffered. Barbara Synge died in 1767 according to the papers, yet she was apparently commended to the care of relatives thirty years later. Years of silence, of unrepresented pain. What art could assuage this double horror?

The twentieth-century Irish rewriter of mythology, James Stephens, said of JMS that 'his approach to knowledge was – to be silent'.[10] Yet Synge's drama is more splendidly vocal than anything before Sean O'Casey. It provided an example of modern tragedy for the author of 'Juno and the Paycock' not only through the sombre 'Riders to the Sea' and 'Deirdre', the tragi-comic 'Well of the Saints' but also the inverted 'Laocoön' in the final act of 'The Playboy' where Christy Mahon

The wounded dramatist takes a bow

is caught up in coils spun by fathers – fathers of the community, father of Pegeen who would be his father-in-law and in time grandfather to 'gallant little swearers' – and, by temporary inaction, spun by his biological father also. Comparing JMS with O'Casey, one might note the comprehensive absence of pregnancy from the life JMS depicts. His figures are terminal, face to face with some end-of-time crisis, yet enduring to be commended as they repeatedly take their bow.

When Edmund Wilson named a collection of essays on modern literature, *The Wound and the Bow*, he saluted Philoctetes on the eve of the Second World War. His heroes were troublesome – the Kipling nobody read, the Joyce who wrote *Finnegans Wake*. Synge might now be added to the list, as much for the history and illness he silently overcame as for the screams of Christy, the curses of Martin Doul, and the studied lamentations of Maurya and Deirdre.

A personal appendix

Method, error and offence in literary history

> We shall not cease from exploration
> And the end of all our exploring
> Will be to arrive where we started
> And know the place for the first time.
> (T. S. Eliot, 'Little Gidding', 1942)

LITERARY history has suffered a double eclipse in recent years and in ways which affect the writing and reading of *The Silence of Barbara Synge*. Practitioners of history have come to acknowledge the importance of literature, the arts and what is still rather grandly called culture. In the Irish context, the work of Louis Cullen, Roy Foster and Oliver MacDonagh has made the point repeatedly and valuably. Meanwhile, literary studies have decisively moved the other way, abandoning historical perspectives in favour of post-structuralist, post-modern and post-colonial ones. If only these two major changes in approach cancelled each other out, returning the literary historian to a *status quo ante bellum*.

But there has always been a contradiction, or creative tension, in the background of literary history. Having routed the scholars for leadership in departments of English, the new critics proceeded to elevate detail and nuance even in the appreciation of form. Historians, released from their long devotion to high politics and war, still aspire to synthesis, even while acknowledging the particularities of documentation. The literary historian might be forgiven for suspecting that his/her profession is a hybrid, whereas in truth it employs a reflexive methodology accommodating bibliography, critical and editorial theory, social criticism and ethical judgement.

'What is truth?' said jesting Pilate, and did not wait for an answer. The author of that observation (Francis Bacon) has combined the reputations of empirical philosopher and corrupt judge. In both regards, it is likely that Bacon has been excessively described. Nevertheless, the reputation of truth is hardly less compromised today than in James I's day. Without capitulating to post-modern tantrums,

A personal appendix

I feel it appropriate negatively to formulate one's responsibilities in this regard – as the obligation to reduce error.

Scaled down to the present context, the problem can be subdivided into its two principal aspects – error which is assimilated from an external source and error which is committed within the work in progress. In each case, it is assumed that the behaviour is unconscious, though even a tepid appreciation of Freud's ideas will qualify any confidence in a wholly objective practice. But what might be called 'conscious error' requires vigorous definition as intellectual dishonesty, a definition broad enough to cover acts of omission – the deliberate exclusion not only of facts but of issues, relationships, concepts and contexts.

Let us take the case of a secondary figure in the story of Barbara Synge – her nephew, George, who married Mary MacDonnell and settled in the Irish midlands. According to the published records, George Synge of Rathmore died in 1806. However, a more recent family chronicler has established that George lived on for another thirty years, that his will was disputed at great expense until declared invalid, and that his estate was divided amongst his acknowledged sons.[1] While the last detail may conceal some explanation of the mistaken or erroneous date given for his death, the Rathmore Synges lie too far from the central line of enquiry to earn further attention in themselves.

However, a second case of misreported death – if that is what we find – begins to look like carefulness. Barbara, there is reason to think, did not die in 1767 but was alive in 1792. Her brother's son, we have even more reason to believe, did not die in 1806 – which might be a typographical error (say for 1836) – were it not for the unpleasant contestation of his will. Barbara's sister-in-law, Mrs Sophia Synge (née Hutchinson), went to great lengths in her own will to distinguish between grandsons 'legally born' and those 'legally conceived' to the point where a third category might be implied.

Of course George Synge's unexpectedly prolonged life does nothing to confirm his aunt's survival of her death notices. But it colours one's sense of the possibilities, dissolving uniqueness in the earlier instance, and casting another light on John Hatch, the presumed widower, particularly on his failure to remarry. His father, Henry Hatch, and both his sons-in-law re-married after their first wife's death, a common practice at the time. Was Hatch obliged to avoid bigamy? Even the confusion as to whether Hatch left a will (which might have benefited a surviving but incapacitated wife) earns a further moment's thought in the light of her nephew George's uncertain behaviour and invalidated will. As Francis Synge (MP), who administered the Hatch estate in the early nineteenth century, was himself a direct ancestor of JMS, the new date for his brother's death impinges (however slightly) on the playwright's moral inheritance.

The historian's practice of seeking independent verification of contentious matter is not always possible in the literary field where the unique existence of a

Method, error and offence in literary history

text complicates things. But literary history brings disparate material together, and the general principle of verification deserves respect. In the particular case of *The Silence of Barbara Synge*, the element of genealogy raises other ethical questions. Mr and Mrs John Hatch have a myriad descendents alive to-day. Do their susceptibilities constitute grounds for omitting questions about the possible confusion of two 'Babas' – one drowned in infancy and the other untraceable to her grave? If it is argued that, even after the passage of two hundred years, questions of personal health remain sensitive, would we not then find ourselves compromised in dealing with John Hatch's conduct with regard to Samuel M'Cracken's will in 1769, or Francis Synge's with regard to church lands? To turn a blind eye can lead to impairment of vision.

Sensitivity deserves to be respected, but not to the point where it censors historical enquiry into remote events and generations. If independent verification were to be required in all cases, history would become a subspecies of scepticism. Yet there are complicated entanglements where one skein is difficult to distinguish from another. Somewhere between issues of personal health and those of financial aggression lies that of illegitimacy. Like ill health, illegitimacy is not in itself a fault in the person, though it certainly denotes a moral judgement of one or perhaps two others. A bastard may live a blameless life, procreate lovingly within the Ten Commandments, and yet feel prejudice to gather round him or her. Financial irregularity has the longer pedigree, because its fruits are sought and contested by succeeding generations.[2]

A response must surely address the intention of the author or the purpose to which the present book is intended. Repetitive attention to 'When the Moon Has Set' was designed to act as a bridge between the historical and literary areas of concern. Indeed, the play was my original prompt to this enquiry. J. M. Synge's inability to resolve the aesthetic questions at its heart testifies to his strange and touching fidelity to historical documentation. Within his own development as a dramatist, early failure led through creative reaction to the extraordinary plays which followed. To illuminate that transformation or – as I would prefer to call it – *creative reflection*, it was necessary to examine in all such detail as presented itself the complex and obscure history I have emblemised in the mystery of Barbara Synge's life and death.

That mystery could not be limited to verifiable events of the day. It implicates her children; and, as sensibility altered with the decades, the attitudes of her brother and sister-in-law, and her daughters' husbands, became prisms through which a family history was refracted. A major aspect of that (essentially eighteenth-century story) is a transition from ecclesiastical to secular wealth, from high responsibility in the church to limited honour bestowed by the crown or state. But the story could not be left there, even if the mystery of Barbara Synge's death had been clarified. And one should stress in these closing pages, that the case remains

A personal appendix

unproven. There remain the processes of transmission by which JMS in the late nineteenth century obtained access to, or was drawn into, a particular historical consciousness. Once again, a paradoxical change occurs for, in the transition of Francis Synge to his John, his Pestalozzian son, there develops an anticipation of certain proto-modernist valorisations – of the minor yet elect, for example. But we are left with a virtual blank between that John Synge and the one whom Yeats called friend.

Such blanks might not resist eternal vigilance. Would further consideration of George Synge's contested estate cast any light on history-less Thomas of Tomriland? In a will drawn up on 31 July 1828, he had evidently arranged to leave 'the lands of Ballatry' to an unknown Reverend Thomas Synge, adding thereafter ample provision for his sons. The conventions of historical verification do not encourage us to identify this intended beneficiary with the equally untraced Thomas Synge of Tomriland (see Chapter 18 above). If one cannot positively discern an impact of Rathmore upon Glanmore, then the double vacancy, a pair of doubtful Thomases, constitute a greater unease in the nineteenth-century declension of Irish landed estate and church establishment.

'Things fall apart ...' The post-war world that Yeats visioned in January 1919 was Victorian Ireland writ large and writ in blood. The ceremony of innocence was drowned, and other ceremonies with it. When JMS's land-agent brother had evicted the Careys in 1887, using Tomriland as his mustering point, the future dramatist was playing tennis in Greystones, Wicklow's Protestant resort village, while his mother noted the steady decline in her income from rents in Galway.[3] Through the family's solicitor, and mooching in Glanmore's library, young JMS gradually learnt of the larger history of the Synges. Exactly what he learned is unlikely ever to be established. Nor can we assume he felt either embarrassment or guilt. His treatment of family history as a topic of folklore is at once frank in manner and vague in substance, leaving us none the wiser as to which kinswoman rode through Roundwood 'on a curious beast'. But it is legitimate to draw inferences from 'When the Moon Has Set' and from the mature work – *The Aran Islands*, 'The Playboy' and 'Deirdre of the Sorrows'. The bridge between apprenticeship and maturity can be located on a map of County Wicklow, south of Roundwood. During the summer of 1902, when JMS wrote 'In the Shadow of the Glen' in Tomriland, he commenced that drama of creative reflection in the townland one Thomas Synge had held so elusively. Tomriland was his starting place.

The hiring of that small farmhouse as holiday home mildly embarrassed Mrs Kathleen Synge, the playwright's mother. In due course, his plays gave greater offence. It is not easy to prove that any member of his immediate family attended a performance during his lifetime. The offence taken was registered mutely, but its nature can be inferred. Strong language, free-flowing drink and sexual innuendo damned the work in the eyes of a pious and conventional household. Nevertheless,

Method, error and offence in literary history

JMS's nonconformity can scarcely be reduced to authorship, dramatic words attributed to imaginary characters. It was more active, intimate and positive than the term 'nonconformity' suggests, while remaining good-mannered at home and uncompromised. It was indeed an act of revolt, rejection and re-appropriation in the course of which an inherited literalism – traceable back to John 'Pestalozzi' Synge – was overturned to disclose radically different senses of 'fact', 'story' and 'truth'. These gave greater offence, for they went beyond practice to challenge principle. If, in the latter half of the eighteenth century, secular land had replaced the Word of God as the source of visible worth, now at the end of the nineteenth century, a new landless word was coined. Instead of Saint Patrick's Cathedral, the Abbey Theatre.

I have proposed that J. M. Synge's influence can be traced into the foundation of the Irish Free State twelve years after his death.[4] This may seem an affront to political history, which speaks of Sinn Fein, Patrick Pearse and Arthur Griffith. It may also seem a deliberate attempt to eclipse W. B. Yeats whose involvement in the day-to-day politics of independence is well known and undeniable. For good or ill, the new state did not adopt a Yeatsian imagery nor follow a Yeatsian programme. Rather, it adapted itself to the acerbic humour of Synge's vision and, in the course of doing so, it sought – through subsidy of the Abbey – also to tone down that vision. If Synge embraced a questionable history, he also enabled a workable future, imperfect, even at times ugly, but a future in which important changes were possible.

One site of these was York Street, Dublin. From old Sam M'Cracken's day onwards, the street had come increasingly into the possession of the larger family, augmented particularly by the acquisition of Vicars Choral property c. 1807. The process of drastic change had begun as JMS was dying, with a Housing of the Working Classes Act (1908). Renewal was accelerated under the Free State government, with the compulsory acquisition of tenement buildings and the buying out of ground rents. Henry Flood and the Reverend Mr Scoffier of M'Cracken's day were no longer even ghosts flitting through the broken fanlights. But before official dismantling was set in motion, the present writer's father was born in one of these tenements (No. 19, York Street) on 30 July 1897.

Notes

INTRODUCTION (pp. 1–10)

1 See his article 'Colleges on the Continent', in W. J. Mc Cormack (ed.), *The Blackwell Companion to Modern Irish Culture.* Oxford: Basil Blackwell, 1998. pp. 119–120.
2 This revisionary view was expressed by Dr Marie-Louise Legge at a seminar in the Institute of English Studies, January 2001, citing evidence in Archbishop King's papers: she continues to pursue the matter, which need not detain the present argument any longer.
3 See *Freeman's Journal*, 16–19 September 1769.
4 A. Norman Jeffares (ed.), *Yeats's Poems*. London: Macmillan, 1989. p. 308.
5 *Works* 4, p. 79. Synge's drafts – see p. 78 – indicate that the playboy had originally intended to use a false name, Fitzsimon Henry, a good deal more fanciful than demotic Christy Mahon.
6 Inevitably this is a compacted – but basically accurate – account of a multi-stage transfer of papers into the public domain. The materials now available include several later benefactions orginating in the Synge/Stephens family, together with other papers deriving from more remote sources. See the list of sources for the present book on p. xii. For an account of the TCD holdings, see Nicholas Grene, *The Synge Manuscripts in the Library of Trinity College Dublin*, Dublin: Dolmen Press, 1971, including the foreword (p. 5) by the then provost of the College, A. J. McConnell.
7 Andrew Carpenter (ed.), *My Uncle John: Edward Stephens's Life of JM Synge*. London: Oxford University Press, 1974.
8 Sean O'Faolain, *Vive Moi* (2nd edn), London: Sinclair-Stephenson, 1993. p. 270.

CHAPTER 1 (pp. 18–23)

1 *Pue's Occurrencess*, 11 August 1741 (re Usher); 29 August (re elderly man); 13 and 17 October (re Kerwin). Three men had been executed on 5 September at Wicklow for murder.
2 Ken Hannigan, 'A Miscellany of Murder: Violent Death in 19th Century Wicklow', *Wicklow Historical Society Journal*, vol. 1, no. 7 (1994), pp. 22–34.
3 J. M. Synge, 'People and Places', in *Collected Works: Volume 2*, Prose (ed. Alan Price). London: Oxford University Press, 1966. p. 198. See also Ken Hannigan, 'An Analysis of County Wicklow's Irish Speakers in 1901', *Wicklow Historical Society Journal*, vol. 1, no. 1 (1998), pp. 20–27.
4 See Thomas McFarland, *Romanticism and the Forms of Ruin*. Princeton: Princeton University Press, 1981.
5 A seven-fascicle work, *The Place-Names of Co. Wicklow*, was compiled by Liam Price, a district court judge, and published by the Dublin Institute of Advanced Studies between 1945 and 1967. Reference is made to it as *Price*, with vol. and page number.
6 NLI: Ms. 11, 333.
7 For the original transaction, see DRD: Mem: 136: 55: 90488. (In these citations, the first of the three numbers indicates the volume, the second the page within the volume, and the third the serial number of the memorial.) Probate of the will of a John Ximenes, diocese of Ossory, was granted in 1773.
8 *Proceedings of the Royal Irish Academy* (1908), vol. 27, Sect. C.

Notes

9 See *The Gonne-Yeats Letters 1893-1938* (ed. A. MacBride White and A. Norman Jeffares). London: Hutchinson, 1992. pp. 520, 527.

CHAPTER 2 (pp. 24–37)
1 Walter Benjamin, *The Arcades Project* (trans. Howard Eiland and Kevin McLaughlin). Cambridge, Mass.: Belknap Press, 1999. p. 833.
2 See the list as published by John O'Hart, *The Irish and Anglo-Irish Landed Gentry when Cromwell Came to Ireland*. Dublin: Gill, 1884. pp. 372–411 (esp. p. 391 col. 2). However, neither Hatch nor Synge appears in the lists appended to Karl S. Bottigheimer, *English Money and Irish Land: The 'Adventurers' in the Cromwellian Settlement of Ireland*. Oxford: Clarendon Press, 1971. The highly influential mid-Victorian work by J. P. Prendergast (1865), which interacted powerfully with the new political concern with Irish land, similarly makes no reference to either name.
3 For details of the Revd John Hatch, I am grateful to the Representative Church Body (RCB) library staff for showing me Ronnie Wallace's work in progress on the clergy of Dublin and Glendalough. Cf., however, a Revd John Hatch said to have been curate of Balruddery in 1748, also vicar of Julianstown.
4 See *Freeman's Journal*, 28–31 July 1764 and 3–7 May 1768.
5 M. Pollard, *A Dictionary of Members of the Dublin Book Trade 1550–1800*. London: Bibliographical Society, 2000. pp. 278, 522.
6 See Aubrey J. Toppin, 'The Personal Marriage and Baptismal Register of the Reverend Michael Thomas Merritt, Catholic Curate, Dublin, 1800–1805', *Irish Genealogist*, vol. 1, no. 4 (October 1938), p. 107.
7 Details of Hatches buried or commemorated in Old Saint Mary's, Ardee, are taken from Dermot MacIvor, 'Monumental Inscriptions at Old Saint Mary's, Ardee, Co. Louth', *The Irish Genealogist*, vol. 3, no. 1 (July 1956), p. 37, etc. See also two articles by Father Diarmuid Mac Iomhair (i.e. Dermot MacIvor) in *The Journal of the County Louth Archaeological Society*, 'The Family of Hatch of Ardee' (vol. 16, no. 4, 1968, pp. 205–223) and 'More on the Family of Hatch of Ardee' (vol. 17, no. 1, 1969, pp. 19–21).
8 For the list of 1600, see *County Louth Archaeological Society Journal*, vol. 4 (196), pp. 308–310; for 1717, see PRONI: D.562/1155.
9 For the Fortesque list, see *County Louth Archaeological Society Journal*, vol. 1 (1906), p. 53; for William Hatch, see *Freeman's Journal*, 16–19 September 1769.
10 See *Two Letters from the Most Rev. Dr Curtis*. Dublin: Grace, [1822]. It is significant that Curtis, a Catholic bishop, lays responsibility for sectarian outrage specifically at the door of William Magee, who will feature later in this narrative.
11 Thomas Wright, *Louthiana*. London: Payne, 1758. Book II, plate XVII.
12 See PRONI: D.562/1476 and 1478–1479.
13 'To Mr William Hatch, the Soi-disant Turf Man, and ex-Hearth Money Collector, of Ardee Castle' (no imprint, but dated 2 April 1832). This rare item is preserved in the BL: 11621 k 4 (vol. 1.2, previously HS 74 1251).
14 *Drogheda Journal*, 2 July 1831.
15 See the typescript summary for Louth, p. 100 (cf. Ms f. 185) in the Royal Irish Academy.
16 Friedrich Nietzsche, *The Use and Abuse of History* (trans. Adrian Collins). Indianapolis: Bobbs-Merrill, 1978. p. 18.
17 John D'Alton, *Illustrations Historical and Genealogical of King James's Irish Army List (1689)*. Dublin: the author, (n. d.).
18 See *Freeman's Journal*, 18–22 February 1766.
19 See *Freeman's Journal*, 11–15 November 1766.
20 The others were Edward Hatch Hoare (1790–1873, MA, TCD) and John Hatch Hoare (1825–1880, of Gloucester).

Notes

21 Cf. Paul Klee's angelus novus in 'Theses on the Philosophy of History', in Walter Benjamin, *Illuminations* (trans. Harry Zohn). London: Cape, 1970. p. 259. Not all is apocalyptic. Another Duleek grouping relates to William Hatch (born 22 June 1848, died 18 November 1912). His parents were John Hatch (died 8 December 1876, aged 82) and Elizabeth Hatch (died 5 February 1883, aged 58). This John Hatch evidently had two brothers – Nicholas (died 18 May 1863, aged 50) and Charles (died 10 December 1860, aged 50). A younger Nicholas Hatch (died 14 March 1901, aged 54) was brother of William Hatch.
22 For an account of the relationship, see NLI: Ainsworth Report No. 206 f. 2027.
23 Rosemary Ffolliott, *The Pooles of Mayfield and Other Irish Families*. Dublin: Hodges Figgis, 1958. p. 151ff.
24 See *The Blundells of Bedfordshire and Northamptonshire. With an account of some of the religious houses in Bedfordshire, to which they were benefactors*. Printed for subscribers only, 1912. p. 173.
25 See Margaret Blundell (ed.), *Blundell's Diary and Letter Book, 1702–1728*. Liverpool: Liverpool University Press, 1952. pp. 262–263. See also W. A. Coppinger, *History of the Coppingers*. Manchester: Sotheran, 1884.
26 Editorial comment in *My Uncle John*, p. 4.
27 In 1732, Henry Hatch effectively bought out William Fold (of Dunbo, County Londonderry) of lands at Kilberry, County Meath. Early deeds, etc., indicate that some lands acquired in the same vicinity had been part of the estates of William Domville and perhaps also of the Barnwall family – see NLI: D. 19,439–19, 658 (years 1706–1707).
28 TCD: Ms. 6184, f. 10.
29 W. A. Maguire, *The Downshire Estates in Ireland, 1801–1845*. Oxford: Clarendon Press, 1972. pp. 155, 192. The second marquis of Downshire (Arthur Hill, 1753–1801) was earl of Hillsborough for the period 1789–1793; he bore the additional titles Viscount Fairford (in the English peerage) during the years 1772–1789 and Viscount Kilwarlin (in the Irish) between 1756 and 1772.
30 PRONI: D.607/455, John Hatch to Miss Blundell, 30 January 1793; for the immediate family context, see W. A. Maguire, 'Missing Persons, Edenderry under the Blundells and Downshires, 1707–1922', in William Nolan and Timothy O'Neill (eds), *Offaly, History and Society*. Dublin: Geography Publications, 1998. p. 517.
31 The archives department in the library, University College Dublin, possesses a collection of documents (S6/28) relating to the property of Sir Samuel Synge-Hutchinson (1756–1846), his forebears and some descendents. These include papers relating to County Meath holdings of Henry and John Hatch, and also a small file on Coolmodry.
32 See BL Add. Ms. 72868, which is the second (or B) volume of the original series. A preliminary note (f. v), 'Six Folio Volumes, lettered respectively A, B [etc.] each containing Maps of the part of the Down Survey made under the direction of Sir W Petty in the years 1657 & 1658 – the above six Volumes are in a chest at Sir F Hutchinson of which I have the key 27 June 1797.' It was about this time that Hutchinson ceased to act for Lansdowne as before; according to f. vi, the missing volume was said to contain maps for most if not all of County Wicklow but 'Those baronies though named in the Index are not Mapd in this Volume. There are a number of Blank leaves in it apparently designed for them.' Lansdowne died in 1805, and his manuscripts were bought by the British Library two years later. When Sir Francis died in 1807, much of his east Wicklow property went to Francis Synge. It is at least possible that the Wicklow maps, deriving from Petty's Down Survey and held (with the others) by Hutchinson as Lansdowne's representative, disappeared from the collection publicly sold because they covered the area of greatest interest to Hutchinson and – in time – to Francis Synge.
33 NLI: Ms. 21 F. 112. The map of 1731 may have passed later to Hatch, when he acquired some of the property: it does not in itself establish so early an involvement in Roundwood land.

Notes

34 PRONI: D.562/4687–8.
35 *Faulkner's Dublin Journal*, issues for 30 January to 2 February, and 2 to 6 February 1762. A later 'Abstract of the ... property of Miss Morgan' (23 October 1770) mentions that Henry Hatch's will devised to John Hatch 'all his real and personal estate'. See NLI: Ms. 11,334.
36 Maguire, 'Missing Persons', pp. 518, 522.
37 Jonathan Swift, *Correspondence* (ed. Williams), vol. IV (1732–1736). Oxford: Clarendon Press, 1965. pp. 410–411.
38 Sir Robert Reading (died 1689) had a new dwelling in Aungier Street, Dublin, in 1674: his daughter married the 6th earl of Abercorn. Three members of the family sat in the Irish House of Commons – John for Swords, 1692–1695; Daniel for Newcastle (Co. Dublin), 1692 and 1703–1711, when he was succeeded by his namesake, till 1715. In *The Whole Case and Proceedings in Relation to Bridget Reading, an Heiress* (London, 1730), one reads how a London resident, Daniel Reading, sent a friend to Dublin to escort his twelve-year-old daughter, Bridget, back to England in 1727. Instead, the friend abducted the girl (a sole surviving daughter whose unnamed mother was dead) and forced her into a clandestine marriage. Thomas Reading surveyed lands for the Hatches in County Meath, 1723–1741, etc.: see NLI: 21 F. 112 and 16 I 9(4).
39 *An Abstract of the Proceedings of the the Incorporated Society in Dublin, for Promoting English Protestant Schools in Ireland, from ... 1733 to ... 1737*. London: repr. from the Dublin edition by M. Downing, 1737. pp. 4–5. The modern authority on the Charter Schools is Kenneth Milne, whose 1997 monograph says little about the particular school built on land subsequently absorbed into the Synges' Wicklow estate.
40 According to a privately published family tree Edward Hoare (1723–1788, barrister, of Royal Crescent, Bath) married in Dublin on 4 August 1744 Elizabeth Hatch, daughter of John Hatch Esquire of Dublin, and sister of John Hatch, sometime MP for Swords. The parish register of Saint Bride's would suggest that the date was 15 September 1744. The Hoare family tree-surgeon, however, was intemperate and occasionally inaccurate, whose nomination of a John (*recte* Henry) Hatch as father of John Hatch MP is a simple error. Other colourful details deriving from this source suggests that the will of the Bath barrister was 'believed a forgery': Edward Hoare, *The Families of Hore and Hoare*. London: Smith, 1883. p. 19. See *Gentleman's Magazine*, 9 October 1788 (p. 1028) and 11 November 1790 (p. 1057) for some further Hoare details.
41 'In Harcourt Street, Dublin, in his 75th year, John Hatch Esq., seneschal of St. Sepulchre's and many years M.P. for the borough of Swords': *Gentleman's Magazine* (October 1797), vol. 67, p. 897. The impression of exhausted old age conveyed in Hatch's last year is consistent with his being older than this obituary states, and I have therefore preferred the date of birth deducible from his TCD matriculation.
42 At the time of the Restoration (1660), a Christopher Hatch was listed among the Lincoln's Inn porters to be retained in its employment: he may be a forebear of the Hatches who marry in 1728/1730. No relationship with the Irish family can be established. See *Records of ... Lincolns Inn. vol. 3 1660–1775* (1899), p. 343.
43 NLI: Ms. 11, 343 contains detailed accounts for the construction of the mill, including receipts for payment to individual tradesmen.

CHAPTER 3 (pp. 38–45)
1 Aidan Clarke, *Prelude to Restoration in Ireland: The End of the Commonwealth, 1659–1660*. Cambridge: Cambridge University Press, 1999. p. 194 n. Giffard (of Castle Jordan, County Meath) died almost immediately after the wedding, leaving Martha a widow who passed the rest of her life with the Temples.
2 Swift to John Temple, 15 June 1706, Jonathan Swift, *Correspondence*, vol. 1 (1690–1713). Oxford: Clarendon Press, 1963. p. 53 Or *Correspondence* (ed. David Woolley). Frankfurt:

Notes

Lang, 1999. vol. 1 (1690–1714), p. 160.
3 See L. J. Arnold, *The Restoration Land Settlement in Counties Dublin and Wicklow, 1660–1688*. Ph.D. thesis, Trinity College, Dublin, 1967. Appendix E. In 1688, Sir Henry Temple held 139 acres of Wicklow land, Dr Abraham Yarner (with whose family the Temples were related by marriage) 831 acres and Sir William Flower 2,639 acres. Henry Hatch had protracted business connection with the Flowers.
4 See Special Collection list in NLI.
5 See NLI: Ms. 11,476.
6 Swift to Revd Thomas Sheridan, 15 and 16 June 1735; Swift to Benjamin Motte [25 October 1735], *Correspondence* (ed. Williams), vol. 4 (1732–1736). Oxford: Clarendon Press, 1965. pp. 351 and 410–411.
7 Swift to John Temple, [February] 1737, Jonathan Swift, *Correspondence* (ed. Williams), vol. V (1737–1745). Oxford: Clarendon Press, 1965. pp. 5–6.
8 Journal to Stella, p. 113; quoted in Irvin Ehrenpreis, *Swift: The Man, His Works, and the Age*. Cambridge, Mass.: Harvard University Press, 1983. vol. 3, p. 440.
9 TCD: Ms. 6184 f. 9. Stephens subsequently corrected 'adjoining' to 'near'.
10 Ehrenpreis, *Swift*, vol. 3, p. 325. Talbot's Castle was built on the site of an Augustinian priory at Trim, County Meath.
11 TCD: Ms. 6184 ff. 9–10. Stephens cites *A Continuation of the Proceedings of the Incorporated Society* ... Dublin: Grierson,1738. The Society's records consistently cite both Temple and the Acton family as the school's sponsors, while its local name (Templestown) suggests the primacy of the absentee's role in the manner.
12 TCD: Ms. 6184 f. 30.
13 Kenneth Milne, *The Irish Charter Schools, 1730–1830*. Dublin: Four Courts Press, 1997.
14 *A Continuation of the Proceedings of the Incorporated Society*. Dublin: Faulkner, 1738. pp. 9–10.
15 TCD: Ms. 5419.
16 *A Sermon Preach'd at Christ-Church, Dublin on the 28th Day of March 1742* ... By George [Ferns]. Dublin: Grierson, 1742. p. 23. 'Copy of a Report from the Charter-School at Templestown ... 27 October 1740' appears on pp. 22–32 and is initialled D. S.
17 *Ibid*. p. 25.
18 See Joseph Robins, *The Lost Children: A Study of Charity Children in Ireland 1700–1900*. Dublin: Institute of Public Administration, 1980. p. 32; see pp. 60–100 for his extended account of the Charter Schools which, characteristically, has little to say about the Roundwood establishment.
19 I draw here on papers preserved in Moore, Kiely & Lloyd (Solicitors), Dublin, which I consulted by kind permission of their client, Ms U. Brown.
20 Robert Steven, *An Inquiry into the Abuses of the Chartered Schools in Ireland*. London: Underwood, 1817. p. 23.
21 See Jeremiah Fitzpatrick's 1785 report, pp. 89–90, quoted by Steven; the girls were 'filthily kept' and taught by young and untrained staff, the one master being immediately dismissed on inspection. Sir Francis Hutchinson's 1788 report is cited in John Howard, *An Account of the Principal Lazarettos in Europe*. Warrington: Eyres, 1789.
22 See *Freeman's Journal*, 18–22 October 1763, etc.
23 TCD: Ms. 6184 f. 89.
24 Elias Thackeray, *General Report of the Charter Schools of Ireland*. Dublin: printed by L. Tute, 1818.
25 *Rules for the Government of the Protestant Charter Schools of Ireland*. Dublin: printed by John Jones, 1826. pp. 54–55. 'The Evil' may have been epilepsy, sometimes called the falling evil, or simply scrofula (King's evil).
26 Templestown features in the report published as an appendix to Isaac Mann's *Sermon Preached at Christ-Church, Dublin on the 15th of May 1774 before* ... Simon Earl Harcourt,

Notes

President, and the rest of the Incorporated Society ... Dublin: Powell, 1775. p. 42. The school is said to have 40 pupils, and John Hatch continues to feaure as a donor to the Society.

27 For Hutchinson's unfavourable report on the schools in 1773, see Milne, *The Irish Charter Schools*. pp. 177–178.
28 Quoted by Howard in *An Account of the Principal Lazarettos in Europe*.
29 Joan Kavanagh, 'The Case of Eliza Davis', *Wicklow Historical Society Journal*, vol. 1, no. 7 (1994), pp. 36–42.
30 Richard Musgrave, *Memoirs of the Different Rebellions in Ireland* (4th edn). Fort Wayne, Indiana: Round Tower Books, 1995. p. 866.

CHAPTER 4 (pp. 46–49)
1 Arthur H. Cash, *Laurence Sterne: The Early and Middle Years*. London: Methuen, 1975. pp. 19–20. Church of Ireland records, however, indicate that Fetherstone (1684–1772) was married to Pamela Parry.
2 For example, a document of c. 1783 bears a note in Edward Stephens's hand, 'Letters Francis Synge To John Hatch June 1787', though these have yet to be located: see NLI: Ms. 11,334.
3 NLI: Ms. 11,323 (i), S. M'Cracken to J. Hatch, 18 November 1761.
4 NLI: Ms. 11,323 (iv), S. M'Cracken to J. Hatch, 26 June 1764.
5 See NLI: Ms. 11,343. No modern internal numbering of the documents within this dossier has been established, though a contemporary serial number is entered on many of them. Unless otherwise stated, all material in the present chapter is to be found under the call-number given here.
6 NLI: Ms. 11, 323 (v), S. M'Cracken to J. Hatch, 21 January 1765.
7 DRD: Mem: 275: 505: 178618. See also Mem: 285: 119: 185724 for another post-mortem registering of an agreement dating back to 1757.

CHAPTER 5 (pp. 50–55)
1 Note dated 4 September 1780, preserved with the papers detailing repair of the mill in 1765.
2 See *Freeman's Journal*, 23–26 February 1765.
3 Ruán O'Donnell, *The Rebellion in Wicklow 1798*. Dublin: Irish Academic Press, 1998. pp. 227–228.
4 For Harcourt Street (named after Simon, 1st earl Harcourt, 1714–1777; viceroy from 1772 till his death), see Douglas Bennett, *Encyclopaedia of Dublin*. Dublin: Gill & Macmillan, 1991. p. 94.
5 Quoted in Greg Laurego, 'Infrastructures of Enlightenment: Road-Making, the Public Sphere, and the Emergence of Literature', *Eighteenth-Century Studies*, vol. 29, no. 1 (1995), p. 48. See *The Rights of Man* (Part One), in *The Thomas Paine Reader* (ed. Michael Foot and Isaak Krammick). London: Penguin, 1987. p. 217.
6 TCD: Ms. 6184 ff. 50–51.
7 TCD: Ms. 6184 ff. 51–52.
8 See David Broderick, *An Early Toll-Road: The Dublin-Dunleer Turnpike, 1731–1855*. Dublin: Irish Academic Press, 1996. I am grateful to Paddy Gillan for going through surviving records in the offices of Fingal County Council in a vain search for references to Hatch.
9 *The Post-Chaise Companion*. Dublin: printed for the author, 1786. p. 294.
10 TCD: Ms. 6184 f. 53.
11 TCD: Ms. 6184 ff. 57–58.
12 O'Donnell, *The Rebellion in Wicklow*, p. 76. Hugo and Holt fell into financial disputation over road building, which added spice to their political differences in 1798; for some

Notes

general comments on Wicklow roads in the 1780s and 1790s, see *ibid.*, p. 21.
13 Robert Fraser, *General View of ... County Wicklow*. Dublin: Graisberry & Campbell, 1801. p. 7.
14 *Ibid.*, p. 37.
15 See Ruán O'Donnell, *Aftermath: Post-Rebellion Insurgency in Wicklow 1799–1803*. Dublin: Irish Academic Press, 1999. pp. 14–16.
16 Fraser, *County Wicklow*, p. 38.

CHAPTER 6 (pp. 58–72)
1 PRONI: D607/A/161. John Hatch to Anna Maria Blundell, 12 April 1757 (copy). For an account of the interconnection by marriage, etc., of the Blundell estates (in King's County) and the Downshire estates (in County Down and elsewhere), see W. A. Maguire, 'Missing Persons: Edenderry under the Blundells and the Downshires, 1707–1922', in William Nolan and Timothy P. O'Neill (eds), *Offaly: History and Society*. Dublin: Geography Publications, 1998. pp. 515–541.
2 I have traced records of four Hatches admitted to the rolls of Dublin freemen – John Hatch (butcher, 1727, by fine), John Hatch (joiner, 1767, by service), John Hatch Esq (currier, 1774, by Grace Especial) and Richard Hatch (glover, 1792, by service).
3 *Freeman's Journal*, 2–5 July 1768; see the issue of 2–5 December 1769 for Hatch and Damer's ultimate election.
4 *Freeman's Journal*, 16–20 February 1768; *ibid.*, 28 June–2 July 1768.
5 The printed bond (5 January 1757) is preserved in a file marked undated items in NLI: Ms.19,439–658.
6 W. A. Maguire, 'Missing Persons, Edenderry under the Blundells and Downshires, 1707–1922', in William Nolan and Timothy O'Neill (eds), *Offaly, History and Society*. Dublin: Geography Publications, 1998. p. 523.
7 DRD: Mem: 247: 28: 158030 (28 September 1765), the term of the lease being twenty years and nine months.
8 See *Fool*, p. 144. The phrase 'gently hated ...' is Stephen Mackenna's. Synge's familiarity with Hatch family history is evident in his first attempt at drama, 'When the Moon Has Set'.
9 See Hatch's diary (NLI: Ms. 18,562) where the event and the place and the date are jointly recorded, though the marriage may have been conducted in a nearby church. The comment on weather is recorded on the front fly-leaf. The marriage was also recorded in *Pue's Occurrences*, 14–18 May 1765 (describing the bride as 'amiable'), and in *Freeman's Journal*, 21–25 May 1765, without giving the bride's Christian name.
10 NLI: P. C. 344 (9). The witnesses were Christopher Abbott and Adam Williams, the latter an attorney with whom Hatch did business over many years.
11 The note relating to Meath land is preserved in a file of undated items within NLI: Ms. D 19,439–658, where its companions include the (dated) Hatch/Shiel bond of 1757. In 1764, a James Shiel (counsellor at law) was elected a freeman of the Corporation of Barber Sugeons; he later was defeated candidate in the 1766 elections for the post of City Recorder; see *Freeman's Journal*, 16–20 October 1764, etc.
12 For Quin and the others, see Elizabeth Batt, *The Moncks and Charleville House: A Wicklow Family in the Nineteenth Century*. Dublin: Blackwater, 1979. pp. 5–7 ff.
13 NLI: P. C. 344 (9). An odd feature of the codicil as recorded here relates to the date of Nicholas Synge's original will which was apparently made on 4 June 1765; the codicil refers to a date of 13 June.
14 See *Freeman's Journal*, 21–25 April 1767, p. 267, column 3.
15 *Ibid.* col. 2.
16 In fact, the second report tells of a pregnant woman who, with a two-year-old in her arms, leapt to their deaths in the Liffey, *Dublin Mercury*, 31 March–1 April 1767, arguably an act

Notes

explicable in terms of genuine distress rather than the callousness of exposing an infant corpse in public.
17 NLI: Ms. 11,323.
18 Elizabeth was born on 21 January 1766, married in 1786, and died on 31 July 1810. She was buried at Glenealy, County Wicklow.
19 See Letter 139 (14 June 1751) in *Elphin Letters*, pp. 296–302.
20 In terms of presentation, there is ambiguity as to how children who died young (at birth or in infancy) are treated. Among the children of Nicholas Synge and Elizabeth Trench, for example, it is puzzling to say the least to find that Edward (born 1726) was followed by another boy who (though he died young) was also named Edward. An error of a more grievous kind lists Barbara Synge (drowned 1792) as the child of a (second) marriage celebrated in 1812 whereas she was unambiguously the child of her father's first marriage. These uncertainties and (fewer) blunders will take on their own significance when different sources of Synge family history are explored. See *Family*.
21 The compiler of *Family* was Mrs Katherine Synge, The Old Rectory, Great Barrow, near Chester. The book was evidently published at the expense of one or more members of the Synge Hutchinson branch. Prefatory matter is dated June 1937. The copy in the Society of Genealogists (London) was annotated by the compiler in January 1963. See p. xii of the printed text for the story of 1897.
22 Quoted in Robert Steven, *An Inquiry into the Abuses of the Chartered Schools in Ireland*. London, 1817. pp. 34–5. For the incident at Drumcliff, see A. N. Jeffares, *W. B. Yeats, Man and Poet*. London: Routledge, 1949. p. 3.
23 Steven, *An Inquiry*, p. 22.
24 Walter Benjamin, *The Arcades Project* (trans. Howard Eiland and Kevin McLaughlin). Cambridge, Mass.: Belknap Press, 1999. p. 473.
25 NLI: Ms. 18,562. OED gives a purely veterinary definition of freemartin – 'an imperfect female of the ox kind, twin-born with a male'.
26 See Anon., *A True and Genuine Narrative of Mr. and Mrs. Tenducci* … London: Pridden, 1768. I am grateful to Rolf Loeber and Magda Stouthamer-Loeber for an account of this rare novel. Tenducci, it seems, conformed to the Church of Ireland (*Dublin Mercury*, 30 June–4 July 1767): in an apparently unrelated incident, the castrato also fathered a child. On the relative normality of reproductive powers among women born co-twins with men, see James Y. Simpson, 'On the Alleged Infecundity of Females Born Co-twins with Males; with Some Notes on the Average Proportion of Marriages without Issue in General Society', *The Edinburgh Medical and Surgical Journal*, no. 158, 16pp.
27 DRD: Mem. 18.6496, witnessed by John Mecum (Hatch's clerk) and Adam Williams (an attorney), both of Dublin.
28 William Monck Mason, *The History … of … the Cathedral Church of St. Patrick*. Dublin: Folds, 1820. p. 48. Associated with this church property was the 'demesne and court land of Lissenhall' (*ibid.*, p. 50n.)
29 *Freeman's Journal*, 20–24 December 1768.
30 In 1742, Christopher Robinson had succeeded Boleyn Whitney on his retirement (*Freeman's Journal*, 15 May 1742). There is a reference to a seneschalship in a letter of 31 May 1766 and to the (then) uncompleted transfer of authority, but it is not clear that this refers to Hatch (PRONI: D/607/A/271). Robinson was subsequently a justice of the King's Bench: (how was he related to the Revd Christopher Robinson of West Wicklow in 1798?). Saint Sepulchre's had been the archiepiscopal palace in Dublin, its liberties lying immediately around Saint Patrick's Cathedral, which gradually slipped into decay during the eighteenth century. I am grateful to the cathedral archivist, Dr Kate Manning, for guidance on this topic. On the seneschal's legal role, I am grateful to Brian Jackson for his comments.

Notes

31 *Belfast Newsletter*, 13–16 January 1784.
32 *Correspondence of Viscount Castlereagh*. London, 1848–1853. vol. 3, p. 60.
33 NLI: Ms. 18, 562.
34 See E. M. Johnston, *Great Britain and Ireland 1760–1800*. Edinburgh: Oliver and Boyd, 1963. pp. 328, 348, 374.
35 *Commons Journal*, vol. 10, part 2, p. dxxii.
36 NLI: Ms. 10,211.
37 A marriage between a Samuel Hatch and Ann M'Cormick in 1770 is listed in Dublin diocesan records. From letters of October 1784, it is clear that our Samuel Hatch was married at that date; see NLI: Ms. 11,328.
38 See G. O. Sayles, 'Contemporary Sketches of the Members of the Irish Parliament in 1782', *Proceedings of the Royal Irish Academy*, vol. 56, section c (March 1954), p. 247.
39 Johnston, *Great Britain and Ireland*, p. 397.
40 PRONI: D/607/A/348, John Hatch to Kilwarlin, 12 October 1787 (copy).
41 *Freeman's Journal*.
42 *Commons Journal*, vol. 12, pp. 357, 386. Eight MPs were excused fines on the same ground. This occasion is the only one on which Hatch is mentioned in vol. 12 of the *Journal*, which covers the years 1786–1788.
43 NLI: Ms. 10,212, Kilwarlin to J. Hatch, undated.
44 *Biographical Sketch of the Struggles of Pestalozzi*. Dublin: Folds, 1815.
45 PRONI: D/607/A/461, J. Hatch to Hillsborough, 24 October 1793. Jebb became President of the Royal College of Surgeons of Ireland in 1800.
46 PRONI: D607/A/370, J. Hatch to Arthur Hill (later marquis of Downshire), 3 September 1788; quoted in Maguire, 'Missing Persons', p. 524.
47 NLI: Ms. 11,984. See also *The Charter of the Royal Canal Company*. Dublin: Chambers, 1789. p. [ii]; *Report of the Committee Appointed by the Royal Canal Comapny 12th June 1793* (n.p., n.d.). p. [1]; Ruth Delany, *Ireland's Royal Canal, 1789–1992*. Dublin: Lilliput Press, 1992. pp. 24–25, 200–201. For evidence of Hatch's perception of the economic value of navigation canals c. 1784, see PRONI: Downshire Papers, Corresp. 272. The Royal Canal Company went bankrupt before being taken over in 1814 by the Directors-General of Inland Navigation.
48 Maguire, 'Missing Persons', pp. 523–524.
49 Yeomanry lists were published in *The Court and County and City Calendar* (Dublin, 1797), and a consolidated typescript is preserved in the Society of Genealogists (London). If the captain was not in fact the ageing seneschal, then others of the same name include the John Hatches listed in note 2 above. The presence of one of these in a yeomanry unit within the Liberty would indicate John Hatch's degree of contact with humbler members of his extended family.
50 PRONI: D/607/A/524, J. Hatch to Downshire, 13 January 1797; and D/607/A/532, John Hatch to Anna Maria Blundell, 20 February 1797. The term 'prime minister' had no official sanction, and here refers to Sir John Parnell (1744–1801), chancellor of the Irish exchequer. Though a younger man, he had like Hatch been a student at Lincoln's Inn, and held land in Wicklow. He was an opponent of Catholic Relief and the Union with Britain. Parnell had travelled to London to seek a loan, following the Bank of Ireland's admission that it was down to its last £20,000. I am grateful to Gillian O'Brien (Institute of Irish Studies, Liverpool) for her discussion of the financial background.
51 NLI: Ms. 11,992 – Loose copy of a letter from Hatch to Captain Mills, dated Saturday, 19 August 1797.
52 NLI: Private Collection Reports, no. 179: f. 1926.
53 NLI: Ms. 11, 995. Robert A. Synge made copies of various Synge wills in 1902: for his notes, see TCD: Ms. 6,199.

Notes

54 NLI: Ms. 11,300, Synge to Downshire, 29/9/1797 (copy); PRONI: D607/A/539, Synge to Downshire, 7/10/1797, quoted in Maguire, 'Missing Persons', p. 524.

55 PRONI: D607/A/23; the resumé quoted here proceeds to complain that Hatch 'died very rich, much of his wealth having been accumulated out of the estates of absentee proprietors'.

CHAPTER 7 (pp. 73–79)

1 Other freemen of the same name include William McCracken (carpenter, Christmas 1733, by Grace Especial), Thomas McCracken (bricklayer, Christmas 1744, by service) and John McCracken (barber, Michaelmas 1765, by service). In 1808, the will of Bernard McCracken (a Dublin hairdresser) was proved.

2 DRD: Mem: 115:77: 79310 (7 October 1743) and Mem: 158: 303: 106005 (15 December 1752). By the end of the 1760s, M'Cracken also had property in Fownes Street, Dublin: see DRD: Mem: 263: 605: 173114 (24 February 1768).

3 The lease, dated 11 May 1749, features in a list of deeds, etc., prepared in August 1846 in the aftermath of John 'Pestalozzi' Synge's death at Glanmore in 1845: see file of so-called undated items in NLI: Ms. D. 19439–658. Glassnamullen consequently was the oldest part of the Synge inheritance in Wicklow.

4 To judge from the one obituary I have traced, John Hatch was born in 1723 or 1724, and died September 1797 at his home in Harcourt Street, Dublin, in his 75th year (see *Gentleman's Magazine*, October 1797, vol. 67, p. 897, and NLI: Ms. 11,300, Francis Synge to Downshire 29/9/1797 (copy); PRONI: D607/A/539, Synge to Downshire, 7/10/1797.

5 Kenneth Milne, *The Irish Charter Schools 1730–1830*. Dublin: Four Courts Press, 1997. pp. 143–146.

6 DRD: Mem: 165:18: 108074 (11 January 1753), Mem: 189: 397: 125916 (22 October 1756), and Mem: 200: 112: 132197 (1 March 1759). Mercer is mentioned in the Incorporated Society's accounts as early as August 1750, and thus appears to have served a relatively long period at the school. In that month, he was instrumental in remitting money on behalf of the Revd Holt Truel, one of the family which supplied the mill-building project and which, in the nineteenth century, married into the Synges.

7 DRD: Mem: 213: 365: 141552 (22 January 1762).

8 In keeping with the eighteenth century's casual attitude towards spelling, the name is variously Stuart or Stewart in the source material cited in this and the succeeding chapter: I have standardised to Stuart throughout, except when quoting directly. The *Freeman's Journal* records (9–12 March 1771) the death of a 'Miss Stewart' of Marlborough Street, Dublin, at Drummin, County Wicklow. This may indicate some connection between the Stuarts and Thomas Hugo, who lived at Drummin in the barony of Ballinacor North: there are other Drummins in Wicklow, however, and other Stuarts in Dublin. Ann Stewart of Marlborough Street married Nathaniel Johnson of Bordeaux, see *Freeman's Journal*, 28–31 January 1769.

9 For Stuart, see DRD: Mem: 220: 332: 145016 (15 January 1763) in which I cannot decipher Stuart's father's Christian name. For the Glassnamullen accounts, which were drawn up much later probably to demonstrate M'Cracken's honest stewardship on Hatch's behalf, see NLI: Ms. 11,340.

10 NLI: Ms. 11,323 (i), S. M'Cracken to J. Hatch, 30 December 1761; Ms. 11323 (ii), S. M'Cracken to J. Hatch, 1 February 1762; Ms. 11,323 (v), 8 March 1765.

11 *Freeman's Journal*, 29 March–1 April 1766; *ibid*., 30 September–4 October 1766; 6–9 December 1766. Mary Keightly died in Janauary 1767, at Drummin, which may be the place of that name in Ballinacor North (*ibid*., 31 January–3 February 1767). Mount Nebo is not recorded in Price's *Place Names of Wicklow*, though in the 1790s the north Wexford Orangeman, John Hunter Gowan so styled his place.

12 TCD: Ms. 5668 (list of children, 1765–1792).

Notes

13 NLI: Ms. 11, 323 (iv), S. M'Cracken to J. Hatch, 7 February 1764.
14 NLI: Ms. 11,232 (ii), S. M'Cracken to J. Hatch, 28 January 1762, 26 September 1762, 11 July 1762; Ms. 11,323 (v), S. M'Cracken to J. Hatch, 8 December 1765.
15 NLI: Ms. 11,333. This is taken from a summary of the events leading to M'Cracken's death, drawn up in connection with Hatch's efforts to obtain possession of the Wicklow property.
16 NLI: Ms. 11,323 (v), S. M'Cracken to J. Hatch, 22 December 1765. It is true that 'cousin' had been used in English (including Shakespeare's English) as a synonym of 'friend', and that this usage persisted in Ireland, especially in what are now the border counties. But the evidence of M'Cracken's letters does not suggest that he ever had this broad meaning in mind. See S. M'Cracken to J. Hatch, 8 December 1765 for the postscript reporting Salmon's sentiments, the letter in which pistols had been requested.
17 NLI: Ms. 11, 323 (v), S. M'Cracken to J. Hatch, 22 December 1765. The Revd David Stephens had died in February 1765 (see *Pue's Occurrences* and *Freeman's Journal*); his birthplace having been Carrickmacross, he may have shared something of the County Monaghan background which emerges among M'Cracken's relatives.
18 NLI: Ms. 11, 323, S. M'Cracken to J. Hatch, 2 February 1769. Mary Salmon disappears from the chronicle, and cannot be identified elsewhere, unless she is the Mary Salmon who married Michael Mooney and lived at Derrintown, County Kildare (see DRD: Mem: 291: 98: 189870). However, the marriage of a Miss Salmon of Wicklow to a Mr Hore (no Christian name given), as reported in *Freeman's Journal* of 2–6 April 1765, suggests a kinship with the family of Henry Hatch's second wife.
19 NLI: D. 19, 439–19,658 (in the file marked 1760–1780.)
20 NLI: Ms. 11,333.
21 The *Dublin Mercury* of 10–12 August 1769 carried a brief news report, 'We hear from the county of Wicklow, that a gentleman of easy fortune, and who seemed to labour under no discontent, shot himself one day last week.' A formal death notice on the same page reads 'Suddenly at Roundwood, co. Wicklow, Mr M'Cracken, formely an eminent peruke-maker of this city.' The death was also noted in the *Freeman's Journal*, 8–12 August 1769.
22 See *Dublin Mercury*, 24–28 March 1767: a decade later, M'Cracken's nephew whinged on paper in letters to Hatch written from a Francis Street address.
23 Wills (proven 1769 and 1771) indicate M'Cracken had property in more than one county, though the texts of these (assumed to have been destroyed in 1922) are unlikely to emerge after more than two centuries. For Hatch's taking possession, see NLI: Ms. 11,335 with details of expenses incurred, 9–10 February 1774.
24 NLI: Ms. 11, 328.
25 NLI: Ms. 11, 323 (v), S. M'Cracken to J. Hatch, undated; the date stated derives from the endorsement of Hatch or his clerk.

CHAPTER 8 (pp. 80–91)
1 *Freeman's Journal* records (17–21 April 1764) the death of a man named Bowles, formerly of Wicklow, late of Chequer-Lane, Dublin.
2 NLI: Ms. 11, 333.
3 NLI: Ms. 11, 335.
4 The capital letter D after two names may indicate that these persons had died between the making of the will and the testator's own death, in which case the Sam Hatch listed was not Adam Williams's assistant but the older Samuel Hatch of Kells.
5 NLI: Ms. 11,323. In 1765, Delamour had been paid by M'Cracken for plastering and related work on Annamoe Mill, and so was almost certainly a local man. On 10 March 1784, a number of Roundwood worthies (including Thomas Hugo and the Revd Ambrose Weekes) signed a statement of good character for Delamor, as a resident in the parish for seventeen years, 'an Honest Sober and Industrious tradesman and Reasonable in his

Notes

charges'. The last detail would suggest that he required such testimony to extract payment from Hatch (see NLI: Ms. 11,343.)

6 NLI: Ms. 11,323.
7 NLI: Ms. 11,323 (6).
8 NLI: Ms. 11,323 (18).
9 See 'demesne continued' in NLI: Ms. 11,340.
10 See TCD: Ms. 4351 f. 50, etc. For an account of 'When the Moon Has Set' as drama and psychic history, see *Fool*, pp. 160–171.
11 Surviving church records for Kells commence in 1773: the only occurrence of the name records the death of a 'Widow Mc Cracken' (no other details) on 8 September 1775. No instance of the name, Hatch, is to be found in these records, for details of which I am grateful to Carmel Rice of the Meath Heritage Centre. For details of the funeral arangements, see four documents in NLI: Ms. 11,335.
12 See NLI: Ms. 11,331. The wife of a Robert Wisdom, of Liffey Street in Dublin, died in the autumn of 1768 (see *Freeman's Journal*, 8–11 October 1768). He may have been related to the Revd John Wisdom, vicar of Luske and a Justice of the Peace, who resigned as assistant librarian at Marsh's Library, beside Saint Patrick's Cathedral, in October 1767.
13 NLI: Ms. 11,323 (vi) I. Shiel to J. Hatch. It seems that Mrs H[atton?] was related to Rooney, an 'atty of a low class' and that the Hattons were initially suspected of some foul play.
14 Material in this paragraph from various documents in NLI: Ms. 11,323.
15 NLI: Ms. 11,331. Adam Williams to [unknown, but almost certainly John Hatch, the address being Saint Stephens Green], 15 November 1773.
16 NLI: Ms. 11,323. See in particular James Rooney to J. Hatch, 30 July 1774.
17 NLI: Ms. 11,323 (18, letter of 6 December 1777). This provision for the Suttons of Glasnamullen cannot be reconciled with the £5 annuity listed in the Hatch Papers.
18 NLI: Ms. 11,323, John Ardill to J. Hatch, 25 July 1778.
19 From documentation preserved in NLI: Ms. 11,333. The lawyer's name may have been Radcliffe. The papers established that Samuel Hatch was the son of James Hatch (of Kells), and that Joseph was a cousin of Samuel's. In November 1782, Joseph Hatch did in fact make some effort to sell his interest in M'Cracken's estate.
20 NLI: Ms. 11,323, Francis Vesey (of Stephen Street, Dublin) to J. Hatch, 30 April 1778.
21 For a statement sworn before a magistrate for a debt owed to one Thomas Jolley (and dating back to 1774), see NLI: Ms. 11,333. The promissory note of 7 December 1775 was made out in favour of Chrisopher Nerey (see NLI: Ms. 11,332, unsorted).
22 NLI: Ms. 11,323, W. Stuart (at 44, Francis Street, Dublin) to J. Hatch, 23 September 1779. 'Long confinement' perhaps indicates that Stuart had been imprisoned (for debt, most likely) and that Hatch may have come to his aid.
23 NLI: Ms. 11,323, F. Stoddard to J. Hatch, 18 November 1773.
24 NLI: Ms. 11,323, F. Stoddard to [?John Hatch], 1 February 1776.
25 NLI: Ms. 11,323, F. Stoddard to J. Hatch, 22 March 1774.
26 NLI: Ms. 11,331.
27 NLI: Ms. 11,323. The remark about delicacy remains inscrutable. On 10 September 1772, Joshua McCracken (a Dublin peruke-maker like Samuel M'Cracken, and almost certainly a relative) married Catherine Riely (spinster) in Saint Bride's Church. Back in February 1719, Richard Riely married Barbarah [sic] Synge. Herein may lie some sense of impropriety, though the name Riely (Reilly, Riley, etc.) is so common as to make it unlikely that the two events were in any way linked or that there had been some marriage between the ecclesiastical Synges and Hatch's humble relatives.
28 NLI: Ms. 11,331. The addressee is not identified in the letter, but its preservation in the Hatch Papers would argue that either Hatch or someone acting on his behalf had assisted M'Cracken relatives.

Notes

29 NLI: Ms. 11,323. In another undated letter to Hatch, she complains of receiving no reply to an earlier letter, mentions preparations to go to Lisbon where her brother is, and signs off 'Anne Kennedy whose maiden name was Mc Cracken'.
30 NLI: Ms. 11,331. Zacharias Brown to S. M'Cracken, 16 April 1765.
31 See *Commons Journal*, vol. 12, part 2, p. cccviii.
32 NLI: Ms. 11,323, Thomas Emerson to J. Hatch, 2 June 1787 (reply drafted on Emerson's letter to Hatch). For Synge on the list of nominees in 1777, see *Commons Journal*, vol. 10, part 2, p. ccccvi.
33 For the death of Barbara Synge (1790–1792) on 19 May, see the annotated copy of *The Family of Synge* in the Society of Genealogists, London. See also the diary of [Sir] Robert Synge (c. 1760–1804) for 19 May 1792 – 'Brother Frank's Daughter Bab was drowned in the River at the bottom of the shrubbery at Syngefield' – quoted in Ainsworth Report No. 378.
34 PRONI: D.607/A/443, J. Hatch to Anna Maria Blundell, 26 May 1792. For Hatch's activities as agent for the Blundells at Edenderry and in County Down, see Martin Dowling, *Tenant Right and Agrarian Society in Ulster, 1600–1870*. Dublin: Irish Academic Press, 1999. pp. 63–64ff; also W. A. Maguire, 'Missing Persons', Edenderry under the Blundells and the Downsires', in William Nolan and T. P. O'Neill (eds), *Offaly; History and Society*. Dublin: Geography Publications, 1998. pp. 515–541.
35 NLI: Ms. 11,328, Copy/draft of letter from John Hatch in Dublin to Thomas Clarkson at Roundwood, 31 May 1796.
36 NLI: Ms. D. 19,439–658 does contain a copy of a second will in M'Cracken's name, dated [blank] day of August 1769. It appoints John Hatch and William Stuart as executors; most of the bequests are as in the 1762 will, but it leaves the balance of the estate to William Stuart and then to the first and every son, etc., of William Stuart, then to Samuel Stuart, then to Henry Hatch of Kells (son of James Hatch of Kells). In other words, it casts John Hatch in role simply as executor.
37 NLI: Ms. 11,328, S. Hatch to 'Respected Sir' (i.e. John Hatch), 'Sunday 1/2 past three 17th October 1784'; see also Ms. 11,328 (10), S. Hatch to J. Hatch, 7 October 1784 for a decidedly less frightened submission ten days earlier. John Hatch, however, had drawn up 'Sam Hatch's Acct of Money recd & not pd over to me' totalling £118, collected during the years 1781–1784 from Roundwood tenants such as Clarkson, Harding, Polland, amongst others (see NLI: Ms. 11,334).
38 NLI: Ms. 11,328. Copy/draft J. Hatch in Dublin to Samuel Hayes at Avondale, 6 June 1783.

CHAPTER 9 (pp. 92–95)
1 Unless otherwise stated, evidence of Hatch's borrowings derives from NLI: Ms. D. 19,439–658, a large collection of documents broken down into separate dated files.
2 See, for example, the declarations in relation to the April 1771 elections, *Calendar of the Ancient Records of the City of Dublin*. vol. 12. Dublin: Dollard, 1905. p. 122.
3 Documentation preserved by Moore, Kiely & Lloyd (Solicitors), Dublin, includes several leases from Lord Milltown to Hatch in 1769, etc.
4 Note also Simeon Boileau, a merchant in Phrapper's Lane, Dublin, who died in 1767: see *Freeman's Journal*, 4–7 July 1767.
5 NLI: Ms. 11, 323, Elizabeth Redwill to J. Hatch, 18 March 1790. Redwill was a sister of the Stuart brothers, a niece of M'Cracken, though she does not appear to have featured in his will.
6 NLI: Ms. 11, 323, Mrs Stuart to J. Hatch, 5 September 1792.
7 NLI: Ms. 11,332 is a large bundle of unsorted receipts, promissory notes, and other fragmentary evidence of financial affairs, covering the careers of both Henry and John Hatch, with a small amount of material relating to Francis Synge's administration of his father-in-law's affairs. It includes J. Theophilus Boileau's receipt for the loans to John Hatch.

Notes

CHAPTER 10 (pp. 98–107)

1 *An Abstract of the Proceedings of the Incorporated Society in Dublin, for Promoting English Protestant Schools in Ireland, from … 1733 to … 1737*. London: reprinted from the Dublin Edition by M. Downing, 1737. pp. 5, 10. *A Continuation of the Proceedings … . from 1737 to 1738*. Dublin: printed by Geo. Grierson, 1738. p. 8. *Ibid.* (1740), pp. 12–13.

2 Some time c. 1856, Arthur Guinness acquired Roundwood, though not directly from the Synges (see DRD).

3 Mark Bence-Jones, *Burke's Guide to County Houses. Volume I – Ireland*. London: Burke's Peerage Limited, 1978. pp. 248–249.

4 Written on the back of a set of stitched pages, in NLI: Ms. 11,331.

5 For this paragraph cf. NLI: Ms. 11, 341. Pollard appears to have paid rent to Wm. Stewart up to 1 May 1774 (see Ms. 11, 340).

6 In NLI: Ms. 11,332 (unsorted). The crucial falsification changed the word 'last' to 'next' with reference to a date.

7 NLI: Ms. 11, 334.

8 NLI: Ms. 11, 334. The date of survey was 29 January 1788.

9 NLI: Ms. 17, 275.

10 TCD: Ms. 6184 ff. 43–45.

11 In NLI: Ms. D 19,439–6 58 (file for 1781–1790).

12 The graveyard at Derrylossary contains a headstone on which the name of Frances May Weekes 'alias Stephens' (died 28 January 1793 aged 60) appears. If she was the daughter of the Revd David Stephens, then she was born when he was c. thirty-six years old. One might presume with greater confidence she was the wife of Revd Ambrose Weekes, but for the absence of any record on this stone or elsewhere of his death or burial. The same stone commemorates William Sutton Weekes, by implication a son of the rector: his second Christian name would suggest that his mother had been a Sutton, a large family in the parish. Suggestion hovers round Ambrose Weekes like a brimstone halo.

13 TCD: Ms. 6184 f. 55. Francis Synge to John Hatch, 8 June 1787 (typed copy made for Edward Stephens). This item of correspondence does not appear to have found its way into NLI with the bulk of the Hatch Papers. A 'nigger' *(recte niggard)* was a metal device used for economising on fuel burnt in the open grate.

14 NLI: Ms. 17, 275 (Diary of Robert Synge); see entry for 13 May 1789 in connection with the marriage of Mr Bolton and his bride (Eliza McDonnell) at Saint Andrews church, Dublin; the Synge/Ormsby wedding took place on 26 December 1794.

15 W. D. Macray, *A Register of the Members of St. Mary Magdalen College, Oxford*. New Series vol. 3. London: Frowde, 1901. p. 221.

16 See NLI: Ms. 17, 275 (diary of Robert Synge). Entries for 11 October 1793 and 10 July 1794 indicates that while the Revd Samuel Synge did indeed sleep at the inn, his daughter Fanny stayed with her Synge relatives in the town. For the background to Fanny's birth and upbringing, see chapter 12 below.

17 Maurice Craig, *Classic Irish Houses of the Middle Size*. London: Architectural Press, 1976. p. 127 (with photograph).

18 NLI: Ms. 17, 275. Entries for 20 May and 11 June 1800.

19 TCD: Ms. 6184 f. 66. For details of Synge's compensation claim, see *Commons Journal*, vol. 19 (appendix.)

20 TCD: Ms. 6184 ff. 71, 74, 76.

21 The cheques are preserved in NLI: Ms. 11332 (unsorted).

22 Sir John Carr, *The Stranger in Ireland*. London: Phillips, 1806, p. 147. The description of Glanmore, which includes a reference to 'the celebrated Devil's-glen', faces an illustration showing the plate engraved by Phillips of Bridge Street, Blackfriars, in June 1806.

23 See a note by Edward Stephens contributed to *Family*, p. xv.

Notes

24 TCD: Ms. 6184 f. 71.
25 Charles Orpen, *The Claim of Millions of Our Fellow-Countrymen of Present and Future Generations to be Taught in Their Own and Only Language, the Irish: Addressed to the Upper Classes in Ireland and Great Britain*. Dublin: Tims, 1821. prelims.
26 NLI: Ms. 11,337 (2) includes a memo dated 1751 re. Samuel M'Cracken 'engrossing a Deed of Release from Mr Morgan to You [i.e. John Hatch] of Lands of Roundwood' – receipt for £1 9s 8d signed by Christopher Dalton, 6 July 1751. Ms. 11, 332 (unsorted) includes a small memo book recording Gardiner's receipts (via M'Cracken) from Morgan, beginning April 1752.
27 NLI: Ms. 11, 991 f. 22v.
28 NLI: Ms. 11, 991 f. 8v.
29 George O'Malley Irwin, *The Illustrated Guide to the County of Wicklow*. Dublin, 1844.

CHAPTER 11 (pp. 108–112)

1 See Jonathan Swift, *Correspondence* (ed. Harold Williams), vol. V (1737–1745). Oxford: Clarendon Press, 1965. p. 124n.
2 Mary Granville (i.e. Mrs Delaney), *The Autobiography and Correspondence*. London: Bentley, 1861. vol. 3, p. 87 (Mrs Delany to Mrs Dawes, 15 February 1752).
3 John S. Crone, *A Concise Dictionary of Irish Biography*. London: Longman, 1928.
4 See biographical note in *Elphin Letters*, p. xliii.
5 Quoted in Robert Steven, *An Inquiry into the Abuses of the Chartered Schools in Ireland*. London, 1817. p. 66.
6 The will was proved late in 1792 in Canterbury Prorogative Court and thus – unlike wills related solely to Irish property – has survived the ravages of war.
7 'for my daughter Elizabeth Synge one thousand pounds part of said eight thousand pounds for my second son Samuel Synge three thousand pounds part of said eight thousand pounds for my third son George Synge fifteen hundred part of said eight thousand pounds for my fourth son Robert Synge one thousand pounds part of said eight thousand pounds and for my youngest son Francis Synge fifteen hundred pounds the remaining part of said eight thousand pounds'.
8 The Hutchinson brothers had both married – Francis to Elizabeth Trench, James to Elizabeth Tottenham – but without issue in either case.

CHAPTER 12 (pp. 113–126)

1 *Works* 2, p. [26] – 'The People of the Glens'.
2 Joseph Holt, *Rebellion in Wicklow* (ed. Peter O'Shaughnessy). Dublin: Four Courts, 1998. pp. 20–21. For the importance of the Manning family in mid-nineteenth-century Rathdrum, see chapter 19 below.
3 See PRONI: D/607?A/537, Richard Annesley to Downshire, 23 September 1797.
4 PRONI: Dl607/A/536, Henry Stewart (Dublin) to Downshire, 23 September 1797.
5 PRONI: D/607/A1544A, Henry Stewart (Westmeath) to Downshire, 12 December 1797. Stewart/Stuart may have been the nephew at Edenderry alluded to by Hatch in 1793.
6 PRONI: D/607/A1538, Francis Synge to Downshire, 29 September 1797.
7 PRONI: D/607/A/539, Francis Synge to Downshire, 7 October 1797.
8 See *Faulkner's Dublin Journal*, 8 March 1798, p. 3 col. 3.
9 PRONI: D/607/A/560, 13 October 1798.
10 PRONI: D/607/A/ 557, Francis Synge to Miss Blundell, 14 June 1798. The family disasters remain unidentified.
11 PRONI: D/607/A/23.
12 NLI: Ms. 11, 330. For a fuller account of Mrs Sophie Synge, see n. 45 below.
13 See PRONI: D.607/A/23.

Notes

14 The note on the course of the rebellion begins on the blank leaf facing the printed month of May, and covers events from 26th to 30th May. Its summary character is well exemplified in: 'they had another large Camp at Carrigburn Hill, near to which, at Scullabogue, they murdered 193 protestants, by shooting about 20, & shutting up the rest in a large Barn cruelly Burned them to death'. The note (perhaps 200 words in all) continues up to the arrival of the army in Wexford town.

15 Ruán O'Donnell claims that Synge was out of the country at the beginning of the Wicklow rebellion but does not cite evidence; see his 'Roundwood in 1798', *Roundwood History and Folklore Journal*, no. 3 (1990), p. 7.

16 Between 1775 and 1782, Harvey had kept twelve terms at the King's Inns, after his graduation from Trinity College Dublin; he does not appear to have been called to the bar.

17 For evidence of the Synges employing servants of this surname – but different Christian names – at Syngefield, near Birr, see Mrs Sophia Synge's will.

18 The diary is NLI: Ms. 11,994.

19 The family connections linking Stephens and Colclough also involved the Hearns. William Stephens (born 1749, 'manager Dixon's Mt Temple') had two children: one, Susan, married Colonel Colclough of Tintern Abbey (Wexford); her brother, John, was the father of Henry Colclough Stephens (1826–1901) referred to above who married Jane Hearn and had four children: of these, Susan married [?] Oulton, and Henry Francis married Annie Synge.

20 The edition used remains unidentified.

21 PRONI: D.607/F/416, Robert Ross to Downshire, 18 September 1798.

22 For Kingsborough's role in suppressing the rebellion in the Roundwood area, see Ruán O'Donnell, *The Rebellion in Wicklow 1798*. Dublin: Irish Academic Press, 1998. p. 187. O'Donnell refers to the burning of 'Sir Francis Hutchinson's plantation on the south slope of the glen'; since the Hutchinson-Synge marriage of 1752, the two families had come to possess adjoining properties in Wicklow. The Kingsborough at work here is, of course, the killer of Henry Fitzgerald in his bedroom less than a year earlier.

23 When T. Crofton Croker's heavily edited version of Holt's *Memoirs* appeared in 1838, the *Dublin University Magazine* (*DUM*) published a brief but deeply hostile review, attributed (not without dissent) to Isaac Butt. The anonymous reviewer waxed sarcastic at Holt's preference for the company of rebels rather than 'his friends, Messrs Synge and Tottenham [who] were as near at hand as the gang to which he attached himself', and proceeded 'to say nothing of the Amazon in the green habit, who appears to have "ruled the camp" in the absence of Mrs. H.' (*DUM*, vol. 12, July 1838, pp. 72 and 74.)

24 O'Donnell, *The Rebellion*, pp. 242, 292.

25 *Commons Journal*, vol. 19 (appendix). The columns detailing the amount allowed against the claim, any deductions made and the sum raised through a specific fund are, in Synge's case, blank.

26 Documentation held by Moore, Kiely & Lloyd (Solicitors), Dublin, and quoted by kind permission of Ms U. Brown (Donegal).

27 John D'Alton, *History of Drogheda*. Dublin: the author, 1844. vol. 1 p. xcix.

28 Francis Synge's anti-Unionism in 1800 was well publicised in lists of voters incorporated in Sir John Barrington's *Rise and Fall of the Irish Nation*, reissued at regular intervals throughout the nineteenth century.

29 Fredric Jameson, *The Political Unconscious: Narrative as a Socially Symbolic Act*. London: Methuen, 1981. p. 9.

30 The mother was Jane Caufeild (died April 1784), half sister of 'Mrs Jordan', celebrated actress and mistress of the future William IV.

31 See N. F. Lowe, 'Mary Wollstonecraft and the Kingsborough Scandal', *Eighteenth-Century Ireland/Iris an Dá Chultúr*, vol. 9 (1994) pp. 44–56.

Notes

32 He was the second eldest son of Hans Widman Wood, and died unmarried.
33 See vol. 8 p. 39 of W. E. H. Lecky's *History of England in the Eighteenth Century*. London, 1878–1890. For an earlier account, see the *Recollections of Skeffington Gibbon*. Dublin, 1829.
34 NLI: Ms. 17,725.
35 NLI: Ms. 17,725. Margaret Synge (née Wolfe) continued her husband's diary after his death in 1804; the entry is found under 25 April 1825.
36 NLI: Ms. 10,212. This collection of letters includes four written between August 1790 and September 1792, when both Kilwarlin and Kingsborough sat in the Irish House of Commons. Hatch and Kingsborough had been simultaneously members of the House, following the election of 1783.
37 If the valedictory *Peerage* insists that Frances Synge (born 1788) died in 1885, then she presumably is the person of that name who died in Dublin's Whitworth Hospital (see Mount Jerome re. no. 494). In contrast, see also the recording of a birth in Paris in 1825 ('24 April – a visit from my sister [-in-law] she told me of the birth of a grandson for my brother Saml Synge Hutchinson in Paris on 31st of March name Samuel.' Diary of Lady Margaret Synge) and another grand-child named Frances two years later. See NLI: Ms. 17,275 – entries for 24 April 1825 and 26 December 1827.
38 Francis Synge Hutchinson (1802–1833), later distinguished as a founder among the Brethren: see chapter 16 below.
39 See *Family* p. 7, where the three names are placed at the left (or elder) side of the descendants' list. The *Peerage* of 1906 uses the phrase 'and by her had issue' to introduce the son and daughter of Samuel Synge and Dorothy (née) Hatch; this leaves open the interpretation that he had other issue by another woman. Together these verbal and typographical infelicities generate unnecessary uncertainty.
40 At first glance it might seem reasonable to accept that the disasters referred to by Francis Synge included Hatch's death, the absence of a will and resulting complications. But Synge mentioned these as a distraction from the business of taking over Hatch's responsibilities, and so they must be regarded as external to it. Edward Stephens, writing in the 1930s, states that round the time of Hatch's death, his elder daughter was expecting a child, and implies that this child did not survive (see TCD: Ms. 6184 f. 62.)
41 UCD: S6/28/27.
42 The Kilwarlin/Hatch correspondence (now NLI: Ms. 10,212) was likewise withheld when Edward Stephens deposited the bulk of the Hatch Papers: it was subsequently donated by his widow.
43 The archbishop of Dublin in 1762 was Charles Cobbe (1687–1765), who had risen steadily from bishop of Killala in 1720, translated to Dromore in 1727, Kildare in 1732, and finally Dublin in 1743.
44 See vol. 8, p. 1926 of Sir John Ainsworth's Special Reports, typescripts preserved in the NLI manuscript room. The ellipses are Ainsworth's.
45 Though Samuel Synge appears to be the first 'black sheep' to emerge in the family, there had been earlier concern. Before his father (Edward Synge, 1725–1792) had married in 1752, there was much distress about a 'silly love-affair'. Whether she was the object of his ardour, the woman whom he married was Sophia Helena Maria Hutchinson (died 24 January 1799), daughter of Samuel Hutchinson (d. 27 October 1780), bishop of Killala and his wife Sophia (née Hamilton). For the distress, see Edward Synge (1691–1762) to Alicia Synge, 14 June 1751, in *Elphin Letters* pp. 296–301. In July 1759 Mrs Delany makes an arch comment about Edward of Elphin's letters 'to his nephew Neddy' which may encode a later incident of rebuke (see Mary Granville, *The Autobiography and Correspondence*. London: Bentley, 1861. vol. 3 p. 561.) For an account of the return (via Pill) of Mrs Sophia Synge's body for burial at Birr, see the diary of her son, Robert – later Sir Robert Synge, Bart (c. 1760–1804) – quoted in Ainsworth's Report No. 378.

Notes

46 UCD Archives: S6/28/26–27 (Synge-Hutchinson papers).
47 Dating as most of them did from before the Reformation, Irish country graveyards constituted a rare and quiet meeting place for the rival denominations. However, 'There is a Protestant Church in the Village of Glenealy with a burial ground attached. exclusively for the interment of members of that communion, who appear to be numerous, as the yard, tho' extensive, is well stocked with graves.' (Ordnance Survey Letter, written from Rathdrum 24 January 1839; see typescript summary, Wicklow, p. 119 (c. Ms. f. 365) in the Royal Irish Academy.
48 William Monck Mason, *History ... of ... the Cathedral of St. Patrick*. Dublin: Folds, 1820. pp. 98–99n. For the text of Charles I's grant of the Vicar's Choral (1640) see *ibid.*, pp. xxxvi–xlvi of the Appendix with a list of properties.
49 As late as December 1949, Revd Samuel Synge (brother of JMS) swore a statutory declaration re 8 Ely Place to the effect that he had never heard of any claim adverse to his title or the title of other family members to the Synge property (then being sold).
50 See Timony Stunt, 'John Synge and the Early Brethren', *CBRF Journal*, no. 28 (1976), pp. 39–41. Also *My Uncle John* p. 8.
51 NLI: Ms. 11,330 (1) Mary Tuke (servant to Mrs Synge), 8 September 1830 to Francis Synge, Glanmore. 'My mistress desired Mr Edward to tell you to keep two pounds out of this half year & two pound at next March 1831 for the use of poor Nurse Cullin who with her six Children are great objects [.] God Almighty will bless you Sir for your goodness to them.' Also John Synge to his children, 27 January 1832 writing from Dublin.
52 NLI: Ms 11,991.

CHAPTER 13 (pp. 127–132)
1 *Works* 2 p. 221 – 'The People of the Glens'.
2 'Albert Widman, of an old Suabian family ... purchased the estate of Hanstown from Lord Wharton in the reign of William III' (Burke's *Landed Gentry*, 1847, vol. 3, p. 278). He married Barbara Lyons, by whom he had Hans Widman. For Widman of Hanstown, County Westmeath, see memorials of 1718 onwards (e.g. DRD: Mem: 22: 322:12141 witnessed by Mary Widman). By 1733, the name is 'Wood alias Widman', and the latter name has disappeared by 1757. The Hans Wood of 1765 onwards is presumably from a younger generation.
3 A deed of assignment (20 March 1765) refers specifically to Hans Wood of Rosmead and his wife (Frances King), evidence that the property, if not the house, was already in his possession. The deed, witnessed by William Frizell, tided up outstanding details of the late Sir Henry King's estate, the surviving executor being Robert French (see DRD: Mem: 236: 317:154777). In 1781 Wood appears as a trustee of the marriage settlement for Hugh O'Reilly of Westmeath and his bride Catherine Mary Ann Mathew (a minor) of the notable Tipperary family (see DRD: Mem: 339: 348: 229034).
4 W. B. Yeats, 'Coole Park, 1929', in *Yeats's Poems* (ed. A. N. Jeffares). London: Macmillan, 1989. p. 358.
5 *The Complete Baronetage*, vol. 5 (1707–1800). Exeter: Pollard, 1906. pp. 410–411. Hans Widman had been the co-heir at law of John Wood of Rosmead who died c. 1733. The only other Widman I have traced is an Ensign of that name in Hope's Regiment of Foot (see PRONI: D. 108 and T.1060).
6 On the question of special provision, see the will of Mrs Sophia Synge (née Hutchinson, died 1799) which left only £200 in consols to her granddaughter Frances Synge, because she had been amply provided for by Samuel Hutchinson, formally bishop of Killala. (I rely here on Sir John Ainsworth's summary in Report No. 162.) The will was proved in the Canterbury Prerogative Court, 1799.
7 *Family*.

Notes

8 *Morning Post*, 15 September 1792.
9 I am grateful to Dr Mary Sokol, University of Sussex, for her detailed comment on the law in this connection and on Mrs Sophia Synge's will. Illegitimate children could not *inherit* until the 1969 Family Law Reform Act, so that any provision for them had to be made by way of *gift*. In this case, the testatrix is also taking great care to avoid problems which arose due to differences of definition with regard to illegitimacy as between the ecclesiastical courts and the Common Law.
10 The dash reproduced here is a lengthy one, and it occurs at a delicate point in the (copy of the) will. The term 'granddaughter' is accurate, and the next identification should be 'daughter of my said son ...' But the word 'daughter' has been anticipated and thus repeated in the manner reproduced here. Is this an unconscious transmission by the copyist of a hesitation or other emotion on the part of the testator?
11 Mornington is situated just east of Drogheda town, on the south bank of the Boyne estuary, a valuable property with commercial potential. Colp (as it is now spelled) lies further inland.
12 There may have been a degree of family kinship between the Synges and Darbys: John Nelson Darby's mother was Anne Vaughan; Archdeacon Synge's youngest sister, Mary (b. 1742) married William P. Vaughan of Golden Grove, King's County.
13 NLI: Ms. 17, 275 – entries for 12 December 1798, 24 and 31 January 1799.

CHAPTER 14 (pp. 134–156)

1 NLI: Ms. 17,275 – entries for 10 September and 2 October 1793, and 9 November 1794.
2 NLI: Ms. 17,275 – entries for 8 August 1807; 24 February, 14 May, 7 June, 15 August 1809.
3 TCD: Ms. 6206, undated draft letter. Mrs Synge's letter is dated 1 April 1809.
4 In 1821, W. Russell edited the *Sermons* of John Hough (1651–1743) who, as a stout protestant, had been ousted from the presidency of Magdalen by James II. A different William Russell, Moravian minister in Dublin, associated with many (including John Synge) who contributed to the establishment of the 'Plymouth' Brethren; see T. C. F. Stunt, *From Wakening to Secession: Radical Evangelicals in Switzerland and Britain 1815–35*. Edinburgh: Clark, 2000. p. 174.
5 TCD: Ms. 6206, Mrs Elizabeth Synge (in London) to John Synge (at Glanmore), 1 April 1809.
6 This was the widow of Major Arthur Wolfe (1786–1813) of the Kildare Militia, who gave birth to her child Elizabeth (died 1822) on 20 September 1813, that is less than a month after her husband's death.
7 TCD: Ms. 6205. Journal of John Synge, ff. 5–6.
8 TCD: Ms. 6205. Journal of John Synge, f. 24v.
9 See W. J. Mc Cormack, 'Language, Class and Genre', in Seamus Deane *et al.* (eds), *The Field Day Anthology of Irish Writing*. Derry: Field Day, 1991. vol. 1 p. 1101.
10 W. F. P. Napier, *A Letter to General Lord Viscount Beresford*. London: Boome, 1834. p. [3]. Beresford had foolishly got himself involved in a pamphlet skirmish twenty years after the events in which he was accused of playing a less than glorious part.
11 Journal of John Synge, f. 28 (15 April).
12 TCD: Mss. 6207–6209.
13 For some observations on Borromeo's nineteenth-century significance in literature and thought see the present writer's 'Introduction' to J. Sheridan Le Fanu, *Borrhomeo [sic], the Astrologer*. Edinburgh: Tragara Press, 1985. pp. 5–17.
14 Walter Benjamin, *The Arcades Project* (trans. Howard Eiland and Kevin McLaughlin). Cambridge, Mass.: Belknap Press, 1999. p. 648. I have reduced some editorial matter within the passage quoted, for the sake of immediate comprehensibility, a procedure Benjamin would have condemned out of hand.
15 *Ibid.* pp. 901 and 916.

Notes

16 'Goethe' [1928], in Walter Benjamin, *Selected Writings: Volume 2, 1927–1934* (trans. Rodney Livingstone *et al.*; ed. M. W. Jennings *et al.*). Cambridge, Mass: Belknap Press, 1999. pp. 183–184.

17 In the aftermath of R. L. Edgeworth's death, the family wished to get one of his sons into Charterhouse school, and succeeded with Grey's (by implication, financial) assistance; see M. Edgeworth to Charles Grey (1764–1845, 2nd earl, whig prime minister 1831), in Durham University Library.

18 See Mrs F. A. Edgeworth to Mary Sneyd, 18 January 1803: Christina Colvin (ed.), *Maria Edgeworth in France and Switzerland: Selections from the Edgeworth Family Letters*. Oxford: Clarendon Press, 1979. pp. 84–86. The editor of this volume observes cautiously in a footnote that many of Pestalozzi's 'practical ideas were evolved independently on an empirical basis by [the Edgeworths] and published in *Practical Education* (1798). Some ideas in RLE's later educational writing may have been influenced by Pestalozzi' (*ibid.* p. 86 n.1.) In fact, RLE specifically notes Pestalozzi in connection with the teaching of 'anatomy' to six-year-olds; see R. L. Edgeworth, *Essays on Professional Education*. London: Johnson, 1809. pp. 210–211.

19 It may seem that the novels by Maria Edgeworth cited in this paragraph scarcely lie far enough apart in time to permit the kind of radical development between them which Benjamin found in Goethe's Wilhelm Meister series. However, Edgeworth's fiction should not be tied to the dates of its publication: most of her significant work underwent extended periods of gestation, the points of origin lying in concealed earlier moments. See W. J. Mc Cormack, *Ascendancy and Tradition in Anglo-Irish Fiction from 1789 to 1939*. Oxford: Clarendon Press, 1985. pp. 97–168; and *idem*, 'The Tedium of History: An Approach to Maria Edgeworth's *Patronage*', in Ciaran Brady (ed.), *Ideology and the Historians*. Dublin: Lilliput Press, 1991. pp. 77–98.

20 W. Benjamin to G. Scholem [20 December 1931], *The Correspondence of Walter Benjamin 1910–1940* (ed. Gershom and Theodor W. Adorno; trans. Manfred R. Jacobson and Evelyn M. Jacobson). Chicago, London: University of Chicago Press, 1994. p. 388. The *document humain* to which Benjamin referred was probably Herman Escher (ed.), *Pestalozzi and His Times: A Pictorial Record*. Zurich: Buchdruckerie Berichthaus; London: J. M. Dent, 1928.

21 Kate Silber, *Pestalozzi, the Man and His Work*. London: Routledge, 1960. p. 2. For a more thorough biography in German, see Peter Stadler, *Pestalozzi: Geschichtliche Biographie* (2 vols). Zurich: Neue Zürcher Zeitung, 1993, especially vol. 2 pp. 466–473 for the Anglophone interest shown by such diverse figures as Maria Edgeworth, Robert Owen and John Synge.

22 See L. G. Seeger, *The 'Unwed Mother' as a Symbol of Social Consciousness in the Writings of J. G. Schloeer, Justus Möser, and J. H. Pestalozzi*. Berne: Lang, 1970. pp. 28–34.

23 Maria Edgeworth to Mrs Ruxton, 29 April 1820, and to Honora Edgeworth, 19 August 1820, in *Maria Edgeworth in France*, pp. 106, 222.

24 When Allen visited Ballitore School (the alma mater of Edmund Burke) in October 1826, he met Mary Lecky and her daughter (*Life*, vol. 2 p. 420). Among Orpen's circle of friends and supporters was 'Mr John Leckey': see C. Orpen, *The Claims of Millions of Our Fellow-Countrymen of Present and Future Generations to be Taught in their Own and Only Language, the Irish; Addressed to the Upper Classes in Ireland and Great Britain*. Dublin: Tims, 1821. p. 128.

25 De Vesci employed Louis Albert du Puget, a former pupil of Pestalozzi's, in his Abbeyleix school. See du Puget, *Intuitive Mental Arithmetic, Theoretical and Practical, on the Principles of H. Pestalozzi*. Dublin: Printed by William Folds, 1821. 244pp. (The TCD copy was once the property of John Synge.)

26 Charles Mayo, *Memoir of Pestalozzi* (2nd edn). London: Hessey, 1828. p. [1].

27 Kate Silber, 'Pestalozzianism in Britain and the United States', in *idem*, *Pestalozzi*, Appendix 1.

Notes

28 See *Report of the Proceedings at the Several Public Meetings held in Dublin by Robert Owen.* Dublin: Carrick, 1823. p. 39. The plate, 'A View of the Plan of Mr Owen's Proposed Village' faces p. 1. In the face of hostility, Owen and Cloncurry appear to have organised an impromptu Hibernian Philanthropic Society which met on 3 May 1823 in Morrison's Hotel. Archibald Hamilton Rowan was among those who attended.

29 Quoted in Silber, *Pestalozzi*, p. 291.

30 No connection has been established between this Harding (probably not a Quaker), and the family at Roundwood and Castle Kevin which features in the lives of John Hatch and J. M. Synge. In October 1826, Allen attended a Friends' meeting in Wicklow town, which he thought a low place though the surrounding county was attractive (*Life*, vol. 2 p. 419).

31 Emma Le Fanu, *Life of the Reverend Charles Edward Herbert Orpen, M. D.* London, 1860. p. 48. In William Allen, A Life ... London: , 1846. vol. 2 'about five hundred and twenty' schools were regarded as being in communion with Kildare Place in April 1820.

32 See Thomas Wyse, *Historical Sketch of the Catholic Association*), quoted in Hugh Kingsmill Moore, *An Unwritten Chapter in the History of Education, Being the History of the Society for the Education of the Poor of Ireland, Generally Known as the Kildare Place Society 1811–1831*. London: Macmillan, 1904. pp. 92–93. Francis Wyse took part in one tumultuous meeting at New Ross, County Wexford, when between two and three thousand people crammed into the unfinished Catholic chapel to hear a debate; see Philip Dixon Hardy, *A Full and Impartial Report of the Prooceedings at New Ross, Convened by the Roman Catholic Magistrates and Gentry of that Town to Oppose the Bible and Kildare-St. Schools.* Dublin: R. M. Tims, [n.d.].

33 Richard Davis, *Revolutionary Imperialist, William Smith O'Brien, 1803–1864.* Dublin: Lilliput Press, 1998. p. 25.

34 Allen, *Life*, vol. 3 p. 164.

35 See *ibid.* vol. 2 pp. 431–433 for the text of this letter, dated 19 January 1827.

36 Edgeworth to Allen, 19 January 1827, in Allen, *Life*, p. 432; Allen had been in Ireland several times before he received this admonition.

37 Any reassessment of Maria Edgeworth is hampered by the curious way in which her vast correspondence was edited in the twentieth century, with two volumes selected on the basis of Edgeworth's travels outside Ireland, and the great bulk of her letters left unpublished. Marilyn Butler's *Maria Edgeworth, a Literary Biography* (Oxford, 1972), out of print for many years, deserves revision and republication.

38 E.g. 15 July 1831 when both Daniel and Maurice O'Connell spoke against these provocations to violence.

39 George Vicesimus Wigram, *Memorials of the Ministry of G. V. W.* London: Brown, 1881. vol. 1 p. [iii]. For his influence at Avondale, see R. F. Foster, *Charles Stewart Parnell: The Man and His Family.* Hassocks: Harvester, 1976. p. 129.

40 See my 'Between Burke and the Union: Reflections on PRO: CO.904/2', in John Whale (ed.), *Burke's Reflections on the Revolution in France: New Interdisciplinary Essays.* Manchester: Manchester University Press, 2000. pp. 60–93.

41 J. H. Pestalozzi, *Letters on Early Education Addressed to J. P. Greaves ... With a Memoir of Pestalozzi.* London: Sherwood *et al.*, 1827. p. xxiv (of the memoir).

42 [John Synge], *A Biographical Sketch of the Struggles of Pestalozzi.* Dublin: Folds, 1815. p. 6, n.

43 Synge, *Sketch*, pp. xvi–xvii.

44 See [John Synge,] *The Relation and Description of Forms, According to the Principles of Pestalozzi. Part I, with four Copper-plate Engravings.* Dublin: Sold by Martin Keene, Bookseller, College Green – Thomas Bowes, 67 Lower Gardiner Street – and at the Committee House for Charitable Societies, 16 Upper Sackville Street, 1817. 106, 64, 38pp. (with 1 folding plate at rear). The verso of the title-page reads 'Entered at Stationers Hall.' and 'George P. Bull, Printer: Roundwood, Wicklow.' The final page of the second

Notes

sequence carries the imprint 'G. P. Bull, Printer, Roundwood, Co. Wicklow.' The final leaf of the third sequence bears errata. That three pagination sequences were used indicates the experimental nature of the enterprise. The TCD copy has an informal bookplate with 'John H Synge' (i.e. John Hatch Synge, the dramatist's father) printed in an oblong frame of links with a crown in each of the four corners.

45 For Thomas Lewis O'Beirne and the Union, see W. J. Mc Cormack, *The Pamphlet Debate on the Union Between Great Britain and Irland 1797–1800*. Dublin: Irish Academic Press, 1996.

46 See F. E. Bland, *How the Church Missionary Society Came to Ireland*. Dublin: Church of Ireland Printing and Publishing Company, 1935. p. 129.

47 The four are: i) [John Synge], *Pestalozzi's Intuitive Relations of Numbers*, Part I (with a large table). Sold by Martin Keene, Bookseller, College Green – Thomas Bowes, 67 Lower Gardiner Street – and at the Committee House for Charitable Societies, 16 Upper Sackville Street, 1817. 240pp. The title-page version reads 'Printed by G. P. Bull, Roundwood, Co. Wicklow.' (TCD copy presented by R. A. Synge in October 1935.) ii) *ibid*. Part II. 154pp. iii) *ibid*. Part III. Containing the Use of the First Table of Fractions (with a large Plate), 1818. 180pp. iv) *ibid*. Part IV. Containing the Use of the Second Table of Fractions (with a large Plate.) Dublin: Sold by R. M. Tims, 85 Grafton Street (opposite Duke Street), 1819. 192pp.

48 T.C. F. Stunt, *From Awakening to Secession; Radical Evangelicals in Switzerland and Britain 1815–35*. Edinburgh: Clark, 2000. pp. 150, 173. For the item of 1828, see *The Infant School Teacher's Assistant on Pestalozzian Principles, No. 1: Lessons on the Bead Table or Arithmometer*. Teignmouth: sold by L. B. Seeley and Son; Seeley and Burnside, London; and R. M. Tims, Dublin, 1828. The copy of this 12-page pamphlet in pink wrappers, preserved in TCD library, is inscribed 'Jane Synge a Present from dear Papa'.

49 For Isabella Synge's role on the Ladies Committee of the ISPENIML, see the preliminaries to Charles Orpen's *The Claims of Millions* (1821).

50 Verse three has special appeal to hard-pressed academics; it promises 'the long Sabbatic morrow'.

CHAPTER 15 (pp. 157–167)

1 *Fool*, pp. 160–171, which also establishes that JMS had read 'Rosmerholm' in a German translation; see also Frank McGuinness, 'John Millington Synge and the King of Norway', in Nicholas Grene (ed.), *Interpreting Synge; Essays from the Synge Summer School 1991–2000*. Dublin: Lilliput, 2000. pp. 57–66. In 1951 Jan Setterquist had observed a debt to 'Rosmersholm' in Synge's 'Riders to the Sea'; see his *Ibsen and the Beginnings of Irish Drama* (2nd edn). New York: Gordian Press, 1974. pp. 332–335.

2 Cherrie Matheson's reminiscences of JMS are cited in *Fool*, p. 187: it should be conceded that her memory, as well as his, is questionable.

3 See W. J. Mc Cormack, *From Burke to Beckett: Ascendancy, Tradition and Betrayal in Literary History*. Cork: Cork University Press, 1994. pp. 94–122.

4 Introduction (p. xii) by Douglas Grant to C. R. Maturin, *Melmoth the Wanderer*. London: Oxford University Press, 1968. Grant is mistaken in locating these scenes on the west coast of Ireland, just as he misjudges the theological orientation of the Church of Ireland. He is, however, acute in recognising that the novel is more concerned with the initiating place of action than has previously been acknowledged. The novel's dedication – 'to the most noble the Marchioness of Abercorn …' – refers to Lady Anne Jane Gore (1763–1827), daughter of the 2nd earl of Arran and widow of Henry Hatton of Clonard, County Wexford, whom the 1st marquis of Abercorn (John James Hamilton) had taken as his third wife in 1800. His lordship's second wife (his cousin, Cecil Hamilton) left him and was divorced: their daughter married the 3rd earl of Wicklow in 1816.

Notes

5 Maturin, *Melmoth*, p. [7].
6 Ibid., *Melmoth*, pp. 256–257 nn. William Hamilton (c. 1755/1757–1797) was the son of a merchant ship's captain, John Hamilton (c.1725–1780); see the biographical notice prefacing the son's *Letters Concerning the Northern Coast of the County of Antrim*. Belfast: Simms & M'Intyre, 1822.
7 [Anon.], *The Absentee: a Poem*. Dublin, Milliken, 1830. p. 37.
8 C. R. Maturin died in October 1824; see *The Annual Biography and Obituary for the Year 1826*, vol. 10. London: Longman, 1826. p. 450.
9 NLI: Ms. 17, 725 – entries for 20 December 1799 and 18 February 1810.
10 Maturin, *Melmoth*, p. 257 n.
11 Sigmund Freud, 'Moses and Monotheism', in *The Penguin Freud Library Volume 13: The Origins of Religion*. Harmondsworth: Penguin, 1985. pp. 345, 381.
12 Maturin, *Melmoth*, p. 26.
13 A recent short study of the Protector's Irish reputation suggests that J. P. Prendergast's *The Cromwellian Settlement in Ireland* (1865) 'did more than any [other] book to create and perpetuate nascent nationalist perceptions of the man, while conceding that 'numerous folk-tales which centre on Oliver Cromwell ... connect him with the Devil'. See Jason McElligott, *Cromwell, Our Chief of Enemies*. Dundalk: Dundalgan Press, 1994. pp. 17,15.
14 REBECCA (*gathers her crocheting*): They cling to their dead here at Rosmersholm.
MRS HELSETH: If you want my opinion, miss, it's the dead who cling to Rosmersholm.
Henrik Ibsen, *Plays: Three* (trans. Michael Meyer). London: Methuen, 1988. p. 32.

CHAPTER 16 (pp. 168–183)
1 Henrik Ibsen, *Brand* (trans. Michael Meyer. London: Eyre Methuen, 1967. p. 93.
2 Quoted from notes in *Stephens*, TCD: Ms. 6206.
3 W. Elfe Tayler (ed.), *Passages from the Diary and Letters of Henry Craik*. London: Shaw, n.d. p. 109 (entry for Monday 10 August 1829).
4 *Family*, pp. 20–21. Of the three daughters, only Jane (1825–1895) is assigned a year of birth. The several published versions of *Stephens* differ oddly in placing John Hatch Synge on the family tree, the first edition (1959) describing him as the third son, and the second (1989) as the fourth son – p. 4 in each edition.
5 Elfe Tayler, *Henry Craik*, pp. 116, 113.
6 Ibid., p. 119.
7 Elfe Tayler, *Henry Craik*, pp. 122–123. According to the editor, a new edition, revised by Edward Hodges of Bristol, was published in 1864.
8 John Synge to Miss Bridson, 29 December 1831, quoted in *My Uncle John*, p. 9.
9 See editorial note in *My Uncle John*, p. 10.
10 For a good account of the period, see Desmond Bowen, *The Protestant Crusade in Ireland 1800–1870*. Dublin: Gill & Macmillan, 1978. esp. pp. 62–67.
11 See T. C. F. Stunt, *From Wakening to Secession: Evangelical Radicals in Switzerland and Britain 1815–1835*. Edinburgh: Clark, 2000.
12 R. S. Brooke, *Recollections of the Irish Church*. London: Macmillan, 1877. pp. 34–35.
13 I give the title as indicated on the standard-sized (octavo) version. This declared itself published in London and sold there by various booksellers, including Seeley; Dublin distribution was effected through R. M. Tims of Grafton Street, a bookseller strongly committed to 'bible education' and controversial pamphleteering. The author's name was given as Parens. The printer was Barnett, of Teignmouth (as indicated on the verso of the title-page). It is likely that Synge did not set the type (Barnett's task) but did participate in printing sheets. Three distinct pagination sequences (64, 56, 46pp) suggest that the work was assembled over a period of time.
14 Ibid. pp. iv–vi.

Notes

15 The Early Printed Books Computerised Catalgue in TCD ascribes all of the titles following to John Synge, gives 'c. 1832' as a date, and implies Clash (i.e. Ballinaclash) as the place of publication/printing: (1) Alphabet Lessons; (2) Hymns for Children; (3) [Lesson Sheets, 6 items in all]; (4) Lessons on Geography 1–17; (5) Reading Lessons from the Instructor; The Three Kingdoms of Nature; (6) Reading Lessons of One Syllable. Given the bulk of material and the limited means of production, it can be accepted that printing was sustained over a period of at least one year. No evidence of Ballinaclash as a place of publication has ever been adduced, and evidence on the broadsheets themselves clearly indicates Glanmore as the printing press's location.

16 Information on Rhind derives for the most part from the anonymous *Faithful Unto Death: A Memoir of William Graem Rhind*. London: Yapp, [1863]. see p. 28 re Cambridge.

17 *Faithful Unto Death*, p. 41.

18 *Ibid.*, p. 43.

19 *Ibid.*, pp. 44–46.

20 Documentation preserved by Moore, Kiely & Lloyd (Solicitors), Dublin.

21 Quoted in *Faithful Unto Death*, p. 49. I have been unable to trace a copy of the original handbill.

22 W. G. Rhind to W. R. O'Byrne, 5 November 1844. BL. Add Ms. 38,051 f. 52.

23 TCD: Ms. 7225.

24 The inscription is cut in small capitals, thus eliminating the issue of spelling Lord, etc., with or without an initial capital; punctuation is largely effected by line-breaks with some consequent syntactical looseness. To avoid excessive emphasis, quotation here is given in lower case lettering. Another plaque in the Nun's Cross church commemorates Lieutenant-Colonel R [sic] Casement of the Royal Field Artillery who died 21 December 1917 aged 53.

25 See F. R. Coad, *A History of the Brethren Movement*. Exeter: 1968. p. 58 n. 39; A. J. Gardiner, *The Recovery and Maintenance of the Truth*. Stow Hill Bible and Tract Depot. p. 50.

26 I am grateful to Howard Caygill for showing me an unpublished paper on 'Leadership and Schism among the Exclusive Brethren' from which I have drawn some of this material.

27 See correspondence from G. S. Herbert (stockbroker) to Gardiner, 11 October 1890, etc., in NLI: Ms. 11,329 (1).

28 Adolphe Monod, *The Way of Patience Better than that of Secession*. London: Seeley, 1850.

29 For example, *l'Eglise du Dieu Vivant* (etc.). Nîmes: Boissier; Vevey: Prenleloup; Paris: Meyrueis; Lausanne: Duret, 1860. 120pp. A summary (and hostile) history of Darby's impact in this sphere of Francophone protestantism may be found in G. Nicole and R. Cuendet, *Darbysme et Assemblées Dissidentes*. Neuchatel: Delachaux et Niestlé, [1962].

30 See the article in Paul Harvey and J. E. Heseltine (eds) *The Oxford Companion to French Literature*. Oxford: Clarendon Press, 1959. pp. 99–100.

31 'Wherefore come out from among them, and be ye separate, saith the Lord, and touch not the unclean thing, and I will receive you.'

32 Anon., *'Exclusivism' Unveiled: A Handbook of Sixteen Questions on the Tenets Peculiar to Darbyism*. London: Macintosh; Dublin: Herbert, 1872. pp. 5 & 9. Edward Nagle (1799–1883), an evangelical pillar of the Established Church condemned 'the unscriptural schism of Plymouthism' saying that it was equal to that of 'Popery': Nagle, *Revision of the Prayer Book*. Dublin: Robert White, [n. d.] p. 8.

33 No modern, independent study of the widespread stigmatic, hysterical and pentecostal phenomena has been attempted. But for an account written from within the Irish Presbyterian establishment at the time, see William Gibson, *The Year of Grace: A History of the Ulster Revival of 1859* (jubilee edition). Edinburgh, London: Oliphant, [1909].

34 There had been earlier initiatives, associated in England variously with Charles Kingsley, F. D. Maurice and E. V. Neale. The founding of the Guild of Saint Matthew in 1877 is sometimes thought of as the moment of renewal, linked through Stewart Headlam, with

Notes

the Fabian Society.
35 Quoted by Stunt, in *From Wakening to Secessions*, p. 164.
36 *Ibid.*, pp. 164–165.
37 Francis William Newman, *Phases of Faith*. Leicester: Leicester University Press, 1970. p. 17.
38 Eric Hobsbawm, 'Identity History is Not Enough', in *idem, On History*. London: Weidenfeld & Nicolson, 1997. pp. 351–366.
39 See W. J. Mc Cormack, *From Burke to Beckett: Ascendancy, Tradition and Betrayal in Literary History*. Cork: Cork University Press, 1994. pp. 123–163.

CHAPTER 17 (pp. 186–193)
1 Small advertisement taken by John Hugo in *The Wicklow News-Letter* (24 July 1858, etc.).
2 Joseph Robins, *The Lost Children: A Study of Charity Children in Ireland 1700–1900*. Dublin: Institute of Public Administration, 1980. p. 32. See also *Commons Journal of Ireland*, vol. 15 pt (431) cciii.
3 Fanny Taylor, *Irish Homes and Irish Hearts*. London: Longmans, 1867. pp. 5–6. Taylor founded the Order of the Poor Servants of the Mother of God, and was known by her name in religion as Sister (later Mother) Mary Magdalen.
4 RCBL: P. 251/5/1. All material relating to Dunlavin derives from this source, unless otherwise stated.
5 Diarmuid Mac Iomhair, 'The Family of Hatch of Ardee', *Journal of the County Louth Archaeological Society*, vol. 16 (1968) p. 211. The *Belfast News-Letter* of 20 November 1855 records the marriage of Rose Anna Mary Hatch (of Wicklow) to Patrick Moore (of Raheny, County Dublin); while it is not clear how seemingly mobile combinations of Christian names can be resolved to identify individual daughters, the appearance of the item in a Belfast newspaper suggests surviving links between the Wicklow Hatches and their northern kinsfolk. A further marriage recorded in the same paper (20 February 1854) – Adelaide Bryant Hatch to Dr T. H. Dillon – adds to the family's involvement with professional medicine.
6 Harold O'Sullivan, 'Ardee Dispensary Minute Book, 1813–1851', *Journal of the County Louth Archaeological Society* loc. cit., pp. 5–27. In 1832, when cholera broke out in Ardee as everywhere else, the Board of Health then established included William Hatch, Dr Hatch's brother.
7 Minutes of Rathdrum Union, 1 January 1850 (vol. 6 p. 186). John Synge's son, Francis, who played an occasional role in local administration was absent when Hatch's appointment was approved.
8 A death notice in the *Belfast News-Letter*, 20 May 1858, for Thomas William Hatch of Akyab, East Indies; note the inversion of Christian names between the death notice and the commemorative tablet. This branch of the Hatches seems to have had a cavalier attitude to nominal order.
9 See *First Half-Yearly Report Presented to the Mining Company of Ireland*. Dublin: printed by Chambers and Hallagan, 1825. Among the directors was Whitley Stokes, of Trinity College, Dublin.
10 In the 1830s, one traveller observed that 410 people in 63 houses lived in 'wretched, dirty and filthy habitations' on the east side of the valley; see Des Cowman, 'The Mining Community at Avoca, 1780–1880', in *Wicklow Essays*, pp. 761–788.
11 See 'John Gower, Roundwood Park to Dublin Castle, 4th July 1843', *Roundwood and District History and Folklore Journal*, no. 9 (1997) p. 12.
12 The description is taken from an unidentified source in William Nolan, 'Land and Landscape in County Wicklow c. 1840', *Wicklow Essays*, p. 685; for the skeleton discovered on 2 June 1874, see Ken Hannigan, 'Violent Death in 19th Century Wicklow', *Wicklow Historical Society [Journal]*, vol. 1, no. 7 (July 1994) pp. 28–29.

Notes

13 'People and Places', in *Works* 2, p. 195.
14 Documentation in Moore, Kiely & Lloyd (Solicitors), Dublin.
15 See Document 25 in Mac Iomhair, 'The Family of Hatch of Ardee', p 221.
16 *Irish Generalogical Sources No. 1*. Dun Laoghaire: Dun Laoghaire Genealogical Society, 1997.

CHAPTER 18 (pp. 194–200)
1 For Lynch, see *Irish Book Lover*, July/August 1936, pp. 84–85.
2 NLI: Ms. 11,991.
3 NLI: Ms. 11,991.
4 Journal of Caroline Synge, 9 February 1842: TS (copy) in the possession of Richard Synge, quoted by permission of Robert and Jane Tottenham (gratefully acknowledged).
5 UCD Archives: S6/28/37.
6 The last quoted phrase is taken from the calendar of the Synge-Hutchinson papers in UCD rather than from the will itself.
7 See Joseph Robins, *Fools and Mad: A History of the Insane in Ireland*. Dublin: Institute of Public Administration, 1986. p. 69. See also *Administration*, vol. 7, no. 2, pp. 146–165.
8 Documentation preserved in Moore, Kiely & Lloyd (Solicitors), Dublin, and quoted by kind permission of their client, Ms U. Brown (Donegal). The property was said to be held under a lease from the Vicars Choral of Saint Patrick's Cathedral.
9 See *Fool* pp. 55ff.

CHAPTER 19 (pp. 201–208)
1 Stanza Two of 'To Ireland' by SMM, dated August 1872 when the author – see n. 12 below – was in Ireland.
2 Eva Ó Cathaoir, 'The Poor Law in County Wicklow', in *Wicklow Essays*, p. 538. I shall be repeatedly indebted to this lengthy article (*ibid.*, pp. 503–579) in the pages which follow. See also the more narrowly focused piece by the same author, cited in n. 8 below.
3 Ó Cathaoir, 'The Poor Law in County Wicklow', pp. 510–511.
4 Details of Union minutes are taken from records preserved by Wicklow County Council; for access to these I am grateful to Joan Kavanagh and Mary Fitzpatrick. The disciplining of Captain Stewart (the Master) occurred in August 1844.
5 Rathdrum Union Minutes, vol. 5, pp. 15–16 (25 January 1848).
6 It is possible that Isaac Flower was connected with the Kilkenny family of the same name, ennobled as viscount Castledurrow; Henry Hatch had been closely associated with them in the early part of his career. In 1668, a Captain Flower was listed in the Hearth Money Rolls as a resident of Wicklow town.
7 The most notable member of this Wicklow family was Robert Manning (1816–1897), who worked (1856–69) as an engineer for the marquis of Downshire, and then moved to the Board of Works. See Joseph Robins, *Custom House People*. Dublin: Institute of Public Administration, 1993. pp. 72–74.
8 Eva Ó Cathaoir, 'Rathdrum Workhouse, Part I (1838–1888)', *Wicklow Historical Society [Journal]*, vol. 1, no. 4 (July 1991), pp. 11–12.
9 Rathdrum Union Minutes, vol. 6, pp. 148–150 (11 December 1849).
10 Ó Cathaoir, 'The Poor Law in County Wicklow', pp. 518, 520.
11 *Ibid.*, p. 526.
12 *Ibid.*, pp. 529, 526, 523.
13 David Thomson and Moyra McGusty, *The Irish Journals of Elizabeth Smith*. Oxford: Clarendon Press, 1980. p. 229.
14 Ó Cathaoir, 'The Poor Law in County Wicklow', p. 533. (The figures cited relate to the year 1881.)

Notes

15 Rathdrum Union Minutes, vol. 2, p. 114 (20 February 1844); these minutes were signed by John Synge, grandfather of JMS.
16 Ó Cathaoir, 'The Poor Law in County Wicklow', p. 549.
17 For Jane Elliott, see *Wicklow News-Letter*, 6 October 1866. The Rathdrum Union Minutes (vol. 39, p. 130v, etc.) noted Captain Truell's involvement in the Ashford Cholera Dispensary (26 November 1866), through which Dr John Hatch appears to have augmented his annual income (a quarter of salary being listed as £22). The nuns are therein described as Infirmarian Sisters; see also *Wicklow News-Letter*, 1 December 1866.
18 *United Ireland*, 2 October 1886, p. 2 and supplement. I am grateful to a speaker at the Irish Historians in Britain conference, Brighton, 2000, for a spirited account of the episode.
19 F. C. Devas, *Mother Mary Magdalen*. London: Burns Oates, 1927. pp. 376, 355.

CHAPTER 20 (pp. 210–220)
1 *Works* 2, pp. 218–219 – 'The People of the Glens' from which the epigraph for this chapter is also taken.
2 Mary C. King (ed.), 'J. M. Synge's When the Moon Has Set', *Long Room*, nos 24 & 25 (1982), p. 19.
3 *Ibid.* p. 20.
4 John D'Alton records a memorial in Bath Abbey to a Costello family which had prospered in Spain: this is no longer to be seen being, we conclude, covered by the floored pews since installed. A second memorial (near the porch), commemorating Bartholemew Costello who died in 1806, links him to the barony of Costello in Mayo.
5 See *Fool* pp. 232–235. It is possible that the gentry were present simply because the funeral coincided with the usual Morning Service, hardly a normal practice.
6 'When the Moon Has Set', p. 35.
7 *Wicklow News-Letter*, 2 January 1864. The victim's name appears to have been Townley. A 'tramp-painter' was probably an itinerant tradesman who made something of a living by painting farm sheds, etc.
8 'When the Moon Has Set', p. 18.
9 *Ibid.*, p. 21.
10 *Ibid.*, pp. 32–33.
11 *Ibid.*, p. 23.
12 *Works* 3, pp. 171–173.
13 *Ibid.*, pp. 165, 175.
14 *Ibid.*, p. 173.
15 *Ibid.*
16 Mary C. King, *The Drama of J. M. Synge*. London: Fourth Estate, 1985. pp. 160–196.
17 *Works* 3, p. xv.
18 *Ibid.*
19 *Ibid.*, p. 21.
20 *Ibid.*, p. 173. Stage directions have been omitted in order to focus on Mary's contradictory utterance about unbirth.

CHAPTER 21 (pp. 221–225)
1 See *Fool*, p. 229.
2 David Grene and Richmond Lattimore (eds), *Sophocles II*. Chicago: University of Chicago Press, 1969. p. 16.
3 See *Fool*, pp. 233–238 for an analysis of the origins of 'In the Shadow of the Glen' with reference to the death of Winterbottom and another Wicklow shepherd.

Notes

CHAPTER 22 (pp. 226–240)

1 The fullest account is Angela Bourke, *The Burning of Bridget Cleary: A True Story*. London: Pimlico, 1999. Bourke, however, relied on Hubert Butler's essay 'The Eggman and the Fairies', in *idem*, *The Sub-Project Should Have Held His Tongue and Other Essays*. London: Penguin, 1990. pp. 102–112.
2 E. F. Benson, 'The Recent "Witch-Burning" at Clonmel', *The Nineteenth Century* (June 1895).
3 *Fool*, p. 314.
4 *Works* 4, p. 97.
5 Bourke, *The Burning*, p. 42. In this account it is not conclusively established that Bridget Boland (as she then was) attended the Sisters of Mercy convent in Drangam, but the presumption seems reasonable.
6 Butler, 'The Eggman', p. 104.
7 *Works* 4, pp. 170–171, incorporating a word from drafts preceding Synge's final text.
8 For James Lynchahaun's attack on his employer (and lover?) Mrs Agnes MacDonnell in October 1894, see *Fool*, pp. 254–255.
9 Bourke, *The Burning*, pp. 115, 121, etc.
10 'Pat' (i.e. Patrick Kenny], in *Irish Times*, 30 January 1907, reprinted in James Kilroy (ed.), *The Playboy Riots*. Dublin: Dolmen, 1971. p. 38.
11 For an intriguing account of modern literary utopianism see Fredric Jameson, 'Of Islands and Trenches', in his *Ideologies of Theory: Essays 1971–1986. Volume 2, Syntax of History*. London: Routledge, 1988. pp. 75–101.
12 'In the Shadow of the Glen', *Works* 3, p. 41.
13 Jameson, 'Of Islands and Trenches', p. 89.
14 Brian MacDermot, *Leigh of Lara': A Romance of a Wicklow Vale*. Dublin: M. H. Gill; London: Simpkin, Marshall, 1899. p. 10.
15 See *Fool*, pp. 123–124 for a transcript including various cancelled words and phrase. The notebook entry cannot be dated precisely.
16 MacDermot, *Leigh of Lara'*, pp. 10–11.
17 *Ibid.*, p. 114.
18 *Ibid.*, p. 23.
19 *Ibid.*, p. 9.
20 *Ibid.*, p. 134.
21 Major Bookey of Derrybawn, a friend of the young C. S. Parnell, was drowned in 1875, which may have facilitated MacDermot in using the name of the estate for fictional purposes.
22 John H. Edge, *An Irish Utopia*. Dublin: Hodges, Figgis and Co., 1906, p. 61.
23 Standish O'Grady, *All Ireland*. Dublin: Sealy, Bryers & Walker, [1898].
24 Edge, *An Irish Utopia*, p. 23.
25 Bourke, *The Burning*, p. 136.
26 See William Nolan, *Fassadinin: Land, Settlement & Society in South East Ireland 1600–1850*. [n. p., n. d.] and William E. Hogg (ed.), *The Millers & Mills of Ireland, 1850: A List*. Sandymount: Hogg, 1998.
27 'Rathdrum is a town in Ireland; it would be merely a village in England', Edge: *An Irish Utopia*, p. [1].
28 *Ibid.*

CHAPTER 23 (pp. 241–247)

1 *Works* 2, p. 3.
2 The writings of Louis Marin are highly suggestive as a starting point for further inquiry along these lines; see his *Utopics, Spatial Play* (trans. R. A. Vollrath), Atlantic Highlands:

Notes

Humanities Press, 1984, but also *Etudes sémiologiques* (Paris: Klincksieck, 1971) and *Sémiotique de la Passion* (Paris: Aubier Montaigne, 1971). I have examined JMS's debt to the American Nicholson in *Fool*, pp. 246–249.

3 George O'Brien, 'Who Fears to Speak', *Times Change* (Dublin), no. 20 (Summer 2000), pp. 27–29.
4 Jean-Paul Sartre, *The Family Idiot, Gustave Flaubert*. Chicago: Chicago University Press, 1981. vol. 1, p. x.
5 For an analysis of *Letters to My Daughter*, see *Fool*, pp. 6–7, 414–418.
6 The suggestion was made by the poet, Brian Lynch, following the publication of *Fool* in 2000.
7 See *Fool*, pp. 283–286. Lebeau disappeared to a teaching post in South America, taking with him (one presumes) JMS's side of their correspondence; his papers have yet to be traced.
8 G. E. Lessing, *Laocoön, an Essay on the Limits of Painting and Poetry* (trans. E. A. McCormick). Baltimore: Johns Hopkins University Press, 1984. p. 8.
9 See Paul Rabinow (ed.), *The Foucault Reader*. New York: Pantheon Books, 1984. p. 179.
10 See *Fool*, pp. 430 and 481.

A PERSONAL APPENDIX (pp. 249–253)
1 Richard Synge, of Cambridge, in private communications. I am grateful to Mr Synge for his generosity and courtesy.
2 Sources of this kind, quoted in *The Silence of Barbara Synge*, are available in publicly accessible libraries, notably Trinity College, Dublin, the National Library of Ireland, and the Public Record Office of Northern Ireland. In most cases, these papers were donated by publicly spirited members of the families concerned.
3 See *Fool*, pp. 71–73.
4 See also *Fool*, pp. 409–415.

Index I

General index

Wicklow place-names, members of the Hutch and McCracken families, and members of the Synge family are indexed separately (Indexes II–IV). Unless otherwise indicated cross-references are to the corresponding index; 'n' after a page reference indicates a note number on that page.

Abbey Theatre, 19, 226, 239, 253
Action française, L', 180
Acton, Thomas, 41
Acton, Thomas, 202
Acton family, 34, 98, 207
Adams, Robert M., vi
Addison, Joseph, 144
Agar, Charles, 124
Ainsworth, Sir John, 123, 271n44
Allen, Henry, 55
Allen, William, 146, 147, 149, 274n24
Allgood, Molly, 243, 244
Ancienne dissidence, 173
Anderson, George, 170
Anderson, Mary, 169
anonymous communications, 73; 76, 83, 85–86, 91
Archer family, 212
Ardee (Louth), 12, 25, 26–29, 30, 31, 58, 88, 89, 92–94, 168, 188, 189, 204, 281n5, 281n6
Aspel, Widow, 25
Augustan tradition, 38, 55
Austen, Jane, 160

Bach, J. S., 200
Bacon, Francis, 249

Ball, Benjamin, 48
Ball, John, 123, 124
Barnett (printer), 174, 175
Barny, Mr and Mrs, 102
Barrington, Sir Jonah, 270n28
Barton, Anna Maria, 237
Barton, Hugh, 235
Barton, Robert Childers, 237
Barton, Thomas (Johnson), 236
Barton family, 8, 22, 48, 212, 235, 236
Beethoven, Ludwig, 241
Belton, John, 42
Benjamin, Walter, 24, 65, 141–143
Benson, E. F., 226
Bentham, Jeremy, 146
Beresford, J. C., 115
Beresford, W. C., 137–138, 139, 145, 165, 273n10
Beresford, William, 139
Berkeley, George, 34
Bertie, Robert, 61
Bewley, Samuel, 146
Blount, John, 128
Blundell, Anna Maria, 32, 90, 116
Blundell, Mary, 31
Boccaccio, 164
Boileau, J. Theophilus, 267n7

Index I

Boileau, Magdalane, 94, 95
Boileau, Simeon, 267n4
Boileau, Solomon, 94
Bonafous, M., 103, 134
Bonham, John, 59, 92
book trade, 150, 151, 152–153, 175, 230, 275–276n44
Bookey family, 236, 282n21
Booth family (of Laragh), 212
Borromeo, Carlo, 140, 273n13
Boucicault, Dion, 240
Boundary Commission, 8
Bourne, Daniel, 37
Bowen, Elizabeth, 8
Boxol, Jane, 118
Boyle, James, 25
Brady, James, 53
Brady, Mr (labourer), 85
Bridgnorth (Shropshire), 1, 2, 4, 68, 128, 145
Brien, James, 48
Brocas, Mr, 99
Brontë, Charlotte, 63
Brooke, R. S., 173, 174
Broomfield, John, 75
Brown, Zacharias, 89
Browne, Albert William, 192
Browne, Mrs, 89
Buckridge (Devon), 168, 170, 171
Bull, George P., 151, 152–153, 175
Burbridge, Margaret, 75
Burke, Edmund, 150, 164, 274n24, 275n40
Burke's Irish Families, 128
Burke's Landed Gentry, 5, 62, 64, 122, 160
Burke's Peerage, 128, 271n39
Burney, Frances, 162
Bury, Phineas, 128
Butler, Hubert, 227
Butler, Samuel, 229
Butt, Isaac, 54, 202, 270n23

Caldwell, Hannah Tynte, 188, 192
Calvin, Jean, 180, 181

canal investment, 71
Carey, Hugh, 196, 252
Carey, Mat, 196
Carpenter, Andrew, 31
Carpenter, Catherine, 68
Carr, Sir John, 100–101
Carrickmacross (Monaghan), 73, 89
Carroll, Mr, 84–85
Casement family, 155
Castell, Alexander, 93, 95
Catholic emancipation, 28, 125, 154, 168, 176, 207, 263n50
Celtic Revival, 6, 27
Charter Schools, *see* Incorporated Society
Chartism, 179
Chateaubriand, F. R. (vicomte de), 149, 158
Cheney, Bradson, 27
Childers, H. C. E., 237
Childers, Robert Caesar, 236, 237
Childers, Robert Erskine, 237
Childers family, 8
Clarkson, Thomas, 88, 90
Cleary, Bridget, 225, 226–229, 235
Cloyne (Cork), 2
Coffey, John, 4
Colclough, John, 119
Coleman, William, 202
Coleman family, 195
Coleridge, S. T., 149, 158, 166
Collins, Michael, 8
Collins, Thomas, 175
Collins, W. W., 229
Complete Baronetcy, 62, 127
Concordia Society, 80
Connolly, James, 23
Connor, Cornelius, 22
Cooke, William, 192
Cooper, Edward, 66
Cooper, Joshua, 61
Cooper, Richard, 66
Cooper, Richard Synge, 64
Cooper, William, 152

General index

Coppinger family, 31
Corbut (or Corbett), Miss, 88
Corry, Isaac, 115
Costello, James, 212
Costello, Susan, 206
County Councils, 221
Craig, Maurice, 103
Craik, Henry, 169–170, 207
Critchley, Mr, 55
Croker, T. Crofton, 270n23
Cromwell, Oliver, 2, 26, 28, 166, 277n13
Cullin, Nurse, 125–126, 272n51
Curtis, Jane, 3
Cunningham, Robert, 20, 22, 53
Cuthbertson, James, 27, 192, 193
Cuthbertson family, 23

Dalton, Christopher, 23
Dalton, John, 29
Daly, Robert, 146, 171, 181, 182
Darby, J. N., 21, 44, 132, 153, 178–183 *passim*, 273n12
Darby, John, 132
Darby, Susannah, 181
Davis, Eliza, 45, 260n29
decadence, vi, 4, 7, 215
Decluzeau, Revd, 28
degeneracy, 214–215
Delany, Mrs Mary, 271n45
Delemere family, 23
Delemere, Isaac (or Delemor), 83, 265–266n5
Depositions (of 1641), 25, 33
De Valera, Eamon, 23, 103
De Vesci, *see* Vesey
Dickens, Charles, 230
Dingley, Rebecca, 40
disestablishment (church), 7
Doran, Mr, 204
Dowse, Mr, 48
Downshire estates, 32
Doyle, James Warren, 172; in *An Irish Utopia*, 236
Doyle, Phoebe M., 200

Drogheda, 1, 25, 273n11
Dublin Foundling Hospital, 42, 45
Dublin Society, The, 54, 55
Dublin University Magazine, 28–29, 270n23
Duff, Mr (of Liffey Street and/or Cope Street), 78, 79, 80
Dunne, Jack, 238
Du Puget, L. A., 274n25

Eadin, Widow, 75
Ecclesiastical Commissioners, 198
Edge, John H., 4, 172, 230, 231, 236, 239
Edgeworth, Anne, 2, 3, 108, 163
Edgeworth, Mrs Frances Anne, 142, 267n18
Edgeworth, Francis, 2
Edgeworth, Maria, 1, 2, 51, 103, 142, 144, 145, 148–149, 155–156, 158, 160, 162, 205, 239, 274n17, 274n19, 275n37
Edgeworth, R. L., 51, 142, 143, 148, 149, 174, 274n17, 274n18
Eliot, T. S., 249
Elliott, Jane, 206, 281n17
Ellwood, John, 34
Ely, marquis of, 208
Emerson, Mrs Catherine, 90, 102
Emerson, Thomas (alderman), 89–90, 98–99, 101, 155, 160, 230
Emmet, Robert, 157, 161
Encumbered Estates Court, 7
Erasmus Smith School (High School Dublin), 51
evangelicalism, 6, 19, 44, 132, 152, 153, 154, 175, 176, 207; and good works, 177
'Evil, The', 259n25
evolution, 214, 215, 228

Family of Synge, The (1937), 64, 122, 169, 171, 196, 262n20, 271n39
family trees, vi, 25, 197; of Synge, 3, 5; of Hatch, 35

Index I

famine, 7, 103, 155, 169, 176, 177, 194, 197, 202, 207; Brethren behaviour during, 178, 181; in *An Irish Utopia*, 236–237; Rathdrum Union during, 203
Fenton, Mrs (née Swift), 33–34, 40
Ferguson, Samuel, 29, 105–106
Fetherston, Revd Thomas, 46
Fichte, J. G., 145
Fitzgerald, Lord Edward, 239
Fitzgerald, Henry, 121–122
Fitzgibbon, Elizabeth, 139
Fitzgibbon, John, 101, 138–139
Fitzwilliam Estates, 239
Flaubert, Gustave, 242–243, 245
Fleming, Richard, 74, 101
Flood, Henry, 69, 73, 253
Flower, Isaac, 203–205, 280n6
Flower, William, 39
Flower family, 203, 259n3, 280n6
Foot, Lundy, 92, 93
forgery, 83, 84, 85
'49 Officers, 25, 30–31
Foster, Anthony, 33
Foster, James (miller), 47, 48, 49
Foster, John (Lord Oriel), 28
Foucault, Michel, 224, 246
Foundlings, 42–43, 186–187, 204
Fourier, Charles, 141, 143
Fox, Mary, 36
Fraser, Robert, 54–55, 155
Freeman, Harriet, 27
Freeman, Mary Harriet, 188
Freeman, Mr (of Tomdaragh), 19
Freeman, Miss (of Tomdaragh), 75
Freeman, Robert, 120
Freeman, Simeon, 188
Freemartin twins, 65–66, 213, 262n25
French, Robert, 34, 116, 124, 131, 137
French, Robert (jnr), 134, 137
French, Mrs, 100
Freud, Sigmund, 157, 159, 165–166, 167, 250
Frizell family, 36, 55, 189, 233, 272n3

Fröbel, Friedrich, 143

Gaelic language, 3, 21, 105, 174, 269n25
Gardiner, Luke, 34, 73, 106
Gardiner, T. W., 179, 196; for Mrs Gardiner, *see* Index IV, Synge, Mrs Francis
Garnett family (Meath), 62
Gautier, Mme, 145
Gay, John, 38
Gentry republicanism, 8, 237
Giffard, Lady Martha, 39, 40
Giffard, Thomas, 39
Gladstone, W. E., 237
Godwin, William, 121, 158, 163
Goethe, J. W. von, 142, 274n19
Goldsmith, Oliver, 101
Gonne, Henry, 59
Gonne, Iseult, 23, 193
Gonne, Maud, 23, 59, 193, 206
Gonne, Thomas, 59
Goodwin, Michael, 153
Gordon, Mr (of Lissenhall), 52
Gore-Booth, Sir Robert, 64–65
Goring family, 65–66
Gower, John, 190
Grangegorman (hospital), 204, 224
Grattan, Henry, 19
Green, J. A., 145
Gregory, Augusta (Lady), 1, 6, 28, 226, 230, 239
Grey, Charles (2nd earl), 142, 274n17
Grey, Jo, 118
Griffith, Arthur, 253
Griffith's Valuation, 189, 194
Groves, A. N., 169
Guinness (of Roundwood), 99

Hamilton, Alexander, 152
Hamilton, C., 106
Hamilton, Elizabeth, 151
Hamilton, Hugh, 152
Hamilton, Isabella, *see* Index IV, Synge, 1st Mrs John

General index

Hamilton, Sophia, 271n45
Hamilton, William, 161, 163, 277n6
Harcourt Street (Dublin), 51, 52, 72, 74, 104, 117, 120, 124, 198, 199, 200
Harding, Edward Henry, 189
Harding, Harry, 36, 275n30
Harding, John, 36
Harding, John (of Wicklow), 83
Harding, Joseph, 120
Harding, Widow, 83
Harding, William, 146
Hardy, Thomas, 235
Harris, Walter, 34
Harrison, Thomas, 48
Harvey, Bagnal, 118–119
Hatch Castle (Ardee), 10 (illus.), 28
Hatch Street (Dublin), 177, 191–192
Hatton, Mary, 89
Hatton, Mr, 85
Hatton, Thomas, 39
Hatton, Thomas, 120
Hatton, William, 39, 89
Hayes, Samuel, 101, 267n38
Hebrew, 87, 170, 173–174, 277–278n13
Hegel, G. W. F., 182
Hely Hutchinson, Coote, 199
Hely Hutchinson, Francis, 198
Hely Hutchinson family, 72
Hibernian Church Missionary Society, 152
Hill, Arthur (Lord Kilwarlin, then 2nd marquis of Downshire), 68, 69–70, 72, 114, 122, 257n29
Hill family (Down), 31, 32, 68
Hobsbawm, Eric, 182–183
Holt, Joseph, 22, 54, 113–114, 119, 162, 260n12; his Memoirs, 270n23
Home Rule, 8, 180, 194, 202, 237
Hore, Edward, 35, 61, 68
Hore (or Hoare) family, 35, 58, 68, 256n20, 258n40
Houghton, John, 42
Houghton, Thomas, 25
Housing of the Working Classes Act, 42, 253

Howard, Charles (duke of Norfolk), 31
Howard, John, 43, 64, 66
Hugo, John, 186
Hugo (or Hugou), Thomas, 22, 48, 49, 50, 54, 55, 77–78, 119, 260n12, 264n8, 265n5
Hugo, Thomas W., 191
Hume, Gustavus, 95
Hutchinson, Sir Francis, 32–33, 45, 64, 102, 105, 112, 123, 130, 153; maps of, 257n32, 270n22
Hutchinson, Sir James, 112
Hutchinson, Samuel, 34, 64, 109, 130, 161, 271n45
Hutchinson, Sophia, *see* Index IV, Synge, Mrs Sophia
Hutchinson, William, 85
Huxley, Margaret, 189

Ibsen, Henrik, 23, 78, 84, 157, 167, 168, 215, 216, 225, 277n14
identity, 2, 5, 8, 158, 205, 242
Ievers, Peter, 29
Incorporated Society, 34, 35, 40–45 *passim*, 47, 51, 64, 73, 98, 109, 153, 175, 206, 230; carriers for, 74
initialled only communications, 60, 61, 85–86
insanity, 210, 213, 215, 222, 228
Irish Citizen Army, 23
Irish Free State, 8, 253
Irish Society, 105, 153, 160
Irving, Edward, 154, 173

Jacobitism, 29, 31
Jameson, Fredric, 158, 230, 270n29
Jean Paul, 141
Jebb, Sir Henry, 70
Jeffreys, Mrs Arabella, 137–139, 145
Jeffreys, James St John, 138
Jeffreys, Marianne, 139
Jennings, Charles, 86
Jews, Judaism, 6, 143, 158, 164, 165, 175; *see also* Hebrew

Index I

Johnson, Esther, 39, 40
Johnston, Francis, 155, 199
Johnston family, 23
Joyce, James, 1, 6, 7, 8, 9–10, 237, 245, 247

Kane, Nathaniel, 73
Kavanagh, Edmund, 41, 42
Kavanagh, Terance, 48
Kells (Meath), 29–30, 73, 79, 84, 88;
    parish records, 266n11; poor of, 82
Kelly, William, 180
Kemmis, William, 202
Kemmis family, 21
Kempis, Thomas a, 173
Kenny, Patrick, 228
Kerwin, Michael, 19
Kierkegaard, Søren, 182
Kildare Place Society, 146, 148, 154, 172,
    275n31, 275n32
Killala, diocese of, 161
Kilwarlin, Lord, *see* Hill, Arthur (2nd
    marquis)
King, Frances, *see* Wood, Mrs Hans
King, Mary C., 219
King, Robert (vsc. Kingsborough, 2nd
    earl of Kingston), 121, 122, 127
King's County (now Offaly), 31, 33, 58,
    59, 71, 109, 115, 132
Kingsborough family, 31, 119, 121,
    270n22
Kingsmill Moore, Hugh, 275n32
Kipling, Rudyard, 247
Klopstock, F. G., 144
Kneller, Godfrey, 38

Laffarty, James, 47
Lambert, Mr, 122
Land War, 239
landownership as reality, 179
Lansdowne, Lord, 32
La Touche, David, 92, 93
La Touche, James Digges, 160
La Touche, John, 93
La Touche, Mrs Peter, 160

Lavin, Mary, 8
Lawless, Valentine (2nd baron
    Cloncurry), 146, 275n28
Lawrence, D. H., 29
Lawrence family (of Roundwood), 85
Lebeau, Henri, 244
Lecky family, 145, 274n24
Leersen, Joep, 2
Le Fanu, Emma, 147
Le Fanu, Joseph Sheridan, 165, 167,
    273n13
Le Fanu, Thomas, 165
Legislative Independence, 69
Lely, Sir Peter, 40
Lessing, G. E., 245
licenses (for guns, pubs etc.), 221–222
Linen Board, 98
L'Isle Adam, Villiers, 113
Lissenhall (Co. Dublin), 52, 59, 61, 62,
    72, 74, 78, 109
Lloyd, Humphrey, 75
Local Government Act (1898), 221
Loti, Pierre, 157
Lowe, Revd Christopher, 50
Lynch, Brian, 283n6
Lynch, Thomas, 194
Lynchahaun, James, 226
Lynn, Kathleen, 23

MacBride, Maud Gonne, *see* Gonne
McCarthy, Senator Joe, 244
Mc Cormack, C. E., 253
MacDermot, Brian, 230–236 *passim*, 239
MacDonnell, Mary, *see* Index IV, Synge,
    Mrs George
McGuinness, Frank, 157, 167, 216, 276n1
McKenna, James, 202
MacKenna, Stephen, 243
MacLeod, J. A., 200
McQuaid, J. C., 8
madness, *see* insanity
Magdalen College, Oxford, 102–103,
    125, 134, 135
Magee, William, 168, 172

General index

Manners, Charles (4th duke of Rutland), 101
Manning, Ambrose, 236
Manning, Bernard, 204
Manning, Dr, 204
Manning, Francis, 189
Manning, James, 204
Manning, Joseph, 203
Manning, Ralph, 203
Manning, Robert, 280n7
Manning, Samuel, 189
Manning, William, 204
Manning family, 114, 203, 240
Manwaring, Thomas, 74
Manzoni, Alessandro, 230
Martyn, Edward, 6
Marxism, 7–8, 180–181, 207, 245
Mason, Joseph, 36
Matheson, Cherrie, 157, 244, 276n2
Mathew family, 121
Maturin, 'Aunt', 163
Maturin, C. R., 20, 158–165 *passim*
Maturin, Miss E. M., 162–163, 230
Maturin, G. J., 34
Maturin, Henry, 161
Maturin, Peter, 160–161, 163
Maturin, 'Uncle', 163
Maturin, William, 52
Maurras, Charles, 180
Mayo, Charles, 145
Meade, William, 30–31
Meade family, 30
Meath, Lady, 206
Melmoth the Wanderer (Maturin), 158–164 *passim*; dedication of, 269–277n4; and Synge family, 166
Memorials of the Dead, 66
Mercer, Samuel, 74
Mercy, Richard, 75
Milliken, Richard, 138
Milltown, Lord, 93
Minerva Press, 158
mining, *see under* Wicklow
Modernism, 29

Monck, Anne, 61
Monck Mason, William, 125, 272n48
Mooney, 'Big' Peter, 195
Mooney, 'Little' Peter, 195
Moore, George, 1, 6, 8
Moore, Marianne, 31
Moore, Michael, 31
Moore, Robert (glazier), 47
Moore, Thomas, 20
moral agency, 7, 175
More, Sir Thomas, 229
Morgan, George, 34, 106
Motherwell, Robert, 113
Municipal Reform Act (1840), 28
Murdock, Miss, 207
Murphy (servants), 129
Murphy, James and Susan, 118
Musgrave, Sir Richard, 45, 115

National Education system, 176
National Library of Ireland, 6, 33, 46, 123
Needham, Thomas N., 198
Neville, Jacob, 74
Newman, Frank, 182–183
Newman, John Henry, 182
Nicholson, Asenath, 206, 242
Nietzsche, Friedrich, 29, 215
Nordau, Max, 215
Norris, Richard, 102
Nugent, George Frederick, 139
Nuttall, Mary, 46

O'Beirne, Thomas, 152, 276n45
O'Brien, Sir Edward, 148
O'Brien, George, 242
O'Brien, William, 208
O'Brien, William Smith, 148
O'Byrne, Fiach Mac Hugh, 4
O'Byrne, Mr, 178
O'Carolan, Torlough, 4
O'Casey, Sean, 8, 193, 200, 246
O'Connell, Daniel, 125, 154–155, 168, 275n38

Index I

O'Connor, Frank, 8
O'Doherty, Miss, 3
O'Faolain, Sean, 8; 'A Broken World', 9–10, 18, 19–20, 38, 73, 108, 113, 134, 194
O'Flaherty, Liam, 8
Ogilvy, Mary, 203
O'Grady, Standish James, 20, 237
O'Kelly, Sean T., 99
Orange Order, 153, 190, 194
Ordnance Survey, 29, 191, 272n47
Ormsby, John, 102
O'Rourke, Mr, 203
Orpen, C. E. H., 145, 146–147, 148, 269n25
Ossory Clerical Association, 152
Owen, Robert, 14, 146, 155, 181, 229, 275n28

Paine, Tom, 51
Parnell, C. S., 8, 22, 91, 149, 194, 202, 239
Parnell, Sir John, 263n50
Parsons, Sir Lawrence, 115
Pastorini, Prophecies of, 172
Pearse, Patrick, 253
Pennefather, Edward, 181, 182
Peppard, Henry, 31
Peppard, Nicholas, 31
Peppard, Thomas (MP), 31
Percivall, Mary, 94
Persse family, 1
Pestalozzi, Carl, 145
Pestalozzi, J. B., 144
Pestalozzi, J. H., 7, 44, 107, 125, 141–147 *passim*, 150–151, 154, 155, 160, 169, 174, 181; influence on Edgeworths, 274n18
Petty, Sir William, 33, 257n32
Philoctetes, 242, 245
Pim family, 146
place-names, 21
Platonov, Andrei, 241
Plunkett, James, 8

Plymouth Brethren, 7, 19, 21, 87, 107, 132, 149, 152, 154, 169, 172–174, 207; anti-territoriality, 173, 177; origins of, 173; the splits of 1848 and 1879, 178–179;
Pollard, Thomas, 74, 99
Pollard, William, 74, 99
Pollard family, 23
Ponsonby faction, 67
Poor Law Commission, 201, 203, 221
Poor Servants of the Mother of God, 208
Pope, Alexander, 38
Portarlington, 103, 134
Pound, Ezra, 29, 147
Power, John, 30
Power, John Hatch, 30
Prendergast, J. P., 256n2, 277n13
Price, Liam, 21, 22
Pritchard, Thomas, 36
Pro-Cathedral (Dublin), 6
Protestant ascendancy, 28, 164–165, 183
Protestantism, 2, 7
Proud, Jane, 3
Pue's Occurrences, 18
Pullen, Mary, 25

Quin, Henry, 61
Quin, Wyndham, 128

Radcliffe, Mrs, 158
rates of pay, 47–48
Rathmines School, 26, 193
Rawlings, J., 106
Reading, Daniel, 34
Reading family, 258n38
Reformation, 3, 21
Regency crisis, 70
Reilly, Mary, 199
Rhind, W. G., 175–178, 189, 191, 202, 205, 207
roads, 20, 50–55 *passim*, 77, 260n5
Roberts, Samuel, 177, 191
Robinson, David, 237

General index

Rooney, Edward, 40, 83–84, 99
Rooney, Mrs Edward, 40, 83, 85
Rooney, James, 83–84, 85, 86, 91
Ross, Robert, 119
Ross, Robert (d. 1918), 158, 166
Rousseau, J. J., 143
Rowan, A. H., 275n28
Royal Irish Academy, 152
Russell, Matthew, 208
Russell, William, 135
Ruxton (magistrate), 28
Ruxton, Ann, 93–94
Ruxton, Ann (Baroness Kilwarden), 103, 163
Ruxton, John, 93
Ruxton family, 103, 204

Saddlemyer, Ann, 217
Saint Patrick's Cathedral (Dublin), 4, 12 (illus.), 22, 62, 66, 104, 109, 116, 123, 125, 187, 200, 275n48
Saint Sepulchre, 65, 66–67, 93, 104, 116, 136, 198
Sartre, Jean-Paul, 242
Schleiermacher, Friedrich, 149, 158
Scoffier, Revd Lewis, 73, 253
Scott, Walter, 20, 68, 230
Scullabogue (Wexford), 118
Shaw, George Bernard, 1, 6, 231
Sheehan, Daniel, 228
Sheridan, Thomas, 34
Shiel, Isaac, 60, 85
Shiel, James, 59, 60, 92, 261n11
Shute, Mr, 137
Sinn Féin, 253
Sister Julia, 207
Sister Marcella, 207
Sisters of Mercy, 206–207
Smalley, Caleb, 75
Smith, Elizabeth, 205
Smith, James, 48
Smith, Thomas, 48
Smyth, Isabella, 94
Smyth, Thomas, 100

Société des Étudiants Protestantes, 181
Sophocles, 224, 225, 246
Spanish Inquisition, 161
Stearne, Henry, 23
Steele, Frances, *see* Index IV, Synge, 2nd Mrs John
Stephens, Revd David, 41–42, 50, 77, 89, 98
Stephens, Henry Colclough, 119, 123; *see also* Index IV for Stephens family
Stephens, James, 246
Stephens, William, 270n19
Sterne, John snr, 46
Sterne, John jnr, 46
Sterne, Laurence, 21, 46, 98
Sterne, Richard, 46
Stewart, Mrs, *see* Index IV, Synge, 2nd wife of Francis (MP)
Stock, Joseph, 161
stroke (in childbirth), 63
Stuart, Francis, 23, 193, 232
Stuart, Iseult, *see* Gonne, I.
Stuart family (of Roundwood), 33; *see also* Index III
Sutton, John, 84
Sutton, John, 204
Sutton family, 23, 86, 268n12
Swift, Jonathan, 4, 7, 28, 33, 34, 38, 39, 46, 187, 245
Swords (Co. Dublin), 58, 66, 67, 70, 86, 92, 104, 109, 115, 120–121, 123–124, 126, 198
Synnot, Mr (teacher), 41

Tagmon (Wexford), 58
Taylor, Fanny, 208
Teignmouth (Devon), 169, 175
Temple, Henry (viscount Palmerston), 33
Temple, Henry (3rd viscount Palmerston), 94
Temple, Sir John, 25, 33, 38–39, 108, 154, 163

Index I

Temple, the Hon. John ('Jack'), 34, 39, 40, 41, 44, 73, 98
Temple, Sir William (d. 1627), 38
Temple, Sir William (d. 1699), 7, 39
Thompson, Joseph, 119–120
Thom's Directory, 189
Tillotson, John, 43, 119, 124
Tims, R. M., 152, 175
Tone, T. W., 113, 163
Toole, Clothilda, 50
Tottenham, Charles, 53
Tottenham, Col. Charles, 202
Trench, Elizabeth, 3, 59
Truell family, 264n6; *see also* Index IV, Synge, Mrs Francis (née Truell)
Tuke, Mary, 272n51
Turnbull, Mary, 31
Turnpike roads, 51

Ulster, 238
Ulster Rebellion (1641), 2
Ulster Revival (1859), 181, 278n33
Union (act of etc.), 8, 53, 54, 103–104, 120–121, 143, 149, 150, 151, 152, 157, 158, 207, 237, 263n50, 275n40, 276n45
United Ireland, 208
United Irishmen, 54, 118, 119–120, 157, 161, 207, 221
Usher, Robert, 19

Vesey, John (2nd viscount de Vesci), 145, 146, 181, 274n25
Voltaire, 58

Waller, Mr, 25
Walpole, Horace, 158
Waterloo, Battle of, 135, 149, 165
Weekes, Revd Ambrose, 37, 50–55 *passim*, 77, 101, 120, 160, 236, 265n5
Weekes, Mrs Ambrose, 101, 160
Weekes, Frances May (alias Stephens), 50, 268n12

Weekes, James, 50
Weekes, William Sutton, 50, 268n12
Wellesley, Arthur (duke of Wellington), 137, 139–140, 165, 172, 236
Weston, Galen, 99
Wexford, 22, 113, 117, 155, 162, 208
White, Ann, 94, 95
Whiteboys, 139
Whitmore, Joy, 74
Wicklow (county), 4, 7, 8, 18–23 *passim*; cholera, 177, 186, 192, 206, 211; development of, 101, 210; as fictional setting, 158–159, 161, 276n4; gaelic spoken, 19, 106; 'Irish Reformation' in, 183; map of (part), 16; mental illness in, 44, 210, 213, 215, 239; mining in, 55, 101, 189–191, 229, 279nn9–10; parliamentary constituencies, 197; Petty's maps of, 257n32; Poor Law provisions, 201–202, 210; rebellion and, 19, 102, 113, 127, 155; sexuality in, 205–206; Temple property in, 39, 73, 94, 259n3; vagrancy in, 201, 210; *see also* Index II
Wicklow Tenants' Association, 202
Widman (later Wood) family, 121, 127, 272n2
Wigram, G. V., 149, 275n39
Wigwell, Mr, 213–214
Wilberforce, William, 149
Wilde, Oscar, 1, 6, 92, 158, 219
William III, 38, 39
Williams, Adam, 61, 74, 77, 85, 86, 261n10, 262n27
Williams, Ann, 203
Williams, Raymond, 7–8, 10, 245
Wilson, Edmund, 247
Wingfield, Theodosia viscountess Powerscourt, 177, 182, 207
Wingfield family, 22, 48
Winterbottom, John, 225

General index

Wisdom, Revd John, 266n12
Wisdom, Robert, 84–85, 86, 266n12
Wolfe, Arthur, lord Kilwarden, 102, 137, 161, 163, 164
Wolfe, Arthur, 137
Wolfe, Mrs Arthur (widow), 137
Wolfe, Elizabeth, 103
Wolfe, Margaret, *see* Index IV, Synge, Mrs Robert
Wolfe, Marianne, 137
Wolfe, Richard, 137
Wolfe, Theobald, 163
Wollstonecraft, Mary, 121, 270n31
women as source of credit, 94
Wood, Frances, *see* Index IV, Synge (later Synge Hutchinson), 1st wife of Samuel
Wood, Hans, 127
Wood, Mrs Hans (née Frances King), 121

Wood, Robert, 121–122
Wood family, 121
Woods, Anthony, 75
Wordsworth, William, 20
Wright, Thomas, 28
Wybrants, William, 48
Wyse, Thomas, 147
Wyse, W. C. B., 147

Xemenes, Charles, 23
Xemenes, John, 23, 255n7

Yarner, Abraham, 259n3
Yeats, Revd John, 64–65
Yeats, William Butler, 1, 4–5, 6, 7, 8–9, 27, 28, 29, 55, 59, 103, 113, 122, 127, 221, 226, 228, 229, 230, 238, 239–240, 244, 252
York Street (Dublin), 42–43, 65, 73, 80–81, 106, 120, 125, 200, 253

Index II

Wicklow place-names

Aghowle, 196; rent-roll of 1832, 196
Altidore, 155
Annamoe (or Animo), 21, 22, 36, 37, 46–49 *passim*, 50, 51, 75, 189–190, 196, 212, 231, 235
Arklow, 19, 22, 43, 44, 45, 74, 206
Ashford, 107, 155, 207, 211, 281n17
Aughavanna, 46
Avoca, 19, 101, 190, 279n10
Avonbeg (river), 22
Avondale, 21, 202

Ballagh, 193
Ballinaclash, 278n15
Ballinacor North, 16 (map), 21, 22
Ballinacor South, 21, 193
Ballinacorbeg, 21, 47, 51–52, 89
Ballinagonéen, 23
Ballinatone, 8, 23
Ballycullen, 196
Ballycurry, 155
Ballynacor, 39, 76, 202
Baltinglass, 205
Bray, 20, 197
Brockagh, 190, 235; in fiction, 233, 234; list of miners, 191

Calary, 21, 23, 181, 182
Camadery, 191
Carrarasticks, 193
Castle Kevin, 21, 23, 37, 40, 189, 211, 233, 240

Castle Sallagh, 130, 187
Clonmannon, 48, 196, 207
Clorah and Clorah Cottage, 175, 176, 177, 191
Coolmodry, 32, 257n31
Cronelea, 45
Cronemore, 8
Cronroe, 155

Delgany, 20, 213
Derrybawn, 236
Derrylossary, 22, 37, 41, 50, 75, 86, 98, 100, 102, 190, 268n12
Devil's Glen, 22, 53, 105, 119, 154, 162, 175, 211
Djouce Mountain, 23
Donard, 194
Drumgoff, 21
Drumeen (or Drummin), 22, 48, 235–236, 237, 264n8
Dunlavin, 43, 186, 187, 188, 189, 190, 192
Dunran, 119

Enniskerry, 19, 20, 21, 22, 100, 181, 182; *see also* Powerscourt

Gibbstown, 197
Glanmore, 5, 14 (illus.), 22, 45, 72, 100, 101, 104–105, 106, 124, 125, 126, 132, 135, 153, 154, 155, 171, 182, 186, 194; education in, 148, 173–175; eve-of-famine account, 107;

Wicklow place-names

Francis Johnson works on, 124;
and *Melmoth the Wanderer*, 162;
mystical incident, 178; quarry, 202;
rent-roll of 1832; re-purchased, 169;
Synges no longer occupants, 226
Glassnamullen, 23, 73, 74, 75, 80–81;
tenants of, 82, 86, 264n3
Greenane, 22, 55
Glen of the Downs, 53
Glendalough, 18, 19, 21, 22, 55, 188, 190–191
Glendalough House, 237
Glenealy, 125, 136, 272n47
Glenmalure, 22, 23, 36, 46, 229, 237
Glenmouth, 22, 53, 105, 124, 162
Greystones, 252

Kelshamore, 197
Kilfee, 45, 105; printing at, 153
Killiskey, 136, 153, 194, 202
Killough House, 8
Kilmacurragh, 98, 207
Kilpeddar, 155
Knockanarrigan, 197
Knockrath, 231

Laragh, 22, 54, 188, 190, 230, 231
Laragh Castle, 23, 189, 232
Laragh East, 22, 189
Leitrim, 98; *see also* Roundwood
Lough Nahanagan, 46, 189
Luganure, 189–190
Luggala, 155

Macreddin, 8
Moneystown, 40

Newcastle, 16 (map), 93, 183
Newtownmountkennedy, 20, 22, 101, 139, 183
Nun's Cross, 13 (illus.), 107, 125, 136, 153, 183

Paradise Glyn, 22
Powerscourt, 19, 100, 171, 173, 175

Rathdown, 21, 42, 203, 205

Rathdrum, 19, 21, 22, 282n27; Poor Law Union etc, 188, 189, 192, 202–204, 208, 212, 224, 225, 246, 280n2, 280n8–10, 280n14–16
Rathnew, 210
Rathsallagh, 187
Rossanagh, 155
Roundwood, 8, 12 (map), 13 (illus.), 22, 33, 36, 40, 42, 46, 51, 53, 54, 61–62, 73–79 *passim*, 80–91, 92, 98, 100, 105, 106, 113, 124, 127, 147, 153, 154, 155, 168, 182, 188, 190, 194, 202, 212; 'the curious beast' in, 127, 252; description of in 1778, 99–100; in 1798, 120; and *Melmoth the Wanderer*, 162, 166–167; printing in, 150–151, 163; receipts etc., c. 1752, 269n26; rent-roll in 1832, 195; tenants of, 85
Rustyduff, 197

Seven Churches, 22, 191
Shillelagh, 20, 193, 206
Sugar Loaf Mountain, 211

Templestown (school), 41–42, 43, 44, 47, 74, 82, 98, 105, 153, 175, 207; closure, 99; M'Cracken's bequest, 80; pupils, 75; teachers, 84
Tiglin, 114
Tiglin South, 194
Tinahely, 20
Tinnepark, 75
Tochar, An, *see* Roundwood
Tomdaragh, 19, 75, 188
Tomriland, 22, 120, 188, 194–197, 202; in JMS's literary development, 252; rent-roll in 1832, 195; as sign, 196; tenants, 195
Tynte Park, 187

Vartrey (river), 53

Wicklow (town), 19, 37, 44, 46, 75, 78, 88, 275n30
Woodenbridge, 19

Index III

Members of the
Hatch and McCracken families

Bowles, Elinor, 80, 82, 265n1

Edwards, Edward, 79
Edwards, Sarah, 80, 82

Hatch (of Dublin, 1640), 25
Hatch (freemen of Dublin), 261n2
Hatch (of Duleek), 257n21
Hatch (of Dundalk), 58
Hatch (of Sycamore Alley), 25
Hatch, Adelaide Bryant, 279n5
Hatch, Ann (Ardee, 1760), 26
Hatch, Ann (Ardee, 1793), 27, 188
Hatch, Ann (Mrs Boyle), 25
Hatch, Mrs Ann, 25
Hatch, Anna Maria, 188
Hatch, Benjamin, 25
Hatch, Bridget, 26
Hatch, Mrs (Brookville), 26
Hatch, Mrs Catherine, 25
Hatch, Charles, 25, 80, 82
Hatch, Christopher, 258n42
Hatch, David (Dublin), 25
Hatch, Debby, 26
Hatch, Dorothy, *see* Index IV, Synge, 2nd wife of Samuel
Hatch, Mrs Dorothy (née Reading), 34, 35
Hatch, Edward (Ardee), 26
Hatch, Elizabeth (Mrs Hore), 35
Hatch, Elizabeth (Mrs Power), 30

Hatch, Elizabeth (d. of John Hatch of Kells), 80, 82
Hatch, Elizabeth, *see* Index IV, Synge, 1st wife of Francis
Hatch, Mrs Elizabeth (formerly Widow Hore), 34, 35
Hatch, George, 25
Hatch, Mrs H (Blackrock), 26
Hatch, Mrs Harriet (née Freeman), 27
Hatch, Henry, 4, 23, 31–33, 39, 40, 68, 76, 257n27; died, 33, 59, 71; marriages, 34, 35, 58, 250; relationship to M'Cracken, 36, 73, 74, 75, 213; and Roundwood, 41, 47, 53
Hatch, Henry (of Kells), 267n36
Hatch, James (Kells), 29, 79, 81, 82, 83
Hatch, Jane (d. of Dr J. Hatch), 188
Hatch, Mrs Jane (née Pepper), 27
Hatch, Mrs Jemima, 30
Hatch, Jeremiah, 27
Hatch, Jeremiah (jnr), 27, 188
Hatch, Jeremiah (b. 1797), 27
Hatch, Jeremiah Anthony, 188
Hatch, Jeremiah Simon, 188
Hatch, John (1690), 29
Hatch, John (Ardee, 1717), 26
Hatch, John (Ardee, 1760), 27
Hatch, John ('49 Officer), 25, 26, 29
Hatch, John (of Kells), 80
Hatch, John (d. 1819 'an Honest Man'), 27

Members of the Hatch and McCracken families

Hatch, John (doctor), 27, 186–193 *passim*, 232, 235, 240; appointed to Laragh, 279n7; children, 188; civil and religious marriages, 188; in Dunlavin parish, 187; property dealings, 192

Hatch, John (MP), 3, 7, 11, 23, 24, 25, 26, 29, 74, 101, 154, 160, 173, 192–193, 200; administers M'Cracken's affairs, 78, 81, 83, 136; as ancestor of JMS, 6; anonymous letters to, 83; and Blundell/Downshire estates, 59, 61, 67, 71, 114; and Blundell family, 31, 58; canal development, 71; career in Commons, 69–70, 83, 150; church property, 120, 124, 125; corresponds with Francis Synge, 260n2; death, 8, 20, 68, 71–72, 114; debts, 59, 92–95 *passim*, diary, 11 (illus.), 61–62, 65, 67, 213; Dublin property development, 51, 67, 104; elected to Commons, 58, 69, 92; enters TCD, 35; as executor of will, 267n36; freeman of Dublin, 261n2; and Glanmore, 105; grants land to Elizabeth Synge, 66; and Hill family, 32, 65, 122; and Incorporated Society, 65; inheritance from M'Cracken, 80–81, 213; at Lincoln's Inn, 35–36; marriage, 5, 22, 47, 59–60, 71, 75, 250; name in yeomanry lists, 71; obituary, 257n4; pays for London trip, 68–69; preferred residences, 74; on road development, 50, 51–53; and Roundwood, 22, 33, 44, 46–47, 53–54, 73, 79, 100, 106, 134, 155, 162; Saint Sepulchre's Liberty, 65, 66–67, 93, 104, 116, 136, 198; succeeds his father, 33; (in)testacy, 104, 106, 114, 115, 117, 123; uncertain date of birth, 66; unknown grave, 50

Hatch, (Revd) John, 25, 36
Hatch, John (of St Michan's), 25
Hatch, John (s. of George), 25
Hatch, John (Middlesex), 36
Hatch, John (s. of Dr J. Hatch), 188
Hatch, John Anthony Freeman, 193
Hatch, Jonathan, 82
Hatch, Jonathan, 27
Hatch, Joseph, 80, 82, 86
Hatch, Joseph (West Arran St.), 193
Hatch, Joyce (Kells), 29
Hatch, Margaret (New Street), 25
Hatch, Mark, 30
Hatch, Mark Pendry, 30
Hatch, Mary (Ardee), 26
Hatch, Mrs Mary, 25
Hatch, Mary Harriott [sic], 188
Hatch, Minnie, 30
Hatch, Nicholas, 25
Hatch, Nicholas (1840s), 26
Hatch, Nicholas Stephen, 30
Hatch, Richard (Ardee), 27
Hatch, Richard (Dublin), 25
Hatch, Mrs Rose (née Williams), 27
Hatch, Rose Anna Mary, 279n5
Hatch, Rose-Anne, 27, 192
Hatch, S., 29
Hatch, Samuel (of Kells), 80, 82, 86
Hatch, Samuel, 36, 52, 74, 85, 86–87, 88, 91, 92, 263n37; accounts for London trip, 68–69, 110–111
Hatch, Samuel (of Ballagh, Co, Wicklow), 193
Hatch, Sarah, 26–27
Hatch, Susannah, 36
Hatch, Terence, 27
Hatch, Thomas, 27, 58
Hatch, Thomas (d. 1778), 27
Hatch, Thomas (MB), 27
Hatch, William, 80
Hatch, William (d. 1769), 27
Hatch, William (b. 1795), 27, 28, 192
Hatch, William Thomas, 188
Hatche, William de, 24

Index III

Kennedy, Ann (née McCracken), 3, 88–89, 160, 267n29

Lovett, Thomas, 80, 82

McCracken, Mr (not Samuel), 86
McCracken, Widow, 266n11
McCracken, Bernard, 264n1
McCracken, John (barber), 257n1
McCracken, John, 88
McCracken, Mrs John, 88
McCracken, Joshua, 266n27
M'Cracken, Samuel, 22, 50, 77, 92, 98, 101, 188; admitted freeman, 73; and Annamoe, 47–49; and Ballinacorbeg, 47; confesses to affair, 76, 213; death of, 49, 78, 162, 246; flees to Hatch, 76, 78; funeral arrangements, 81, 83, 84; and Glasnamullen, 23; literacy of, 75, 77; property in Dublin, 42; relationship to Hatch, 36, 53; and Roundwood, 33, 40–41, 73, 106; subject of rumour, 76; threats of suicide, 79; wills of, 77, 78, 80–1, 83–87 *passim*, 106, 136, 212, 218, 230, 251, 267n36; writes to Hatch, 63, 75, 76, 77, 79

McCracken, Thomas (bricklayer), 264n1
McCracken, Thomas, 89
McCracken, William (1733), 264n1
McCracken, William, 82, 86
McCracken, Mrs William, 86
Metge, Joyce (alias Hatch), 29
Metge, Peter, 80, 82

Nugent, Catherine (otherwise Hatch), 26

Radwell (or Redwill), Mrs Elizabeth (née Stuart), 88, 94, 267n5

Salmon, Mrs Mary (widow), 48, 76, 77–78, 82, 83, 86, 89
Stoddart, Francis, 82, 85, 88, 89, 98, 160
Stuart, Eliza, 82
Stuart, Henry, 82, 114
Stuart, Jane (sister of M'Cracken), 80, 82
Stuart, James, 74–75, 80, 82, 83, 87, 99
Stuart, Mrs James, 99
Stuart, Mary, 82–83, 87, 94–95
Stuart, Samuel, 82, 267n36
Stuart, Samuel Charles, 94
Stuart, William, 78–79, 82, 83, 87, 99, 267n36
Stuart brothers, 48, 84–85, 86, 213

Index IV

Members of the Synge family

Baba, 110, 131; *see also* Synge, Barbara (Mrs John Hatch)

Hutchinson, Francis Synge, *see* Synge-Hutchinson, Francis

Stephens, Edward, 6–7, 8, 31, 40, 43, 44, 52, 89, 90–91, 98, 101, 103, 105, 123
Stephens, Harry, 189, 245
Stephens, Lilo, 6, 217
Stewart, Mrs Elizabeth, 105, 125
Synge (hatter of Drogheda), 1, 4
Synge, Alexander Hamilton (uncle of JMS), 169, 177, 191–192
Synge, Alicia (Mrs Cooper), 1, 61, 66, 108, 271n45
Synge, Annie (Mrs Harry Stephens, sister of JMS), 270n19
Synge, Barbara (Mrs John Hatch), 2, 3, 4, 8, 24, 34, 61, 64, 72, 76, 102, 107, 110–111; her brother's will, 110; daughters, 66, 70; death and death notices, 11 (illus.), 62–63, 251; marriage, 5, 47, 59–60, 75, 109; pregnancy, 61; and Roundwood, 22, 99, 127; as significant forebear of JMS, 246; her silence broken, 220; suspected trip to London, 68–69, 110; unknown grave, 50, 62, 66

Synge, Barbara (child, d. 1792), 90, 102, 110, 111, 128, 251
Synge, Barbarah (Mrs Richard Riely), 266n27
Synge, Caroline, 197, 198, 280n4
Synge, Charles (lt-col.), 2, 110, 130, 132, 135, 136, 137, 197
Synge, Edward (Bp. of Cork etc.), 3, 108
Synge, Edward (Bp. of Elphin), 1, 3, 4, 33, 34, 60, 103, 105, 108, 271n45
Synge, Edward (Abp. of Tuam), 3, 34, 43, 64, 108, 161
Synge, Edward (archdeacon), 61, 62, 63, 64, 70, 102, 111, 123–124, 161; his children, 109; marriage, 271n45; 'silly love affair', 271n45; his will, 109–112, 128, 132
Synge, Edward (of Carhue), 147–148
Synge, Dr Edward (of Syngefield), 62, 64, 102–103, 109, 112, 128, 129, 130, 131, 132
Synge, Edward (brother of JMS), 26, 196, 243, 244, 252
Synge, Edward (uncle of JMS), 168, 169
Synge, Edward Hutchinson (nephew of JMS), 243
Synge, Edward Millington, 125
Synge, Mrs Eliza (of Great Britain St), 200
Synge, Elizabeth (unmarried sister of Barbara), 64, 66, 95

Index IV

Synge, Elizabeth (Mrs John Ormsby), 102, 109, 110, 111, 129, 130
Synge, Elizabeth (d. of Robert Synge), 110, 131
Synge, Frances (eldest child of Samuel Synge (-Hutchinson)), 112, 122; alleged illegitimacy, 128; in her father's will, 198–199 in her grandmother's will, 129–130; possibly her cousin's inamorata, 136
Synge, Frances Dorothy, 105
Synge, Frances Mary, 171
Synge, Francis (MP), 5, 7, 8, 22, 31, 32, 43, 46, 53, 54, 64, 70, 103, 123, 124, 127, 129, 131, 142–143, 200, 207, 208; administers Hatch's estate, 72, 95, 103, 104, 115–117, 121, 123, 200; assigned, 120, 125, 136; builds Glanmore, 103–105, 155; in Commons, 71, 115, 150; corresponds with John Hatch, 260n2; death, 106, 125–126, 171; describes Hatch to Downshire, 114–115; diary for 1798, 118; Hatch's Dublin church property assigned, 120, 125, 136; investments etc., 71; and rebellion, 55, 72, 102, 104, 117–119; remarriage, 105, 125; at Roundwood, 90, 101, 160; siblings, 109, 129; and Union, 104, 120–121, 125, 157
Synge, 1st wife of Francis (MP), née Elizabeth Hatch, 5, 46, 63, 70, 90, 104, 105, 116, 121, 124, 125, 126, 134–137, 151, 200
Synge, 2nd wife of Francis (MP) (formerly Stewart, widow), 105
Synge, Francis (d. 1878), 45, 154, 167, 169, 195; afforestation, 191; and cholera crisis, 207; guardian of Rathdrum Union, 279n7
Synge, Mrs Francis (née Editha Truell; later Mrs T. W. Gardiner), 48, 179, 196, 207

Synge, Francis (s. of George Synge), 110, 130, 135, 136
Synge, Francis (of Chapel Lane), 199–200
Synge, George (Bp. of Cloyne), 2, 3, 108, 250
Synge, Revd George, 31
Synge, George, 109, 129, 130, 131, 132, 136, 250, 252
Synge, Mrs George (née Mary MacDonnell), 109, 132, 250
Synge, George (1842–1926), 171
Synge, Henry, 171
Synge, Isabella (d. of John Synge, 2nd marriage), 171
Synge, John (grandfather of JMS), 5, 44, 70, 105, 107, 116, 125, 126, 134–156 *passim*, 170–171, 207, 253; assists [Plymouth] Brethren, 132, 138, 173, 182, 183, 272n50; birth, 102, 134; chair of Rathdrum Union, 188, 202, 221; children of 2nd marriage, 171; commemorative plaque, 178; condemns proselytism, 202; continental tour, 125, 137–141; drawing by, 15 (illus.); Dublin property, 177; early desire to marry, 135–136; as educator, 173–175, 271–279n13, 279n15; first marriage, 151–152, 155; inherits Glanmore, 106; journal quoted, 138–139; moves to Devon, 168; Pestalozzian writings, 145, 150–152, 162, 275–276nn42–44, 276n47; sketch-books, 139–140
Synge, 1st Mrs John (née Isabella Hamilton) 105, 135, 151–152, 153, 154, 168, 171, 276n49
Synge, 2nd Mrs John (née Frances Steele), 135, 171
Synge, John Hatch (father of JMS), 5, 30, 95, 154, 169–170, 171, 177, 186 mystical experience, 178; photograph of, 15; property dealings, 191–192

Members of the Synge family

Synge, John Millington (dramatist), 1, 2, 4, 6, 7, 8, 24, 28, 30, 31, 72, 95, 145, 200; *The Aran Islands*, 5, 210; cultural nationalism and, 103; decadence and, 7, 45, 113, 229; 'Deirdre of the Sorrows', 219, 238, 246; and Paris, 179, 181; on Pierre Loti, 157; 'The Playboy of the Western World', 5, 28, 109, 210, 221–225 *passim*, 226–228, 242, 246–247; early poetry, 208; his reading of history, 50, 118, 215, 245; 'Riders to the Sea', 210, 219–220, 246; 'In the Shadow of the Glen', 22, 23, 190, 195, 211, 224, 230, 252; Stephens's life of, 8, 40, 52, 55, 64; in Tomriland, 195, 252; on vagrancy, 201, 203, 210, 213; 'The Well of the Saints', 183, 190, 231, 246; 'When the Moon Has Set', 63, 65, 84, 157, 167, 189, 210–220 *passim*, 251; his Wicklow essays, 210–211, 229; Wicklow folklore, 37, 45, 113, 127, 182, 252; on Wicklow Gaelic, 19, 46

Synge, Joseph (apothecary), 4

Synge, Julia, 200

Synge, Mrs Katherine (genealogist), 62, 262n21

Synge, Mrs Kathleen (née Traill), 183, 252

Synge, Nicholas (Bp. of Killaloe), 3, 34, 59, 60–61, 62, 66, 109, 261n13

Synge, Richard (of Bridgnorth), 3

Synge, Richard (d. 1874), 171

Synge, Richard (of Cambridge), 283n1

Synge, Robert, 100, 102, 103, 109, 111, 122, 129, 131, 132, 134, 137, 163, 272n45

Synge, Mrs Robert (née Margaret Wolfe), 100, 132, 137, 161, 163

Synge, Robert Anthony (brother of JMS), 26, 118, 244, 263n53

Synge, Robert Daly, 171

Synge, Samuel (dean of Kildare), 3, 108, 109

Synge, Samuel (later Synge Hutchinson), 5, 70, 72, 103, 104, 109, 110, 112, 117, 127, 129, 170, 173, 187; changes name, 124; children, 123, 136, 197; death, 197; 1st marriage, 121; 2nd marriage, 122, 124, 132; in his mother's will, 129–131; papers of, 257n31; his will, 198–199

Synge, 1st wife of Samuel (later Synge Hutchinson), 112, 121, 127, 136, 198; birth of twins, 122; died, 122

Synge, 2nd wife of Samuel (later Synge Hutchinson), 5, 63, 70, 72, 95, 102, 104, 121, 135, 170, 200; marriage, 117, 122, 124, 132

Synge, Samuel (died s. p.), 171

Synge, Samuel (brother of JMS), 26, 50, 72, 152, 200, 208, 243, 272n49

Synge, Mrs Sophia (née Hutchinson), 62, 64, 70, 109, 110, 111, 112, 128; burial, 272n45; her children listed, 129; death, 123, 132; implies J. Hatch made will, 115, 117; her will, 115, 128–132, 250

Synge, Sophia Helena Maria, 131

Synge, Revd Thomas, 252

Synge, Thomas (of Tomriland), 171, 194–197, 252

Synge family (of County Clare), 149

Synge Hutchinson, Sir Edward, 197

Synge Hutchinson, Elizabeth, 123, 197

Synge Hutchinson, Francis, 72, 170, 173, 198

Synge Hutchinson, John Hatch, 123, 197

Synge Hutchinson, Samuel, 123, 197

Synge Hutchinson, Sophia Elizabeth, 123, 198–199

EU authorised representative for GPSR:
Easy Access System Europe, Mustamäe tee 50,
10621 Tallinn, Estonia
gpsr.requests@easproject.com

www.ingramcontent.com/pod-product-compliance
Lightning Source LLC
Chambersburg PA
CBHW050135240426
43673CB00043B/1676